The Routledge Dictionary of Modern British History

John Plowright

Routledge
Taylor & Francis Group
LONDON AND NEW YORK

First published 2006
by Routledge
2 Park Square, Milton Park, Abingdon, Oxon OX14 4RN

Simultaneously published in the USA and Canada
by Routledge
270 Madison Avenue, New York, NY 10016

Routledge is an imprint of the Taylor & Francis Group, an informa business

Typeset in Times New Roman and GillSans by Taylor & Francis Books
Printed and bound in Great Britain by MPG Books Ltd, Bodmin

British Library Cataloguing in Publication Data
A catalogue record for this book is available from the British Library

Library of Congress Cataloging in Publication Data
A catalog record for this book has been requested

ISBN10: 0-415-19243-9 (hbk)
ISBN10: 0-415-19244-7 (pbk)
ISBN10: 0-203-08846-8 (ebk)

ISBN13: 978-0-415-19243-9 (hbk)
ISBN13: 978-0-415-19244-6 (pbk)
ISBN13: 978-0-203-08846-3 (ebk)

The Routledge Dictionary of Modern British History

The Routledge Dictionary of Modern British History is an essential guide to the last two centuries, which have witnessed democratization, international decline, devolution, the rise of the welfare state, and New Labour challenging the Conservatives as the natural party of government.

Includes:

- every Prime Minister from Pitt the Younger to Tony Blair
- protest movements from Chartism to CND
- military conflict from the French Revolutionary Wars to Iraq
- milestones from the Act of Union to the Northern Ireland peace process

John Plowright is Head of History at Repton School in Derbyshire. He is the author of *Regency England* (Lancaster Pamphlets, Routledge, 1996) as well as numerous articles.

Also available from Routledge

Ancient History: Key Themes and Approaches
Neville Morley
0-415-16509-1

Fifty Key Thinkers on History
Marnie Hughes-Warrington
0-415-16982-8

Fifty Key Medieval Thinkers
G.R. Evans
0-415-23663-0

The Routledge Companion to Fascism and the Far Right
Peter Davies and Derek Lynch
0-415-21495-5

The Routledge Companion to Postmodernism (Second Edition)
Edited by Stuart Sim
0-415-33359-8

Who's Who in Europe 1450–1750
Henry Kamen
0-415-14728-X

Who's Who in Military History
John Keegan and Andrew Wheatcroft
0-415-26039-6

Who's Who in Modern History
Alan Palmer
0-415-11885-9

Who's Who in Nazi Germany
Robert Wistrich
0-415-26038-8

Who's Who in Jewish History
Joan Comay, new edition revised by Lavinia Cohn-Sherbok
0-415-26030-2

Who's Who in World War I
John Bourne
0-415-14179-6

Who's Who in World War II
Edited by John Keegan
0-415-26033-7

Who's Who in Gay and Lesbian History
Edited by Robert Aldrich and Garry Wotherspoon
0-415-15983-0

Who's Who in Contemporary Gay and Lesbian History
Edited by Robert Aldrich and Garry Wotherspoon
0-415-29161-5

Who's Who in Russia since 1900
Martin McCauley
0-415-13898-1

Who's Who in Twentieth-Century Warfare
Spencer Tucker
0-415-23497-2

Who's Who in Naval History
Alastair Wilson (UK entries) and Joseph Callo (US entries)
0-415-30828-3

To Sue

My wife and the love of my life

Contents

Acknowledgments

The authors of books with titles similar to this one seem to share Mr Gradgrind's belief that 'the facts' can speak for themselves. This author believes that it is appropriate and helpful sometimes to express an opinion as well as act as chronicler.

The Rev. Benjamin Jowett, Master of Balliol, once wrote that 'Writing requires boundless leisure, and is an infinite labour, yet there is also very great pleasure in it.' This book has been the product of limited leisure and hard labour. The author, who found some pleasure in researching and writing it, hopes that its intended audience will derive even more pleasure and value in reading it.

Special thanks are due to Sue, Alex and James for keeping me happy and (outwardly) sane during the production of this book.

I would like to thank all those who have helped in a variety of ways to equip me for that task, particularly my late parents but also Miss Kate Allan, Professor Derek Beales, Professor Jeremy Black, Professor David Cannadine, the late Mr Maurice Cowling, Mr Andrew Hewlett, Mr Nicholas Hillman, Mr Benjamin Holt, Mr Andrew Jones, Miss Nela Kashfi, Mr and Mrs Ron Lee, Mrs Gilian Noero, Dr Jonathan Parry, the Reverend William Plowright, Mr Ken Reed, Mr Timothy Toulmin, Miss Caroline Shaw and the Governors, Head Master, colleagues and students of Repton School.

Those at Routledge concerned with the publication of this book have shown the patience of Job. None of the above but myself alone bears the responsibility where what follows fails to match the wisdom of Solomon.

JP Repton

List of entries

Abdication crisis, 1936. Edward VIII was not the first British monarch to shirk his duty but none was more reckless in disregarding the constitutional implications of pursuing his personal happiness.

It was 3 December 1936 when Britain's newspapers belatedly joined the world's press in speculating about the liaison between Edward VIII and Mrs Wallis Simpson. The King's evident desire to marry his mistress created a constitutional crisis not so much because she was an American or a commoner, although these were considered significant disabilities at the time, but rather because she was a divorcée. Although the Church of England came into existence largely in order to facilitate Henry VIII's desire to divorce his first wife so that he could marry his mistress, the fact that the sovereign has henceforth been Supreme Governor of the Church of England has meant that they cannot, in conscience, marry a divorced person and retain the crown.

Baldwin appreciated that Mrs Simpson could never be queen (because this would be unacceptable to Britain and the Dominions); that Edward would not give up the chance of marrying her; that a morganatic marriage (whereby the spouse and any children would not enjoy royal rank or privileges) was impracticable because alien; and that the final decision whether or not to abdicate must be the King's. Moreover, as Jenkins states, Baldwin's handling of the crisis enabled him to step down as prime minister (just sixteen days after George VI's coronation) in 'a glow of achievement'.

The Abdication Bill (with the consent of the Dominions under the Statute of Westminster) was passed on 11 December 1936.

The only real casualty of the whole affair, other than Edward himself, was Winston Churchill, whose abortive efforts to create a King's Party, albeit briefly supported by certain sections of the press, confirmed the widely held view that his judgement was questionable and that he should not therefore return to government.

A recording of Edward's halting abdication speech, penned by Churchill, helped actor Charles Laughton to get into character as the Emperor Claudius.

Aberdeen, George Hamilton-Gordon, fourth Earl of (28 January 1784–14 December 1860). George, the future fourth Earl, was the eldest son of Lord Haddo, the heir to the third Earl of Aberdeen. His father died in 1791 and Dundas (Lord Melville) and Pitt in due course became his guardians. Despite the wishes of the third Earl that he be partly educated in Scotland, his grandson was educated at Harrow and at St John's College, Cambridge. Unlike many members of the aristocracy he did not serve an apprenticeship in the Commons as he inherited the earldom in 1801 and became a Scottish representative peer in 1806.

In August 1813 Castlereagh dispatched Aberdeen to Vienna as special ambassador. This appointment attracted considerable criticism on the grounds of Aberdeen's relative youth, inexperience and imperfect command of French, not least when these led to his being outmanoeuvred by Metternich into allowing freedom of trade and navigation as subjects for discussion. Thus although he was rewarded with a viscountcy in 1814, Aberdeen spent the next fifteen years raising his family (by his second marriage, of 1815), improving his estates and pursuing his antiquarian interests.

He returned to active politics as chancellor of the duchy of Lancaster under Wellington in 1828, becoming foreign secretary later in the year as part of the reshuffle occasioned by the departure of the Canningites. As a philhellene he took joy in the creation of an independent Greece but was unable to prevent Russia from exploiting Ottoman weakness in the aftermath of Navarino.

After serving as secretary for war and the colonies in 1834–35 under Peel, he returned to the Foreign Office under Peel in 1841. His actions in ending the war with China (by the 1842 Treaty of Nanking), and restoring friendly relations with the United States (through the Webster–Ashburton treaty of 1842) and France, were in marked contrast with those of Palmerston: a point emphasized by his criticism of the Don Pacifico affair. Indeed, the two foreign secretaries are customarily depicted as pursuing rival foreign policies, with Palmerston closer to Canning in his willingness to employ force in the assertion of Britain's supposed interests, whilst Aberdeen is more akin to Castlereagh in adopting a non-confrontational, conciliatory aspect.

Aberdeen followed Peel over the repeal of the Corn Laws in 1846, emerged as the leader of the Peelites on Peel's death in 1850, courted unpopularity by opposing Russell over his Ecclesiastical Titles Act in 1851, but in 1852 became prime minister of a Whig–Peelite radical coalition. Had Palmerston been his foreign secretary then Britain might not have drifted into the Crimean War in 1854. However, it was the government's manifest mismanagement of the war that fatally discredited it. Thus when Roebuck moved for a select committee to inquire into the condition of the Army in the Crimea, the government was defeated by 305 votes to 148 and Aberdeen was forced to resign.

Aberdeen was an incompetent diplomat in his youth who developed, under Peel's watchful eye, into a competent foreign secretary. However, his reputation hinges upon the three years of his premiership. To his admirers, such as Muriel Chamberlain, he created a coalition which anticipated the Liberal Party not least in its innovative programme of reform which embraced institutional and fiscal change spearheaded by Gladstone himself. To his detractors he shows why the meek will not inherit the earth, or rather why such an outcome might prove a mixed blessing.

Abortion Act, 1967. The 1966 feature film *Alfie*, which starred Michael Caine as the eponymous anti-hero, reflected changing attitudes towards sexuality whilst its portrayal of backstreet abortion chimed with the growing clamour for legal reform.

The 1967 Abortion Act, which began life as a Private Member's Bill sponsored by Liberal MP, David Steel, received the support of the Labour government and came into force from April 1968. It legalized terminations of pregnancies of up to 28 weeks on four possible grounds, namely, where, in the opinion of two doctors, continued pregnancy could harm the mother's physical or mental health; where the baby might be deformed; where the mother had been raped; and where the baby would be born into undesirable conditions. A million legal abortions had been performed by 1980.

The 1990 Human Fertilization and Embryology Act revised the general limit downwards to 24 weeks, with a number of exceptions.

Adams, Gerry (6 October 1948–). Gerry Adams, the son of Gerard Adams, was born in Belfast and educated at St Finian's on the Falls Road and then St Mary's Christian Brothers' School. Leaving school early, he became a barman. Consistently denying membership of the IRA, Adams certainly comes from a very strong Republican background on both his father's and mother's side and was subjected to internment in 1971 as a suspected IRA leader in the Ballymurphy area. On release from jail he allegedly joined the IRA delegation that secretly met with the British government, in the person of Willie Whitelaw, in London in 1972, and he spent several months on remand after being charged with IRA membership in February 1978, before being released by the Lord Chief Justice.

As vice-president (1978–83) and then (thanks to a coup by northern republicans) president of Sinn Féin (from 1984), Adams has masterminded the policy of supplementing the bullet with the ballot box, arguing as early as 1979 that victory could not be achieved solely by military means: a policy which gained ground when the hunger strikes of the early 1980s yielded electoral gains. Adams himself was elected a Member of the Northern Ireland Assembly 1981, MP for Belfast West 1983–92, and from 1 May 1997, and a Member of the new Northern Ireland Assembly for Belfast West from 1998.

The 1985 Anglo-Irish Agreement can be seen as an attempt to secure the moderate Republican position of the SDLP from the growing electoral threat posed by Sinn Féin but in 1988 John Hume entered into private talks with his Sinn Féin counterpart and the resulting 'Hume–Adams process' led, in due course, to the 1994 IRA ceasefire, which paved the way for the Good Friday Agreement.

The fact that he has carried the bulk of the extreme republican movement with him (notwithstanding the Real IRA and Continuity IRA) is a testament to Adams's persuasive powers. Whether he continues to retain that high level of support, or even comes to attain the sort of stature achieved by other former opponents of the British Crown, like Jomo Kenyatta, only time will tell.

The appeal for the IRA fully to embrace democratic means of achieving their goals, with which Adams launched the Sinn Féin campaign for the 2005 election and which was followed on 28 July by the IRA ordering its members to dump their arms and end the armed campaign, can be viewed, according to taste, as either a statesmanlike gesture or an attempt to regain support at home and internationally which had been lost in the wake of IRA implication in Robert McCartney's murder.

Addington See SIDMOUTH (HENRY ADDINGTON).

Adullamites Radical John Bright christened those Liberals opposed to the moderate Reform Bill introduced by Gladstone to the House of Commons in March 1866 as 'Adullamites': a reference to 1 Samuel 22, where the cave of Adullam provided the collecting point for 'every one that was in distress and every one that was discontented'.

The Adullamites numbered about forty and were united by regret for Palmerston's passing and fears about the impact of extending the franchise upon their own seats and/or upon the ability of the traditional ruling class to govern. The Adullamites joined with the Conservatives to defeat the government on a wrecking amendment by 315 votes to 304 in June 1866.

This rebellion led to Russell's resignation, the formation of a minority Derby–Disraeli administration and the passage of what proved to be a more radical measure in the shape of what became the 1867 Reform Act.

Adulteration of Food, Drink and Drugs Act, 1872. As its name suggests, the Act was intended to protect the pockets and stomachs of consumers from superfluous and possibly harmful substances being added to these commodities. Its principal beneficiaries were the working class, who were obviously most at risk and who received further protection through the Sales of Food and Drug Acts of 1875 and 1899.

Agricultural Holdings Act, 1875. The principle of the Agricultural Holdings Act alienated landlords by extending the terms of the 1870 Irish Land Act to English tenants by offering them compensation for improvements. Moreover, its permissive character failed to satisfy the tenant farmers, who were more attracted to the Liberals in the 1880 election campaign by their promised reform of the land and game laws.

All the Talents, Ministry of, 1806–7. Following the death of Pitt the Younger, Grenville formed what was dubbed the Ministry of All the Talents because it not only included his own followers but those of Charles James Fox and Addington (later Lord Sidmouth). The Ministry manifestly failed to live up to its name despite abolishing the slave trade, either by waging the war more effectively or by making peace. Gravely weakened by Fox's death, it fell in March of the following year, following the King's refusal to accept any concession to Catholics.

Anglo-Irish Agreement, 15 November 1985. The Anglo-Irish agreement was signed at Hillsborough, County Down by Mrs Thatcher for Great Britain and Dr Garrett Fitzgerald for the Irish Republic. They agreed that Northern Ireland would remain a part of the UK according to the wishes of its majority, but that there should be regular consultation between the two governments on several aspects of policy and to this end a small secretariat of civil servants from both countries was established.

Westminster hoped to get better cross-border security from the deal; whilst Dublin, for the first time since 1922, secured acknowledgement that it had a role to play in the North.

Predictably, this last aspect of the agreement resulted in its wholesale condemnation by the Unionists. All fifteen Unionist MPs, other than Enoch Powell, resigned their seats in protest and to allow their electorates to register their disapproval. Ian Gow also resigned from the government.

Anglo-Irish Treaty, 1921–22. The rising bloodshed of the Anglo-Irish War ultimately persuaded both sides to call a truce (9 July 1921) so as to allow a conference in London 'to ascertain how the association of Ireland with . . . the British Empire might best be reconciled with Irish national aspirations'. Realizing that such a conference was unlikely to meet hard-line republican demands de Valera declined to attend, so Michael Collins and Arthur Griffith headed the Irish delegation.

Agreement was reached on 6 December, with the signing of a treaty establishing the Irish Free State as a self-governing dominion within the British Commonwealth (obliging members of the Irish parliament to take an oath of allegiance to the British Crown). The six counties of Northern Ireland could and did retain their status within the United Kingdom.

Collins correctly prophesied that in agreeing these terms he was signing his own death warrant for de Valera led those members of Sinn Féin in the Dáil who rejected the treaty. It was nevertheless ratified in Dublin on 7 January 1922 by 64 votes to 57, with Westminster following suit on 31 March 1922.

In Ireland the treaty led to partition and civil war (1922–23), whilst in Britain it contributed to the Carlton Club revolt and the downfall of the Lloyd George coalition.

Anglo-Irish War, 21 January 1919–9 July 1921. The Irish Volunteers, who were increasingly known as the Irish Republican Army (IRA), waged a guerrilla war against the Black and Tans and other British forces, characterized by raids, ambushes and assassinations. This military campaign, masterminded by Michael Collins, began in 1919 after the elections of 1918 had produced a majority for Sinn Féin (with 73 of the 105 Irish seats), which boycotted the Westminster parliament in favour of its own Dublin-based Irish Assembly (Dáil Eireann).

The Lloyd George government responded to the threat to British sovereignty and law and order by extending the emergency powers created by the wartime Defence of the Realm Act and reinforcing the Royal Irish Constabulary with regular troops and two new forces: the Auxiliaries and the infamous Black and Tans. However, heavy handed tactics such as the 'sacking' of Cork city on 11–12 December 1920 merely alienated much of the civilian population and thus stimulated IRA recruitment. Indeed, the violence escalated, particularly in the western counties of Munster and on the Ulster borders, until a truce was agreed on 9 July 1921. This led to the Anglo-Irish Treaty, which ended the Anglo-Irish War but led to the Civil War of 1922–23 after dividing the island.

Anti-Corn Law League, 1839–46. The Anti-Corn Law League (ACLL) was a predominantly middle-class pressure group which emerged in 1839 out of the Mancunian Anti-Corn Law Association which had been founded the previous year. The ACLL's inaugural conference was held in London at the same time as the National Convention and historians have spent much time comparing the apparent success of the ACLL in securing the Repeal of the Corn Laws (1846) with the failure of Chartism to secure the six points of the People's Charter within the movement's lifetime.

Certainly the ACLL's decision to follow Cobden's advice and confine itself to a single aim, namely, total and immediate repeal of the Corn Laws, appears to have focused its energies, although it is worth pointing out that many ACLL supporters mistakenly regarded this as merely the means of securing an end to the political, economic and social dominance of the landed aristocracy.

In 1842, a time of slump, Bright proposed a general lockout by employers in the belief that this would provoke such extreme hardship and disorder that the government would be forced to make concessions. However, Cobden successfully argued that the ACLL should continue to follow constitutional methods, which was much more to the taste of most of its mostly non-conformist middle-class adherents.

The ACLL adopted the high moral ground in its battle with the forces of agricultural protection, claiming that free trade would pave the way for world peace. However, more selfish and materialistic reasons help to explain the ACLL's popularity amongst the middle classes, namely, the views that the artificially high price of bread resulting from the Corn Laws meant that wages were higher than need be the case, whilst increased importation of foreign grain might stimulate the demand abroad for British manufactured goods.

The ACLL pioneered the methods of modern pressure group organization and the mobilization of opinion, including a permanent headquarters (in Manchester), salaried regional organizers, strict accounting methods and a card index filing system. It also had two advantages compared with earlier pressure groups, namely improved communications through the expanding railway network and the advent of cheap mail through the Penny Post.

In 1841 the ACLL took the radical step of attempting to exert pressure upon the political parties by putting up its own candidate at the Walsall by-election. Although the League candidate was defeated, eight League candidates, including Cobden at Stockport, were returned at the 1841 general election. Bright joined his ACLL colleagues in the Commons in 1843 following a by-election at Durham.

Before one is tempted to sneer at the diminutive size of this parliamentary army it is worth remembering that in the golden age of the independent member powerful oratory might actually influence votes. Certainly in 1845 Peel memorably told his front bench colleague Sidney Herbert '*You* must answer this, for *I* cannot', after Cobden had made a particularly effective speech in favour of free trade. It is, however, now customary to point out that Peel had his own long-standing reasons for wishing repeal and more immediate reasons for wishing to attribute his apparent conversion to the Irish potato blight in Ireland and the persuasiveness of ACLL propaganda.

If the ACLL converted anyone it was not Peel and the Conservative Party but Russell and the Whigs. The latter were fearful of losing urban seats to the League or to the Tories on a split vote and thus Russell tried to pre-empt this danger by announcing his conversion to repeal of the Corn Laws in his Edinburgh letter of December 1845. This was to prove decisive insofar as Peel was ultimately obliged to rely upon Whig votes to carry the measure when his own party divided on the issue.

Notwithstanding the above, many contemporaries made the mistake of overestimating the ACLL's influence in securing repeal. The result was that numerous pressure groups such as the Liberation Society, the Education League and the United Kingdom Alliance modelled their organizations and activities upon the ACLL in the vain hope of emulating its apparent success.

The ACLL is also often erroneously taken as symbolizing the political coming of age of the middle classes newly enfranchised in 1832. In fact, the history of the ACLL shows what a long way the middle classes still had to go in Britain before they achieved political power commensurate with their economic muscle. Indeed, Peel embarked upon the repeal of the Corn Laws like Grey had embarked upon the Reform Act as a means of demonstrating the continued fitness of the landed aristocracy to govern and thus keep the middle classes at arm's length.

Artisans' Dwellings Act, 1875. The 1875 Artisans' Dwellings Act was the work of Richard Cross, home secretary in the Second Disraeli administration. The Act was permissive, allowing local authorities to prepare urban improvement schemes. If parliament confirmed their compulsory purchase orders, the land thereby obtained could be sold, on condition that the original inhabitants were rehoused, and the property redeveloped, with the local authorities themselves undertaking this work if the home secretary gave his permission.

The process of redevelopment was so slow that by 1885 only 10 English and Welsh towns had opted to make use of the Act. Gareth Stedman Jones has argued that the legislation actually worsened the housing situation, at least in London, as it tended to produce very high densities of dwellers in the new buildings.

Ashbourne Irish Land Purchase Act, 1885. Between June 1885 and January 1886 a caretaker minority Conservative government held office under Salisbury purely in order to allow new registers to be compiled to take into account the terms of the redistribution agreed between the leadership of the two major parties. The Ashbourne Act was the only significant piece of legislation passed in this hiatus between the Third Reform Act and the 1886 general election.

The Act, named after Lord Ashbourne, the Irish Lord Chancellor, was the first in a series of Land Purchase Acts by which Unionist administrations sought to solve the Irish land question by making available state funds to allow Irish tenant farmers to purchase their holdings. The 1885 Act provided £5m to allow tenants to borrow the whole sum required to buy their land, which was to be repaid over 49 years at 4% interest.

Asquith, Herbert Henry, first Earl of Oxford and Asquith (12 September 1852–15 February 1928). Herbert Henry Asquith was the second son of a Yorkshire Congregationalist cloth-merchant, who died when Herbert was just eight. His widow brought up their four children with the financial help of her brothers, who helped their two nephews to attend the City of London School. For Herbert this was followed by a classical scholarship to Balliol College, Oxford with firsts in both classical moderations (1872) and literae humaniores (1874), and the Craven scholarship (1874). That same year he was elected to a Balliol fellowship and entered Lincoln's Inn, being called to the Bar in 1876.

He first achieved national prominence in Liberal circles when he researched the Bradlaugh case for Gladstone. This helped him to enter parliament for East Fife as a Gladstonian Liberal in 1886. Two years later, Asquith consolidated his legal and political position thanks to his performance as junior counsel for Parnell before the Parnell commission. He took silk in 1890 but the following year suffered the loss of Helen, his first wife, by whom he had had four sons and one daughter.

In 1892 Gladstone made him home secretary at the age of thirty-nine. This office often proves a political graveyard but Asquith left it in 1895 with his reputation as an administrator and debater enhanced. Moreover, in May 1894 he had married Margaret (Margot) Tennant, who was celebrated in London society for her strength of character and intellect, with whom he would have another five children, although only two survived infancy. Although she brought wealth to their union it was not sufficient to preclude Asquith from defying convention and returning to the Bar, whilst his party remained internally divided and out of office.

Asquith himself appeared to contribute to the Liberal Party's difficulties when in June 1901 he publicly protested against the phrase 'methods of barbarism' as applied by Campbell-Bannerman to Kitchener's counter-insurgency tactics in South Africa, and when, in February 1902, he joined fellow Liberal Imperialists in setting up the Liberal League. In fact, Asquith was becoming increasingly disenchanted by Rosebery and willing to mend bridges within the party: a process facilitated by the ending of the Boer War and by Conservative policies, particularly regarding education and tariffs. Indeed, Asquith became the foremost defender of free trade, following Chamberlain around the country in order to rebut his arguments.

When Balfour's government resigned early in December 1905, and Campbell-Bannerman was invited to form a ministry, Asquith was the first to break the Relugas Compact by accepting the post of chancellor of the exchequer and deputy leader of the House. He was confirmed in these posts following the Liberal landslide of 1906 and his budget of that and the two following years confirmed his reputation as a man of great intellectual resourcefulness. The 1907 budget was distinguished for establishing the difference between earned and unearned income for income tax, whilst the 1908 budget, delivered after he had replaced Campbell-Bannerman as prime minister, provided for means-tested non-contributory old age pensions.

Asquith's first major test as prime minister was the dispute within the cabinet over the level of naval spending. He engineered the compromise which secured an even bigger construction programme for the Admiralty than it had at first demanded, and when Lloyd George as his chancellor sought, in his 1909 budget, to provide £14m in extra taxation to cover both battleships and pensions, he backed him to the hilt when the means chosen to help accomplish these ends provoked the Lords into rejecting the budget.

In the January 1910 general election Asquith secured a majority of 124, which nevertheless rendered his budget vulnerable to a combined Irish–Unionist challenge. However, he refused to amend it and it passed into law in April. He now sought to limit the powers of the peers by means of a Parliament Bill.

Simultaneously with the passing of the budget, Asquith had prepared and presented to the Commons a scheme providing that a Bill which had been passed by the House of Commons in three successive sessions should, after a minimum period of two years from its first introduction, automatically become law in spite of its rejection in each of those sessions by the Lords. Asquith also secured a private undertaking from George V, that in the event of a new general election providing a mandate for reform of the Lords, the King would be willing to contemplate the creation of sufficient peers to overcome continued resistance.

The December 1910 election duly gave the government a majority of 126 but the resistance of the die-hards obliged Asquith to reveal the King's conditional undertaking to use his prerogative if the peers persisted in their opposition to the Parliament Bill. Asquith's critics claimed that he had mired the Crown in political controversy but an objective appraisal of the facts absolves him of this charge and shows him to have acted with strict constitutional correctness in a very delicate situation.

Asquith's powers of diplomacy and tact were further stretched by the Unionist response to his 1912 Home Rule Bill, which threatened a state of civil war, whilst the 'Curragh mutiny' of 1914 resulted in Asquith himself temporarily assuming the secretaryship for war. It is a tribute to Asquith's powers of persuasion that the cabinet and the country were so united in accepting the need to declare war on Germany in August 1914. Moreover, the war placed Ireland and the other divisive domestic issues of the day – the suffragette agitation, Welsh Disestablishment and labour troubles – into a period of enforced limbo.

Asquith worked hard but also played hard. He would consider the arguments on both sides of a question, come to a decision with which he was satisfied and then turn his mind to the pleasures of the day, principally bridge, books and the bottle (occasioning the nickname 'Squiffy'). Margot Asquith records that her husband was determined to read all the Dickens novels 'as they removed his thoughts if only for a short time from Colleagues and Allies'. He had, in fact, already discovered an equally potent distraction that he was less disposed to confide to his wife.

Between 1912 and 1915 Asquith sent passionate love letters to Venetia Stanley who was young enough to be his granddaughter. This correspondence was not only morally questionable but politically imprudent as some letters were not only composed at the cabinet table but divulged what was deliberated there.

Asquith was distraught when in early 1915 Venetia announced her engagement to one of his junior ministers, Edwin Montagu. This decision was probably taken by Miss Stanley as the best means of terminating Asquith's increasingly unwelcome attentions and the attendant distraction was possibly a contributory factor in the collapse of Asquith's Liberal administration and the construction of a coalition government later in May 1915. Personal factors may also have had portentous high political repercussions in the following year insofar as Margot plausibly suggests that Asquith's grief at the death of his eldest son Raymond on 15 September 1916 may have clouded his political judgement at that critical time.

Asquith had reconstructed his ministry on a coalition basis in May 1915 because of the scandal of the shell shortage on the Western Front, the failure of the Gallipoli campaign, and the resignation of Fisher as First Sea Lord. Bonar Law could no longer hold his followers in check as a 'patriotic opposition' because distrust of Churchill had been so greatly magnified by the last two events. Asquith chose the course of coalition with the Conservatives rather than confrontation, although the distribution of offices did little to conciliate them, as Liberals retained all the top jobs, with the exception of the Admiralty (which went to Balfour); Bonar Law and Austen Chamberlain receiving the Colonies and India respectively.

Disputes over strategy became more difficult to resolve, with the full cabinet repeatedly rehearsing arguments first heard in the War Committee. Moreover, the war continued to go badly, with the conscription controversy bitterly dividing the Liberals. The loss of Kitchener provided scope for reconstruction but ended in strengthening Lloyd George's hand, whose position was in any case improving as his friendship with Bonar Law deepened. Beaverbrook played a key role in the second half of November of 1916 in bringing Lloyd George, Bonar Law and Carson together to put pressure on Asquith to relinquish personal control of the conduct of the war to a small war council. When Asquith refused he was manoeuvred into a position where he felt obliged to resign, in the first week of December. Lloyd George took over as prime minister but almost all of the Liberal ministers followed Asquith and the new government became predominantly Conservative.

Asquith fell because he was tired, too often in his cups, unwilling to cultivate the press and generally loath to create the appearance of vigorous activity. The phrase 'wait and see' came back to haunt him. To his family and friends his modesty could amount to a deformity but to his foes and ultimately to much of the electorate his equanimity appeared little more than lethargy.

He bestirred himself to no avail at the time of the Maurice debate and the marginalization of the Asquithian Liberals was made manifest at the 'Coupon Election' of December 1918 when Asquith himself lost his seat and only 26 of his 253 candidates were successful: a poorer showing than that achieved by either Sinn Féin or Labour.

Asquith re-entered Parliament in 1920 as a result of a by-election at Paisley. Once there he condemned the actions of the 'Black and Tans' and urged Dominion Home Rule for Ireland. The break-up of the Coalition, the return of a Conservative government following the November 1922 general election, and Baldwin going to the country on the issue of tariff reform, facilitated formal reconciliation between the 64 Asquithian Liberals and 53 supporters of Lloyd George. The December 1923 election left the Liberals in third place but holding the balance of power between Conservatives and Labour. In opting to provide support for Labour to take office, Asquith displayed a sense of constitutional correctness and fair play but a lack of political common sense. Labour was now seen as capable of holding office, whilst its inability to achieve more in legislative terms could be blamed upon the conditional support it received from the Liberals. In short, Asquith ensured that the Liberals got the worst of both worlds: the brickbats of high office with none of the rewards.

The 1924 election, which appeared to be dominated by the Zinoviev letter, played badly for the Liberals and Asquith was amongst those losing his seat. In 1925 he entered the Lords as Earl of Oxford and Asquith.

Although remaining leader of the Liberal Party until October 1926, this period was one of increasing tension with Lloyd George. As his health gradually declined, Asquith increasingly sought to augment his income by publication of a series of memoirs until his death on 15 February 1928.

For most of his political life Asquith gave an impression of effortless mastery that ultimately served him ill, insofar as the myth grew that he lacked energy. He certainly grew increasingly weary of the strains to which he was subjected over a very prolonged period but many mistook his unwillingness to engage in flashy self-advertisement as signifying arrogance or indolence. His strength of character was most apparent when he refrained from descending to the tactics of those subjecting him to personal abuse. It was said after his death that Asquith was the 'last of the Romans'. It might be more fitting to view him as the last of the high Victorians, combining their intellectual mastery, high moral seriousness and sense of public service with a rather disreputable private life.

Attlee, Clement Richard, first Earl Attlee (3 January 1883–8 October 1967). The seventh child of a prosperous Surrey-based City of London solicitor, Attlee was educated at Haileybury before going up to University College, Oxford. In 1907 he gave up the legal profession to become the residential manager of his old school mission in Stepney, in London's East End, where he became a convert to socialism and a Labour activist, joining the Independent Labour Party (ILP). Unlike most members of his class, including those few who espoused socialism, like Hugh Dalton and John Strachey, he thus experienced the working class at first hand prior to World War One, in which he was twice wounded and rose to the rank of major in the South Lancashire Regiment.

Returning to the East End, he became Mayor of Stepney and then, in November 1922, having married earlier in the year, was elected as MP for Limehouse. Over the next decade he had four children, lectured at the London School of Economics, acted as parliamentary private secretary to Ramsay MacDonald (1922–23), was undersecretary of state for war (1924), served on the Simon Commission on

India (1928–29), and was chancellor of the duchy of Lancaster and then post-master-general in MacDonald's second Labour administration (1930–31).

He served his constituents as dutifully as he had served his Stepney settlement and his troops, and his constituency served him well, for when only forty-six Labour MPs were returned in the 1931 election the fact that he was one of them (with a majority of 551 votes), and one, moreover, with ministerial experience (albeit outside the cabinet), put him on the fast track for preferment within the party and he became deputy leader almost by default. Moreover, when the ailing George Lansbury resigned as leader before the 1935 general election Attlee overcame the challenge of Herbert Morrison and Arthur Greenwood to lead his party (with the latter's supporters overwhelmingly backing Attlee on the second ballot). As leader he was to overcome several attempts by colleagues to displace him and become the longest-serving head of any major political party in twentieth-century Britain.

Peter Clarke writes that Attlee's 1934 conversion from unilateral disarmament to collective security did much to give Labour 'a credible defence policy' but Cowling, among others, would argue that such a claim sits poorly with Attlee's steadfast opposition to rearmament.

By making it clear that he could serve under Churchill but not Halifax in 1940, Attlee did his country a great service and as deputy prime minister (from 1942) and vice-chairman of the cabinet committees on Defence and the Home Front he did sterling but unheroic work of an executive nature. He also forged an extremely effective partnership with Ernest Bevin whose political intuition, massive common sense and deep knowledge of working-class and trade-union life perfectly complemented Attlee's hard-nosed administrative competence and sense of decency.

Labour's election in 1945 took Churchill by surprise, not least because he reasoned that Attlee completely lacked the charisma which he embodied. However, having been engaged in a 'people's war', the electorate looked beyond political personality and wished to use their vote to ensure that their sacrifices had not been in vain, by ensuring that the mobilization of resources and solidarity of the war years endured in peacetime and prevented any repetition of the mass unemployment of the pre-war period.

This dream was fostered by the creation of the National Health Service, the abolition of the means test and widespread nationalization but was placed under strain by the continuation and extension of rationing and dispelled by the convertibility and fuel crises of 1947 although Labour had still done enough by February 1950 to be returned to office, albeit with a greatly reduced majority. Attlee's majority of six seats is all the more impressive when one takes into account the fact that the Conservatives gained an estimated sixty seats through the redrawing of constituency boundaries.

Although Attlee began the liquidation of Empire and obliged Truman's America to assume British responsibilities for the defence of Greece and Turkey in 1947, the decision to build an independent nuclear arsenal and, still more, Britain's participation in the Korean War overstretched Britain's slender resources.

Responsibility for the dispute over National Health Service charges which led to the resignation of Bevan and disfigured the party by splitting it between its right and left wings cannot be laid entirely at Attlee's door, although he created the potential for trouble by passing over Bevan in favour of Gaitskell for the chancellorship and then effectively demoting him to the Ministry of Labour.

In his lifetime Attlee was often treated condescendingly by his peers and the press. Even the electorate were grudging in their approval, for although he won the 1945 and 1950 elections, he lost the 1935, 1951 and 1955 elections: a record number of losses only matched in the twentieth century by Edward Heath. However, history has been far kinder to Attlee to date than to Heath, in part no doubt because the former's achievements were magnified by comparison with those of Wilson and Callaghan, whilst the latter's were outshone when they weren't actually undone by Mrs Thatcher.

Attlee failed to provide inspirational oratory or imaginative thought but his qualities of pragmatism, quiet decency, and common sense chimed with the public mood in the immediate aftermath of the war, and he possessed the ability to harness the diverse talents of his ministerial team, allowing them the space in which they could work effectively, which also allowed him to distance himself from them when they came unstuck, as proved to be the case with Dalton and then Cripps at the Treasury, Morrison at the Foreign Office and Bevan over health charges.

B

Baker Education Act, 1988. The 1988 Education Act is popularly known as the Baker Act after the then Tory secretary of state for education, Kenneth Baker.

It created a National Curriculum, with specified subject content for all children under the age of 16. This innovation was designed to ensure that all students were taught those things which the state considered important and to allow the Department of Education and parents to make meaningful comparisons between schools and teachers when testing of pupils occurred at four key stages. It also allowed schools to opt out of local education authority control by becoming 'grant-maintained' schools, receiving money directly from central government and enjoying the right to control their own budgets.

Baldwin, Stanley, first Earl Baldwin of Bewdley (3 August 1867–13 December 1947). Stanley Baldwin was the son of Alfred Baldwin, a third generation Worcestershire ironmaster who represented the Bewdley division of that county in the Conservative interest from 1892 until his death in 1908. His school career was undistinguished and he achieved only a Third in History at Trinity College, Cambridge.

The young Stanley dutifully followed his father's footsteps into the family business, onto the board of the Great Western Railway and into Conservative politics, succeeding his father as MP for Bewdley.

At the time of the formation of the first World War One coalition (December 1916) Baldwin was parliamentary private secretary to Bonar Law and in July 1917 he became joint financial secretary (with Sir Hardman Lever, for whom he had deputized since February of that year). In this capacity he wrote an anonymous letter to *The Times* (published on 24 June 1919) offering 20% of his own estate to cancel £150,000 of the new War Loan.

In March 1921, after four years in junior office and having turned down the offer of a peerage and the governor-generalship of South Africa in the previous year, Baldwin entered the Lloyd George coalition cabinet as president of the Board of Trade. This promotion came about as a result of the reconstruction of the government necessitated by Bonar Law's resignation through ill health and the fact that Baldwin was so closely identified with his former chief.

The coalition government was hit by the honours scandal and the Chanak crisis. More fundamentally, the Conservative backbenches were restless because Austen Chamberlain, Bonar Law's successor as party leader, was considered too accommodating towards Lloyd George. At the famous Carlton Club meeting on 19 October 1922 Baldwin backed the motion that the Conservatives withdraw from the coalition. The motion was carried by 185 to 88, Bonar Law became prime minister and Baldwin, after a due show of reluctance, continued his meteoric rise by becoming his chancellor of the exchequer.

The two men fell out over American debt settlement, with Bonar Law reduced to stating his case anonymously in a letter to *The Times*. Baldwin won the argument and the succession to Bonar Law when ill health forced the latter's resignation in 1923. That Baldwin should thus become prime minister at the age of fifty-five, after less than three years' cabinet experience, was less a surprise for the wily Baldwin than it was for Curzon his principal, and much more experienced, rival.

Baldwin sought to reunite the Conservative Party and although Austen Chamberlain was unwilling to join the government without Birkenhead, Baldwin secured the next best thing by relinquishing the chancellorship in favour of Austen's half-brother Neville Chamberlain. More fundamentally, Baldwin sought a political realignment whereby Labour would replace the Liberal Party as a moderate, responsible party of government and the chief challenger to the Conservatives.

Baldwin decided to hold an election in 1923 in which he campaigned upon a call for tariff reform for a variety of reasons. Firstly, the hitherto staunchly free trade and electorally crucial North West appeared to be ripe for the taking, given the demand for protection of the woollen and worsted industries. Secondly, such a move would both pre-empt Lloyd George from adopting the issue on his return from the States and drive a wedge between him and his former coalition allies such as Austen Chamberlain. Thirdly, it would secure the support of the Beaverbrook press and promised Baldwin the prospect of winning a personal mandate at the polls.

In the short term the 1923 election was a severe setback for Baldwin. The Liberals (as in 1906) were reunited in the defence of free trade and the Conservatives lost office. More fundamentally, the result represented a setback for Baldwin's long-term objective of replacing the Liberal Party with Labour as the chief source of opposition to the Conservative Party. However, the prospects of this development were considerably strengthened when Asquith played into Baldwin's hands by persuading the Liberals to put Labour into (minority) office insofar as the electorate blamed the Liberals for taking this gamble but were also shown, in the event, that Labour under Ramsay MacDonald was capable of responsible government.

This outcome buried the Liberals even more deeply than it buried the issue of tariff reform, and following Labour's defeat in parliament over the Campbell Case and exploitation of the Zinoviev Letter, Baldwin emerged from the 1924 election with an even more strongly united party (Austen Chamberlain having clambered back on board) and a majority over the Liberals and Labour combined of 228 seats.

Baldwin's Second Ministry of 1924–29 was marked by great events including the return to the gold standard, the signing of the Locarno Pact, and the 1926 Imperial Conference, but only in the case of the General Strike was Baldwin's role greater than that of his cabinet colleagues. He initially postponed confrontation, firstly by effectively killing off a private member's bill in late February 1925, which would have substituted 'contracting in' for 'contracting out' with regard to trade union political funds, and secondly, in

July 1925, by subsidizing the coal industry in order to maintain existing wages and profits whilst the Samuel Commission reported on the industry. However, Baldwin ultimately took steps that provoked industrial action and thus 'justified' his breaking off negotiations with the TUC. During and after the General Strike of 1926, however, Baldwin successfully conveyed an image of restraint, notwithstanding suspension of the legislation restricting miners' hours and the passage of the 1927 Trade Disputes Act, which meant that the degree of bitterness experienced by organized labour in general and the miners in particular was less than would otherwise have been the case.

The electorate found 'Safety First', the Conservative slogan for the 1929 election, singularly uninspiring and Labour emerged as the largest single party but without an overall majority. MacDonald thus formed his second minority government. This result, Baldwin's support for Irwin's October 1929 declaration in favour of eventual Dominion status for India (which provoked the resignation of Winston Churchill from the Shadow Cabinet) and his generally lacklustre performance as leader of the opposition, led to Baldwin's being harassed in the press and at by-elections (where they ran independent Conservatives) by the press lords Beaverbrook and Rothermere, occasioning Baldwin's famous jibe at those enjoying 'power without responsibility – the prerogative of the harlot throughout the ages ... '.

The prospect of a return to office, albeit in a National Government, opened up in 1931 as a consequence of Labour's divisions regarding cuts in unemployment benefit, although it was Neville Chamberlain who headed the negotiations on the Conservative side because Baldwin was holidaying on the continent. Indeed, Baldwin was effectively boxed into a corner because he could hardly reject George V's request that he be prepared to serve under MacDonald. This not only destroyed the realignment of politics which he had carefully nurtured since the 1920s but reduced him to the condition of enjoying power without full responsibility as Lord President of the Council under MacDonald for four and a half years, during which time he negotiated imperial preference at Ottawa.

When MacDonald stepped down in May 1935 the King appointed Baldwin to succeed him and Baldwin managed to ensure that the National Government retained a commanding majority (of 247) after the November 1935 election by simultaneously campaigning upon moderate rearmament and collective responsibility through the League of Nations. Those campaigning for greater military preparedness were temporarily silenced by the appointment, in February 1936, of the Attorney General Thomas Inskip as minister for the coordination of defence. In the meantime, the uproar over the Hoare–Laval Pact had been brought to an end at the cost of forcing Hoare's resignation.

Before he himself stepped down from public office for good in May 1937, there remained one further occasion on which Baldwin exhibited his sureness of touch, namely, in managing to resolve the abdication crisis in such a way as to prevent the issue developing into a major constitutional or political crisis. After resigning Baldwin was made a knight of the garter and became Earl Baldwin of Bewdley. He seemed likely to enjoy his twilight years with his reputation secure in the hands of his former colleagues in the House of Commons, whose salaries he had increased by 50% on the day prior to his departure. However, the outbreak of World War Two meant that Baldwin was soon branded as one of the 'guilty men' who had failed to make adequate preparation to meet the threat posed by foreign dictators. Baldwin thus had to suffer a period of intense public vilification prior to a return to obscurity just before his death in 1947.

Like Salisbury, Baldwin was the dominant figure in British politics for roughly fifteen years. Like Salisbury, too, he brought the Conservative Party electoral dominance by assisting in a fundamental realignment of party politics. However, the differences are as great, or greater, than the similarities. Baldwin, unlike Salisbury, was not a great thinker or particularly interested in foreign affairs, and where Salisbury was abrasive Baldwin was emollient. However, beneath his avuncular, placid and even indolent exterior, Baldwin was a very shrewd operator, with special gifts for projecting an image of himself and of the society that he wished to preserve (not least by exploiting the written medium and the new media of radio and film). Baldwin's bucolic 'Englishness', for example, with its supposed qualities of decency and straight-talking, was originally fashioned in contrast to MacDonald's high-flown Hibernian rhetoric and the Druidical deviousness of the 'Welsh wizard' Lloyd George.

Baldwin was never capable of inspiring passion but he was pre-eminently capable of symbolizing moderation, sanity and patriotism and thereby inspiring widespread affection and trust.

Balfour, Arthur James, first Earl of Balfour (25 July 1848–19 March 1930). Arthur Balfour owed much to his mother, not only because she largely brought him up after his father died when he was six but also because she was a Cecil. Indeed, 'Bob's your uncle' was the expression coined to refer to the advantages he gleaned from being the nephew and political beneficiary of the 3rd Marquess of Salisbury.

After Eton and Trinity College, Cambridge, Balfour, after his mother dissuaded him from a career in philosophy, was elected MP for Hertford in 1874. He acted as private secretary to his uncle (then foreign secretary) in 1878 and became a member of the mischief-making 'Fourth Party' in the early 1880s. However, when Salisbury returned to office he received a series of posts, becoming president of the Local Government Board, 1885–86; secretary for Scotland, 1886 and – most testingly – chief secretary for Ireland, 1887–91. But whereas Ireland proved the political graveyard of most chief secretaries, and the literal one of Lord Frederick Cavendish, it provided the means whereby Balfour made his name or rather changed his sobriquet. No longer 'Pretty Fanny', he became known as 'Bloody Balfour' because of the tough methods by which he pacified the country whilst also seeking to 'kill Home Rule by kindness' by such means as Land Purchase and Congested Districts legislation.

He was made leader of the House of Commons and First Lord of the Treasury in 1891 and thereafter, until he stepped down to make way for his nephew, Balfour acted as Salisbury's elegant mouthpiece in the Commons and even conducted foreign affairs in his place, in the latter stages of his premiership, when Salisbury was absent abroad or ill.

Appalled by the way in which the Boer War had exposed Britain's military unpreparedness and diplomatic isolation, Balfour took action to rectify the situation with measures such as recasting the old Defence Committee of the cabinet into the Committee of Imperial Defence; setting up the War Office (Reconstitution Committee); smoothing relations with the United States (over British Guiana) and agreeing to the Anglo-Japanese alliance in 1902 and the Entente Cordiale in 1904.

Balfour's statesmanlike qualities were also apparent in his passing the 1902 Education Act despite nonconformist protest. However, his gifts proved insufficient to maintain party unity, or power, after Joseph Chamberlain launched his tariff reform crusade in 1903. He tried to hold the party together by accepting the case for retaliatory tariffs whilst keeping the door ajar for full-blooded protectionism should the party approve such a course of action. He also tried, with what appeared to be much double-dealing, to balance the resignation of the Protectionist Chamberlain, with those of the Free Trade ministers Ritchie, Hamilton and Balfour of Burleigh. This was all to no avail, however, and the Tories went down to a massive defeat in 1906. Dissatisfaction with Balfour's leadership reached a climax when he counselled acceptance of the Parliament Bill in 1911 as the price of the party retaining its majority in the Lords. In retrospect it had clearly been a mistake to encourage the Lords to reject the People's Budget but the argument that Lloyd George was abusing the budget appeared plausible and dissatisfaction with the overall Liberal record was sufficiently strong to reduce their position in the 1910 elections from an overall majority of 130 to dependence upon their Irish and Labour allies.

Although Balfour resigned the leadership on 8 November 1911 he remained at the centre of power, being made a permanent member of the Committee of Imperial Defence in 1914; first Lord of the Admiralty when he joined the first Coalition Ministry of May 1915; and foreign minister (1916–19) and Lord President of the Council (1919–22) under Lloyd George. He returned to the latter post between 1925 and 1929 under Baldwin and thus remained in high office until a year before his death aged eighty-two in 1930.

Of independent means both materially and spiritually, 'Nothing matters very much; and very little matters at all' is an aphorism of Balfour's. It conforms both with his rather dilettante manner and with his interest in grand philosophical questions. It is belied by his actions as a politician where he showed himself to be a player whose success was variable but who was always in earnest and who managed to project an image of Olympian detachment whilst engaged in much Machiavellian political manoeuvring. Indeed, Balfour's contemporaries at Cambridge shrewdly took the measure of the man when they nicknamed him 'Tiger Lily': the elegant exterior concealing reserves of mental and physical toughness.

Margot Asquith, a fellow member of the Souls, shrewdly believed that Balfour's weaknesses were that his privileged upbringing and natural charm had denied him the opportunity to shape his character in adversity, whilst the brilliance of his mind and nonchalant air enabled him to argue any case with equal plausibility so that he 'either finessed the ethical basis of his intellect or had none', rendering him 'unintelligible to the average man' and 'unforgivable to the fanatic'. Ultimately Balfour's intellectual detachment was such that his party dispensed with his services as its leader.

Balfour Education Act, 1902. The civil servant Robert Morant (a friend of the Webbs) secretly persuaded a London County Council official to bring a test case over whether the Forster Education Act allowed school boards to fund secondary education. As he anticipated, the ruling was that only elementary education could be lawfully funded under the terms of the 1870 Education Act. Morant thus ensured that the Balfour government would legislate on the matter and the result was the 1902 Education Act, popularly known as the Balfour Education Act.

This Act charged county councils in England and Wales with the responsibility, hitherto discharged by 2,500 locally elected school boards, for providing elementary education through Local Education Authorities (LEAs), as well as investing them with the responsibility for funding education 'other than elementary', which embraced secondary and technical education as well as teacher training. The new municipal grammar schools created under the terms of the Act were modelled on the public schools.

Henceforth a Board of Education with a minister as its president would replace the Privy Council subcommittee as the body with overall responsibility for education. Church schools were to have sole responsibility for their capital spending but would receive grants for current spending from local government in return for a third of the seats on their governing bodies.

The most contentious aspect of the Bill, however, was the proposal that all elementary schools with approved educational standards were to be eligible to support from a local property tax. This raised the spectre of 'Rome on the rates' which had lain behind much of the opposition to Clause 25 of the Forster Education Act. This was an acute embarrassment to the Unitarian Joseph Chamberlain who had made his name in national politics through the Education League campaign against the 1870 Act and who continued to represent the 'nonconformist conscience' in its Liberal Unionist manifestation. The Balfour Education Act thus provoked a nonconformist revolt, eroded the position of the administration returned at the 'Khaki election' of 1900 and helped to sour the already strained relations between the new prime minister and his colonial secretary who avoided a direct confrontation with his leader on the issue by touring the empire in the winter of 1902–3 but who returned to challenge the party leadership, fiscal orthodoxy and the electoral mould by launching his crusade for tariff reform in 1903.

Once elected, in 1906, the Liberals tried to undo what they regarded as the worst aspects of the Balfour Act but the Birrell and McKenna Education

Bills of 1906 and 1908 respectively both fell foul of the Unionist majority in the Lords.

Ballot Act, 1872. Radicals had long campaigned for voting by ballot as a means of eliminating electoral bribery and corruption. Indeed it formed one of the six points of the People's Charter.

Gladstone, like many of those first elected without benefit of the ballot, was sceptical of the merits of the proposal but a bill was introduced under the auspices of his administration in 1871 following a favourable select committee report and became law the following year. Its impact was particularly noticeable in Ireland where ironically the Liberal Party was the chief victim of its introduction, being gradually supplanted by an Irish Home Rule party.

Bank Charter Act, 1844. When Peel entered into his second ministry in 1841 the financial system was unstable and there appeared to be a high risk of bank failure. The 1844 Bank Charter Act went a long way towards rectifying this situation and completing the work of stabilizing the currency which he had begun in 1819 when he chaired the Bullion Commission which recommended a phased restoration of the gold standard.

The Bank Charter Act increased the powers of the Bank of England by giving it the sole right of issuing banknotes in the London area. New banks were banned from issuing banknotes and provincial banks lost this right if they either opened a London branch or amalgamated with a London house, or increased their partners to more than six. Furthermore it was stated that all notes in circulation above the sum of £14m (the fiduciary or 'on trust' issue) were to be backed by gold deposited in the Bank of England's vaults.

Bedchamber Incident, 7–13 May 1839. On 7 May 1839, the Melbourne cabinet agreed to resign office on the grounds that the Commons vote of the previous day, when their majority fell to just five votes, showed them to be incapable of carrying their anti-slavery policy into full effect.

Melbourne doubtless anticipated a repetition of the events of 1834–35, with Peel wrestling with the problems of governing with a minority administration, whilst Melbourne recreated the coalition of anti-Peelite forces. However, it was not to be as Victoria refused to accede to Peel's request that she replace certain Whig Ladies of the Bedchamber with Conservative ones, as a mark of royal confidence. This was the so-called Bedchamber Incident or Bedchamber Crisis.

Victoria refused, and then led Melbourne to understand that Peel had requested the resignation of the entire Household and persuaded him to return to office. The whole affair illustrates the residual power of the Crown and the wilfulness of Victoria.

Bentham, Jeremy (15 February 1748–6 June 1832). Jeremy Bentham was an infant prodigy, studying Latin and French at the age of six, for example. He went to Queen's College, Oxford at twelve years of age to study law and was admitted to Lincoln's Inn at the age of fifteen. Although admitted to the Bar he did not practise law but embarked upon a critique of the legal system which expanded into a discourse on the relations between law and morality.

Bentham's *Introduction to the Principles of Morals and Legislation* (published 1789) best represents the quality of his thought in a single volume. Although he received the patronage of the Earl of Shelburne, Bentham's influence in his own lifetime was, however, severely circumscribed by the outbreak of the French Revolution and the general distrust that it bred of radical ideas.

Bentham nevertheless attracted the support of a number of devoted followers, including James Mill, Joseph Parkes and Edwin Chadwick who, variously known as Philosophic Radicals, Benthamites, or Utilitarians, were to have a profound impact upon the administration and government of nineteenth-century Britain, especially with regard to the penal system, the poor law, policing and local government, through their contributions to the *Westminster Review* and a series of royal commissions in the 1830s.

The term 'utilitarians' derives from the fact that Bentham claimed that the principle of utility provided an objective means of assessing human actions. Insofar as an action tended to produce 'the greatest happiness of the greatest number', Bentham considered that action desirable. Bentham equated happiness with pleasure and its antithesis with pain, and believed that a felicific calculus informed by this understanding provided a practical means of assessing the desirability or undesirability of all actions. Such a view had the merit of discountenancing claims to natural rights but was flawed philosophically because of the asymmetrical nature of response to the pleasure–pain antithesis (the fact that it is easier to empathize with the person who suffers pain than the individual who experiences pleasure). Moreover, in practical terms the crude psychology underpinning Bentham's thought resulted in his followers sanctioning a great deal of unnecessary suffering, most notably through their application of the less eligibility principle to the 1834 Poor Law Amendment Act.

Bentham's crankishness was apparent for all to see in the terms of his will. In accordance with his wishes, his body was dissected in the presence of his friends and his fully clothed skeleton provided the basis for a wax effigy which at the time of writing still adorns University College, London (which he was largely responsible for founding as a non-Anglican alternative to Oxbridge and Durham).

Beveridge Report on Social Insurance and Allied Services (Cmd 6404), 1 December 1942. The Beveridge Report, entitled *Social Insurance and Allied Services*, had its origins in the interdepartmental committee on the coordination of social insurance set up in June 1941 by Arthur Greenwood, the minister for reconstruction. Beveridge was appointed chairman in large part because Bevin, for whom he was working at the Ministry of Labour, saw it as a means of ridding himself of an arrogant and awkward subordinate. Beveridge exceeded the committee's terms of reference to produce a report that effectively laid the foundations of the modern British welfare state.

Its Bunyanesque language, such as the determination to slay the 'five giant evils' of Want, Disease, Ignorance, Squalor and Idleness, owed much to the future Mrs Beveridge, Jessy Mair. This appealing populist style, cleverly engineered advance publicity (orchestrated by the future Lord Longford, Frank Pakenham), the decision to publish separately a cheap edition of the concluding twenty-page summary, and the fact that the victory of El Alamein boosted morale and focused minds on what would happen after the war was won all helped to ensure that the report had an enormous impact.

There was thus strong reaction to the popular perception that Churchill sought to shelve or kill the report to which he responded by promising, amongst other things, the abolition of unemployment and 'national compulsory insurance for all classes for all purposes from the cradle to the grave' after the war, in a broadcast on 21 March 1943.

More practically, a Whitehall committee was established to consider implementation of Beveridge's report which was involved in producing four White Papers, including the 1944 White Paper on Employment Policy (which committed government to 'the maintenance of a high and stable level of employment') and two major pieces of legislation (the Butler Education and Family Allowance Acts) before the 1945 general election.

Bevin, Ernest, (7 March 1881–14 April 1951). Ernest Bevin was the youngest and illegitimate son of Mercy Bevin who was midwife for the small Somerset village of Winsford on the edge of Exmoor. To support herself and her family (she had six sons in all) she also worked as a domestic help and in the village public house but was nevertheless obliged to apply for parish relief on several occasions. She died when Ernest was eight. He lived with his half-sister Mary, leaving school at the age of eleven to work as a farm boy.

At thirteen Bevin moved to Bristol to join two of his brothers in casual labour. A measure of stability, respectability and modest prosperity arrived when he became a van driver with a mineral water firm. After flirting with the idea of becoming a Baptist minister or even a missionary, Bevin joined the Bristol Socialist Society, which was affiliated to the Social Democratic Federation, and became active from 1908 on the Right to Work committee which sought to combat rising unemployment. During the Bristol docks strike of 1910 a carmen's or carters' branch of the Dockers' Union, with Bevin as its chairman, was formed and in 1911 he became a full-time official in the union.

The failure of a series of strikes persuaded him of the need to develop a stronger centralized authority and by 1914 he was helping to create it as one of the union's three national organizers. To the men he appeared as their uncompromising champion and displayed great skill in negotiating compromise solutions which nevertheless satisfied them.

In 1915 Bevin represented his union at the Trades Union Congress for the first time and in 1916 was elected to the executive council of the Transport Workers' Federation. The war years also saw him develop as an able administrator, not least on the joint committees to secure the efficient use of manpower. In 1920 he became assistant general secretary of his union and a national figure by winning the dockers' claim for 16s (80p) a day, and by leading the Council of Action which successfully boycotted the export of arms for use against the Bolsheviks.

Bevin played the leading role in the process whereby fourteen unions were merged to create the Transport and General Workers' Union on 1 January 1922 with a membership of 300,000. Moreover, this colossus continued to grow and provided Bevin with a powerful base, together with his membership of the general council of the TUC from 1925, from which to influence the whole climate of industrial relations. Assisted by Walter (later Lord) Citrine, the TUC general secretary, Bevin brought about a decisive shift away from confrontation towards industrial conciliation, beginning with the Mond-Turner talks in 1928.

He also assisted the labour movement more generally, for example in helping turn the Daily Herald into a successful newspaper jointly owned by the TUC and Odhams Press, and combating pacifism within the Labour Party, forcing Lansbury into resigning in 1935 after publicly castigating him for carting his conscience round from conference to conference. When rebuked by a colleague for this harsh personal attack an unabashed Bevin characteristically replied, 'Lansbury has been going about dressed up in saint's clothes for years waiting for martyrdom. I set fire to the faggots.'

Bevin shared with Churchill an appreciation of the need for total war and he was uniquely qualified to mobilize the country's manpower and industrial resources. Thus he was appointed Minister of Labour and National Service in May 1940 and entered the War Cabinet five months later. Bevin maximized production not only by negotiating the 'dilution' of industry (breaking down skilled jobs in factories and having them performed by large numbers of semi- and unskilled workers, including women) but also by improving working and living conditions. As the mine workers known as 'Bevin boys' shows, he was not unwilling to conscript labour but this was done as a last rather than first resort. In mobilizing labour and ensuring harmonious labour relations Bevin played a decisive role in securing British victory and in so doing won Churchill's admiration.

When Labour was elected in 1945 Bevin coveted the chancellorship and Attlee initially considered offering him the post. In the event, however, he decided to offer Dalton the Treasury and Bevin the Foreign Office, not least because this would distance Dalton from the King and keep Bevin away from Herbert Morrison who had a general oversight of domestic affairs and with whom he notoriously did not get on. When someone said of Morrison that 'he is his own worst enemy' Bevin is famously said to have responded, 'Not while I'm alive he ain't': a sentiment which Attlee would have echoed.

Bevin's close partnership with Attlee, who relied upon him as guarantor of trade union support and loyal defender of his leadership, meant that he was given a very free hand in determining policy even, as with the Middle East, when Attlee did not fully share his views. However, Bevin faced a new world order from a position in which Britain possessed moral authority but lacked the sinews of power, with roughly 10 per cent of prewar national wealth destroyed, the merchant marine 30 per cent smaller than at the outbreak of war, and exports running at little more than 40 per cent of their total in September 1939. Lend–Lease was ended abruptly in August 1945 and ultimately replaced by an American loan whose onerous conditions were to provoke a convertibility crisis. Although the British Empire and Commonwealth comprised roughly a third of the globe's population and nearly a quarter of its land surface it was manifestly in a process of unravelling, which the Americans, no less than the Russians, were keen to assist.

The 1947 withdrawal from the Indian subcontinent was managed with minimal loss of goodwill but the 1948 withdrawal from Palestine was a humiliation, which was only partially offset by defence agreements with Egypt and Jordan in 1949.

Bevin had expressed the hope that in dealing with Russia it might be possible for 'Left to speak to Left' but his experiences at Potsdam rapidly disabused him of this notion and convinced him that Stalin wished to exploit every opportunity to expand Soviet territory and influence. He also came to appreciate that the Left's talk of building a 'third force' of western European powers counterbalancing the Soviet and American power blocs was based upon a misreading of the situation and that Britain's interests lay in persuading the US to assume Britain's traditional role of throwing its weight onto the continent to restore a balance of power, given the disequilibrium arising from British weakness and Soviet ambition.

In February 1947 he successfully made his pitch, pointing out that America would have to step into Britain's shoes in providing economic and military support for Greece or Turkey or risk their falling within the communist orbit. The result was the 'Truman doctrine': a decisive rejection of traditional American isolationism (although Churchill deserves some credit for bringing about this change of heart through his Iron Curtain speech at Fulton, Missouri, in Truman's presence, the previous year).

Bullock identifies three phases in Bevin's five-and-a-half years at the Foreign Office. The eighteen months between the summer of 1945 and the spring of 1947 he characterises as one of frustration arising from the realisation that Britain was too weak to act alone. Britain's decline from great power to supplicant status was marked by the request that America share the costs of running the British zone in Germany and assume the cost of supporting Greece and Turkey, the announcement of withdrawal dates from India, Ceylon and Burma, and the referral of the Palestine Mandate to the United Nations. The turnaround came with America's realisation that Britain needed greater assistance if it, and large swathes of territory both inside and outside Europe, were not to run the risk of being overrun by communism.

The period from April 1947 to the February 1950 election Bullock describes as one of achievement for Bevin, arising from closer relations with, and more generous resources from, the US marked by the formation of the Organization for European Economic Cooperation, in which Bevin played a key role, in response to Marshall Aid. Bevin appreciated the need to create an economically viable and independent West German state in order to ensure the economic recovery and security of western Europe as a whole and played a decisive role in facilitating this process with the Americans (through, for example, the merging of the British and American occupation zones and the Berlin Airlift) whilst also reassuring the French (through the treaties of Dunkirk, Brussels and NATO).

Bevin's foreign policy in the period from February 1950 until his March 1951 resignation is characterised as controversial by Bullock and the arguments regarding Bevin's foreign policy as a whole continue to this day. There are basically two broad, overlapping, charges levelled against him, namely, that he missed the opportunity to take Britain into the European Economic Community, and that he failed to adjust Britain's foreign policy to the fact that she was no longer a front-ranking world power.

In fact, as shown above, Bevin was painfully aware of Britain's diminished power and hence acceded to such actions as the transfer on power in India and Palestinian withdrawal. His achievement was to ensure that Britain was able to continue to punch above its weight by drawing upon support from both Europe and the US. It was precisely because of the 'special relationship' and relations with the Commonwealth that Britain was reluctant to commit itself further to Europe in this period. Nor is it true to say that Bevin sacrificed Britain's independence to American paymasters. Marshall Aid was dispensed with in 1950, two years ahead of schedule, and Britain's foreign policy under Bevin was sometimes opposed to Washington's. For example, Britain was swift to recognise the People's Republic of China and exercised its influence over the Americans during the Korean War to help ensure that the war didn't spill over into Formosa or mainland China. In short, Bevin was nobody's lapdog but rather embodied the bulldog spirit and helped Britain recover its self-respect and enjoy the respect of other nations.

In March 1951, plainly in ill health, Bevin relinquished the Foreign Office to become Lord Privy Seal. He died the following month.

Bevin essentially had three careers: as trade union leader, wartime Labour minister, and as Foreign Secretary. He rose magnificently to the challenge which each of these roles presented. A giant of a man, he created a colossus in the shape of the TGWU but used the muscle which this provided to facilitate rather than disrupt industrial relations. As Minister of Labour and a War Cabinet member Bevin arguably did more than any other man, after Churchill, to equip Britain to fight the war successfully. It is thus entirely fitting that a famous cartoon by David Low depicts Bevin as striding in the front rank next to Churchill at the head of the wartime coalition as they roll up their sleeves for the fight. As Foreign Secretary he played a very weak hand with extraordinary skill in order to ensure that Britain remained a Great Power, albeit in a lower league than the superpowers. In all that he did, the integrity, humour and humanity of the man shines through. He described himself as 'A turn-up in a million' but 'Ernie' was also the salt of the earth writ large.

Black and Tans In 1920 the Irish authorities placed advertisements to recruit auxiliary units to strengthen the regular Royal Irish Constabulary, which was under-strength and over-stretched as a result of increasing IRA violence, much of it directed against the men of the RIC and their families. Those who joined up were mostly ex-servicemen attracted by the prospect of combining a relatively well-paid job with the camaraderie which they had found in the forces. However, they were ill-equipped to cope with the conditions of guerrilla warfare which they found in Ireland and this, together with the relative laxity of police discipline, compared with that of the army, conspired to produce a policy of reprisals which culminated in outrages such as the massacre at Croke Park football stadium and the destruction of the centre of Cork.

The Black and Tans were so named by their opponents partly after a Limerick pack of hounds and partly with reference to their motley uniforms, which combined army khaki with dark green police belts and caps. There was also a separate Auxiliary Division, comprised of ex-officers who, in the opinion of Skidelsky, committed many of the outrages commonly attributed to the Black and Tans.

The activities of the Black and Tans and the Auxiliaries certainly became a source of acute embarrassment for Lloyd George, not least at the hands of Mosley, because his government appeared to have approved their excesses.

'Black Wednesday', 16 September 1992. On 'Black Wednesday' the chancellor, Norman Lamont, made the humiliating announcement that Britain was suspending its membership of the Exchange Rate Mechanism (which pegged the pound to the ECU and a basket of European currencies).

This U-turn came about because sterling was rendered vulnerable to speculation on the currency markets because it was trapped between a weak dollar, which acted as a drag on its exchange rate, at a time when the costs of German reunification led the Bundesbank to keep its – and hence Europe's – interest rates high.

This effective devaluation destroyed the government's economic policy and fatally undermined the credibility of both the chancellor and the Major government. Devaluation and cuts in interest rates also helped produce economic recovery but the Conservatives were unable to reap the rewards of the 'feel-good factor' because 'Black Wednesday' had shattered the Conservatives' reputation for economic competence. The fact that the British economy apparently performed better outside the ERM was a powerful weapon in the armoury of those who disliked the Maastricht Treaty and argued against a single European currency. Such commentators accordingly refer to 'White Wednesday'.

Blair, Anthony (Tony) Charles Lynton (6 May 1953–). Tony Blair was born in Edinburgh, into the middle class. The family settled in Durham, where Blair's lawyer father suffered a debilitating stroke when Tony was 11 years old. He was educated at Durham Choristers School and Fettes College in Edinburgh before reading law at St John's College, Oxford.

Blair graduated in 1975 with a second-class degree, and was called to the bar the following year and entered into practice. In 1980 he married Cherie Booth, a fellow barrister, with whom he was to have four children.

In 1982 he failed as Labour candidate in the Beaconsfield by-election but won Sedgefield in the following year. Together with Gordon Brown he was regarded as a coming man, becoming the youngest member of the shadow cabinet in 1988 and being elected to the National Executive Committee in 1992 after spells as shadow spokesman for energy, employment and the Home Office. In the latter capacity he was widely credited with having 'stolen' law and order as a vote-winning issue from the Tories. His catchphrase 'Tough on crime, tough on the causes of crime', with its blend of toughness and compassion (implying a connection between crime and social deprivation), nicely illustrated Blair's ability to appear all things to all men.

When John Smith died in 1994, Blair was elected leader (after Brown swung behind his bid), and followed the tactics of Neil Kinnock in establishing his credentials for ruling the country by imposing his grip upon his party. More specifically this process of modernization meant reducing the powers of the trade unions and diluting the commitment to socialism by the repeal of Clause 4 of the party's constitution.

Like Peel in the 1830s, Blair in the 1990s repackaged and relabelled his party in order to broaden its appeal and make it electable. Thus Labour became 'New Labour', and 'new' became a mantra to tap into the increasingly widespread feeling that it was time for a change, given that the Conservatives had held office continuously since 1979. The youthful, dynamic Blair skilfully won support for New Labour amongst many 'Middle England' voters who regarded the Major government as sleaze-ridden and lacking either inspiration or direction. Under Blair it became clear that Labour would not turn back the clock on the curbing of union powers or the privatization associated with Thatcherism, whilst the fundamental novelty at the heart of New Labour was that it was supposedly no longer going to be the party of high taxation and high spending.

Thus Labour won a landslide victory on 1 May 1997, winning 419 seats to the Conservatives' 165. Blair, the youngest prime minister since Lord Liverpool, then entered into the longest honeymoon period enjoyed by any premier in living memory. The Bernie Ecclestone affair, when the government appeared to be willing to allow preferential treatment to Formula One racing regarding restraints on tobacco advertising, threatened to tarnish Blair's image but his gravitas at the time of the death of Princess Diana, when the House of Windsor itself appeared in danger of losing its hold over the public's affections, helped give him a statesmanlike image which was burnished by his willingness to intervene to prevent 'ethnic cleansing' in Kosovo.

Domestically Blair's first parliament was characterized by a series of regional referenda: on the peace settlement for Ireland; on a parliament for Scotland (with tax-raising powers) and an assembly for Wales; and on a mayor for London. It is notable that the English – the overwhelming majority within the United Kingdom – were not offered a referendum on an English parliament and that the talk about English regional assemblies remained just that. Another notable feature of these referenda is that although power was formally devolved, Blair appeared unwilling to face the consequences of the people freely exercising their new-found powers. Institutional reform also included the 'freeing' of the Bank of England to set its own interest rates and the abolition of the voting rights of hereditary peers in the House of Lords.

The most important referendum for the future of the United Kingdom was put on hold. Party divisions over Europe were papered over by the promise that the referendum on entry to the Euro (the European single currency) would only take place early in the next parliament if all five economic convergence criteria had been met and the government therefore considered it to be in the national interest to recommend joining.

By accepting for two years the spending limits proposed by their predecessors in office, Blair and Brown bought time for policies such as debt reduction to bear fruit, whilst disarming critics – at least from the right. Critics on the left were pacified by the ending of the assisted places scheme (to fund improvements in primary school class size); a windfall tax on public utilities (to fund welfare to work schemes); the bashing of Oxbridge colleges for alleged elitism; and promises of an ethical foreign policy, a Freedom of Information Act and the opportunity to outlaw hunting with dogs.

In fact, Labour left wingers were disinclined to snap at Blair's heels and demand a new Jerusalem so long as he appeared to be the man capable of offering them the electoral Holy Grail of a second term and assisted by an indifferent performance from the Conservatives under William Hague this was duly delivered in 2001. Indeed, the landslide victory of 1997 was hardly dented, with Labour taking 413 of the 659 seats.

Blair's second term was dominated by foreign policy issues, notably the 'war on terror', which involved the invasion of Afghanistan and then Iraq. Although Lord Hutton's inquiry into the death of Iraq arms expert Dr David Kelly exonerated the government and criticized the BBC it was popularly seen as a 'whitewash'. As a result of this and other inquiries Blair was obliged to admit that Britain had gone to war on a false prospectus insofar as Iraq did not pose a clear and present danger to British interests. However, retrospective efforts to claim that the war was about regime change rather than removing non-existent weapons of mass destruction damaged Blair's credibility.

In September 2004 Blair announced that he would serve a full third term as prime minister if he won an historic third term, the popular expectation being that then Brown would take over. In accordance with this fact the Conservatives campaigned in May 2005 on the slogan 'Vote Blair, Get Brown!' before realizing that this was a formula appealing to many voters.

Blair's biography at the No. 10 website stated that 'The Labour Party went on to win a third term for Mr Blair in May 2005 … ' The author may have sought to indicate modesty on Blair's part or imply that he had become an electoral liability. However, the loss of 47 seats still left Labour with a comfortable majority and Blair clearly retained an appetite to leave his mark in the history books before making way for Gordon Brown or anyone else.

Blanketeers, 1817. The Seditious Meetings Act of March 1817 outlawed large public meetings. The Blanketeers were distressed cotton weavers from the Manchester area who sought to circumvent this law in order to register their condition and need for relief. Their chosen mode of protest was to march from St Peter's Fields to London in small groups in order to petition the Prince Regent. They were equipped for the journey with blankets for sleeping rough and hence their name.

Fearful of any protest, following Spa Fields (December 1816) and the mobbing of the Prince Regent's coach (January 1817), the authorities took no chances and with little or no legal justification broke up the march. A single Blanketeer got through to petition Sidmouth, the home secretary.

'Bloody Sunday', 13 November 1886. The February 1886 mass meeting of the unemployed in Trafalgar Square led to disorder which prompted the resignation of the Commissioner of the Metropolitan police force. His successor, Sir Charles Warren, was determined to re-impose order in the capital and banned meetings in Trafalgar Square. The mass meeting called there by the Metropolitan Radical Federation for Sunday 13 November 1886 was therefore always likely to result in violence. Warren certainly took extensive preparations, backing up his police with the military. Two protesters died in the street-fighting, prompting critics of the police and the government to label the affair 'Bloody Sunday', although many supported Warren's uncompromising line, as indicated by the fact that 30,000 volunteered as special constables in the immediate aftermath of the disturbance.

'Bloody Sunday', 30 January 1972. Thirteen were shot dead and thirteen wounded (one of whom died later) by men of the 1st Battalion of the Parachute Regiment when arrest squads entered the Bogside after attempts to contain an illegal Londonderry march against internment by the Civil Rights Association had resulted in stone throwing.

None of those killed and wounded was shot whilst handling firearms or bombs, although the Paras claimed that they only opened fire after coming under fire themselves. When Lord Chief Justice Widgery's public enquiry into these events alleged that there was a 'strong suspicion' that some of those killed 'had been firing weapons or handling bombs in the course of the afternoon' and that 'others had been closely supporting them', it was regarded as a whitewash by the nationalist community.

In 1998 Tony Blair set up a new inquiry under Lord Savile to try to lay the matter to rest.

Boer War, First, 1880–81. The First Boer War, also known as the Transvaal War, was a conflict in which the 8,000 Boers of the Transvaal fought to regain their independence from the British Crown just three years after annexation of the Transvaal and just one year after British arms at Ulundi removed the Zulu threat which had provided a major reason for the Boers acceding to annexation in the first instance.

Sir Bartle Frere, the High Commissioner for South Africa, warned Westminster of the likelihood of armed rebellion if some form of self-government was not granted to the Transvaal but he was out of favour in official circles for his role in promoting the Zulu war and Wolseley, who was handed his responsibilities for the Boers, told them that 'the Vaal River would flow backwards ... sooner than the British would be withdrawn from the Transvaal'.

Statements made by Gladstone during his Midlothian campaigns had, however, given encouragement to the Boers that they would not have to take to arms to resume their independence and the area quietened down in the immediate aftermath of Gladstone's victory in the 1880 general election. Wolseley misinterpreted this as a response to his show of force in building redoubts at eight locations and he was allowed to hand over his command to Major-General Sir George Pomeroy-Colley, who proceeded to reduce British forces in the area. However, it soon became clear that the Liberals hankered after the Transvaal remaining within a Canadian-style federation and the Boers were finally disabused of the notion that they would be handed back their independence when Gladstone announced that 'the Queen cannot be advised to relinquish her sovereignty over the Transvaal'.

Gladstone made this mistake because he was distracted by Irish affairs, was lulled into a false sense of security by the complacent reports of men on the spot, and because he was swayed by the arguments of those who said that the continued presence of the British was necessary to avert maltreatment of the blacks by the Boers.

The Boers proclaimed their independence on 13 December 1880, laid siege to British garrisons in the Transvaal and sought to block reinforcements coming up through Natal. Last-minute negotiations might well have averted any bloodshed for on St Valentine's Day 1881 the cabinet received an offer from Kruger (via Colley) indicating his willingness to accept the adjudication of a Royal Commission if British troops were withdrawn in the meantime. On 16 February the cabinet instructed Colley to inform Kruger that his proposal would be acceptable if an immediate ceasefire was called. Moreover, the cabinet secretly agreed in principle to restore Transvaal independence subject to retaining sovereignty over the native border districts.

However, Colley sought to put Britain into a strong negotiating position by delaying the transmission of the cabinet's message to Kruger until he had secured a victory in the field. In the event Colley was killed and his force of roughly 360 men were comprehensively defeated at Majuba Hill (27–28 February 1881). Colley's replacement, Evelyn Wood, was all for teaching the Boers a lesson but Gladstone approved a truce that came into effect on 6 March after he received Kruger's conciliatory reply to his original offer.

A Royal Commission was duly appointed and the provisional peace terms negotiated by Wood were essentially ratified by the Pretoria Convention in August 1881.

Boer War, Second, 1899–1902. For Britain the Second Boer War had a threefold rationale, namely, serving strategic interests (in protecting the trans-oceanic route to India), serving plutocratic interests (by securing the world's richest goldfield in the Witwatersrand), and serving political interests (in providing Joseph Chamberlain with the opportunity to promote imperialism as a popular cause). Thus in 1899 the newly appointed Governor of the Cape and High Commissioner Sir Alfred Milner pushed the Boer republics of the Transvaal (established 1848) and the Orange Free State (established 1854) into war as effectively as Sir Bartle Frere had pushed the Zulus into conflict with the British Empire twenty years earlier.

Whereas the British government had been caught by surprise by the outbreak of the First Boer War the ground was studiously prepared for the resumption of that conflict. Firstly, the Boers were cut off from any prospect of German assistance which the Kaiser's telegram had once seemed to hold out, when the promise of Angola in the Anglo-German agreement of 1898 persuaded the Kaiser to renounce any interest in Afrikaner affairs. Secondly, a meeting of Milner and Paul Kruger (the Transvaal president) at Bloemfontein in the summer of 1898 to discuss the problem posed by the uitlanders allowed Britain to give the appearance to the outside world of having exhausted all the diplomatic options whereas in fact Kruger had offered to make concessions to the uitlanders' demands for representation. Thirdly, the successful conclusion of the Sudan campaign with the victory at Omdurman enabled Britain to concentrate its attention and its troops upon the veldt. Thus British troops in southern Africa increased from 12,000 to 50,000. Indeed, it was the build up of imperial troops upon the Transvaal's borders that provoked Kruger into issuing an ultimatum on 9 October 1899 that gave 48 hours for their withdrawal. British rejection of this demand precipitated the Boer declaration of war on 12 October.

However, just as the Zulu War had begun with humiliation for the British at Isandhlwana, so the imperial forces received a series of reverses at the hands of the Boers, with the British territories of Natal and Cape Colony invaded, and Ladysmith, Mafeking and Kimberley besieged. Furthermore, in December British forces were defeated at Colenso, Magersfonetein and Stormberg, in the so-called 'Black Week'.

Eventually, however, the weight of superior numbers began to tell, with reinforcements meaning that nearly 450,000 imperial troops were ranged against roughly 45,000 Boers and by January 1901, with the relief of Ladysmith, Mafeking and Kimberley and with both Bloemfontein and Pretoria (respectively the capitals of the Orange Free State and Transvaal) firmly in British hands, Lord Roberts (who had replaced Sir Redvers Buller as commander-in-chief) felt that the war was as good as won and left the mopping up operations to Kitchener. However, as many as 15,000 Boer commandos continued to operate very effectively as guerrillas and it was not until their land was covered by blockhouses and barbed wire, their farmhouses had been destroyed, and their families had been interned in concentration camps in appalling conditions that they entered peace negotiations on 23 March 1902 and the Treaty of Vereeniging brought the war to an end on 31 May.

Notwithstanding staunch support from the Dominions, the war raised questions about the policy of 'Splendid Isolation' and acted as a spur to a search for friends on the international stage which resulted in the Anglo-Japanese alliance of 1902, the Entente Cordiale with France of 1904, and the Anglo-Russian Entente of 1907.

The war also stimulated military and social reform including the creation of the Committee of Imperial Defence and legislation to enable local authorities to provide free school meals (many recruits having had to be refused because malnourished).

The British lost approximately 28,000 soldiers in the conflict, compared with 4,000 Boer troops and 20,000 civilians (who mostly succumbed to epidemic diseases in the concentration camps). In addition, roughly 12,000 black Africans died serving as non-combatant auxiliaries to the two sides or as inmates of the camps.

Bonar Law, Andrew See LAW, ANDREW BONAR.

Bradlaugh affair, 1880–88. Charles Bradlaugh (1833–91) was elected MP for Northampton in 1880. As an atheist he wished to affirm rather than take the oath before taking his seat. This precipitated a dispute within parliament which was exploited by the Fourth Party. Indeed, the issue brought its four members (Sir Henry Drummond Wolff, John Gorst, Arthur Balfour and Lord Randolph Churchill) together and into national prominence. The quartet exploited the issue as a means of embarrassing the leadership of Sir Stafford Northcote and the 'old gang' in the Commons by being more active than he in embarrassing the Gladstone administration (Gladstone being prepared to indulge Bradlaugh's scruples).

Attacking the republican Bradlaugh incidentally helped Churchill to repair his relations with the Prince of Wales as well as helping to preserve his relations' finances as the £4,000 per annum received by the Duke of Marlbrough was one of the state pensions criticized by Bradlaugh.

Bradlaugh accordingly failed to gain admission to the Commons during the second Gladstone government of 1880–85, and was elected seven times in all before the issue was finally resolved in his favour in 1886.

The ability to affirm was formally recognized by the 1888 Oaths Act.

Bright, John (16 November 1811–27 March 1889). John Bright was brought up in a Quaker family in the Lancashire textile town of Rochdale, and attended Quaker schools at Ackworth and York. His first successful foray into politics came in 1840–41 when he successfully campaigned against church rates in Rochdale but it was as the right-hand man of Richard Cobden in the Anti-Corn Law League that he won national prominence and, in 1842, a seat in parliament representing Durham. The two men were widely seen as possessing complementary qualities, with Cobden embodying reason whilst Bright communicated passion, so that 'it was Bright's task to excite the emotions after Cobden had convinced the understanding' (Briggs).

Bright believed that much remained to be done after the 1846 repeal of the Corn Laws and in 1847 he returned to Lancashire as MP for Manchester. The Manchester School was to pass, however, from widespread acclaim in 1846 to almost universal opprobrium in 1854, with Cobden and Bright's opposition to Britain's involvement in the Crimean War and in 1857, ten years after being returned unopposed, Bright was bottom of the poll in Manchester, almost three thousand votes behind his principal opponent. However, later in the year he moved to Birmingham and was returned unopposed.

Having largely lost a middle-class radical constituency thanks to Palmerston, the Crimean War and the Indian Mutiny, Bright turned to the working class, reinvented himself and revived his political career as the tribune of the people. He forged links with national trade union leaders in support of the North during the American Civil War (1861–65) and then helped provide a respectable front for the extra-parliamentary agitation to enfranchise the respectable working class which culminated in the 1867 Reform Act.

Bright tended to see issues in black and white terms and it is not surprising that the judgement which contemporaries and posterity have made of Bright himself have been correspondingly stark. To those of a cynical cast of mind such as Palmerston, Bright was nothing more than a humbug, whose campaigns to repeal the Corn Laws, propagate peace, reduce taxation and extend the franchise, no less than his consistent opposition to factory reform, were motivated by nothing more than the desire to serve the material interests of his – the manufacturing – class. To those like his fellow-Quaker A. J. P. Taylor, by contrast, Bright was an heroic figure who was prepared to risk all in the pursuit of what he knew to be right. It is no surprise that Gladstone, about whom similar controversies rage, sided with those who gave Bright the benefit of the doubt, stating that 'The supreme eulogy which is Bright's due, is that he elevated political life to a higher elevation … '. However, Gladstone's word should be taken with a pinch of salt insofar as Bright, by the second half of the nineteenth century, represented the acceptable face of radicalism, and as such he served in Gladstone's cabinets in 1868–70, 1873–74 and 1880–82.

His contribution to legislation in this period was largely limited to the Bright clauses of the 1870 Irish Land Act, not least because his political energies were largely confined to threatening resignation over a variety of issues: a threat which carried out in relation to the bombardment of Alexandria in 1882 finally brought his career in public office to an end. In 1886 he was the standard bearer of 'old' radicalism in opposing Irish Home Rule but in this, as in all other respects, he had by this stage been completely eclipsed by the representative of 'new' radicalism: Joseph Chamberlain.

British and Foreign Schools Society Founded in 1810 in response to the problem of growing godlessness, particularly in the growing urban areas, the British and Foreign Schools Society sought to provide a non-conformist or free (Protestant non-Anglican) church education both at home and overseas. It helped inspire the Established Church to respond by setting up the National Society in 1811 and the two voluntary societies became bitter rivals.

British Nationality Act, 1948. The British Nationality Act of 1948 was the first attempt to define British citizenship and in so doing confirmed the legal right of over 800 million Commonwealth citizens to reside in the United Kingdom.

British National Party (BNP) The British National Party (BNP) was formed by John Tyndall in 1982 following a split in the National Front and the accession of a faction from the British Movement and the British Democratic Party. Its supporters call for withdrawal from the European Union and admire Jean-Marie Le Pen but have been unable to emulate his success. Despite efforts to make themselves more respectable, their electoral highlight prior to the new millennium consisted of a local council by-election victory in the Millwall Ward of Tower Hamlets in September 1993.

British Union of Fascists (BUF) On 1 October 1932, on his return from Mussolini's Italy Sir Oswald Mosley launched the British Union of Fascists. It initially received financial support from Lord Rothermere and from Mussolini himself. Although numbering perhaps as many as 40,000 members at its peak it failed to unite all fascist organizations within Great Britain, whilst many were alienated by the violence between the party's blackshirted stewards and anti-fascist demonstrators at its Olympia rally on 7 June 1934. This factor, together with the BUF's growing anti-Semitism and Mosley's increasingly autocratic direction, led to a further waning of support and the party's increasingly turning its energies to local and sectional issues. In particular it sought to exploit anti-Semitic sentiments in the East End of London, causing further disorder, such as the Battle for Cable Street and drawing down upon itself the 1936 Public Order Act (banning political uniforms).

The BUF's increasing radicalization and identification with Nazi Germany rather than fascist Italy was symbolized by the addition of the words 'and National Socialists' to the party name from 1936. This change occurred at the prompting of William Joyce (the future Lord Haw-Haw) who nevertheless broke away to set up his own National Socialist League in 1937.

Before and after the outbreak of World War Two, the BUF campaigned for peace through negotiation, until Mosley and many leading party members were interned on 23 May 1940, and the party was proscribed in July 1940.

Brown, Gordon (20 February 1951–). Gordon Brown is the son of a Labour-voting Church of Scotland minister, and was educated at Kirkcaldy High School and Edinburgh University where he gained 1st Class Honours and a Doctorate. His schoolboy dream of becoming a professional footballer disappeared with the loss of the use of his left eye in an accident and his ambitions thereafter focused upon politics. Already at the age of 12 he was volunteering to canvass against Sir Alec Douglas-Home at the 1963 Kinross and West Perthshire by-election, and at Edinburgh he became rector and chairman of the University Court between 1972 and 1975.

From 1976 to 1980 Brown lectured at Edinburgh and then Caledonian University before working at Scottish TV from 1980 to 1983. His involvement in Labour politics saw him elected to Labour's Scottish Executive in 1977 and become MP for Dunfermline East and Chair of the Labour Party Scottish Council in 1983.

His air of authority and competence and his intellectual and political abilities resulted in his serving on the Opposition front bench as shadow chief secretary to the Treasury (1987–89), shadow trade and industry secretary (1989–92) and shadow chancellor from

1992. In these years Brown's closest political associations were with Peter Mandelson and Tony Blair, with Brown widely perceived as the most likely from their generation ultimately to become Labour leader. However, following the untimely death of John Smith in 1994, Mandelson decided to back Blair rather than Brown for the succession, and Brown, appreciating that the more telegenic Blair's bandwagon had acquired a critical momentum, stepped aside in return for an understanding that he would have the Exchequer in the event of Labour's victory at the polls.

Gordon Brown was duly appointed as chancellor of the exchequer on 2 May 1997. His first act in office (which had not been so much as hinted at in Labour's manifesto) was to establish an independent Bank of England. This symbolized the willingness of New Labour to embrace certain key features of Thatcherism: a point driven home by Labour's sticking to Conservative spending plans for its first two years in office (cutting the overall level of public spending by 0.5% in each of the first two years so that public spending represented the lowest proportion of GDP since the 1960s).

Brown therefore played a pivotal role in allowing Labour to shed its 'tax and spend' image, and he appeared to relish his image as the 'Iron Chancellor'. However, Brown did not wish to alienate Old Labour and therefore stressed that his prudence was for a left-wing redistributive purpose. Thus budgetary surpluses ultimately allowed for the release of more money for health and education as well as helping to finance measures such as the working families tax credit, the children's tax credit, the minimum pension guarantee and increases in child benefit. New Labour's acceptance of the need for a competitive market economy was also tempered by the introduction of the minimum wage.

How History will ultimately judge Brown depends upon two factors: his continuing success as chancellor and his relationship with Tony Blair. The two overlap insofar as one source of tension between the two men concerns the timing of joining the euro. A provisional judgement is that Brown has played a key role in overseeing a substantial improvement in the nation's finances and a radical improvement in the political fortunes of the Labour Party. The key to success in both areas has been Brown's willingness to be a sort of 'Rab' Butler in reverse: moving Labour into a position of occupying and redefining the new political middle-ground established by the Tories in the 1980s (embracing the market, privatization and low taxation), just as Butler helped persuade the Conservative Party of the 1950s to accept the key features of the welfare state and the mixed economy embraced by the Attlee governments. Whether Brown will ultimately fare better than Butler in terms of his political career remains to be seen.

Bruce's Licensing Act, 1872. The 1872 Licensing Act was disliked intensely by the liquor trade, its many customers, and defenders of personal liberty such as Bishop Magee, who famously said he would prefer to see Britain free than sober. However, Gladstone was exaggerating when he remarked 'We have been borne down in a torrent of gin and beer' with respect to the Liberal defeat in the 1874 general election. He nevertheless continued this theme in March 1880 stating, when parliament was dissolved, that the government came in on beer but went out on water (the government's Water Bill to unify the private water companies of London into a single municipal monopoly having been savaged by the Conservative press).

One of the first actions of the Second Ministry headed by Disraeli was to amend the 1872 measure in a manner pleasing to the liquor trade by the 1874 Licensing Act.

Bulgarian atrocities agitation, 1876. In 1875 Gladstone retired from the Liberal leadership and was succeeded by Granville in the Lords and Hartington (later Devonshire) in the Commons. However, in 1876 he returned to the centre of the political stage over what he described as 'the Bulgarian horrors', namely, Turkish massacres of the Sultan's Christian subjects in Bulgaria. Gladstone was not the first to protest against this action. An unholy alliance of nonconformists and High Churchmen had already begun to agitate on the issue, and W. T. Stead along with Bishop Fraser of Manchester, H. P. Liddon, the canon of St Paul's, and the historian Edward Freeman were amongst those luminaries who publicly expressed their indignation prior to Gladstone. Nevertheless he soon came to head the agitation by virtue of his eminence and his eloquence in condemning the atrocities in his pamphlet entitled 'The Bulgarian Horrors', which sold 40,000 copies in a few days and 200,000 copies in its first month. In it he described the Turks as an 'anti-human species of humanity', condemned their 'abominable and bestial lusts', and called for their removal 'bag and baggage' from the Bulgarian province which they had 'desolated and profaned'.

Cynically-minded historians such as Michael Bentley have suggested that Gladstone was perhaps motivated less by moral outrage than the realization that Bulgarian atrocities represented an issue comparable to Irish disestablishment which had the capacity of uniting the chronically fissiparous Liberal Party under Gladstone's leadership and discomfiting his arch-rival Disraeli as the Conservative approach to the Eastern question meant turning a blind eye to Turkish excesses for fear of doing anything which might weaken the Ottoman Empire to Russia's eventual advantage.

Burgage boroughs Prior to the passage of the Great Reform Act in 1832 which swept them away, this form of franchise, conferred the right to vote in some boroughs by virtue of possessing certain specific pieces of property. There were thirty-nine such burgage boroughs out of the 203 English parliamentary boroughs before the reform of parliament.

Butler Education Act, 1944. Rab Butler went to Education in 1941 determined to pass a measure of reform and was assisted in this aim by several powerful officials as well as by the 1942 publication of the Beveridge Report, as Butler's proposal became a means whereby the Conservative Party could demonstrate its willingness to undertake social reform without incurring great expense.

Asked before the passage of the Education Bill, in a Central Office of Information film, what he considered its long-range effects would be, Rab answered that he anticipated its consequences being 'as much social as educational', namely, 'welding us all into one nation'. This is ironic given that the Act created the tripartite secondary school system of grammar, secondary modern and technical schools which came to be regarded as socially divisive because the principle of selection ensured that they did not enjoy parity of esteem (or funding). In essence, grammar schools existed for the academic elite (as determined by the 11+ examination), secondary moderns for the unskilled majority and technical schools for the residue. Butler also did nothing of substance to weld one nation by addressing the public school issue.

However, he was more successful in tackling an even more powerful vested interest in the shape of the voluntary sector, which still ran more than half the schools in England and Wales. Butler tackled the problem of substandard education in church schools by offering financial inducements for them to surrender greater control to local education authorities.

The Act also involved a host of useful reforms regarding such matters as free school milk, meals and transport, as well as its central achievement of making secondary education to the age of fifteen freely available for all (although fees were retained in direct grant independent grammars for non-state aided places).

Given budgetary constraints and limited room for manoeuvre, given the interests of local authorities, the independent sector and the churches, Butler achieved a radical overhaul of the educational system that for all its flaws – such as the failure to develop the technical schools – was a major achievement.

'Butskellism' In February 1954 *The Economist* coined the term 'Butskellism' in order to imply that there was an essential continuity between the economic policies of the Conservatives and their Labour predecessors, as epitomized by R. A. Butler as chancellor (1951–55) and his Labour counterpart, Hugh Gaitskell, who had been chancellor, 1950–51.

More generally, the term came to be applied to the alleged post-war consensus comprising a commitment to Keynesian demand management, full employment, a mixed economy, the welfare state, and Britain's posture as a global power as symbolized by a strong pound and possession of an independent nuclear deterrent.

The origins of the consensus of what came to be referred to as 'Butskellism' can be discerned in the wartime coalition. Thus Quintin Hogg (the future Lord Hailsham), for example, welcomed the Beveridge Report as 'a relatively Conservative document', tabled a motion calling for the immediate creation of a Ministry of Social Security which won the support of over forty Conservative MPs, and was a member of the Tory Reform Committee which was tacitly encouraged by Butler, Eden and Macmillan. Indeed, Macmillan's 'Middle Way', with its determination to plot a middle course between socialism and *laissez-faire* capitalism, could be regarded as a foundation text for 'Butskellism'.

K. O. Morgan argues, however, that the concept of 'Butskellism' obscures important differences between the two men and their parties regarding social, industrial and fiscal policy but adds that the term is of value in referring to a shared 'state of mind' implying 'a coherent attempt to maintain a social consensus and ... "set the people free" ... without dismantling the popular welfare and industrial fabric of the Attlee years'.

The post-war consensus held despite the challenges represented by 'ROBOT' in 1952, the foundation of the Campaign for Nuclear Disarmament (CND) in 1957, and the 'little local difficulty' caused by Thorneycroft, Powell and Birch in 1958. The election of Mrs Thatcher in 1979 symbolized the end of this consensus although the last rites had actually been intoned over its corpse by James Callaghan in September 1976, at least three years before the uncollected litter and unburied bodies of the 'winter of discontent' when he told a Labour Party conference that 'You cannot now, if you ever could, spend your way out of a recession'.

C

Callaghan, Leonard James (Jim), Baron Callaghan of Cardiff (27 March 1912–26 March 2005). Jim Callaghan was born in Portsmouth and received a strict Baptist upbringing mostly at the hands of his mother, as his father was a petty officer in the Navy at sea for long periods, who died in 1921 as a consequence of wounds incurred in World War One. The fact that MacDonald's 1924 Labour government ensured that his mother received a war widow's pension was a strong factor in Callaghan becoming a socialist.

Leaving school at seventeen, Callaghan became a tax clerk in the Inland Revenue but gave it up to become a full-time trade union official with the Inland Revenue Staff Federation. He soon demonstrated his skills as a negotiator in this capacity.

During World War Two he followed his father's footsteps into the navy and rose from being an ordinary seaman to become a lieutenant in the Atlantic patrol service.

In the 1945 Labour landslide Callaghan took the seat of Cardiff South from the Conservatives, and was to represent it for the next forty-two years. On the backbenches he was, like other talented individuals, cultivated by Hugh Dalton. With this patronage, Callaghan began his ascent of the ministerial ladder, being made parliamentary secretary to the Ministry of Transport.

During the thirteen years of opposition that began with the 1951 Conservative victory, Callaghan consolidated his power base in the party through his close contacts with the unions. He also sought to keep open his channels of communication with both the party's left and right during the civil war between Bevanites and Gaitskellites, although he was perceived as moving more towards the right as time went on (and the position of the right within the party generally strengthened).

When Wilson won the 1964 election Callaghan became chancellor, only to discover that Britain was facing a record balance of payments deficit. Wilson and Callaghan took the fateful decision not to devalue. A sterling crisis ensued within a month, when an emergency budget failed to win the City's confidence. Callaghan temporarily recovered the situation and began a radical redistributive reform of the tax system, including the introduction of capital gains, corporation and selective employment taxes, but the vulnerability of sterling was such that in November 1967 the government was forced to devalue by nearly 15%. It was an enormous blow to Callaghan both personally and politically.

Callaghan offered to resign from the cabinet but instead exchanged places with Jenkins at the Home Office. Although this meant that Callaghan had effectively been devalued by four places in the then cabinet hierarchy, he faced a more pressing problem with the start of the Troubles in Ireland. It was thus Callaghan who sent British troops into Ulster in 1969, although the real problem consisted in getting them out again once they had been dispatched.

Labour's mainland troubles centred on the unions' hostility towards the White Paper *In Place of Strife*. It was Callaghan who led the cabinet rebellion on behalf of the unions against Castle that resulted in the delay of significant trade union reform until Thatcher became prime minister. Callaghan nevertheless claimed that his action was more than merely a reflex defence of vested interest, insofar as the Donovan report had come out against statutory curbs of union powers. Nevertheless, in sabotaging the government's industrial relations policy Callaghan is a prime contender for having lost Labour the 1970 general election, although Jenkins is more usually held responsible, given his failure, as chancellor, to produce a 'giveaway' budget.

Callaghan became foreign secretary when Labour returned to office under Wilson in 1974 and thus played a key role in renegotiating the terms of Britain's entry into the EEC prior to the referendum on membership. When Wilson resigned in 1976 Callaghan defeated four Oxford graduates – Jenkins, Healey, Foot and Benn – to become party leader and prime minister. He thus became the only politician to have held all four modern major offices of state: home secretary, foreign secretary, chancellor of the exchequer and prime minister.

Callaghan was to discover, however, that he had inherited from Wilson a financial position similar or worse to that which he had inherited from the Conservatives in 1964, with sterling in crisis and inflation at 30%. He applied for a massive loan from the International Monetary Fund (IMF) but this was made conditional upon massive public spending cuts that left-wing cabinet colleagues such as Benn intensely disliked. Callaghan was haunted by fears of a repetition of 1931but managed to maintain cabinet unity and secure a breathing space by means of the IMF loan.

In the autumn of 1978 Callaghan's political instincts left him when he refused union advice to call an early general election. Instead, the 'winter of discontent' destroyed the government's credibility and helped Mrs Thatcher into power. Callaghan never appeared more out of touch than when he stepped off the plane from the Caribbean into snow-swept and strike-torn Britain and told the waiting reporters that, in effect, the situation had been overdramatized: a performance which prompted the famous 'Crisis? What Crisis?' headline.

Labour lost the May 1979 election and Callaghan resigned as party leader in October 1980. Labour was not to return to office until 1997. It is the great irony of Callaghan's career that he, who worked more closely with the trade unions than any leading Labour politician since Bevin and who more than anyone else was responsible for burying *In Place of Strife*, should have fallen foul of his former friends in the winter of discontent.

Like his contemporary, Lyndon Baines Johnson, Callaghan was a big man with a short fuse, whose avuncular manner and occasional hint of menace rendered him a superb negotiator. Also like LBJ, he lacked a mind which had been trained by the discipline of higher education but more than compensated for this with a fund of common sense that made him a formidable political operator, until his touch deserted him in 1978.

Campaign for Nuclear Disarmament (CND) CND was formed in 1958 in order to secure the abolition of British nuclear weapons and thereby set an example to other nations. It was thus based upon an entirely unrealistic assessment of the operation of international relations. Its reading of domestic politics was equally flawed, as annual marches to Aldermaston were no substitute for bringing direct power to bear on the major political parties by contesting parliamentary seats in the manner of the Anti-Corn Law League.

CND nevertheless impacted upon internal Labour politics and the October 1960 Labour Party conference endorsed unilateralism, prompting Gaitskell to declare his determination to 'fight and fight and fight again to save the party we love'.

By 1961 CND itself was showing signs of schism between the constitutionally minded majority and supporters of Bertrand Russell and the Committee of 100 who advocated civil disobedience. The latter's alienating tactics and astute political management enabled the Gaitskellites to reverse Labour's endorsement of CND policy and it was not until the deployment of cruise missiles in the early 1980s that the organization's fortunes temporarily revived.

Campbell-Bannerman, Sir Henry ('C-B') (7 September 1836–22 April 1908). The future prime minister was Henry Campbell until 1872 when he assumed the additional name and arms of Bannerman under the will of his maternal uncle, Henry Bannerman. Henry Campbell was the second son, and youngest of the six children, of Sir James Campbell, the co-founder of the Glasgow firm of J. & W. Campbell, wholesale drapers and warehousemen.

Educated at Glasgow High School and University, he then proceeded to Trinity College, Cambridge, where he graduated in 1858, as twenty-second senior optime in the Mathematical Tripos, and a Third in Classics. Joining the family business he became and remained a partner until 1868 when he unsuccessfully contested the Stirling Burghs as an advanced Liberal. However, he won the seat at the 1868 general election and retained it until his death.

Recognition of Campbell's political ability came in November 1871 with his appointment as financial secretary to the War Office: a post to which, as Campbell-Bannerman, he returned on the formation of the second Gladstone government in 1880, becoming secretary to the Admiralty in May 1882 in the reshuffle occasioned by the Phoenix Park murders. He was appointed chief secretary for Ireland (without a seat in the cabinet) in October 1884: a post which he occupied without major incident for eight months before the government came to an end.

When Gladstone formed his Third Ministry in February 1886, Campbell-Bannerman, a staunch supporter of Irish Home Rule, entered the cabinet as secretary of state for war. However, the defeat of the First Irish Home Rule Bill resulted in a speedy return to the opposition benches for what proved to be six years (1886–92).

Campbell-Bannerman returned to the cabinet as secretary of state for war when Gladstone formed his fourth administration (July 1892) and served on the cabinet committee that drafted the Second Irish Home Rule Bill.

When Rosebery succeeded Gladstone as prime minister on 3 March 1894, Campbell-Bannerman retained his office, where he was generally regarded as doing a good job, establishing what amounted to an eight-hour day in the Woolwich Arsenal ordnance factories and smoothing the retirement of the Duke of Cambridge as commander-in-chief. However, on the very day that the Duke's retirement was announced (21 June 1895) the Conservatives successfully moved a reduction of Campbell-Bannerman's salary on the ground that the reserves of cordite and other small arm ammunition were inadequate, and thereby brought down the government (Rosebery resigning the following day).

Campbell-Bannerman on leaving office expressed an interest in becoming Speaker until persuaded by his colleagues to remain on the opposition front bench. Campbell-Bannerman joined Harcourt in signing the majority report of the select committee of inquiry into the Jameson Raid that basically exonerated the imperial and South African governments, despite Liberal left wingers baying for Joseph Chamberlain's blood.

Following Rosebery's resignation in 1896 and Harcourt's in 1898, Campbell-Bannerman was elected Liberal leader in the Commons early in 1899. Although a popular figure on both sides of the Commons, he did not inspire affection, in equal measure, from both wings of his party, and Liberal Imperialist distrust of Campbell-Bannerman was enhanced by his criticizing both the necessity of the Boer War and the manner in which it was waged. These feelings were heightened in 1901 by Campbell-Bannerman's speech condemning 'methods of barbarism in South Africa' and by his expression of continued support for Irish Home Rule, leading, in early 1902, to the creation of the Liberal League.

Heart was put into the Liberal Party by the policies pursued by the Unionist governments of Salisbury and Balfour following the 'Khaki election' of 1900, notably with regard to education, licensing and 'Chinese Slavery'. However, the factor which did most to reunify and revivify the Liberal Party was the schism within Unionist ranks over tariff reform from 1903. For the sake of party unity Campbell-Bannerman also indicated, in response to pressure from Rosebery, Grey, Asquith and Bryce, that consideration of Home Rule should be postponed.

This was not, however, sufficient to prevent Haldane, Grey and Asquith from plotting (in what became known as the Relugas Compact) to prevent Campbell-Bannerman from exercising real power as prime minister. However, when Balfour resigned and Campbell-Bannerman was invited to form a government, on 5 December 1905, he managed, fortified by his wife, to outmanoeuvre the plotters and construct an administration representative of all sections of the party (including the three conspirators). Furthermore, he won a landslide victory at the polls in January 1906, with the Liberals enjoying a majority of 273 over the Unionists, independently of the broad support which they enjoyed from the Irish and Labour parties.

Campbell-Bannerman's two-year premiership achieved much that was worthy, notably passing the Trade Disputes Act and conferring full responsible government on the recently defeated Transvaal and Orange Free State. In general, however, it failed to live up to expectations because of 'C-B's poor health and spirits (following the death of his wife in 1906) and the determination of the Unionist-dominated House of Lords to block or emasculate Liberal legislation. The Plural Voting, Land Values (Scotland) and Small Landholders (Scotland) Bills all fall into the first category, whilst the 1906 Education Bill falls into the second. Moreover, the Irish members rejected a scheme to create a series of Irish councils.

On 4 April continuing ill health obliged Campbell-Bannerman to resign his office, and Asquith succeeded him. Just under three weeks later, Campbell-Bannerman died at 10 Downing Street.

Campbell-Bannerman had a long career and rose higher than he himself appeared to anticipate or his talents at first appeared to justify. In the event, however, and against the odds he helped heal the (mostly self-inflicted) wounds from which the Liberal Party had been suffering since the split over Irish Home Rule and managed to take the Liberals into office in 1906 with a majority greater than any enjoyed by Gladstone. His tragedy was that this came too late for him personally, as shown by the fact that he became 'father of the House of Commons' in the course of his premiership. Nevertheless, in his leadership of the Liberal Party and the country he managed to exhibit a quiet dignity, courage and authority and excited widespread affection by virtue not just of these qualities but also through his equable temperament, good humour, loyalty and natural modesty. Like Attlee he may seem a pygmy compared with his parliamentary rivals and colleagues but his patent sincerity and principled progressivism (tempered by pragmatism) render him worthy of posterity's positive re-evaluation.

Campbell Case, October 1924. J. R. Campbell was arrested for a *Workers' Weekly* article in which he urged soldiers not to fire upon their fellow workers. When the Attorney General dropped the prosecution following protests within the Labour Party, the Conservatives and Liberals combined to defeat MacDonald's minority government on a censure motion, thereby precipitating an election in which, assisted by the Zinoviev Letter, the Conservatives romped home to an overall majority of 223.

Canning, George (11 April 1770–8 August 1827). Although educated at Eton and Christ Church, Oxford, Canning's background was hardly typical for a future member of the governing class as his father had died in penury (in 1771) and his mother had been forced to become an actress. His uncle, the Whig and City banker, Stratford Canning, rescued his nephew from insolvency and obscurity but the stigma attaching to his early years was never completely expunged and became a barb in the hands of those whom Canning alienated by virtue of his conversion (at Oxford) to Pittite policies and his consistently abrasive personality.

After two years on the backbenches, Canning was rewarded in January 1796 for his loyalty to, and oratory in the service of, Pitt by being made one of two undersecretaries at the Foreign Office. After two years he moved to the Board of Control and thence to the Treasurership of the Navy. In December 1805 Pitt told him that he intended to bring him into the cabinet but died before he was able to honour this promise. Canning thereafter became the self-appointed guardian of the Pittite legacy. His refusal to serve under Grenville and Charles James Fox in the 'Ministry of All the Talents' in 1806 was, however, widely interpreted as motivated less by devotion to Pitt's memory than manoeuvring in pursuit of his own prospects. Canning did become foreign secretary when Portland formed his purely Tory administration in 1807 but his attempt to have Castlereagh removed from the War Office led to their joint resignations and celebrated duel (in which Canning's pride and jacket were the only casualties).

In 1812, following Spencer Perceval's assassination, Canning was invited to return to the Foreign Office but declined the offer when Liverpool refused his request that Castlereagh be displaced as leader of the House of Commons. Having bid himself out of the market in 1812, Canning had to accept demotion when he returned to the cabinet in 1816 as president of the Board of Control, only to resign in 1820 in protest at the government's handling of Queen Caroline. Canning was on the verge of setting sail to India in August 1822, when Castlereagh's suicide provided him with the opportunity of assuming the dual role he had coveted a decade earlier.

Liverpool desperately wanted to enlist Canning's debating talents in order to bolster his Commons front bench but he had to fight hard to persuade George IV to re-appoint a friend (and alleged lover) of his detested wife. However, in the course of a few years Canning was able to win over his royal master by a combination of flattery, placing patronage at his disposal, and manifestly successful and popular policies including complete disengagement from the Congress system, recognition of the new Central and South American republics and military assistance for the constitutionalist cause in Portugal in 1826. Moreover, he was clearly Liverpool's chosen successor and the Ultras did more harm than good in heavy-handedly pressing Wellington's claims. Thus when Liverpool was forced to resign through ill health in February 1827 George turned to Canning as his successor.

Although Canning agreed that Catholic Emancipation would remain an open question, such was his identification with the cause as well as the personal dislike and distrust which he engendered that forty office holders refused to serve under him, including about half of Liverpool's cabinet. Canning nevertheless formed an administration by becoming his own chancellor of the exchequer and recruiting the Whigs Lansdowne, Devonshire, Tierney and Carlisle.

Canning's premiership was to last just one hundred days. In domestic terms it achieved nothing of significance (bills to emancipate the Catholics and modify the Corn Laws both coming to grief). His death on 8 August 1827 left the Tory party and foreign policy regarding the Eastern Question in considerable disarray, as cooperation with France and Russia, pursued through the 1826 St Petersburg Protocol and 1827 Treaty of London, was to lead to the battle of Navarino, which weakened the Turks relative to the Russians much more than Canning had ever envisaged or desired.

As MP for the prosperous and relatively large Liverpool constituency 1812–22, Canning possessed an insight into the interests of the mercantile middle classes which many of his contemporaries lacked and he was a pioneer in presenting his policies to the public. It is difficult not to feel, however, when contemplating his career that office came first and his principles a very poor second.

Captain Swing riots, 1830–31. The Captain Swing riots were a species of Luddism in the arable farming areas of the South, East Anglia and the Midlands. They began in Kent at the end of August 1830 with the destruction of threshing machines. However, new machinery was not the only cause of rural distress and the unrest took a variety of forms, including assault and arson. The protesters commonly demanded a reduction in tithes and rise in wages.

The very day after entering office in November 1830, Melbourne as home secretary offered a reward of £500 for bringing arsonists and machine-breakers to justice, and two days later instructed magistrates to display greater vigour in enrolling constables. Troops were also used more widely and effectively.

Although the last incident of machine-breaking occurred in September 1832, the Swing riots proper effectively ended early the previous year. 1,967 men and women were put on trial over 34 counties, of whom 19 were hanged, 644 were imprisoned and 481 suffered transportation.

The protest was not entirely barren insofar as the higher wages obtained under duress sometimes persisted when peace returned, and farm mechanization was delayed in the affected areas, apart from East Anglia, until the 1850s. Arguably Swing also had a hand in stimulating the Poor Law Amendment and Tithe Commutation Acts. On the other hand, the severity with which the authorities treated the rioters may have retarded agricultural trades unionism as it was not until 1872 that Joseph Arch created the first national union of agricultural labourers.

Cardwell army reforms When Gladstone formed his first government in 1868, he appointed his fellow Peelite, Edward Cardwell, secretary for war. The need for radical reform of the military had been exposed by the Crimean War and emphasized by the Austro-Prussian war of 1866. Reform would go hand in hand with retrenchment, although Cardwell had already laid the foundations for reduced estimates as colonial secretary under Palmerston, 1864–66, when he had introduced the policy of withdrawing imperial troops from those colonies unwilling to pay for their upkeep.

The chief feature of his reform of the army was the abolition (by royal warrant) of the purchase of commissions, in favour of promotion by merit.

Conscription was not ideologically acceptable, politically possible or, at this stage, militarily necessary, but the creation of a trained reserve and the attraction of a better class of recruit were both recognized as highly desirable and to this end the Army Enlistment Act of 1870 created a system of short service, comprising six years with the colours and six with the reserve. Removing some of the harsher forms of military discipline (such as flogging on home service and branding deserters) may also have done something to encourage enlistment. The Regulation of Forces Act of 1871 sought to encourage recruitment and stimulate *esprit de corps* by linking regiments with specific counties or regions, and ensuring that one battalion served at home whilst the other was overseas.

Last but not least, the department of the commander-in-chief was brought under the more effective control of the War Office and steps were taken to improve military education. In bringing these changes into effect Cardwell exhibited to the full his energy, patience, firmness of purpose and courtesy. The effort, however, undermined his health and he died, as Viscount Cardwell of Ellerbeck, in 1886.

Carlton Club revolt, 19 October 1922. The Carlton Club is the club of the Conservative Party. Its most famous meeting, held on 19 October 1922, provided an occasion for dissident elements within the party, including Baldwin, Bonar Law and the bulk of the backbenchers, to express their discontent with the continuation of the wartime Lloyd George coalition. This discontent focused upon policies such as the handling of the Chanak crisis and the general air of sleaze which surrounded Lloyd George, particularly given the honours scandal.

The meeting was originally fixed for the day of the Newport by-election when it was anticipated that the intervention of an anti-Lloyd George Conservative would let in the Labour candidate by splitting the coalition vote. In the event, however, this threat failed to materialize and thus the stick with which the party hierarchy had intended to discipline the dissident backbenchers was dashed from their hands. Nor was the carrot of promotion effective. On the contrary, the coalition bred discontent because it increasingly appeared to block the prospects of young hopefuls. Moreover, a number of old hands, including the party's chief whip, chief agent and chairman, together with Salisbury and Derby, were equally disillusioned with the status quo. Thus the vote went against Austen Chamberlain by 185 to 88 (including 10 ministers), obliging him to resign as Conservative Party leader, which in turn obliged Lloyd George to resign as prime minister.

Caroline affair, 1820–21. In 1794 the future George IV had married his first cousin, Princess Caroline of Anspach. It was not a love match. Indeed, George had only consented to the project because promised financial assistance by his father. Having produced an heir – the Princess Charlotte Augusta – the couple separated by 1796 and Caroline returned to the continent in 1814. George as Prince Regent repeatedly requested his ministers to arrange a divorce on the grounds of his wife's alleged adultery. Matters came to a head in 1820 with George III's death and Caroline's decision to return to Britain to claim her rights as queen.

Caroline was very popular with the British people not so much because personally endearing but because George was so despised and honouring the queen provided a means of snubbing him. Thus Caroline's progress to London was greeted by cheering crowds who turned to rioting once she reached the capital. More serious still, there were even signs of disaffection amongst some of the soldiery. Those posted outside Carlton House saluted Caroline as she passed and the 3rd regiment of Foot Guards were so open in their attachment to their royal mistress that they were immediately dispatched to Portsmouth.

Liverpool had reluctantly conceded to George's wishes for a divorce by bringing forward a Bill of Pains and Penalties into the Lords, which would deprive Caroline of the title and rights of queen. The Bill passed its third reading by just nine votes which suggested certain defeat if it was to pass down to the Commons. To avoid this humiliation Liverpool dropped the Bill, thereby angering George and provoking more rioting in London.

Caroline was refused admission to George's coronation in July 1821 and died of peritonitis the following month. Shortly before her death she had accepted a financial settlement, which would have minimized her potential to embarrass the Crown, but in death she still managed to discomfort the authorities. She was to be buried in Brunswick and to this end her corpse was to be transported through London to Harwich. However, her supporters objected to her funeral procession's route because it avoided the City itself as a notorious centre of pro-Caroline sentiment. Thus at Cumberland Gate a crowd sought to intercept the cortège by stoning the accompanying Life Guards, who responded by killing two demonstrators and wounding many others. This incident became known as 'Carol-loo', in reference to the earlier 'massacre' of Peterloo. The rioters nevertheless succeeded in their objective and the procession went by the more popular route.

Thus on three occasions between 1820 and 1821 Queen Caroline was the occasion of serious disorder in the capital. The whole affair weakened the Liverpool government in three important respects and nearly brought it down by distracting it from more important business, by provoking Canning's resignation, and by souring the King's relations with his prime minister. Indeed, Liverpool only survived because the King's indolence outweighed his anger.

Carson, Edward Henry, Baron Carson of Duncairn (9 February 1854–22 October 1935). Edward Carson was born in Dublin on 9 February 1854, the second son of an architect. 'Ned', as he was known in the family, exhibited both a reserved and passionate nature. At Portarlington boarding school he was nicknamed 'Rawbones' because he was so ungainly and was excused games on account of his frail constitution. At Trinity College, Dublin he studied law, being called to the Irish bar in 1877, appointed counsel to the Attorney General for Ireland in 1887 and taking silk in 1889. He was appointed solicitor-general for Ireland in June 1892 because Balfour had been so impressed by him.

The following month he was elected to parliament as a Liberal Unionist for one of the Dublin University seats, which he was to hold for the next twenty-six years. He was called to the English bar by the Middle Temple in 1893 and proceeded to become the youngest QC in the country (aged 35) and the first Irish QC to take silk in England. His parliamentary reputation was secured by his participation in the debates on the Second Irish Home Rule Bill in 1893, whilst his reputation at the English bar was made by his success in defending the libel action against the Marquess of Queensberry brought by Oscar Wilde in 1895. He was less successful in defending Dr Jameson of Jameson-raid fame in 1896.

Despite having strongly attacked the 1895 Land Purchase Act, in 1900 he was appointed solicitor-general for England (which also involved his being knighted) and he performed this function until the Balfour government resigned in December 1905. However, it was in early 1910 that Carson assumed the role for which he became most famous, succeeding Walter Long as leader of the Irish Unionists in the Commons.

Realizing that the Parliament Act removed the veto of the Lords over Irish Home Rule, on 23 September 1911 Carson spoke at a rally at Craigavon at which he asserted: 'We must be prepared ... the morning Home Rule passes, ourselves to become responsible for the government of the Protestant Province of Ulster.' In other words, the jurisdiction of any Dublin parliament would be denied and Ulster would seek to rule itself through its own provisional government. Bonar Law publicly pledged his party's support for Carson's stand against the Third Irish Home Rule Bill (which was due to become law in June 1914).

28 September was designated 'Ulster day', during which 237,368 Ulstermen signed the Covenant and 234,046 of their womenfolk signed their own declaration solemnly pledging themselves to resist the imposition of Dublin rule. The creation of the Ulster Volunteer Force in January 1913 and the gun-running at Larne in April 1914 gave practical expression to this determination, whilst the Curragh 'mutiny' (March 1914) had suggested that the armed forces could not necessarily be relied upon to crush any revolt.

The principle of Ulster's exclusion was admitted by Asquith when, on the second reading of the Home Rule Bill, he offered 'county option' with a time limit of six years, which Carson described as 'sentence of death with a stay of execution'. Carson and James Craig (later Viscount Craigavon) were, however, unable to secure the permanent exclusion of the whole province of Ulster when they attended the Buckingham Palace conference (21–24 July) nor to prevent the passage of the Home Rule Bill into law but its operation was suspended until after the war and Asquith promised an amending bill which would address the question of exclusion prior to implementation. Although he considered that the Liberals had treated Ulster shabbily, Carson recognized Ulster's duty to the country upon the outbreak of World War One and offered the authorities the services of the Ulster Volunteer Force.

Carson made his own contribution to the war effort by serving in Asquith's ministry of May 1915 as Attorney General, although he found himself increasingly at odds with the administration on a number of issues, culminating in its decision, following the Easter Rebellion in 1916, to re-open negotiations with a view to bringing the Home Rule Act into immediate effect, subject to an amending bill excluding all or part of Ulster. The talks foundered and Carson resigned from office in October 1916: a step that marked the break up of Asquith's government.

Carson soon returned to office under Lloyd George as First Lord of the Admiralty, leaving this post to become a member of the war cabinet in July 1917. However, in January 1918 he resigned from the government on learning that Lloyd George was intending to introduce legislation for Ireland which he considered likely to be inimical to the cause of Ulster. Reassured by Bonar Law on the eve of the coupon election, Carson was returned to Westminster for the newly created Duncairn division of Belfast, and with a heavy heart he accepted the 1920 Government of Ireland Bill as a lesser evil than earlier versions of Home Rule.

Recognizing the need for young blood, he announced his resignation as leader of the Ulster Unionists on 4 February 1921 and on 24 May left the House of Commons on his appointment as a Lord of Appeal in Ordinary (taking the title Baron Carson of Duncairn): a post from which he resigned in October 1929. Falling badly ill in early 1934 he died on 22 October 1935 and was given a state funeral in Belfast. He had previously told a friend, 'I died on the day I left the House of Commons and the bar'.

As a lawyer and politician Carson's powerful advocacy arose from his physical and moral courage, commanding presence and passionate sincerity. It was thanks to these gifts that he, more than any other man, helped ensure the maintenance of Ulster within the United Kingdom.

'Cat and Mouse Act', 1913. The Cat and Mouse Act is the popular name for the Prisoners' Temporary Discharge for ill health Act. The home secretary, Reginald McKenna, passed it on 25 April 1913 in order to counteract the unfavourable publicity generated by the policy of force-feeding suffragettes on hunger strike. Under the terms of the Act they could be released when unwell but could be re-arrested to serve out their sentence once they had recuperated. Hence the 'cat and mouse' tag, as the state appeared to possess the power to toy not only with the liberty but also with the very life of its citizens.

Catholic Association Daniel O'Connell made Catholic Emancipation an umbrella issue for a whole range of Catholic Irish grievances. On 5 May 1823 he founded the Catholic Association 'to adopt all such legal and constitutional measures as may be most useful to obtain Catholic Emancipation'. Assisted by the Catholic priesthood and financed by the Catholic rent, the organization grew to be very powerful.

In 1825 it dissolved itself in order to pre-empt suppression by the authorities, only to be reformed in modified form. O'Connell's election at the 1828 County Clare by-election led to the achievement of the association's immediate objective in 1829, whereupon it again dissolved itself, just ahead of a legal ban.

Catholic Emancipation, 1829. The Dublin parliament was persuaded to abolish itself by passing the Act of Union by a mixture of bribery and promises, the chief of which was Catholic Emancipation. This would involve the repeal of those Test Acts which effectively excluded Roman Catholics from holding certain offices. However, George III claimed that Catholic Emancipation was contrary to his coronation oath and thus Pitt was unable to honour his promise and accordingly resigned as prime minister in 1801.

Agitation in favour of Emancipation increased in 1823 with the creation of the Catholic Association. However, Liverpool was personally opposed to Emancipation and, realizing it to be a divisive issue for the Tories, he made it a condition of holding office under his premiership that the issue was treated as an open question, thereby effectively muzzling pro-Emancipationists like Canning and the Grenvillites.

However, the Tory party fell into disarray following Liverpool's resignation in 1827, whilst the 1828 repeal of the Test and Corporation Acts by granting civil equality to Dissenters made it more difficult to deny that status to Catholics. O'Connell's defeat of the popular Protestant landlord Vesey Fitzgerald in the 1828 County Clare by-election brought matters to a head, facing Wellington and Peel with what appeared to be a choice between endangering the Union by allowing massive bloodshed in Ireland or accepting Emancipation. They reluctantly chose the latter as the lesser of the two evils.

New oaths obliged Catholics to swear allegiance to the Crown in its Protestant succession and to disavow the deposing power of the Pope as well as his assumption of any temporal jurisdiction in the United Kingdom. This was acceptable to the consciences of Catholics and thus they were rendered eligible for all offices of state except those of Regent, Lord Lieutenant and Lord Chancellor. However, this was counterbalanced by other measures designed to reassure the Ultras and the Protestant Ascendancy by limiting the electoral influence of Catholicism in Ireland. These measures included the outlawing of the Catholic Association and raising the Irish county franchise from 40 shillings to £10 per annum, which greatly reduced the Irish electorate and the number of O'Connellite MPs.

Nevertheless, Emancipation provided an enormous boost to the confidence of the Catholic Irish and deepened Tory divisions. The Ultras felt betrayed and were converted to parliamentary reform as they realized that parliament had failed to reflect the strength of anti-Catholic feeling amongst the general public. The affair also helped convert Peel to the policy, later followed by Gladstone, of attempting to conciliate moderate Irish Catholic opinion but in the short term he had to tread very carefully for fear of appearing unprincipled. Hence his declining Wellington's request, at the behest of the King, to form an administration to pass a moderate measure of parliamentary reform.

Cato Street Conspiracy, 23 February 1820. The Cato Street Conspiracy takes its name from the fact that the main conspirators – Spenceans led by Arthur Thistlewood – were arrested in Cato Street, Marylebone. They were plotting insurrection centred upon the murder of the entire cabinet as it dined at the Earl of Harrowby's. However, an agent provocateur ensured that the King's government was in no real danger.

Thistlewood was one of five of the plotters executed, whilst another five were transported for life. The Conspiracy's broader significance was that it appeared to provide retrospective justification for the Six Acts.

Chadwick, Sir Edwin (24 January 1800–6 July 1890). Edwin Chadwick was born at Longsight, near Manchester, the first child of James Chadwick, a Francophile radical and failed businessman turned journalist. When his father moved to London he was educated at home by his father and private tutors. After apprenticeship as an attorney's clerk he entered the Middle Temple, supporting himself before he was called to the Bar by journalism for various papers.

An 1829 article on *Preventive Police* made such an impression upon the ageing Bentham that shortly afterwards he engaged Chadwick as his secretary, with special responsibility for writing the police and health sections in his 'Constitutional Code'. Chadwick was so close to Bentham by 1830 that he offered him an annual income for life as the authorized mouthpiece of his teachings when he died; an offer Chadwick respectfully declined in order to retain his freedom of expression.

Chadwick's public career began in earnest in 1832 when he was persuaded to investigate the operation of the poor law first in the metropolis and then in Berkshire. His investigations led him to argue that the chief problem was the rise in able-bodied pauperism, compounded by the fact that the allowance system drew men from the labour market. Chadwick sought to reverse this process by applying the less-eligibility principle (making the receipt of poor relief less attractive than even the lowest paid work). In order to ensure effective national implementation, Chadwick called for the plan to be carried out by paid officials acting under the supervision of a central agency with comprehensive powers. This was the essence of the scheme advocated in the Royal Commission report and implemented in the 1834 Poor Law Amendment Act. Chadwick was rewarded by being appointed secretary to the Poor Law Commission, as well as being given a place on the Royal Commission into child labour in factories.

Chadwick's brief in the latter capacity was to provide the cabinet with a credible alternative to Ashley's Ten Hour Bill without alienating the manufacturers by reducing adults' hours of work. Chadwick's solution was to reduce the hours of children between the ages of nine and thirteen so drastically that two shifts or relays of children could be used to work alongside adults, thereby occasioning no reduction in their hours. Although the cabinet rejected the recommendation that employers be made liable for accidents, and the Commons amended the Bill so that those aged between fourteen and eighteen were limited to a twelve-hour day, the measure that became law as the 1833 Factory Act was still recognizably that proposed by Chadwick.

Chadwick's feuding with the Poor Law commissioners, however, diminished his influence with government whilst he suffered increasing unpopularity nationally, as chief author of the New Poor Law and assumed author of the 1836 Registration Act.

However, Chadwick had not completely exhausted his usefulness to the Whigs. He regarded a strong rural police force as an essential corollary to the New Poor Law and the Whigs were increasingly alarmed by the threat to law and order posed by anti-poor law demonstrations and Chartism. They were accordingly receptive to Chadwick's suggestion of the Royal Commission which served as the prelude to the 1839 Rural Police Act, although the legislation was but a pale permissive shadow of the bold centralizing measure Chadwick originally conceived.

Chadwick became increasingly absorbed in public health issues and persuaded the Poor Law Commission to undertake the enquiry that ultimately produced the ground-breaking 'Report on the Sanitary Conditions of the Labouring Population'.

This proved to be an enormous success and led, not least through Chadwick's demonstrating the close correlation between life expectancy and class, to his authoring a report on intra-mural internments (1843), facilitating the Health of Towns Commission (which reported in 1844–45), aiding in the Public Health Bills of 1847–48, and finally being appointed England's first paid Commissioner for Public Health.

Chadwick would have achieved more had he not attracted the criticism of the engineering profession and *The Times* and had it not been the case that the Metropolitan Commission broke free of both his control and that of the General Board established under the 1848 Public Health Act with the result that sanitary arrangements for London were contested between the Commission, the Board and the vestries.

In 1854 a coalition of London's threatened interests resulted in parliament placing the Board of Health on the same basis as the Poor Law Board, with a president seated in the House and a salaried full-time staff under him. Chadwick retired from the expiring Board with £1,000 per annum compensation. During the Crimean War he hankered after a return to public service through some new enquiry but actually did nothing more than advise the Administrative Reform Association on civil service reform.

Chadwick continued to publish a stream of reports, addresses and pamphlets, successfully campaigning with Florence Nightingale for a Royal Commission into the health of the Indian army, helping create the Sanitary Institute (1876), and playing an active role in numerous learned societies.

Knighted in 1889, Chadwick died the following year. In the course of his life he had revolutionized both local government and the social services. He had achieved so much because he was, in Lord John Russell's words, 'A man of the greatest energy . . . with a spirit of enquiry which induced him to labour by zeal . . . ' His vision was often original, his writing invariably lucid and his plans could be breathtakingly bold, but he was not a man to whom it was easy to warm, being priggish, precipitate and constitutionally incapable of suspending judgement. Opinionated, obstinate and lacking in a sense of proportion, he dedicated himself to the public good but was himself fundamentally lacking in humanity, preferring to deal with people in the abstract rather than as flesh and bone.

Chamberlain, Arthur Neville (18 March 1869–9 November 1940). As the son of Joseph Chamberlain it might be claimed that Neville Chamberlain was born into 'the purple of commerce' but in fact it was his stepbrother Austen who was marked down as his father's standard-bearer and Neville was packed off for seven years by his father to the family's ill-fated Bahamian sisal plantation. On his return to Birmingham he went only marginally more successfully into the copper-brass business before finding his feet and proving himself his father's son in municipal politics, where he rose in the course of four years to become Mayor, in 1915. His first experience of national politics as director-general of National Service, 1916–17, was a bruising experience that merely encouraged him in a lifelong dislike of Lloyd George.

Entering parliament in 1918 he attained ministerial office (as postmaster-general) in 1922 but made his name at Health, particularly between 1924 and 1929, during which time he passed twenty-one of the twenty-five measures which he identified as desirable when he entered office. His administrative zeal and competence was also apparent during his time at the Treasury, notably 1931–37, during which time he came to be regarded as heir apparent to Stanley Baldwin. It was his misfortune upon entering into his inheritance in 1937 that foreign affairs assumed greater significance than domestic affairs.

Chamberlain's determination to keep the direction of foreign policy in his own hands, rather than his policy of appeasement, in itself led to the resignation of Eden as foreign secretary in February 1938. Appeasement itself passed from near universal acclaim at the time of Munich to near universal denigration shortly thereafter. The debate still rages, although it is the defenders of Chamberlain's reputation who are currently most vocal.

Although Chamberlain's record prior to the war is at least defensible there can be no question that his record as a wartime leader was disastrous. He failed to inspire or unite the nation. Hence his forced abdication in favour of Churchill in May 1940 after his majority fell from 200 to 80 on a vote of confidence. However, his hold on his supporters within the Conservative Party remained tight and it is to his credit that he used his position as party leader, in the relatively brief remainder of his life, to help consolidate Churchill's position as premier rather than intrigue against him.

Chamberlain, Joseph (8 July 1836–2 July 1914). Joseph Chamberlain came from a prosperous non-conformist Birmingham family and by the age of 38 his business acumen in manufacturing screws allowed him to retire. He first achieved national prominence leading the non-conformist agitation of the National Education League against the 1870 Education Bill in general and Clause 25 in particular.

Chamberlain became an innovative mayor of Birmingham, 1873–75, engaged in slum clearance, the municipalization of gas and water supplies ('gas and water socialism') and fostering civic pride through a variety of other projects.

This local power base provided Chamberlain and his allies with a launching pad for Westminster, with Joseph entering parliament in 1876. The following year he helped found the National Liberal Federation, a union of local Liberal Party organizations, which was widely disliked as imitating American 'caucus' politics and as a device for imposing radicalism and Chamberlain himself upon the parliamentary party. Its role in the 1880 Liberal victory was exaggerated by contemporaries but helped secure Chamberlain's appointment as president of the Board of Trade. His ally Sir Charles Dilke joined the cabinet and threatened to outshine him by virtue of the role he played, alongside Gladstone, in framing the parliamentary reform of 1884–85, only to have his career ruined when he was cited as co-respondent in a divorce case. W. E. Forster, another potential challenger to Chamberlain on the party's centre-left, had already had his prospects blighted when Chamberlain negotiated the Kilmainham Treaty behind his back and thus forced his resignation as Irish chief secretary.

'Radical Joe' reaffirmed his radical credentials and most obviously set out his stall as a future party leader by means of the Radical or Unauthorized Programme of 1885. It was partly in order to pre-empt such socialistic legislation, some have suggested, that Gladstone converted to the cause of Irish Home Rule by December 1885. Chamberlain was not prepared to go farther down the road of devolution than his central board scheme but irreconcilable differences were not apparent at the beginning of Gladstone's Third Ministry of 1886, which Chamberlain initially joined as president of the Local Government Board. However, he resigned as soon as the shape of Home Rule became clear. Thereafter Chamberlain and his former rival for the succession, the Marquis of Hartington, became Liberal Unionists.

By 1895 the Liberal Unionists entered into office with the Conservatives, with Chamberlain becoming colonial secretary under Salisbury. Chamberlain's restless mind and desire to give the lie to the proposition that the Liberal Unionists had been swallowed whole, led to his making radical suggestions, such as old-age pensions, and passing radical measures such as the 1897 Workmen's Compensation Act.

Chamberlain's colonial policy was aggressive, as shown by his complicity in the Jameson Raid of 1895 and in helping provoke the Boer War of 1899–1902. The latter helped convert him to the need to end Britain's 'Splendid Isolation' (through alliance with Germany or the United States) and strengthen the empire (and finance social reform) through the imposition of tariffs. Chamberlain resigned from the cabinet on 9 September 1903 to be better able to campaign on the issue of tariff reform but he was frustrated in his ambition by Balfour's manoeuvring to preserve party unity, the strength of the popular attachment to free trade (which contributed to the Liberal landslide of 1906) and by his suffering a stroke in July 1906.

Chamberlain had the qualities, which Margot Asquith summarized as 'Political bruising, perfect speaking, artistic self-advertisement, audacity and courage ... ', to put certain issues on the political agenda, but he ultimately lacked the flexibility and the following required to implement that vision. In the final analysis his gifts were destructive rather than creative, and he holds the unique distinction of having split both the Liberals (over Home Rule in 1886) and the Unionists (over Tariff Reform in 1903).

Chamberlain, Sir Joseph Austen (16 October 1863–16 March 1937). As the eldest son of Joseph Chamberlain, Austen, unlike his half-brother Neville, was groomed for high office. So keen was he to follow his father's footsteps, he adopted all of his props, including the monocle, orchid buttonhole and wing collars. After an education at Rugby, and Trinity College, Cambridge, he spent time in France, Turkey, Greece and Germany before entering parliament in the ranks of the Liberal Unionists in 1892. Largely thanks to his father he was to represent Birmingham for his entire political career, of thirty-eight years, and spend all but two of them occupying the government or opposition front benches.

By 1902 he had entered the cabinet alongside his father as postmaster-general. The posts which he went on to hold included chancellor of the exchequer (1903–5 and 1919–21), secretary of state for India (1915–17), and First Lord of the Admiralty (1931). Austen's elevation to the front rank of politics in being appointed chancellor to succeed C. T. Ritchie in 1903 was less through his own merits than because Balfour considered it to be the best means of keeping a line open to Austen's father, as Joe had just resigned from the cabinet in order to be able to pursue his tariff reform campaign unmuzzled.

Austen was the favourite to become party leader following Balfour's resignation in 1911, as he was the preferred candidate of the outgoing leader, the chief whip, the party chairman and a majority of shadow cabinet colleagues (despite his alleged disloyalty as a 'ditcher'). However, the rival candidacy of Walter Long eventually resulted in the success of Andrew Bonar Law as a 'compromise candidate'.

However, when Bonar Law resigned through ill health in March 1921 Austen was the only possible successor and was duly acclaimed as Conservative Party leader. The post of prime minister nevertheless continued to elude him, chiefly because he attached himself too closely to his father's former arch-rival, Lloyd George, attempting to prolong the coalition government well beyond the point at which it appealed to most Conservatives. He might just have managed to keep a lid on discontent within the ranks of his own party if he had agreed to Lloyd George's suggestion in February 1922 that he, as leader of the majority party in the coalition, become prime minister. However, he declined and the result was the Carlton Club revolt of 19 October 1922, which forced his resignation as party leader and brought down the coalition. Out of loyalty to the likes of Birkenhead, Austen refused to join the purely Conservative administration formed by Bonar Law in 1922 and hence he lost out to Baldwin, when the latter stepped into Bonar Law's shoes following a second (and terminal) collapse in his health in 1923.

Together with his French counterpart as foreign minister, Aristide Briand, Austen won the Nobel Peace Prize for his work in formulating the Locarno Pact. However, the Pact manifestly failed to preserve peace and may even have made the outbreak of war more likely insofar as it did nothing to reaffirm Germany's eastern frontiers as settled at Versailles. Chamberlain's reputation was thus in decline even before his death.

Blake attributes to Churchill whilst Beaverbrook attributes to Birkenhead the same damning summary of Austen's political career, namely, 'He always played the game and he always lost it'. This was due to his loyalty to his father's principles and his erstwhile colleagues. Filial piety and ill-advised political friendships, together with a rather starched and stiff personal manner, thus conspired to prevent him from achieving power in his own right. This had always been his father's ambition rather than his own and this fact, more than any other, explains why it was unfulfilled. Ultimately he lacked the physical stamina, the robustness of temperament and the sheer willpower to shin to the top of the greasy pole. Austen was that classic form of gentlemanly Englishman whose chief quality is the ability to be a good loser.

Chandos amendment In order to offset the loss of nomination boroughs and reinforce landlord influence in the county seats (which would be increased under the terms of the 1832 Reform Act), Viscount Chandos successfully proposed that the county electorate be increased by adding the 'fifty pound tenants at will': those tenant farmers who occupied but did not own land to that rental value.

Charitable Bequests Act, 1844. The 1844 Charitable Bequests Act rendered it easier for Catholics to endow their Church in their wills. This was one part of the policy of conciliating Catholic Ireland pursued by Peel in his Second Ministry. In the same year, for example, Lord de Grey was replaced as Lord Lieutenant of Ireland by Lord Heytesbury, who was much more willing to appoint Catholics to government positions.

This policy of conciliation was very unpopular with many members of the electorate and the Conservative Party, although their indignation peaked in 1845 over the Maynooth Grant.

Chartism, 1838–48. Chartism was a popular protest movement which took its name from the People's Charter, which was drawn up by the London Working Men's Association (LWMA), published in May 1838, and was thrice the subject of petitions presented to, and rejected by, Parliament in 1839, 1842, and 1848 respectively. The fact that these three years were periods of acute economic distress have led some to regard Chartism as more an expression of socio-economic than political discontent.

The Chartists elected delegates (by a variety of means, ironically excepting secret ballot) to a National Convention 'of the Industrious Classes' which was to open on 4 February 1839 and run in parallel to the Westminster Parliament. The Convention transferred its meetings from London to Birmingham but could not agree upon what strategy to follow in the event of Parliament rejecting its petition to adopt the Charter, with a general strike, the withdrawal of savings and physical force all being considered. On 4 July disturbances erupted in Birmingham's Bull Ring, and this occasioned a series of arrests in the period leading up to the presentation of the petition to parliament by Thomas Attwood on 12 July and its rejection by 235 votes to 46. However, with most Chartist leaders already behind bars the only serious outbreak of violence which this provoked was the so-called Newport Rising of 3 November 1839, when John Frost led a Chartist force into Newport, Wales, in an abortive attempt to spring their comrades from prison.

Divisions over tactics resurfaced as the Chartist leaders were gradually released from jail. True to his vision of moral force Chartism, William Lovett, for example, founded the National Association for Promoting the Political and Social Improvement of the People in April 1841. Joseph Sturge, similarly, set up the Complete Suffrage Union to unite the middle and working classes by demanding both universal suffrage and the repeal of the Corn Laws. However, Feargus O'Connor attempted to use the Charter Association, founded at Manchester in July 1840, as the vehicle for extracting concessions from the authorities by petitions backed by the threat of violence. However, the second petition was rejected in 1842 by 287 votes to 49, whilst 1848 witnessed the eclipse of Chartism as a mass movement with the Kennington Common meeting turning into a damp squib whilst the third petition was laughed out of court, given its many transparently bogus signatories. O'Connor's Land Plan was a similar, although less dramatic, disaster and O'Connor ended his days in an insane asylum.

As Chartism ceased to be a mass movement after 1848 with none of its six demands fulfilled (despite there having been nothing new in 1838), it is easy to dismiss it as having failed. However, subsequently all the points of the Charter, with the exception of annual parliaments, have been granted. More specifically, universal manhood suffrage was granted in 1918 (with both sexes receiving the vote on equal terms in 1928); payment of Members of Parliament was introduced in 1911; equal electoral districts effectively came into being with the redistribution of 1885; vote by ballot was conceded in 1872; and the abolition of the property qualification (of £300 in land) for Members of Parliament disappeared as early as 1858. Thus taking a longer-term perspective, it is possible to argue that the Chartists posthumously enjoyed considerable success and there is no denying that in its own lifetime the movement provided invaluable political experience for thousands of men, thus contributing to what E. P. Thompson calls 'the making of the English working class'.

Chinese Slavery In the aftermath of the Boer War 50,000 indentured Chinese labourers were imported into South Africa. This 'Chinese Slavery' or 'coolie' labour was extremely unpopular in Britain as it not only offended against the conscience of the humanitarians (objecting to exploitation), and the trade unionists (who disliked blacklegs), but also aroused the prejudice of racists (who did not wish to see 'orientals' taking white men's jobs).

In symbolizing the Unionist government's contemptuous attitude towards labour, Chinese Slavery was instrumental, along with Taff Vale and the Tariff Reform League, in cementing the realignment of the forces of the left that culminated in the Gladstone–MacDonald Pact of 1903 and produced the Liberal landslide in 1906.

Churchill, Sir Winston Leonard Spencer (30 November 1874–24 January 1965). Winston Churchill was the eldest son of Lord Randolph Churchill, third son of the 7th Duke of Marlborough, and Jennie, second daughter of Leonard Jerome of New York. It is no reflection on Harrow or Sandhurst to point out that in essentials he was self-taught. He served widely in the 4th Hussars and between his regimental duties exhibited his distinctive style of writing in the press.

Resigning his commission in 1899 his first major stroke of luck arose out of his acting as a war correspondent in the Boer War as he was captured but managed to escape and won Oldham as a Conservative in the 1900 'Khaki election'.

The tariff reform campaign launched by Joseph Chamberlain led to Churchill crossing the floor of the House as a Free Trader in May 1904.

He was made undersecretary of state for the colonies by Campbell-Bannerman in 1905 and under Asquith he served in the pre-war cabinet as president of the Board of Trade (1908–10); home secretary (1910–11); and First Lord of the Admiralty. These years were marked by his close partnership with Lloyd George, who may be regarded as his mentor with regard to the introduction of labour exchanges and unemployment insurance.

He was poacher turned gamekeeper at the Admiralty, having sought to curb the naval estimates in 1909 but championing higher spending once responsible for the department. His energy, determination and vision did much to make the Navy ready and able to assume its responsibilities on the outbreak of World War One but his patronage of the ill-fated Gallipoli campaign gave his enemies, especially amongst the Conservatives in the coalition government, the opportunity to have him demoted as chancellor of the duchy of Lancaster.

Churchill briefly commanded an infantry battalion on the Western Front before being recalled to the Ministry of Munitions shortly after Lloyd George became prime minister. He then served as secretary of state for war (1919–21) and as secretary of state for colonies (1921–22). Churchill considered breaking with Lloyd George over the latter's unwillingness to pursue more vigorously the policy of armed intervention in Russia but was talked out of this course of action by Birkenhead.

In 1924 Churchill stood unsuccessfully as an independent Consitutionalist for the Abbey Division of Westminster. He was more successful at Epping later in the year as a Consitutionalist 'who supports the Tory Party', and on his return to parliament was unexpectedly made chancellor by Baldwin in which capacity he institutionalized the Ten-Year rule, brought pensions down from the age of 70 to 65, brought in the first pensions scheme for widows and orphans and pioneered a De-rating Act to stimulate the creation or relocation of industry. He also supervised the restoration of the gold standard which by rendering British exports less competitive did much to provoke the General Strike, during which Churchill edited the *British Gazette* (a government broadsheet, produced in the offices of the *Morning Post*).

1929–39 were Churchill's 'wilderness years' as his opposition to the 1935 Government of India Act and support for Edward VIII at the time of the abdication crisis confirmed for many the wayward character of his judgement.

However, Churchill's consistent opposition to appeasement of Nazi Germany invested him with enormous moral authority when his warnings were vindicated and he was thus re-appointed as First Lord of the Admiralty on the outbreak of World War Two.

Churchill intended the Norwegian campaign not only to seize the initiative from the Germans but also from his hesitant colleagues, thereby establishing his claim to the succession. The first of these aims was a miserable failure but the blame for the humiliating failure of the expedition came to rest on Chamberlain rather than Churchill and opened his way to the premiership.

Nevertheless, Churchill might well have lost out to Halifax, who was more popular in the Conservative

Party and who would obviously be preferable to George VI, given Churchill's championship of Edward VIII. However, instead of resigning and recommending Halifax as his successor, Chamberlain summoned a meeting of Churchill and Halifax, at which the former's reluctance to defer to the latter, and the latter's recognition that Churchill would be more acceptable to Labour and the public (as well as the calculation that his premiership might well prove short-lived), helped decide the issue. However, it was only in October 1940, in the month before Chamberlain's death, that Churchill secured the leadership of the Conservative Party.

When Britain stood alone in Europe in resisting Hitler between the fall of France in June 1940 and the German invasion of Russia in June 1941, Churchill's leadership was inspirational. His pseudo-Shakespearean broadcasts suited the national mood of defiance. However, a string of defeats by the summer of 1942, in Greece, Crete, Dieppe and Tobruk, fed mounting discontent. Churchill played for time by playing off his chief rivals, Eden and Cripps, but was rendered invulnerable by the tide of war turning decisively in Britain's favour with the successes of Operation Torch, El Alamein and Stalingrad.

Churchill was initially hostile towards the Beveridge Report because sceptical of the merits of universal benefits, because his first priority was winning the war, because opinion within the coalition towards the plan was divided, because he feared that it would prove too expensive and, last but not least, because he resented Beveridge's attempts to railroad his government into supporting the report. He nevertheless recognized the need to plan for peacetime and defuse the criticism which hostility to the report had engendered. Thus without referring to the report by name, he promised 'cradle to grave' social insurance after the war in a broadcast on 21 March 1943, and a month later appointed a committee to consider eventual implementation of the report which resulted in the White Papers on Social Security, a National Health Service, and Employment Policy in 1944 and on Housing in 1945, as well as the Butler Education Act in 1944 and the Family Allowances Act in 1945.

Churchill felt slighted by the electorate when they returned Labour by a landslide in 1945, particularly as the Conservative campaign had centred upon his personality and achievements. However, he embarked upon not only his Nobel prize winning history of the recent war but alerted the American public to the existence of the Cold War with his 1946 'Iron Curtain' speech at Fulton, Missouri.

He returned to power in the October 1951 general election but with the exception of denationalizing steel was disinclined to undo most of the work of the Attlee governments, not least because his majority was only seventeen and Labour had actually secured more votes nationally than the Conservatives. In 1955 he finally stepped down in favour of Eden. The inevitable had repeatedly been postponed: in order to cover the coronation of Elizabeth II; to await the new Queen's return from a long tour of Australia and New Zealand; to give Eden time to recover his full strength after the botched operation on his bile duct; and to promote détente through summit diplomacy after Stalin's death.

The truth is that Churchill was increasingly loath to relinquish the power and prestige of high office and increasingly doubtful whether his heir apparent was up to the mark. Eden was bound to suffer by the contrast with a colossus like Churchill, just as Rosebery had suffered by contrast with Gladstone. Nevertheless, Churchill's last years in office are bound to appear a terrible anticlimax compared with his war years, and the trend in recent years has been for revisionist historians to chip away even at his earlier achievements, arguing that his resistance to Hitler cost Britain its empire and great power status. It is ironic that many of those most critical of Britain 'surrendering its sovereignty' to a German-dominated European Union should argue that Britain should have allowed Hitler's Germany a free hand on the continent. In the words of A. J. P. Taylor, Churchill was simply 'the saviour of his country' and without him we would have no sovereignty to surrender or pool.

Civil Registration Act, 1836. Prior to 1836 the Established or Anglican Church enjoyed a monopoly in recording births, marriages and deaths. The Civil Registration Act broke that monopoly by arranging for the compulsory civil registration of these details. In due course this innovation was to be enormously valuable in supplementing social legislation such as the 1833 Factory Act insofar as it was now possible to establish the precise age of a child. However, the immediate reason for the passage of the Act was the desire of liberal Anglican Whigs such as Lord John Russell to remove what moderate nonconformists regarded as a grievance.

Clapham Sect The Clapham Sect or Saints, as they were derisively nicknamed, was a small but influential evangelical group within the Church of England, which took its name from the fact that several of its members (which included William Wilberforce, E. J. Eliot, Zachary Macaulay, Henry Thornton, Charles Grant, James Stephen and John Venn) resided in Clapham in south London (of which Venn was the rector). The movement had its own organ, the *Christian Observer*, which first appeared in January 1801.

Best known for their contribution to the abolition of the slave trade (in 1807) and the abolition of slavery in the British Empire (in 1833), they also campaigned for causes such as prison reform, the prevention of cruel sports, the suspension of the Game Law and the lottery, and the colonization of Sierra Leone. They supported Bible societies and missionary work, founding the Church Missionary Society in 1799. In short, they were evangelically motivated paternalistic philanthropists who did some good at home and much good abroad.

Cobden, Richard (3 June 1804–2 April 1865). The name of Richard Cobden is inseparably linked with that of his close colleague in the Anti-Corn Law League, John Bright, and it is sometimes suggested that their partnership worked so well because of their complementary qualities: Cobden lucid and rational, able to appeal to a sophisticated and educated audience such as the House of Commons by the force of his arguments, whilst Bright was passionate and emotional, and better able to sway the emotions of a mass meeting by the force of his oratory.

However, such a claim overlooks the degree to which Cobden followed those in the Anti-Slavery Society and the Agency Committee in giving his campaigning a flavour of evangelical moral fervour. Indeed, Cobden went so far as to attempt to exploit residual anti-slavery sentiments by specially importing American speakers prepared to argue that repeal of the Corn Laws would greatly assist the abolitionist cause in the United States by strengthening the mid-western wheat-producing states relative to the southern slave-owning ones. More fundamentally, Cobden and the Manchester School preached a gospel of internationalism through free trade, or peace through commerce. He was, however, prepared to anger the 'nonconformist conscience' by supporting Sir James Graham's 1843 Factory Bill, with its pro-Anglican education clauses, and the pro-Catholic 1845 Maynooth Grant.

When the Corn Laws were repealed in 1846 Cobden appreciated better than many contemporaries and some subsequent historians that the praise which Peel paid him for his part in this success should not be taken at face value, and once he had failed to persuade Peel to put himself at the head of an avowedly free trade party he left for a year-long European tour to preach the gospel of free trade.

In 1857 Cobden lost his seat in parliament through the unpopularity of his opposition to the Crimean War (1854–56) and the Second China War (1856–57). It was indeed Cobden who moved the censure motion critical of the government's persistence in an unjust war, which was carried by sixteen votes in March 1857, and which prompted Palmerston to dissolve parliament. Palmerston having swept back into office and Cobden having returned to parliament in 1858, the former offered the latter the Presidency of the Board of Trade but Cobden refused and instead assisted the government's pursuit of free trade and improved relations with France by negotiating the Cobden–Chevalier Treaty, for which public service he refused a baronetcy in 1860. However, having been ruined by unwise speculations, Cobden gratefully received £40,000 raised by a second public subscription (the first having raised roughly twice that amount in 1846).

Cobden was ultimately no more successful in politics than in business insofar as his fondest hopes – for international peace and for the middle class to displace the aristocracy – seemed as far removed from reality on his death in 1865 as they had briefly seemed plausible in 1846.

Combination Laws, 1799–1800. In the wake of the rebellion of the United Irishmen in 1798 and the naval mutinies at Spithead and the Nore, the authorities feared that industrial combinations or trade unions might prove to be a vehicle of French revolutionary sentiments and thus outlawed them in 1799–1800.

Enforcement of the laws was patchy, so that they appear to have had relatively little impact upon the combinations of London artisans but greater success in hindering the development or extension of trade union activity in the Midlands and North. The laws also meant that no formal extra-parliamentary protest could be made against the 1814 decision to repeal those clauses of the Elizabethan Statute of Artificers, by which entry to certain trades was restricted to those who had served seven-year apprenticeships to them: a move regarded as encouraging the displacement of skilled by unskilled labour.

Trade unions were not legalized again until the repeal of the Combination Laws in 1824–25.

Commonwealth Immigrants Act, 1962. The 1948 British Nationality Act had allowed all Commonwealth citizens the legal right of residence in the UK and the 1962 Commonwealth Immigrants Act was an attempt to control the increasing numbers, particularly of coloured or non-white Commonwealth immigrants, availing themselves of that right by restricting admission to those issued with employment vouchers.

Commonwealth Immigration Act, 1968. In the face of 'Africanization' policies by the governments of Kenya, Uganda and Tanganyika (which would now be labelled 'ethnic cleansing'), the Commonwealth Immigration Act was rushed through the House of Commons in seven days, in an attempt to prevent East African Asians from entering the country by limiting immigration to those who already had 'partial' ties with existing British residents.

Immigration was an especially sensitive issue at this time given the furore provoked by Enoch Powell's 'rivers of blood' speech on 20 April 1968.

Common Wealth Party The Common Wealth Party was founded in 1942 by the ex-Liberal MP Sir Richard Acland, who refused to be bound by the wartime electoral truce agreed between the coalition parties in government. Thus Common Wealth contested and won three by-elections during the war (at Eddisbury in 1943, Skipton in 1944 and Chelmsford in 1945). Although it did not oppose Labour or 'progressive' candidates, membership of Common Wealth was proscribed for Labour Party members from 1943. Twenty-three candidates stood at the 1945 general election of whom only one – Ernest Millington – was successful. He subsequently joined the Labour Party, as did Acland, effectively bringing Common Wealth to an end. It had acted as a stalking horse for Labour, indicating the shift to the left in electoral opinion during the war years.

Communist Party of Great Britain (CPGB), 1920–91. The Communist Party of Great Britain (CPGB) was inspired by the success of the Bolshevik revolution in Russia of October 1917 and was founded in London in 1920. Its success has been closely tied to attitudes towards the Soviet Union. Thus the period of its greatest influence was between June 1941 (the Nazi invasion of the Soviet Union), when Britain and Russia became reluctant allies, to the start of the Cold War in 1945. In 1945 the CPGB had two MPs and 200 councillors but thereafter it suffered decline with internal divisions particularly marked in 1956 (the crushing of the Hungarian uprising), 1968 (the crushing of the 'Prague Spring') and 1987–91 (the collapse of communism in the Soviet Union and the end of the Cold War). By 135 to 72 delegates to the party's 43rd Congress voted to change their name, constitution and outlook and become the Democratic Left, which seeks to marry Marxism with feminism, green politics, anti-racism and other 'progressive' causes.

Competitive examinations for the civil service (4 June 1870). By an Order-in-Council all departments of the civil service, with the exception of the Foreign Office (at the express request of the foreign secretary), were rendered open to competitive examination. On the face of it this represented a blow for the principles of equality of opportunity and efficiency, which was supplemented by the University Tests Act, and the abolition of the purchase of commissions (part of the Cardwell army reforms) in the following year. In practice, however, it was little more than a crammer's charter that in Froude's words acted 'to rescue some parts of the service from jobbery, and to save ministers from the necessity of offending their supporters'.

This should not have occasioned any surprise as Sir Charles Trevelyan, the co-author of the Northcote–Trevelyan Report (which had recommended examinations in 1853), wrote to Delane 'Our people are few compared with the multitudes likely to be arrayed against it and we must prepare for the trial by cultivating to the utmost our superior morality and intelligence … ' As Briggs puts it, 'the reformers did not wish to throw open the civil service to the middle classes but rather to the new educational elite of the public schools and universities'.

Conservative Party The Conservative Party grew out of the Tory party as Peel sought to repair its electoral fortunes. The Tamworth manifesto is the key document in this process of repackaging that helped return Peel to office at the head of a majority administration in 1841. The party split in 1846 and formed only three minority governments between that date and 1880, when Disraeli formed his Second Ministry. Whilst Randolph Churchill later claimed to have revived the party through adhering to Disraelian notions of Tory Democracy, more important than the 1867 Reform Act, social reform or organizational innovation in ensuring continued Conservative success was Disraeli's role in assuming the mantle of Palmerston, so that the symbolism of the Union Jack and the language of jingoism was appropriated by the party. It was, however, Salisbury who transformed the party into the natural party of government, not least by securing the adhesion of the Liberal Unionists.

From 1895, the Conservative Party has held office, albeit often in coalitions, for seventy years in total. This achievement has been due above all to pragmatism: the Conservatives having made political capital out of not being overtly political let alone ideological. Hence the party's willingness to abandon positions including protection, *laissez-faire*, the 1800 Act of Union, the Empire, and the hereditary peers – as soon as they came to be regarded as electoral liabilities. The party's decline, culminating in the election of New Labour for the first time in 1997, has been principally due to an uncharacteristically principled obsession with the issue of European integration, on the part of both Eurosceptics and Europhiles within the party.

As the twentieth century ended the Conservative Party held only 165 seats out of a total of 665. This almost exactly replicates Conservative fortunes near the beginning of the century, when the Liberal landslide victory of 1906 reduced them to 167 seats out of 670.

Conspiracy and Protection of Property Act, 1875. The 1875 Conspiracy and Protection of Property Act was an attempt to reverse the 1871 Criminal Law Amendment Act, or at least the way in which it had been interpreted in the courts. Indeed, the Liberals had not meant their measure to ban peaceful picketing and when this was how judges began interpreting their measure they planned remedial legislation, only to lose office before they could put it into effect.

The 1875 Act protected trade unions from prosecution for conspiracy by repealing the 1871 measure and explicitly legalizing peaceful picketing. In general it greatly clarified what was and what was not permissible in a trade dispute, for example, laying down that no acts done by two or more persons in the course of a trade dispute should henceforth be deemed criminal unless they would have been crimes if committed by individuals.

Continuity IRA The Continuity IRA is a splinter group of the IRA. It emerged in the mid-1980s in opposition to what became the peace process. Its political wing is Republican Sinn Féin

Convertibility crisis, 1947. Britain wished to preserve sterling as a reserve currency as a totem of its global great power status and because of the City's role as the world's banker. For both these reasons the US disliked the idea, whilst the parlous state of Britain's national finances by the end of World War Two, particularly after the abrupt ending of Lease-Lend just six days after the end of the Pacific war, placed the Americans in a position to dictate terms. Thus convertibility was one of the conditions attached to the £3.75 billion loan negotiated in November 1945. More specifically, it was agreed that the pound would become freely convertible against the dollar and other currencies in July 1947 (twelve months after Congress approved the loan).

However, when convertibility came in on 15 July 1947 it precipitated a massive run on the gold and dollar reserves. Moreover, this convertibility crisis came on top of an existing balance of payments crisis. The former was only brought to an end when a halt to convertibility was announced on 20 August and the conditions attached to the American loan were suspended in September.

The crisis furthered the process whereby Hugh Dalton was discredited as chancellor. However, more fundamentally it helped, rightly or wrongly, to discredit the policy of planning, and destroyed the confidence with which Labour had entered office in 1945: a process which was compounded by the devaluation of sterling in September 1949.

Cooperative Movement Cooperative societies had been founded before that set up by the Rochdale Pioneers in 1844. Theirs, however, flourished and provided the inspiration, through the 'Rochdale principles', for the entire cooperative movement, which grew to be particularly strong in the north of England, not least after the 1852

Industrial and Provident Societies Act provided legal protection.

Corn Laws, 1815. With the end of the French Revolutionary and Napoleonic Wars the landed interest – or at least that part of it which had exploited inflated wartime prices to cultivate marginal land – feared their investment would be lost and the jeopardizing of cereal agriculture altogether if they did not receive protection against the anticipated influx of cheap foreign corn. They argued that the national interest would also be served insofar as Britain needed to maximize her domestic supply of foodstuffs in the event of a continental system-style blockade. Moreover, given that agriculture was by far the largest single employer of labour and that corn provided the staple element in the British working-class diet, a Corn Law would also play an important role in guaranteeing social stability.

After canvassing parliamentary opinion, Liverpool decided that free importation would only be permitted once domestically produced corn had reached the price of 80 shillings (£4) per quarter.

Corporation boroughs In 43 of the 203 English parliamentary boroughs before the Great Reform Act, possession of the franchise was dependent upon membership of the town council or corporation. In 1832 these so-called corporation boroughs were removed when the basic borough franchise qualification became the occupation of property valued at £10 per annum.

Corrupt and Illegal Practices Act, 1883. The 1872 Ballot Act having manifestly failed to eliminate corruption, the Third Gladstone ministry addressed the issue through the Corrupt and Illegal Practices Act which limited allowable election expenditure, specified what forms of campaign expenditure were and were not permissible, obliged election agents to account for their spending, and prescribed penalties for the bribery or intimidation of voters.

Coupon election, 14 December 1918. On 12 November 1918 Bonar Law agreed to Lloyd George's offer to continue the wartime coalition into peacetime. It was also decided to hold what amounted to a 'Khaki election': the first under the terms of the Fourth Reform Act. The coalitionist candidates in the 1918 election each received a letter of endorsement signed by both Lloyd George and Bonar Law.

Asquith dubbed this joint letter 'the coupon' in reference to the pieces of paper that had to be cut out of wartime ration books in order to obtain rationed goods. Asquithian Liberals did not of course receive this endorsement and fared disastrously at the polls, fielding 253 candidates yet winning just 26 seats. Asquith himself was amongst those unseated. This put the Asquithian Liberals behind Labour, which fielded 388 candidates and won 59 seats, or even Sinn Féin, whose candidates won 73 seats, although they refused to take them.

474 coalitionist candidates were elected, of whom 338 were Conservatives and 136 Lloyd Georgeite Liberals. The coupon election thus ensured that Lloyd George remained as prime minister at the price of increasing his dependence upon the Conservatives and further embittering his relations with Asquith. Thus, with

the benefit of hindsight it is possible to recognize the coupon election as marking an important staging post in the decline of the Liberal Party and the emergence of Labour as the chief rival to the Conservatives.

Cowper–Temple clause, 1870. The Cowper–Temple clause was an amendment to Forster's Education Act of 1870 accepted by the cabinet on 14 June whereby 'no religious catechism or religious formulary which is distinctive of any particular denomination' could be taught in rate-aided or board schools and a conscience clause was to apply whereby no child would be required to attend any religious observance or instruction from which his or her parent wished him or her withdrawn.

The clause appeased non-conformists opposed to the idea of supporting alien denominations on their rates. Gladstone reluctantly accepted this 'secular' proposal, which meant that outside specific voluntary or church schools dogmatic denominational teaching would now be funded solely by the denominations concerned and take place off the timetable.

Crichel Down affair, 1954. Sir Thomas Dugdale had once been parliamentary private secretary to Baldwin and by 1954 was minister of agriculture. In that year the civil servants in his department made a gross error of judgement relating to Crichel Down in Dorset.

Dugdale did the honourable thing and his resignation was commemorated in countless textbooks relating to the British constitution to show that ministers carried the can for mistakes made by their departmental subordinates. However, the relevance of Crichel Down has diminished over the years as ministers have increasingly exhibited a tendency to cling to office with a limpet-like tenacity whatever their department's shortcomings or personal failings.

Crimean War (28 March 1854–1 February 1856). Fighting between the Turks and Russians in 1853 followed the latter's refusal to respond to an ultimatum issued on 4 October 1853 to withdraw from the Danubian principalities. The Turkish demand for Anglo-French assistance was intensified following the Russian destruction of a Turkish squadron at Sinope on 3 November 1853. The British and French fleets entered the Black Sea on 3 January 1854, and declared war on Russia on 28 March 1854.

When Russia belatedly evacuated the Danubian principalities in response to an Austrian ultimatum, the allied powers decided to land on the Crimean peninsula on the northern shore of the Black Sea (September 1854) and cripple Russia's strength as a power there by seizing the port of Sevastopol (although fighting also took place in the Caucasus and in the Baltic). Had the expeditionary army (joined by a Piedmontese force of 10,000 after 26 January 1855) moved quickly after landing this might have been accomplished relatively easily. However, delay gave rise to a year-long siege of the Russian fortress and several battles to raise that siege, including Alma (20 September 1854), Balaklava (25 October 1854) and Inkerman (5 November 1854). The Russians finally evacuated Sevastopol on 11 September 1855.

The loss of Sevastopol and an Austrian threat to intervene on the side of the allies led to Russia accepting preliminary peace terms on 1 February 1856. The Congress of Paris met from 25 February to 30 March to work out the final settlement. This was enshrined in the Treaty of Paris, signed on 30 March 1856, which guaranteed the integrity of Moldavia, Walachia, and Serbia and obliged Russia to surrender southern Bessarabia, at the mouth of the Danube. Moreover, the Black Sea was neutralized, and the Danube River was opened to the shipping of all nations.

Aberdeen had blundered into the war 'through a series of half-hearted measures of which he only half-approved' (Briggs). However, the war itself was initially very popular with the public not only because Russia was regarded as a threat to the security of the Empire, the balance of power and the cause of 'freedom' (most recently by its 1849 intervention in Hungary) but also because Britain had not been engaged in a major war since Waterloo. However, when *The Times* carried William Howard Russell's reports detailing British disorganization and incompetence (symbolized by the Charge of the Light Brigade), the mood in the country and parliament soured.

Hence the fame achieved by Florence Nightingale through her efforts to relieve the soldiers' suffering and John Arthur Roebuck's success in securing a select committee to inquire into the condition of the army besieging Sevastopol. This manoeuvre helped bring down Aberdeen's government and bring Palmerston to the premiership as the only politician capable of commanding a majority in the Commons who had not (as Aberdeen's home secretary) been implicated in the administration's mismanagement of foreign and military affairs.

Criminal Law Amendment Act, 1871. Some magistrates interpreted the 1871 Criminal Law Amendment Act, which confirmed that threatening or obstructive behaviour by masters or workmen was an offence, as outlawing even peaceful picketing. This was not the intention of the First Gladstone Ministry, which sought to introduce further legislation to make this plain but fell from power in 1874 before this could be done. The construction placed by some JPs upon the 1871 Criminal Law Amendment Act thus alienated those very trade unionists who had reason to be grateful to the government for passing the 1871 Trade Union Act (giving them legal recognition and protection of their funds). It was left to Disraeli and the Conservatives to reap the rewards of trade union gratitude by formally legalizing peaceful picketing in their 1875 Conspiracy and Protection of Property Act.

Criminal Law Amendment Act, 14 August 1885. The 1885 Criminal Law Amendment Act was passed following a series of lurid articles by W. T. Stead in the *Pall Mall Gazette*. Its principal measure was to raise the age of consent for girls from thirteen to sixteen.

'Curragh mutiny', 1914. J. E. B. Seely (later Lord Mottistone), the secretary for war, issued ambiguous instructions to the commander-in-chief for Ireland, which led to his officers being instructed that whereas Ulstermen might 'disappear' all others must obey any order to coerce Ulster into accepting the Home Rule Bill or face dismissal. Brigadier-General (later Sir) Henry Gough, the commanding officer of the 3rd Cavalry Brigade, and 56 of his officers, stationed at the Curragh, outside Dublin, thus announced that they would prefer dismissal to being ordered north to enforce Irish Home Rule. Thus Churchill later described the incident as 'not mutiny in any base sense, but rather an act of conscientious passive resistance'.

D

Davitt, Michael (25 March 1846–30 May 1906). Although born in Ireland in 1846, Michael Davitt was raised in Lancashire, after his father had been evicted from his holding at Straide in County Mayo, and the family migrated. It was there that Davitt lost his right arm in an industrial accident at the age of eleven. Attracted by Fenianism, Davitt joined the movement in 1865 and was arrested in 1870 and sentenced to fifteen years' penal imprisonment for gun-running. Released in December 1877 on ticket-of-leave he immediately rejoined the Irish Republican Brotherhood.

Whilst regarding independence as the ultimate goal, Davitt became persuaded in the meantime to place Fenian support behind the constitutional movement and campaign on the land question. This strategy became known as the 'New Departure'. John Devoy, the Irish–American Fenian, and Charles Stewart Parnell were the other leaders of the New Departure but Davitt was its chief author and the founder of the Land League.

During his imprisonment in Portland prison between February 1881 and May 1882 Davitt rethought his strategy and came out in favour of a policy of land nationalization which he hoped might unite the Irish and British poor. However, it failed to have this result and merely provoked an open breach with Parnell in 1884.

Davitt strongly supported the alliance between the Irish and the Gladstonian Liberal Party but, following the split within nationalist ranks in 1890, became an anti-Parnellite MP for Meath (1892) and then West Mayo (1895–99). The United Irish League which Davitt helped found in 1898 suggested his having fallen behind popular attitudes towards the land question, as did his opposition to the 1903 Wyndham Act.

Death duties, 1894. In his 1894 budget Sir William Harcourt applied death duties to land on a graduated scale ranging from 1% where the capital value of the estate lay between £100 and £500, to 8%, where it was in excess of £1m. Death duties accelerated the process whereby the traditional aristocracy gave up land, especially when World War One resulted in death duties being levied in relatively short succession.

Defence of the Realm Act (DORA), 8 August 1914. In the early days of World War One the Asquith government encountered little opposition in passing the Defence of the Realm Act (DORA), which was subsequently extended on six occasions.

Initially designed to guard against espionage, the demands of total war meant that the legislation was soon extended to empower the government not only to suspend many civil liberties but to intervene in the marketplace, controlling wages and prices and directing manpower and other resources. An early amendment of DORA, for example, gave the government powers to appropriate factories and convert them to producing munitions.

This clearly ran counter to *laissez-faire* ideology but raised few protests, even allowing for the fact that Regulation 27 of DORA forbade reports or statements 'by word of mouth or in writing or in any newspaper, periodical ... or other printed publication' which were 'intended or likely' to undermine loyalty to the King, confidence in the currency or recruitment. The latter also justified the imprisonment of conscientious objectors, such as the Independent Labour Party (ILP) leader, James Maxton.

In short, DORA was rightly regarded by the Liberals as a necessary evil given the conditions of modern total warfare.

Derby (Edward George Geoffrey Smith Stanley), 14th Earl of (29 March 1799–23 October 1869). Edward Stanley, the eldest son of the 13th Earl of Derby, was educated at Eton and Christ Church, Oxford. He first entered parliament in the Whig interest as MP for the rotten borough of Stockbridge in 1820 but served in the ministries of Canning and Goderich as a junior Lord of the Treasury and undersecretary for war and the colonies respectively.

In 1830 he became chief secretary for Ireland under Grey and in 1833 became secretary for war and the colonies, which meant that he was responsible for the abolition of slavery in the British Empire. However, his High Church scruples regarding lay appropriation led, in 1834, to his resignation, along with Richmond, Ripon and Graham, and the formation of the 'Derby Dilly': a short-lived attempt at creating a third force in parliament. By 1837 he had moved into partnership with Peel and in 1841 was rewarded with reappointment to the post of secretary of state for war and the colonies.

Stanley's relations with Peel cooled and in 1844, at his own request, he entered the House of Lords as Lord Stanley of Bickerstaffe. Thus when the breach came with Peel over the repeal of the Corn Laws, Derby entered into partnership with Disraeli who led the protectionist Conservatives in the Commons. The latter was understandably less keen than the former to reunite the Conservative Party by persuading the Peelites to return to the fold. However, the most that Derby (as Stanley had become in 1851 on the death of his father) secured was temporary Peelite goodwill for the formation of his 'Who-who' minority administration in 1852 and his formal abandonment of protection. This goodwill was withdrawn in spectacular fashion when Gladstone savaged Disraeli's budget in December 1852, and brought about the ignominious fall of the ministry.

Derby's political dilettantism – his preference for the racetrack or his estate – rather than for high political manoeuvring at Westminster meant that he was largely inactive until the Crimean War brought about the fall of Aberdeen in 1855 and then failed to seize the moment to form an administration, despite attending upon Victoria. It was only an uncharacteristic error on the part of Palmerston, in the form of the Conspiracy to Murder Bill, which led to the latter's resignation and Derby forming his second minority government in 1858. This fell in its turn in 1859 following the passage of an amendment critical of its parliamentary reform bill, although support for the cause of Italian unification was another factor which led to the coalescing and consolidation of parliamentary forces hostile to the Conservatives.

During Palmerston's first ministry Derby had described him with a fair measure of approbation as 'a Conservative minister working with Radical tools' and it was only after the humiliation over the Schleswig-Holstein question in 1864 that Derby exerted himself to condemn Palmerston's policy of 'meddle and muddle'. However, it was not until the Adullamite split in Liberal ranks over parliamentary reform in 1866 that Derby was able to form his third minority administration. It was Derby who encouraged Disraeli to think in terms of 'dishing the Whigs' by means of taking a 'leap in the dark': promoting a reform bill which would wrong-foot Gladstone and provide the Conservatives with an opportunity of extracting long-term political advantage although in the short term this meant suffering the resignations of General Peel, Lord Carnarvon and Viscount Cranborne (the future Lord Salisbury). The Second Reform Act triumphantly vindicated its authors' long-term expectations, and Derby performed one further service for the rejuvenation of Conservatism before his 1868 resignation through ill health, in ensuring that the party would accept Disraeli as his successor.

'Derby Dilly', 1834. Dilly was an abbreviation for a type of coach called a diligence, and the Derby Dilly was the name applied to the group led by Stanley (later the 14th Earl of Derby) who, together with Richmond, Ripon (formerly Goderich), Graham and about forty MPs, were in parliamentary transit, having left Melbourne's Whig ministry after Russell attempted to commit the administration to the principle of lay appropriation. After having toyed with the idea of creating a new centre party the Derby Dilly (diminished in strength by roughly one half by the 1835 general election) gradually coalesced with Peel's Conservative Party.

Derbyshire rising, 9 June 1817. Unrest in Regency Britain manifested itself in a variety of forms. One of the most ominous, at first sight, was the uprising of several hundred men in what they believed to be a national insurrection on 8–9 June 1817. The Huddersfield rising of 8 June saw several hundred men dispersed by the authorities on the moors before they could march on Huddersfield. The Pentridge, Pentrich or Derbyshire rising of 9 June was more serious insofar as one man was shot in the course of about three hundred men marching upon Nottingham from the foot of the Peak district.

The authorities had been aware of the plot since 23 May, thanks to the work of the agent provocateur W. J. Richards ('Oliver the Spy'), and the rising was easily suppressed. Jeremiah Brandreth and two of the other ringleaders, Isaac Ludlam and William Turner, were executed and some of their followers transported.

E. P. Thompson dismissed White's argument that the rising arose chiefly due to Oliver's provocations, claiming that the rising should be viewed as 'one of the first attempts in history to mount a wholly proletarian insurrection' although he was forced to admit that the affair also illustrates 'the weakness of the revolutionary organization, and the lack of an experienced leadership'.

Devaluation of the pound, 18 September 1949. A downturn in the US economy in the late spring of 1949 aggravated Britain's balance of payments and currency reserve problems, which in turn persuaded Hugh Gaitskell and Douglas Jay to put pressure upon the chancellor, Sir Stafford Cripps, to devalue.

He was finally persuaded by their arguments and Britain's immediate economic difficulties were greatly relieved by the announcement on 18 September that the pound would be devalued by roughly a third, from $4.03 to $2.80. Devaluation, however, also brought Labour's post-war reform programme to an end.

Devaluation of the pound, 18 November 1967. Sterling was an issue for Harold Wilson from the moment he became PM in October 1964, as a run on the pound forced him to choose between shoring up the pound or devaluing and, like Attlee, seeing his programme of social reform run into the sands. Wilson chose the former course but the overvalued currency continued to cause problems even after he succeeded in strengthening his majority in March 1966.

A downturn in the US economy, recession in the German economy, the closure of the Suez Canal, as a consequence of the Six Day War, and a strike by dock workers resulted in Britain recording its worst ever monthly trade deficit figures to date in October 1967 and put such enormous pressure upon sterling that the cabinet resolved on 16 November on devaluation.

Two days later, it was announced that the pound would be devalued by 14.3% from $2.80 to $2.40 and on 29 November it was announced that Chancellor Callaghan would be exchanging places with Roy Jenkins at the Home Office. The general mood of despondency had been materially added to by de Gaulle's announcement two days prior to this reshuffle that he was again exercising his veto over Britain's request for EEC membership.

Export-led growth failed to materialize in time to assist Labour to victory at the polls in 1970 (as import prices initially rose more quickly than export prices) so that in retrospect the decision not to devalue earlier – in July 1966 if not in October 1964 – can be seen as having cost both the economy and the Labour Party dearly.

Devolution Devolution is the process whereby power is decentralized, being removed from the Westminster parliament and placed in the hands of the constituent parts of the United Kingdom. The demand was most vocal in Ireland in the nineteenth century but the creation of the Irish Free State inspired Welsh and Scottish nationalists, for whom home rule was seen as a staging post to complete independence.

The 1973 majority report of the Kilbrandon Commission on the constitution recommended the creation of an elected Scottish parliament and an elected Welsh assembly (with more limited powers). These proposals were taken up in a 1975 White Paper and in 1976 a devolution bill passed its Second Reading by 292 votes to 245, with much cross voting by members of both the major parties. However, the issue was complicated when an expatriate Scot, George Cunningham (Labour, Islington), secured an amendment that required approval by 40% not simply of those voting in referenda but of the Scots and Welsh electorate respectively.

This proved to be an insurmountable obstacle when referenda were held on 1 March 1979, as there was a 4 to 1 majority in Wales against devolution (243,048 in favour and 956,330 against) and in Scotland the vote was 1,240,937 (51.6% of those who voted) in favour and 1,153,502 (48.4% of those who voted) against, with 36% of the electorate abstaining or apathetic. The legislation was accordingly withdrawn.

However, on 12 September 1997 on a 60.4% turnout the Scottish expressed a double affirmative, with 74.3% of those voting agreeing that there should be a Scottish parliament and 63.5% of those voting agreeing that this body should have tax-varying (which is to say, tax-raising) powers.

Six days later 50.3% of a 50.1% turnout agreed that there should be a Welsh Assembly.

Given that the Conservatives are moribund on the Celtic fringe, whilst Labour traditionally draws much of its strength there, it is perhaps only a matter of time before they call the separatists' bluff, like the Czechs did in relation to the Slovaks, and allow the Welsh and Scots to go their own way entirely.

Devonshire (Spencer Compton Cavendish), Marquis of Hartington and Eighth Duke of (23 July 1833–24 March 1908). Spencer Compton Cavendish was the eldest son of the four children born to William Cavendish, second Earl of Burlington, later seventh Duke of Devonshire. Lord Cavendish, as he was first known, was educated at home, chiefly by his father, and then at Trinity College, Cambridge, where he gained a second class in the mathematical tripos of 1854.

In 1856 he went to Russia on the staff of his cousin, Granville George Leveson-Gower, second Earl Granville, who was representing Queen Victoria at the coronation of Tsar Alexander II, and in the following year entered parliament for North Lancashire as a Liberal supporter of Lord Palmerston. In January 1858 Cavendish assumed the title of Marquis of Hartington after his father became the seventh Duke of Devonshire.

In June 1859 Palmerston had Hartington move the vote of no confidence which brought down the government of Lord Derby and resulted in Palmerston returning to office. After a trip to the United States during which he visited the headquarters of both the Union and Confederate armies, Hartington was appointed a junior Lord of the Admiralty in March and in May was promoted to an undersecretaryship at the War Office, where he assisted in the organization of the Volunteer movement. In February 1866 he entered the cabinet as secretary of state for war and when the government of Lord Russell fell in June he visited Germany in the immediate aftermath of the Austro-Prussian war.

When Gladstone formed his First Ministry in 1868 Hartington declined the office of Lord Lieutenant of Ireland but accepted that of postmaster-general, with a seat in the Cabinet. He allowed himself to be persuaded to succeed Forster as chief secretary for Ireland towards the end of 1870 but he found coercion legislation and the 1873 Irish University Bill uncongenial.

At a party meeting at the Reform Club on 3 February 1875, following

Gladstone's announcement of his intention to resign the leadership, Hartington grudgingly agreed to take his place. Like Lord Rosebery later, Hartington's love of racing sat uncomfortably with the 'non-conformist conscience' of many members of his party (although unlike Rosebery his horses never placed him in the embarrassing position of winning the Derby). His effectiveness in leading the opposition to the Disraeli government was also limited by the fact that he basically approved of the Suez Canal share purchase of 1875 and was not greatly agitated by the Royal Titles Act of 1876. Although critical of the policies which led to the Second Afghan war in 1878, Hartington was also markedly more sympathetic towards 'Beaconsfieldism' in its handling of the Eastern Question than many other members of his own party, including Gladstone.

Indeed, the Bulgarian atrocities agitation spearheaded by Gladstone not only undermined the government of Lord Beaconsfield but also Lord Hartington's leadership of the Liberal Party. Thus in April 1880, following the Liberal triumph at the polls, Hartington was obliged to inform Her Majesty that he could not discharge her commission to form a government and Victoria was reluctantly obliged to send for Gladstone.

Hartington was appointed secretary of state for India in Gladstone's Second Ministry, in which role he did much useful work such as helping bring the Second Afghan War to a successful conclusion, despite the grief occasioned by the Phoenix Park murders in May, when his brother, Lord Frederick Cavendish (at that time Irish chief secretary), was assassinated.

From 16 December 1882 until the ministry fell in the summer of 1885, Hartington next served once again as secretary of state for war. In this capacity he helped to take the decision to send General Gordon to supervise the evacuation of Egyptian forces from the Sudan. Once it became clear that Gordon required military assistance, Hartington pressed his colleagues to dispatch an expedition but it was only once he threatened resignation, in July 1884, that he induced them to act, by which time it was too late to save Khartoum from capture or Gordon from death.

Hartington also came close to resignation when it was suggested that a parliamentary reform bill would be passed as soon as possible, whilst a bill for the redistribution of seats would come at some undefined point in the future. Indeed, it was largely thanks to Hartington's negotiations with Sir Michael Hicks Beach (later Lord St Aldwyn), that the political deadlock was broken and the decision was taken to pass the redistribution and franchise bills at the same time. He also participated in the inter-party Arlington Street discussions at which the terms of the redistribution bill were settled.

When the Hawarden Kite signalled Gladstone's conversion to the cause of Irish Home Rule and he formed his Third Ministry in 1886 on the basis of bringing forward such a measure, Hartington declined to serve. He had long been the recognized leader of the Whigs and led them in their opposition to Home Rule. In this he also made common cause with Joseph Chamberlain, the leader of the radicals within the Liberal Party and his great rival for the succession to Gladstone.

By appearing upon the same platform as Lord Salisbury at the Opera House in the Haymarket on 14 April, Hartington helped lay the foundations of the Unionist alliance which was to dominate British politics for the next two decades.

At the 1886 election, following rejection of the first Irish Home Rule Bill in the Commons, the Liberal Unionists campaigned as a distinct party under the presidency and leadership of Hartington and secured 78 seats compared to 191 for the Gladstonian Liberals. Salisbury, with the Queen's approval, asked Hartington to form a government, in which he would serve, or to take office in a government led by Salisbury: an offer repeated in January 1887, after the crisis caused by the sudden resignation of Lord Randolph Churchill. Hartington twice declined, however, for fear that such a step would alienate certain Liberal Unionists whose return to the Gladstonian banner might bring Home Rule closer. Instead, Hartington helped, over the next five years, to keep the Salisbury government in being, whilst the chances of any reconciliation with the Gladstonian Liberal Party gradually disappeared.

On his father's death, Hartington became eighth Duke of Devonshire on 21 December 1891 and left the House of Commons for the upper chamber from whence he successfully moved the rejection of the Second Irish Home Rule Bill in 1893.

When Lord Salisbury became prime minister for the third time in March 1894, the Liberal Unionists entered the government, with the Duke of Devonshire becoming president of the Council, continuing in this office after Salisbury resigned on 11 July 1902 and his nephew, Arthur Balfour, succeeded him as prime minister, although he relinquished his post's responsibilities for education and succeeded Lord Salisbury as government leader in the House of Lords.

On 1 October 1903 Devonshire belatedly joined Charles Thomson (afterwards Baron) Ritchie of Dundee, Lord Balfour of Burleigh, and Lord George Hamilton in resigning from the cabinet in the wake of Joseph Chamberlain's campaign for tariff reform. This issue also led him in May 1904 to resign from the Liberal Unionist Association. These problems within the Unionist alliance, which greatly contributed to its loss of office in 1905, and Devonshire's advancing years meant that his political life declined in significance and he was able to spend more time on his other interests such as managing his estates.

Devonshire, like Balfour, sometimes appeared lethargic but despite, or because of, this manner, he could be a highly effective speaker and political operator. He came to possess great political weight in both Houses of Parliament and in the country at large by virtue of his character as much as his possessions and position in society. Above all, what he said carried conviction because it was difficult to deny that a man who had thrice declined to be prime minister (in 1880, 1886, and 1887) was indifferent to the prospect of reward and was rather motivated by principle.

Direct rule Following the Anglo-Irish Treaty in 1921–22, Northern Ireland was ruled by an elected assembly based at Stormont (a suburb of Belfast). The Stormont Assembly was dominated by the Ulster Unionist

Party and represented the perpetuation of the Protestant Ascendancy in Ulster. However, in the late 1960s the civil rights movement drew attention to the corrupt nature of the Stormont regime in protests which marked the start of the Troubles.

In 1972 the Heath government recognized that the Stormont assembly had irretrievably lost the confidence of the Catholic community and decided to suspend its sittings, reverting to direct rule of Northern Ireland from Westminster, with a secretary of state for Northern Ireland sitting in the Cabinet.

A new Northern Ireland Assembly and the ending of direct rule arose as a consequence of the Good Friday Agreement of 1998.

Disraeli, Benjamin, first Earl of Beaconsfield (21 December 1804–19 April 1881). Benjamin Disraeli was the eldest son of the London-based writer, Isaac d'Israeli. Unlike his great rival Gladstone, Disraeli attended neither public school nor Oxbridge, leaving school at about 15. Between 1822 and 1825, he acted as a solicitor's clerk. His finances collapsed as a result of rash speculations and in 1826–27 he published his first political novel, *Vivian Grey.* It was not, however, until the 1830s that Disraeli's social climbing allowed him to enter the high society which he had previously depicted in print, with the patronage of the Tory Lord Chancellor Lord Lyndhurst winning him membership of the Carlton Club and marriage bringing him personal wealth and representation of the corrupt seat of Maidstone. He criticized the New Poor Law, defended the Chartists and in Young England offered a more romantic, less managerial version of Conservatism than that proffered by Peel.

However, it was the repeal of the Corn Laws that marked Disraeli's emergence as a politician of the front rank. In attacking Peel on the grounds of his alleged betrayal of principle (rather than the supposed merits of agricultural protection) Disraeli brilliantly articulated the sentiments of the largely inarticulate backbench squirearchy, and thereby won the undying dislike of Gladstone and the other Peelites. With the party split, Disraeli emerged as second-in-command to Derby. Between 1846 and 1868 he transformed the Conservatives from an embittered protectionist gentry splinter group into a party of government and transformed himself into Derby's natural successor when the latter fell ill in February 1868. This was achieved principally by abandoning the electoral deadweight of protection in 1852, assuming the mantle of Palmerston in 1865, and exploiting Liberal divisions and passing household suffrage for men in the boroughs in 1867 through the Second Reform Act: a series of manoeuvres which confirmed the impression that Disraeli made up in opportunistic panache what he lacked in settled principle.

In 1874 Disraeli headed his Second Ministry, which was also the first majority Conservative government since 1846. In retrospect great claims were made for the social reforms of this administration such as the Public Health, Artisans' Dwellings and Food and Drugs Act, all of 1875. Taken together with the enfranchisement of the artisan class they have been presented as core elements in Disraelian Tory Democracy. Disraeli was certainly keen to 'gain and retain for the Conservatives the lasting affection of the working classes' but this was principally achieved through trade union legislation at home and imperialism abroad.

Much of the early legislation was hastily improvised and originated with Disraeli's colleagues, notably Richard Cross at the Home Office, rather than with the ailing premier himself. Most of the social reform was permissive and uncontentious (unlike the Public Worship Regulation Act), it was rather in foreign and imperial affairs that Disraeli was most active and imaginative, most notably in the 1875 Suez Canal share purchase, 1876 Royal Titles Act and 1878 Berlin Congress.

It used to be alleged that Disraeli was only a late convert to imperialism, only turning to the cry of 'The Empire in danger' in his 1872 Manchester and Crystal Palace speeches, after his cry of 'The Church in danger' of 1868–69 had failed. However, it is now accepted that the two pieces of evidence usually quoted to show Disraeli's early indifference or hostility to empire (his 1852 letter to Malmesbury and 1866 letter to Derby) have only yielded this interpretation when taken out of context. 'Beaconsfieldism' may have been less enduring than Tory Democracy but it was closer to the essence of the man and the contemporary appeal of his party.

Dissenters' Marriage Act, 1836. The 1836 Dissenters' Marriage Act made it lawful for marriages to be held in nonconformist chapels, provided that they were properly licensed for that purpose and the civil registrar was present. Like the Civil Registration Act of the same year, this measure was an effort by the liberal Anglican Whigs to appease moderate non-conformist opinion.

Divorce legislation See MATRIMONIAL CAUSES ACTS.

Downing Street Declaration, 15 December 1993. The Downing Street Declaration or Joint Declaration of the British and Irish governments was announced by John Major and the Irish Taoiseach (Prime Minister), Albert Reynolds, outside 10 Downing Street on 15 December 1993. It consisted of a statement of principles designed to guide the peace process, which some see as having originated in the Hume–Adams talks.

Jim Molyneaux's Ulster Unionist Party was supportive insofar as Unionists were assured in the Declaration that a united Ireland would not be imposed upon them (although this did not stop Ian Paisley and his DUP from denouncing the Declaration), whilst Nationalists such as the SDLP were reassured that their traditions and aspirations would also be respected. Paramilitaries on both sides were offered the prize of being allowed to enter the peace process if they renounced the use of violence. After stalling for time by asking for 'clarification' of the Declaration, Gerry Adams used his influence to secure an IRA ceasefire from August 1994, which encouraged the Combined Loyalist Military Command to declare a ceasefire of their own on 13 October. This did not prove to be permanent but it was an important milestone in the journey towards the Good Friday Agreement.

E

Easter Rising, 1916. Pearse, the head of the Irish Republican Brotherhood and the Dublin revolt, felt that the cause of Irish nationalism demanded a blood sacrifice whatever the prospects of success. Thus on Easter Sunday 1916 a few score of armed republicans occupied the Dublin Post Office and other strategic points in the city until overwhelmed by superior British force. In the course of the fighting 130 British soldiers and sixty-four rebels were killed. It was however the execution by firing squad of a further fifteen court-martialled rebels, including Pearse himself, which transformed the mood in the Nationalist community in large parts of Ireland from one of indifference or even hostility to the rebels into hostility towards the British.

Ecclesiastical Titles Act, 1851. When Berlin hosted the 1936 Olympic Games the Nazi regime ensured that foreign sensibilities were not distressed by toning down official anti-Semitism. By contrast, when the British hosted the Great Exhibition of 1851 they had no qualms about displaying Britain to the world as the homeland of anti-Catholicism, with the introduction of the Ecclesiastical Titles Bill by the government of Lord John Russell in February of that year.

The Bill was a response to the 'Papal Aggression' of the previous year (which divided Britain into Catholic dioceses) and the popular outcry that it provoked (which was on a par with that excited by the Maynooth Grant), and sought to curb papal pretensions by outlawing the circulation of papal bulls in England and any assumption of Episcopal or territorial titles in England (such as 'Archbishop of Westminster') by the Church of Rome not authorized by Parliament. Popular feeling ran so high because the Anglo-Catholic movement within the Church of England was widely regarded as a sort of clerical fifth column for the papacy.

However, the popularity which the Bill brought the ministry in the country was nullified by the difficulties which it brought Russell in parliament, as the measure alienated, for different reasons, the Catholic Irish led by John Sadleir, the Peelites, led on this issue by Gladstone, and some radicals, including John Bright and John Arthur Roebuck. Indeed, the Bill cost Russell the immediate support of the Irish and the prospective support of the Peelites, which in turn obliged Russell to modify the Bill only to suffer the indignity of having militant Protestants succeed in carrying extreme amendments in committee, in which form the Bill was finally passed by 263 votes to 36.

The whole incident confirmed that Russell was accident-prone and that despite the apparent decline in church- and chapel-going revealed by the religious census of 1851, the cry of 'No Popery' was as resonant as ever.

Eden, Sir Robert Anthony, first Earl of Avon (12 June 1897–14 January 1977). Anthony Eden, like

Macmillan (who was three years his junior), went from Eton and Oxford (in Eden's case Christ Church, where he took a first class degree in Oriental Studies) to distinguished service on the Western Front (where he won the Military Cross) and thence into the House of Commons. But whereas Macmillan's interest in 'progressive' domestic policies resulted in his being shunted into a siding for the inter-war years, Eden's matinee idol looks, charm and enthusiasm for foreign affairs led to his being fast-tracked. Thus four years after becoming an MP he was parliamentary private secretary for three years to the foreign secretary, Austen Chamberlain, served as parliamentary undersecretary for foreign affairs, 1931–34, was Lord Privy Seal and minister for League of Nations affairs, 1934–35, and (following the resignation of Sir Samuel Hoare for his part in the Hoare–Laval Pact) was foreign secretary at the age of thirty-eight by the end of 1935.

As foreign secretary Eden managed to sideline the Germanophobe permanent undersecretary Sir Robert Vansittart but was himself marginalized by Neville Chamberlain and his adviser, Sir Horace Wilson. It was thus less for his work in the post than for his resignation from it (accompanied by his parliamentary undersecretary, Cranborne), in early 1938, that Eden won a reputation as an opponent of appeasement. This does not, however, stand up to serious scrutiny. To be more precise, Eden was opposed to appeasement of Mussolini's Italy but was quite prepared to reach an accommodation with Hitler's Germany, even if this involved substantial concessions (having had the anti-German Vansittart removed from his post as permanent undersecretary precisely in order to facilitate such matters). Eden's February 1938 resignation was thus not so much an expression of the principle of resisting aggression, as recognition of his inability to work harmoniously with Neville Chamberlain, whose 'hands-on' approach to foreign affairs as prime minister contrasted markedly with the 'arm's-length' approach of Stanley Baldwin.

Eden did not speak out from the backbenches on Chamberlain's foreign policy and was duly invited to return to government as secretary of state for the Dominions upon the outbreak of war. However, it was Churchill as premier who gave Eden the opportunity to shine, first as secretary of state for war and later in 1940, when Halifax was dispatched to the States, as foreign secretary. Churchill was just as much inclined to interfere in foreign affairs as Chamberlain but a close identity of outlook and aim rendered this meddling less objectionable to Eden. Indeed, so high was Churchill's regard for his foreign secretary that he groomed him for the succession by, for example, asking him to assume the additional responsibility of acting as leader of the House of Commons from 1942. Eden performed this dual role until Labour won the 1945 election. In the process he became a parliamentarian of the highest order but his health began to suffer. He even twice contemplated withdrawing from party politics, toying with the idea of becoming viceroy of India in 1943 and secretary-general of the United Nations in 1945.

However, Eden stuck with the Conservative Party and returned to the Foreign Office and served as Churchill's deputy leader between 1951 and 1955. His diplomacy appeared as impeccable in this period as his dress sense. He was instrumental in bringing peace in Korea and Indo-China, and in averting war between Italy and Yugoslavia over Trieste, whilst smoothing relations between Britain and both Persia and Egypt, and even contributing to a significant thawing of the Cold War.

When Eden eventually entered into the premiership in 1955 he enjoyed numerous advantages. He was young (at least compared with his predecessor), handsome, debonair, popular, and possessed a good television manner, whilst his 'principles' apparently distanced him from the 'Guilty Men' of the thirties and earned him the right to be regarded as Churchill's successor.

However, Eden was also vain, nervous, unable to take the measure of potential rivals (notably Macmillan), in declining health (particularly after a badly bungled operation on his bile duct in 1953), lacking in experience of domestic affairs (because of his concentration upon foreign affairs) and increasingly querulous and frustrated because Churchill had taken such a long time to stand aside for him (although the charitable have interpreted at least part of Churchill's procrastination as a ploy to allow Eden fully to recover his health before entering Number 10). Eden's irritation with Churchill mounted despite, or because of, the fact that the two men had become closer through ties of marriage: Eden's second wife being Clarissa Churchill (the niece of the great man).

With the benefit of hindsight it is possible to see that Eden made a big mistake in December 1955 when he moved Macmillan from the Foreign Office to the Treasury after he had been in the post that he had coveted for so long for just six months. Macmillan resented this move but it also gave him greater power, which he was to use to good effect during the Suez Crisis.

The peacemaker turned war maker when Nasser nationalized the Suez Canal Company in July 1956 because Eden was determined to escape from the shadow of his illustrious predecessor and because he misread Nasser as another Mussolini or Hitler. The Suez Crisis stripped Eden of his glamorous reputation, which was already wearing thin (as lacking the 'smack of firm government'), and the man who had supposedly stood up to the dictators in the thirties became widely derided as a duplicitous aggressor himself (Eden not only lying to the House but trying to destroy the documents that proved this). Ill health forced Eden to resign and his medical problems can be made to bear much of the responsibility for his policies coming to grief but in reality the flaw lay in his temperament and it is difficult to imagine that he could ever have lived up to the expectations vested in him during his long apprenticeship.

Edinburgh Letter, 22 November 1845. On 22 November 1845 Lord John Russell published an open letter to his constituents (in the City of London) from Edinburgh in which he announced his conversion and committed the Whigs to repeal of the Corn Laws. Superficially this was a triumph for the Anti-Corn Law League but whilst Russell now shared their immediate objective he made it clear in his letter that his motivation was closer to that eventually displayed by Peel than to Cobden and Bright, arguing that the struggle to maintain agricultural protection was 'deeply injurious to an aristocracy which (this quarrel once removed) is strong in property, strong in the construction of our legislature, strong in opinion, strong in ancient associations, and the memory of immortal services'.

When Peel resigned on 6 December he therefore had reasonable grounds to hope that Russell might enter office and pursue those policies which he knew threatened the fragmentation of his own party but Russell claimed, after ten days of negotiations, that he was unable to form an administration and 'passed the poisoned chalice' back to Peel. By Christmas 1845 therefore Peel returned to office set on the path to pass the legislation which would divide Peelite and Protectionist Conservatives and result in his losing office for good.

Education Act, 1891. The 1891 Education Act finally fulfilled the aim of the Education League that all public elementary schooling should be free.

Education Act, 1870 See FORSTER EDUCATION ACT.

Education Act, 1876 See SANDON EDUCATION ACT.

Education Act, 1880 See MUNDELLA EDUCATION ACT.

Education Act, 1902 See BALFOUR EDUCATION ACT.

Education Act, 1918 See FISHER EDUCATION ACT.

Education Act, 1944 See BUTLER EDUCATION ACT.

Education Act, 1988 See BAKER EDUCATION ACT.

Education grant, 1833. In 1833 the sum of £20,000 was made available to voluntary (sectarian) schools run principally by the National Society and the British and Foreign School Society. The sum was paltry when set against the £20m made available in the same year as compensation to the slave owners for the abolition of slavery but symbolically the gesture was very important as signifying, for the first time, that the state accepted responsibility for education.

In 1839 the grant was increased to £30,000 and a special committee of the Privy Council (the Board of Education) was entrusted with ensuring value for money by means of state inspection.

Education League In 1867 Joseph Chamberlain founded the Birmingham Education League which evolved into the National Education League. Its aims were threefold: to secure free, compulsory, non-denominational elementary schooling. Although the Forster Education Act did not go far towards meeting these demands, the agitation brought Chamberlain into national prominence in Liberal circles, whilst the League's organization for Birmingham's school board elections provided Chamberlain with insights which he was later to apply to the National Liberal Federation.

Edward VII (Albert Edward) (9 November 1841–6 May 1910). As the eldest son of Queen Victoria,

Albert Edward was named after his father, Prince Albert, although he was known within the family as 'Bertie'. It is difficult to refer to this as a term of endearment because Bertie was starved of parental affection, instead being subjected from a very early age to a rigorous regime designed to make him worthy to be a king. Not surprisingly Edward, who lacked any intellectual flair but showed some strength of character, rebelled against this effort to mould him in his father's image so that by the time he attended Cambridge he had already developed an appetite for food, cigars, gambling and womanizing. When he allowed Nellie Clifton, a local 'actress', to spend the night in his quarters the ailing Albert personally went to Cambridge to reprimand him and when he died shortly afterwards Victoria blamed her husband's death on a chill contracted in the course of administering this reproof.

A year later Edward married Alexandra ('Alix'), the daughter of the King of Denmark, who was three years his junior. He loved her after his fashion but that did not preclude a long line of royal mistresses. Other than ensuring the succession, Victoria was unwilling to allow Edward to perform any royal duties, so that much of his loose living arose from his being at a loose end.

Edward finally came to the throne aged 59, when Victoria died in 1901. He embraced the ceremonial aspects of the role which he had inherited, for example reviving the State Opening of Parliament. As 'the Uncle of Europe', related to most of Europe's crowned heads, he also played a role in fostering Britain's relations with other states, most notably paving the way for the Entente Cordiale.

Edward died of bronchial asthma in 1910, aged 68.

Edward VIII (Edward Albert Christian George Andrew Patrick David) (23 June 1894–28 May 1972). As Prince of Wales Edward was a popular figure despite, or because of, the fact that he had his own ideas which were at variance with those of the 'establishment'. For example, whilst visiting the Dowlais works he made headlines by remarking, 'These steel works brought the men here. Something must be done to see that they stay here working.'

He was also the subject of endless speculation as the world's most eligible bachelor. However, after the court had vetoed one eligible virgin he embarked upon a series of relationships with older women who could not marry him but who could 'mother' him, including Freda Dudley Ward, Thelma Furness, and Wallis Simpson.

Mrs Simpson is often regarded as a greedy snob who got her claws into Edward, provoked the abdication crisis and thereby drove George VI into an early grave. However, if blame is to be apportioned then Edward was at least as culpable with his 'headstrong obstinacy, ingrained self-centredness, marked preference for pleasure when it clashed with duty and admiration for the new German system of government' (Sir John Colville) which was expressed during and after his October 1937 tour of the Third Reich.

The abdication had been a final triumph for Baldwin and one of a long series of embarrassments for Churchill. The Duke of Windsor (as Edward became upon renouncing his throne) remained an actual or potential embarrassment to Churchill, before and during his wartime governorship of the Bahamas. After the war Edward hankered after some sort of official status but this was blocked by Attlee and the Windsors reverted to a sybaritic existence centred upon their Paris home.

Edward finally succumbed to cancer of the throat on 28 May 1972. His corpse was brought back to Britain by the RAF and after lying in state and the funeral service at St George's Chapel, was buried under a simple stone at Frogmore. The way in which his life would unfold had been foretold by Keir Hardie in the year of his birth: 'From his childhood onward … surrounded by sycophants and flatterers by the score … A line will be drawn between him and the people he is called upon some day to reign over. In due course … he will be sent on a tour round the world, and probably rumours of a morganatic alliance will follow, and the end of it will be the country will be called upon to pay the bill.'

The one distinguished aspect of his life, like that of Charles I, was the manner in which he relinquished his crown.

Elizabeth II (Elizabeth Alexandra Mary) (21 April 1926–). The eldest child of George (later George VI) and Elizabeth Bowes-Lyon, the future Elizabeth II was born on 21 April 1926. She became heiress-presumptive in 1936 as a consequence of the abdication crisis. Educated at home (together with Princess Margaret, four years her junior), she gradually assumed a number of royal duties until in 1947 she made her first official visit overseas and (on 20 November) married Lieutenant Philip Mountbatten, now His Royal Highness, the Prince Philip Duke of Edinburgh. The couple went on to have four children: Charles (born 1948), Anne (1950), Andrew (1960), and Edward (1964).

Elizabeth ascended to the throne as Her Majesty Queen Elizabeth II following the death of her father on 6 February 1952. Her coronation – the first to be televised – took place on 2 June 1953.

Critiques of the monarchy were already being offered by John Grigg and Malcolm Muggeridge in the mid-1950s, and Elizabeth's reign has seen disenchantment with the institution she embodies becoming increasingly widespread, although most of this has arisen through the activities of her children and their spouses rather than through the queen herself. She has always been assiduous, albeit rarely inspiring, in the performance of her duties, although a serious question mark arises over whether she, or her advisers, allowed royal prerogative to be eroded by Macmillan in October 1963 in his efforts to ensure that he was not succeeded as prime minister by Rab Butler. However, given the more serious doubts regarding the soundness of judgement of Charles on a wide range of issues, Elizabeth's greatest service to the crown is simply to abide by her coronation oath and discountenance any thought of abdication.

Empire Free Trade Empire Free Trade was a term popularized in the late 1920s by those in the Conservative Party, industry and the press, notably Rothermere and Beaverbrook, who favoured the cause of imperial preference (reduced tariffs in imperial goods relative to those imported from outside the empire). This change of name was thought expedient as Joseph Chamberlain in 1906 and Stanley Baldwin in 1923 had both discovered that any talk of protection was poison at the ballot box.

Leaving aside domestic difficulties, the scheme was completely impracticable as no Dominion leader was prepared to enter into a reciprocal relationship whereby their markets would be opened to British goods. Beaverbrook nevertheless supported the idea as a means of embarrassing the Conservative leadership. However, the cause was finally laid to rest when Canadian prime minister, Richard Bennett, described Beaverbrook's policy as 'neither desirable nor possible' and Duff Cooper decisively defeated an Empire Crusade candidate at the Westminster St George's by-election.

Employers and Workmen Act, 1875. The Employers and Workmen Act repealed the 1867 Master and Servant Act, abolishing imprisonment for breach of engagement and making employer and employee equal parties to a civil contract. Together with the Conspiracy and Protection of Property Act of the same year, this legislation helped persuade many trade unionists to feel better disposed towards the Conservative than the Liberal Party. As Alexander MacDonald, former president of the Miners' Association and chairman of the Parliamentary Committee of the TUC, stated in 1879, 'the Conservative Party has done more for the working class in five years than the Liberals have done in fifty'.

Employers' Liability Act, 1880. The Employers' Liability Act of 1880 established a right to compensation for workmen for personal injury caused through negligence on the part of the employer. In establishing the principle of compensation the Act represented an important step forward but subsequent legislation would be required to extend its provisions as it did not cover occupations such as domestic servants and sailors, did not provide for injuries caused through the negligence of sub-contractors, and enabled workmen to 'contract-out' of its provisions.

Endowed Schools Act, 1869. The Endowed Schools Act was a response to the widespread feeling, only partly assuaged by the Clarendon Commission Report of 1864 and the Public Schools Act of 1868, that ancient endowments for education were frequently misapplied.

The legislation, predictably, did more for the middle than the working class, whose needs were more directly addressed by the Forster Education Act of the following year.

Established Church Act, 1833 See IRISH CHURCH TEMPORALITIES ACT.

Established Church Act, 1836. During his First Ministry (1834–35) Peel established the Ecclesiastical Duties and Revenues Commission to consider possible reforms of the Established Church. This was a practical expression of the political philosophy which he had outlined in his Tamworth Manifesto but was acceptable to the Whigs when they returned to office under Melbourne. Indeed, the 1836 Established Church Act was based upon the recommendations of Peel's commission and went some way towards standardizing the territorial responsibilities of bishops and redistributing Episcopal incomes. Moreover, it made Peel's commission into a permanent body, known simply as the Ecclesiastical Commission.

Evangelical Tories Evangelical Tories such as Oastler, Sadler and Shaftesbury were moved by the sufferings of the industrial working class to advocate a Tory–Radical alliance of the paternalistic aristocracy and the urban masses against the middle classes, and to campaign for improvements in working conditions. However, Sir Robert Peel was in principle opposed to legislation limiting the hours of work as likely to undermine the ability of employers to compete effectively in the international marketplace. The two therefore clashed, particularly over what became the 1844 Factory Act.

F

Fabian Society The Fabian Society was founded in 1883–84 as a non-Marxist socialist society. It took its name from Q. Fabius Maximus ('Cuncator'), whose legendary patience symbolized the Fabians' gradualist tactics. The Fabians initially thought that they could promote their ideas by winning converts in the traditional political parties but gradually they recognized the desirability of a separate Labour Party.

Fabian influence upon the Labour movement has been out of all proportion to its membership, which has included the Webbs, Annie Besant, Bernard Shaw, H. G. Wells, and R. H. Tawney. The 1918 constitution, with its notorious Clause Four (advocating wholesale public ownership of the means of production distribution and exchange), was, for example, Fabian-inspired, being penned by Sidney Webb.

Factory Act, 1802. The 1802 Factory Act represented the first recognition by parliament of the need to protect child labour. This Act specifically sought to concern itself with pauper children in cotton mills. However, it achieved little more than expressing the good intentions of its authors.

Factory Act, 1819. Robert Owen persuaded the former cotton manufacturer, Sir Robert Peel (and father of the future prime minister), to present his proposals to the Commons for a measure for limiting the hours of children's labour in mills.

The resultant 1819 Factory Act specified that in cotton factories no child below the age of nine should be employed, whilst those aged between nine and sixteen years were not to work at night and were not to work in excess of twelve hours per day. However, parents and employers alike connived to ignore these regulations whilst the state lacked any effective means of enforcing their compliance, as it was not until 1833 that a factory inspectorate was created.

Factory Act, 1833. In 1830 John Wood, a Bradford factory owner with a guilty conscience, invited Richard Oastler, a Tory Evangelical steward of a large estate, to see modern factory conditions for himself. Oastler was so appalled that he wrote the first in what became a series of letters entitled 'Yorkshire Slavery' to the *Leeds Mercury*, in which he pointed out that opponents of slavery should begin by addressing the problem at home.

Oastler and his Tory Evangelical friend, Michael Sadler, threw in their lot with the predominantly Radical and Dissenting Ten Hours Movement, and Lord Ashley (later Earl of Shaftesbury) agreed to lead the campaign in the Commons after Sadler lost his seat in December 1832.

A Benthamite-dominated Royal Commission provided the basis for the Bill drawn up by Chadwick and introduced for the government by Althorp in August 1833. Its major terms (which applied to textile factories) prohibited the employment of children under nine (except in silk factories); limited nine to thirteen year olds to nine hours a day and a 48-hour week; limited youths aged between thirteen and eighteen to twelve hours per day and a 69-hour week; prohibited night work (between the hours of 8.30 pm and 5.30 am) for those under eighteen (except in lace factories); obliged employers to provide two hours schooling a day for those between nine and thirteen; and appointed four full-time factory inspectors (backed by superintendents) to check that the Act was being observed.

The Act was to be phased in over thirty months so as to allow employers time to introduce a relay system of child labour so that the hours worked by adults were not affected. There were other ways in which the Act, although representing a major step forward, still left a lot to be desired. For example, until the 1836 Civil Registration Act it was not possible to establish the age of children with any certainty, whilst their parents were often happy to collude with employers in pretending that they were older than was actually the case.

Factory Act, 1844. The principal features of the 1844 Factory Act were that children under the age of eight were not allowed to work in textile factories; young persons aged between eight and thirteen were limited to six and a half hours per day; women were limited to twelve hours per day; and there were to be no night shifts for young persons and women. Children had to attend school at least three hours each day.

The legislation marked a major step forward in protecting factory workers, and stimulated the demand of those still pressing for a ten-hour day.

Factory Act, 1847 See TEN HOURS ACT.

Factory Act, 1850. The 1850 Factory Act stated that women and children aged between thirteen and eighteen were not to work in textile factories outside the hours of 6 am and 6 pm (2 pm on Saturdays), with 1.5 hours each day allowed for meals.

Factory Act, 1874. The 1874 Factory Act had three main provisions. Firstly, it reduced the working day for women and children so as to satisfy the demand for a nine-hour day for all factory workers. Secondly, it raised the age at which children could work from 8 to 10. Thirdly, it raised the age at which youths could engage in full-time work from 13 to 14.

The measure thereby contributed to the well-being of the working classes and Disraeli's reputation as a social reformer.

Factory and Workshops Act, 1878. Based on the recommendations of the Royal Commission established in 1876, the 1878 Factory and Workshops Act codified all factory legislation since the 1833 Factory Act and abolished the distinction, for legislative purposes, between factories and workshops (the latter hitherto being defined as employing fewer than 50 persons). However, women's workshops and domestic workshops were exempted from the general provisions of the Act regarding cleanliness and sanitation, and were allowed to operate the working day within such a wide limit (between 6 am and 9 pm) that the job of factory inspectors was made very difficult.

Factory Extension Act, 1867. The 1867 Factory Extension Act extended the protection afforded by earlier factory acts to non-textile trades by defining a factory as any building in which 50 or more persons were employed for gain in a manufacturing process. Children under the age of eight were not permitted to work and those aged between eight and thirteen were to receive at least ten hours of schooling a week. In addition, special regulations were laid down for dangerous trades such as glass making.

Falklands War, 1982. There are several instances of one side attacking another before declaring war. One thinks of Japan in relation to Russia in 1904 and the US in 1941. In the case of the Falklands, however, neither side declared war, so that technically this war is classed as a 'conflict'.

There is the additional complication that what was for the British the battle for the Falklands was for the Argentinians, initially at least, a war to liberate the Malvinas.

Argentina never renounced her claim to the islands (dating back to the 1820s), whilst the twentieth-century Foreign Office appeared willing to renounce Britain's. Moreover, the Argentinians interpreted the reduction of the Royal Navy's establishment in the area as signifying that Britain's heart was not really in retaining a presence in the South Atlantic and thus in March 1982 probed Britain's determination to defend her claims in the area by having their flag hoisted over South Georgia. On 2 April 1982 an Argentine invasion force secured the Falklands after defeating a Royal Marine platoon stationed there.

Lord Carrington and his Foreign Office colleagues, Humphrey Atkins and Richard Luce, insisted on resigning, despite the fact that he had previously warned against the withdrawal of HMS *Endurance* from the South Atlantic on the grounds of economy, only to be overruled by Mrs Thatcher backing the Ministry of Defence. He made this self-sacrifice because he considered a scapegoat was required and because he thought that the military response would be compromised unless he drew fire from John Nott (whose offer of resignation was rejected) and Mrs Thatcher.

US secretary of state, Al Haig, attempted to broker a settlement but neither the Argentine president, General Galtieri, nor Mrs Thatcher would back down. President Reagan thus backed the latter, supplying valuable Sidewinder missiles, satellite intelligence and refuelling facilities on Ascension Island. The French also provided Britain with information to enable her to cope better with the weapons which they had sold to Argentina, specifically Super Etendard aircraft and Exocet missiles.

The last hopes of a peaceful solution were effectively torpedoed on 2 May 1982 when Mrs Thatcher altered the rules of engagement to allow the sinking of the *General Belgrano* outside of the 200-mile maritime exclusion zone which Britain had placed around the islands, with the loss of 323 Argentine lives. Two days later 21 British lives were lost when an Exocet missile sank HMS *Sheffield*.

British forces landed at San Carlos Bay on 21 May and by 11 June had fought their way to the outskirts of Port Stanley. The Argentine forces on the Islands surrendered on 14 June. British sovereignty had been reasserted at the cost of 258 dead and roughly 800 wounded.

The conflict proved to the people of Argentina that their government was as incompetent at waging war as it was at managing the economy. The upshot of defeat was thus the downfall of the military junta and the restoration of democracy.

When the Franks Report was published it revealed that Mrs Thatcher had effectively invited the Falklands invasion by supporting HMS *Endurance*'s withdrawal. Any question of blame was, however, swallowed up in the euphoria of victory. Mrs Thatcher resisted the temptation of calling an immediate 'Khaki election' but the 'Falklands factor' was still sufficiently strong the following year to facilitate the Conservatives being returned to power in 1983 with the biggest Commons majority since the Labour landslide of 1945. The Falklands thus completely transformed the prospects for Mrs Thatcher whose intransigence in the face of the return of mass unemployment prior to the conflict was less well regarded than her resolution in the face of Argentine aggression. At least as importantly for the future of Thatcherism, the Falklands immeasurably strengthened Mrs Thatcher in relation to the Foreign Office and the 'Wets' within her own party even if the costs of sending the task-force and creating Fortress Falklands undermined efforts to curb public expenditure.

Cynics said that the war was fought in order to ensure that Britain had a suitable platform in the South Atlantic for future exploration and exploitation of the region's mineral wealth. It would, however, be more accurate to see Mrs Thatcher's response as shaped by a desire to expunge from the national and party memory the appeasement of the 1930s and the Suez fiasco of 1956. Superficially a throwback to 'gunboat diplomacy', the Falklands allowed Mrs Thatcher, like Palmerston, to represent herself as the staunch defender of Britain's interests and capture a renewed mood of national self-confidence. The rhetoric of defending British sovereignty was given a new resonance when deployed by Mrs Thatcher in her relations with her European Community partners. At the same time it helped to cement the Reagan–Thatcher version of the 'special relationship', with the United States able to rely on Britain alone amongst its NATO allies in 1986 for support in its air strike against Libya.

Family Allowances Act, 1945. Churchill, despite his profound reservations regarding the Beveridge report in general and universal benefits in particular, backed what became the Family Allowances Act, which was the first universal benefit of the modern British welfare state, providing five shillings (25p) per week for the second and all subsequent children.

Fenianism Following the failure of Young Ireland, a revolutionary organization was founded in Dublin on St Patrick's Day, 1858 by James Stephens (a veteran of the 1848 rising). At first this body was known by a variety of names but gradually its members came to be known as Fenians, after an American-based branch of the organization which took its name from the Fianna, or army of Finn MacCamhail in the old Irish stories.

The Fenians recruited members in Ireland and from among the Irish immigrant communities in Britain and the United States, particularly once the Civil War there ended in 1865. Risings were launched in Ireland in early 1867 but were easily suppressed. However, the agitation to secure an amnesty for the Fenian prisoners and anger at the execution of the Manchester martyrs all helped mobilize nationalist sentiment, and persuade Gladstone of the desirability of addressing the Irish Question.

First World War See WORLD WAR ONE.

Fisher Education Act, 8 August 1918. When Lloyd George formed his first coalition government in December 1916 he appointed the distinguished historian H. A. L. Fisher to be president of the Board of Education.

The 1918 Education Act raised the school-leaving age from twelve to fourteen, abolished fees in elementary schools, ensured that at least half of the cost of education was met from central government funds, and sought to expand provision for education of those aged between fourteen and eighteen.

However, the Geddes Axe fell particularly heavily upon Fisher's Education Act, as post-war retrenchment meant that expenditure on secondary expansion was cut and certain provisions in the Act never came into being, notably the 'continuation' schools that were to provide education beyond the age of fourteen.

'Food taxes' When Joseph Chamberlain launched his tariff reform crusade his free trade opponents soon claimed that the result would be dearer food. This equation of protection with food taxes was highly effective in electoral terms and the 1906 election was fought against a backdrop of posters comparing the large (white) loaf of free trade with the smaller (brown) loaf of protection.

Foot, Michael Mackintosh (23 July 1913–). Michael Foot's father was the Rt. Hon. Isaac Foot, the Liberal MP for Bodmin, and it was as a Liberal that Michael was elected president of the Oxford Union. He also obtained a second in Philosophy, Politics and Economics at Wadham College, which he entered after attending Leighton Park School, Reading. The school was Quaker although Isaac Foot was a Methodist.

Oxford was followed by clerking in Liverpool (an experience which completed his conversion to socialism), and then an introduction to journalism for the *New Statesman* and *Tribune*. The latter introduced him to Bevan, who in turn introduced him to Beaverbrook, and these two men became Foot's ill-assorted mentors and idols.

Through Beaverbrook Foot joined the *Evening Standard* under the editorship of Frank Owen. These two and Peter Howard produced 'Guilty Men', the influential attack upon appeasement. With the outbreak of World War Two Owen was called up and Foot took over as editor until he fell out with Beaverbrook after falling in love with Lily Ernest, one of Beaverbrook's mistresses. Transferring to the *Daily Herald*, Foot began a political column there which he produced for the next two decades. The breach with Beaverbrook lasted only a small fraction of this time, being repaired in 1948. Foot, an active supporter of CND, also had a falling-out with Bevan over the latter's condemnation of unilateralism as an 'emotional spasm' but once again a reconciliation was effected and Foot went on to become the high priest of the Bevanite cult, producing a hagiographical two-volume life of the man whom he eventually succeeded to represent Ebbw Vale in parliament.

Foot first, however, was elected to parliament in 1945 to represent his home town of Plymouth, after defeating the incumbent, Hore-Belisha. Foot's active political career was to fall into three phases. First came his period of Bevanite rebellion against the Labour leadership in the late 1940s and 1950s. Foot was out of parliament between 1955 and 1960 so the platform for this campaign was provided by the pages of *Tribune* (of which he became co-editor in 1948), and the panel of the BBC television programme 'In the News' (on which he sat in the early 1950s). The climax to this campaign came with Foot having the party whip withdrawn for two years because he voted against the defence estimates in 1961.

The second phase lasted from 1963 to 1970, when Foot traded in his role of gadfly for that of 'responsible' critic of the early Wilson leadership over issues such as Rhodesia, Vietnam, Prices and Incomes policy, *In Place of Strife* and the scheme for reform of the House of Lords proposed by Richard Crossman. The latter was defeated by means of an unholy alliance with Enoch Powell, with whom Foot also found himself in agreement in opposing British membership of the EEC.

From 1970 to 1983 came the third phase, when Foot belatedly became a team player and gradually climbed up the party and ministerial ladders. In 1970 he was elected to the shadow cabinet, served as secretary of state for employment, 1974 to 1976, and then Lord President of the Council and Leader of the House, 1976 to 1979. In 1976 he came second to Callaghan in the leadership election (surviving into the third ballot) and duly became deputy leader (a post he had already contested in 1970, 1971 and 1972).

When Callaghan resigned as leader following defeat in the 1979 election, the contenders were John Silkin and Peter Shore (who were defeated on the first ballot) and Denis Healey and Michael Foot, who went on to become deputy leader and leader respectively (having won 129 and 139 votes respectively on the second ballot). It has been suggested that some future SDP defectors supported Foot because his election would justify their future desertion. Foot's leadership certainly saw the party's fortunes sink to a very low point, as the desertion of the Gang of Four did not see an end to faction. Indeed, it was during this period that the Bennite challenge reached its peak with Tony Benn contesting the deputy leadership with Denis Healey in 1981.

Even if one leaves the Falklands factor out of account, Labour faced an uphill struggle in the 1983 election which the near-seventy-year old Foot was not the man to surmount. The slickness of the Saatchi and Saatchi promotion of the Conservative cause was never seen to better effect than now, when it was set against the ramshackle, tottering figure of Foot with his windy rhetoric, welder's glasses, and walking stick. The result was that Labour won only 209 seats and was fortunate that its share of the votes cast narrowly managed to exceed that of the Alliance. Foot stepped down from the leadership in order to spend more time with his beloved books.

Michael Foot spent the first fifty-seven years as a fully-paid-up member of the awkward squad who then decided that he wished to exercise power and responsibility. Not surprisingly he reached the top too late, lacking the requisite experience and looking like a political dinosaur. In the second half of the twentieth century he has a strong claim to have been Labour's most calamitous leader.

Forgery Act, **1830**. The 1830 Act for the Consolidation of the Forgery Laws was one of the most important of those measures passed by Peel as home secretary (1822–27 and 1828–30) whereby English statute law was consolidated and the number of offences carrying the death penalty reduced.

In the case of the Forgery Act, Peel reduced 120 statutes relating to forgery to one Act comprising four clauses, and removed the death penalty for cases of forgery involving receipts, stamps, orders, other deeds and bonds and banknote paper

Although traditionally cited as evidence of Peel's liberal Tory credentials, such reforms were not in fact motivated by humanitarian considerations. Rather, Peel was aware that juries were increasingly reluctant to convict even the obviously guilty because they considered many punishments disproportionate. Thus in order to combat the rising crime wave Peel reduced the penalty for almost 200 offences from death to imprisonment or transportation.

Forster Education Act of 1870 Robert Lowe, having failed to block the Second Reform Act (1867), told the Commons that 'it will be absolutely necessary that you should prevail on our future masters to learn their letters': a view that became popularized as the phrase 'We must educate our masters'. It was, however, rather a recognition by parliament of the economic desirability of having a literate and numerate workforce and the fear that advances in science were eroding the social cement provided by religious faith amongst the masses that acted as the twin spurs for the passage of the Elementary Education Act of 1870, more popularly known as Forster's Education Act, after W. E. Forster the relevant minister.

The Bill sought to extend the provision of elementary schools so that the entire country was covered, although attendance was not made universally compulsory until the Mundella Education Act of 1883 (board schools alone being empowered under the 1870 Act to make education compulsory for those aged between five and thirteen, with powers of exemption for those over ten having attained certain standards).

In order to keep costs low and not unduly offend vested interests Forster proposed merely to supplement, where necessary, the existing voluntary system of denominational schools with schools administered by locally elected boards, who would levy local rates for that purpose. The boards could also, subject to parliamentary approval, frame by-laws making education compulsory within their jurisdiction for five to twelve year olds and by 1876 roughly half of those eligible were thus compelled.

Opposition to the measure focused on the issue of what, if any, religious teaching would take place in the rate-aided or board schools. The Cowper–Temple clause was an amendment to the Bill which stated that 'no religious catechism or religious formulary which is distinctive of any particular denomination shall be taught' in such schools, whilst a conscience clause applied to all elementary schools, which gave parents the opportunity to withdraw their children from any religious observance or instruction of which they disapproved. However, many non-conformists remained unhappy with the Bill and particularly with Clause 25, which allowed local boards to pay, from the rates, to send poor children to schools of their parents' choice, including Church ones.

The Act was a milestone in the state's recognition of its role in providing education but the decision to fill in the gaps in the existing system rather than create a truly national one proved to be a millstone around the necks of future legislators, with sectarian considerations bedevilling educational policy well into the twentieth century. More immediately, the non-conformist revolt against the 1870 Bill blighted Forster's career and, through the activities of the National Education League, fostered the prospects of his future rival, Joseph Chamberlain.

Fourth Party, 1880–85. The Fourth Party took its name from a piece of parliamentary badinage early in the lifetime of the 1880 parliament. One member had portentously referred in passing to the 'two great parties of state', only to be pulled up by Parnell interjecting 'three' and Lord Randolph Churchill trumping him with 'four'. This last also involved a play on the fact that the Fourth Party had just four members, the others being Sir H. Drummond Wolff, John (later Sir John) Gorst, and Arthur (later Lord Arthur) Balfour.

This dissident Conservative group came together to attack Gladstone's sympathetic handling of the Bradlaugh affair but their real target was the lacklustre leadership of the Conservatives in the Commons by Sir Stafford Northcote and the Tory 'old gang'.

The Fourth Party dissolved when its activities threatened to embarrass rather than assist Salisbury, and his nephew, Balfour, peeled away.

Fox, Charles James (24 January 1749–13 September 1806). Charles James Fox was the third son of Henry Fox, 1st Lord Holland, and his wife, Lady Caroline Lennox, eldest daughter of Charles Lennox, 2nd Duke of Richmond. After Eton, Hertford College, Oxford, and the Grand Tour, Charles entered parliament in 1768. He opposed George III during the revolt of the American colonies, served in Rockingham's brief ministry in 1782 and in 1783 joined with his former enemy Lord North in a coalition ministry, until December when George brought it down by securing its defeat on the reform of the Indian government bill. The rest of his life was spent in opposition, barring the last few months when he was a leading member of the Ministry of All the Talents. This was so not least because the French Revolution rendered all reformers suspect, and particularly Fox who continued to voice his approval of the event long after others had changed their minds.

It is relatively easy to dismiss Fox as a dilettante dedicated to nothing more than high society and high living, embracing gambling, drinking and fornication. Compared with his arch-rival, Pitt the Younger, he can thus appear to be a political lightweight who repeatedly lost the battle for office and consigned himself to the sidelines by his resolute support of relief for dissenters and Catholics and equally staunch opposition to the French Revolutionary and Napoleonic wars (which he opposed on the grounds that those prosecuting the war did so in order to secure themselves in office and destroy English liberties).

However, it was precisely in opposition to the government of the day, or, to be more precise, in opposition to the prerogatives of the Crown claimed by George III, that Fox made his mark, becoming, in the words of A. J. P. Taylor, 'the first leader of a formed and avowed Opposition'. Moreover, he asserted that the Crown must accept as prime minister the political leader who could command a majority in the Commons and this principle was to triumph with the failure of William IV to impose Peel on the country in 1834. He thus became a patron saint for later radicals and earned himself a place of honour in the Whig interpretation of history.

He died a few months after his arch-rival Pitt, and a few months before the abolition of the slave trade, which he had long championed.

Framebreaking Act, 1812. In response to the emergence of Luddism in the previous year, the government of Spencer Perceval in 1812 passed the Watch and Ward and the Framebreaking Acts, the latter of which made machine breaking a capital offence and resulted in the execution of several Luddites.

Freeman boroughs Prior to the Great Reform Act of 1832 the electors in 62 of England's 203 parliamentary boroughs were those who had received the freedom of the borough. Parliamentary reform removed these freeman boroughs.

French Revolutionary and Napoleonic Wars, 1 February 1793–18 June 1815. The enthusiasm for some in Britain for the French Revolution such as William Wordsworth and Charles James Fox was placed under increasing strain by the new regime's increasingly radical rhetoric and actions, culminating in the execution of Louis XVI. However, the decisive factor in bringing war was the threat posed to Britain's commercial interests and national security represented by French annexation of the Austrian Netherlands and the opening of the Scheldt. It was, however, France that declared war on Britain and Holland on 1 February 1793.

In the war of the first coalition (1793–96) Britain successfully asserted its naval dominance (most notably at the Glorious First of June in 1794 and at Cape St Vincent and Camperdown in 1797) whilst many French and Dutch colonial possessions were overrun (the former including Tobago, Martinique and St Lucia, whilst the latter included the Cape of Good Hope). However, all interventions in the decisive European theatre of war (as at Dunkirk and Toulon) were humiliatingly rebuffed.

In 1798 the victory of Nelson at the battle of the Nile (otherwise known as Aboukir Bay) effectively cut off the French forces, which had landed under Napoleon in Egypt, and the rebellion of the United Irishmen was successfully suppressed. The former helped pave the way for the surrender of the French army in Egypt after the battle of Alexandria, whilst the latter provided the final impetus on the British side for the Act of Union (both 1800). In general, however, the war of the second coalition (1799–1801) essentially reflected the course of the first, with successful naval actions (such as the capture of Minorca) offset by ineffective attempts at intervention on the continent (at Belle Ile, Ferrol and elsewhere). Most ominously, Prussia, Sweden and Denmark made peace with France, and were joined by Russia in December 1800 in forming the anti-British Armed Neutrality. However, Nelson's victory at the battle of Copenhagen on 2 April 1801 forced the abandonment of this league.

When Addington replaced Pitt as prime minister (because George III had refused to honour the latter's promise of Catholic Emancipation), he successfully resumed the attempt to negotiate peace with France, the result being the Peace of Amiens (signed on 27 March 1802). The Treaty is commonly regarded as marking the point of transition between the French Revolutionary and the Napoleonic Wars.

The treaty certainly only provided a brief respite in the fighting as war resumed on 18 May 1803 and with it Napoleon resumed his plans for the invasion of Britain which were finally scotched by Nelson's decisive defeat of the combined French and Spanish fleets at Trafalgar (21 October 1805). Napoleon next sought in vain to crush Britain by means of economic warfare, in the form of the Continental System. Instead, by encouraging him to invade Russia in 1812 it helped bring about his own eventual downfall.

In the meantime the disastrous Walcheren expedition of 1809 – the fallout from which provoked the famous duel between Castlereagh and Canning – suggested that Britain still had not learnt the lesson of its earlier abortive continental expeditions. British intervention in the Iberian Peninsula (the Peninsular War) initially went equally badly, with the Corunna campaign of 1808–9 resulting in retreat, evacuation and the death of Sir John Moore. Ultimately, however, British intervention in Spain and Portugal constituted a powerful thorn in Napoleon's side and contributed materially to his defeat.

Equally important in the success of the fourth coalition was Britain's willingness and ability to act as paymaster to her continental allies, Russia, Prussia, Austria and Sweden. However, Napoleon's abdication to Elba and the first Treaty of Paris did not mark the final end of the story as Napoleon returned to France, raised an army and crossed into Belgium. However, at the battle of Waterloo (18 June 1815) Wellington (assisted by the Prussians under Blücher) was able to bring the '100 Days' and the French Revolutionary and Napoleonic Wars to a successful conclusion.

Fuel crisis, 1947. By the end of 1946 unofficial strikes and a shortage of labour had produced severe problems in the coal industry. Moreover, demand for increased coal production rose dramatically as the winter of 1947 was the worst for many years, particularly for the seven weeks from late January to mid-March.

Emmanuel Shinwell, the left-wing minister of fuel and power, had failed to ensure that adequate reserves were stockpiled because he naively assumed that the nationalization of the mines (on 1 January 1947) would solve all the industry's problems. In consequence, power supplies had almost completely broken down by March, so that electricity was cut off from homes, offices and factories for the five daily hours of heaviest consumption. Two and a quarter million people were thrown out of work and the government's reputation fell as low as its coal stocks. The episode resulted in Gaitskell's replacing Shinwell but more importantly discredited the policy of a centrally planned economy and, together with the convertibility crisis later in the year, helps to explain why the Attlee government lost confidence in its mission of building a new Jerusalem and contented itself with 'consolidation'.

G

Gaitskell, Hugh Todd Naylor (9 April 1906–18 January 1963). Hugh Gaitskell's father was a senior official in the Indian civil service. He was thus born into a wealthy upper-middle-class family. After the Dragon School and Winchester he went up to New College, Oxford, where he was taught by G. D. H. Cole, amongst others, and joined the Labour Party during the 1926 general strike. Graduating with a First in PPE, the young Gaitskell took an adult education job in Nottingham before transferring to University College London, where he taught economics between 1928 and 1939.

Dalton invited him to join his Ministry of Economic Warfare as a civil servant, and in 1942 he followed Dalton to the Board of Trade as his PPS. Entering parliament as MP for South Leeds in 1945, Gaitskell's rise was spectacular thanks to Dalton's patronage, his outstanding intellectual and administrative abilities, and the fact that some of Labour's old guard fell by the wayside. He was appointed parliamentary secretary to the Ministry of Fuel and Power in 1946 under Shinwell, whom he replaced the following year. In 1949 he played a leading role in persuading Cripps of the desirability of devaluation and helped implement the measure during the latter's illness. Moving to the Treasury as minister for economic affairs in March 1950, he was promoted to the chancellorship in October.

The fact that Gaitskell replaced Cripps over Bevan's head exacerbated the antipathy between the two men and their supporters, who rightly regarded them as contenders to succeed Attlee and standard-bearers of differing visions of the Labour Party (despite sharing much common ground). This rivalry came to a head when the Korean War led the US to urge Britain to embark upon a £4.7 billion arms programme which it could ill afford. Gaitskell sought to raise £23m of this (per year) through charges on dentures and spectacles. Bevan, believing in the principle that the National Health Service, which he had created, should be free at the point of need, regarded this as a resigning matter. The terminally ill Bevin was unable to effect a compromise, whilst Attlee was unable to provide a firm lead because temporarily ill in hospital. Thus the charges were included in the budget on 10 April, with Bevan resigning on 22 April (and Wilson resigning the following day).

Gaitskell not only won over health charges but also won the race to succeed Attlee, being elected party treasurer in 1954 and Labour leader (and leader of the opposition) in December 1955, when he secured more than double the votes for Bevan (157 to 70), his personal vote also exceeding those for Bevan and Morrison combined (110).

In 1956 Gaitskell, despite being pro-Israeli and highly critical of Nasser's actions, was opposed to British military intervention in the Suez Crisis without UN approval. Opposition to Suez at least allowed Gaitskell and Bevan to patch up their differences.

Defeat in the 1959 election meant, however, that the gulf with the left re-widened as both sides blamed the other. Hence Gaitskell's abortive attempt at the 1959 party conference to repeal Clause 4 of the Labour Party constitution.

The rise of CND also exacerbated left–right tensions At the 1960 party conference the block votes of those unions supporting unilateralism, notably the Transport Workers and the AEU, overturned the party's official defence policy. Gaitskell showed great determination in securing the reversal of that decision at the 1961 Blackpool conference, and in the meantime fended off a challenge to his leadership by Wilson (by 166 votes to 81).

At the 1962 conference Gaitskell pleased the party's left at the risk of antagonizing some of his supporters on the right by speaking against Britain joining the EEC on the terms proposed, declaring that such a move 'means the end of a thousand years of history'.

Nevertheless he had managed to reunite the party on a moderate basis and Labour was ahead in the polls at the time of his sudden death in 1963, so that it was Wilson who led Labour to success in the 1964 election. Gaitskell is thus remembered, like John Smith, as a Labour leader who reunited the party and helped make it electable during its wilderness years, only to die at that most poignant moment when the promised land appeared to be within reach.

Gang of Four See SOCIAL DEMOCRATIC PARTY.

Gaols Acts, 1823–24. Shortly after becoming home secretary in 1822 Peel turned his attention to prison reform. The resulting Gaols Acts of 1823 and 1824 rationalized the prison system and ensured that certain minimum standards were achieved by establishing a system of inspection.

Garden Suburb As well as establishing the first cabinet secretariat, Lloyd George also set up his own informal secretariat which became known as the Garden Suburb because huts to accommodate it were erected in the garden of Number Ten Downing Street.

'Geddes axe', 1922. In 1922, as a Conservative minister in the Lloyd George coalition government, Sir Eric Geddes wielded 'the Geddes axe' when he chaired the economic committee which introduced swingeing public spending cuts (including a cut of roughly one-third in educational spending) which did much to undermine the premier's promise of 'Homes Fit for Heroes'.

General Strike, 1842. In fifteen English or Welsh shires and eight Scottish counties a wave of strikes and protest meetings took place in the summer of 1842. This disturbance, which began on the North Staffordshire coalfield and centred upon industrial districts in the Midlands, Cheshire, Lancashire and Yorkshire, has traditionally been referred to as the 'Plug Plot' or the 'Plug Plot riots' because a popular method of taking action was to force the withdrawal of boiler plugs so as to deprive factories and mines of their steam power. However, because this was only one form of protest and because the talk of a 'plot' implies conspiratorial planning, some historians prefer to refer to these events as the General Strike of 1842. Demands focused upon improved pay and work conditions but the 'People's Charter' provided the banner under which the demonstrators mobilized.

The strike failed for three main reasons. Firstly, in the absence of storekeepers extending credit to the striking workers or their being sustained by contributions from wealthier sympathizers, they were forced back to work by hunger. Secondly, the strike was insufficiently general, failing to include, for example, the Monmouthshire colliers and many Lancashire cotton workers. Last but not least, the authorities took prompt and effective action to restore order, arresting the ringleaders and suppressing large meetings in the disturbed areas.

General Strike, 3 May–12 May 1926. The General Strike had its long-term origins in frustration in the Labour movement with the fact that payment of MPs was the only concession wrung by the parliamentary Labour Party from the Asquith government, despite the fact that the two general elections of 1910 had rendered it dependent upon Labour and Irish votes. The inclination to put greater faith in the industrial arm of the movement was also stimulated by the spread of syndicalist ideas from the continent. World War One brought a truce to the industrial unrest of the Edwardian period, just as it brought a suspension of hostilities for the duration from the suffragettes. However, whilst women got the vote in 1918 peace brought no comparable victory for Britain's trade unionists and industrial militancy returned. The formation of the first Labour administration under Ramsay MacDonald in 1924 did little to dampen the desire for radical change as its minority status sharpened MacDonald's desire to show the electorate that it had little to fear from a supposedly socialist government. Even under MacDonald there was a major transport strike in London that resulted in the cabinet declaring a state of emergency. When MacDonald's government fell in October 1924 and the Conservatives returned to power under Baldwin the gloves were off.

On Red Friday (31 July 1925) the Triple Alliance, acting through the TUC, won from the government a temporary subsidy and a royal commission into the state of the coal mining industry. The Samuel Report (published in March 1926) was, however, unacceptable to the Miners' Federation (whose slogan was 'not a minute on the day, not a penny off the pay') and the TUC backed the miners in their call for a national or general strike when the subsidy ran out and the coal owners threatened a general lock out unless the miners accepted lower wages and longer hours.

The general strike (which was actually limited to 'first-line' industries) began one minute before midnight on 3 May 1926. It soon became apparent that the Baldwin government had been as assiduous in making preparations for industrial action as the TUC had been negligent.

The TUC General Council left the miners in the lurch by unilaterally calling off the general strike on 12 May. Strike-breaking preparations had proved effective and the package offered by Samuel to Jimmy Thomas (acting on behalf of the TUC) differed little from what the General Council had demanded before the strike began. However, the decisive factor was the government's suggestion that the general strike placed the unions outside the protection afforded their funds by the 1906 Trade Disputes Act.

Betrayed by the TUC, the miners fought on in vain for a further six months. The government in turn betrayed the TUC General Council insofar as the 1927 Trade Disputes Act largely removed the protection afforded by the 1906 Trade Disputes Act. The one consolation for MacDonald and his colleagues was that industrial action had been discredited for the foreseeable future, and the initiative passed back to the parliamentary arm of the movement.

George III (George William Frederick) (4 June 1738–29 January 1820). George William Frederick was the eldest son of Frederick Louis, Prince of Wales, the eldest son of George II. His father having died in 1751, George became George III on his grandfather's death in 1760.

Upon his accession he withdrew royal confidence in the Whigs and chose the third Earl of Bute as his chief minister. However, Bute was not up to the job and there followed a period of ministerial instability which only ended with the appointment of Lord North in 1770. The loss of the American colonies in 1783 was a bitter blow and George brought down the Fox–North coalition in December of that year by securing parliamentary defeat of its bill to reform the government of India. William Pitt the Younger whom he appointed in 1784 suited him and brought stability until 1801 when he preferred to accept Pitt's resignation rather than allow Catholic Emancipation, which he regarded as contrary to his coronation oath.

1801 was also a watershed year insofar as George was increasingly prone thereafter to incapacity, latterly identified as porphyria, which gave the king the appearance of having lost his sanity. So serious was his condition that it resulted in his very unpopular son becoming Prince Regent from 1811 until he ascended the throne as George IV upon his father's death in 1820.

In the eyes of Whig politicians such as Fox and Whig historians such as Macaulay, George came to rival Charles I as a monarch who sought to push royal power to tyrannical limits. However, in the public's eyes he soon ceased to be regarded as posing a threat to the constitution, and instead was first admired as a model farmer and upright paterfamilias and then seen as a figure to be pitied as a result of his debilitating illness.

George III thus became Britain's best-loved Hanoverian monarch although given the competition for this title this was hardly a great achievement.

George IV (George Augustus Frederick) (12 August 1762–25 May 1830). Like earlier Hanoverian princes, George Augustus Frederick was on very poor terms with his father (George III), which meant that a reversionary interest battened upon his ample person, consisting of politicians who pinned their hopes of office upon his ultimately ascending the throne or becoming regent.

In the 1780s George patronized the Whigs in general and Charles James Fox in particular. In return he was flattered and encouraged to indulge in a dissolute lifestyle which reached its apotheosis in 1785 in his unconstitutional secret marriage to the twice widowed and Roman Catholic Mrs Fitzherbert (one of his numerous mistresses).

In order to obtain at least temporary relief from the costs of his lavish entertaining and building programme, which was to reach its zenith in the Royal Pavilion at Brighton, George agreed to marry Princess Caroline of Brunswick in 1795. This marriage of convenience produced an heir – the Princess Charlotte-Augusta (1796–1817) – but was in all other respects an unmitigated disaster, with the couple separating soon afterwards.

George had nearly become regent in 1788 but his father recovered and it was not until 1811 that George became Prince Regent and was able to betray the hopes of his erstwhile Whig friends. He also made life very difficult for his prime minister, Lord Liverpool, by virtue of his clear personal dislike of the ministry and disputes over patronage and royal expenditure. However, it was George's strained relations with his estranged wife which provided the greatest scope for tension.

Upon his accession to the throne upon his father's death in 1820 he was chiefly concerned to deny his wife the privileges due to her as Queen of England and to this end forced Liverpool to introduce a Bill of Pains and Penalties. Liverpool managed to limit the damage which George did to the monarchy through his unrelenting antipathy to Caroline and his insensitive extravagance and Sir Walter Scott even managed to use George to strengthen the institution of monarchy in Scotland by his adroit stage-managing of the royal tour there of 1821.

George overcame his initial dislike of Canning to appoint him prime minister upon Liverpool's enforced withdrawal from politics through ill health in August 1827 but then contributed to the discomfiture of the Tory party by first endorsing (1827) and then withdrawing (1828) his confidence from Goderich.

George's death in 1830 and the accession of William IV helped clear the path for the First Reform Act (1832) which took practical steps to reduce the influence of the Crown, the prestige of which had been severely diminished as a consequence of the moral laxity and extravagance of George's regency and reign.

George V (George Frederick Ernest Albert) (3 June 1865–20 January 1936). George Frederick Ernest Albert was the second child of the future Edward VII and Queen Alexandra. Between the ages of six and eighteen he was tutored by the Rev. Dalton (future canon of Windsor and father of the future chancellor, Hugh Dalton). His promising naval career was cut short on 14 January 1892 when the death of his elder brother placed him second in line to the throne. Just as Henry VIII inherited his elder brother's spouse, so George, now Duke of York, inherited his elder brother's betrothed: their cousin, Princess Victoria Mary (May) of Teck. The marriage took place on 6 July 1893 and the union proved to be a happy and fruitful one.

The death of Queen Victoria on 22 January 1901 brought George one step closer to the throne and obliged him to perform more public duties given his father's age.

The death of his father on 6 May 1910 pitchforked George into the constitutional crisis arising from the Lords' rejection of the People's

Budget. The peers had belatedly accepted the budget (on 28 April) but now faced a parliament bill in line with the mandate secured by the Liberals in the January 1910 election. George let it be known that he would not consent to an ad hoc creation of peers to ensure passage of the Parliament Bill until after a second general election, in which the issue had been clearly presented before the electorate.

Asquith and Crewe successfully sought from the King, on 16 November, a secret and 'hypothetical understanding' that sufficient peers would be created should the need arise in the next parliament. Making this promise public (by mutual agreement) helped persuade a sufficient number of peers to drop their opposition to the Parliament Bill so that it could be passed without obliging the King to honour his undertaking.

However, by clearing the way for Irish Home Rule the Parliament Act threatened a new constitutional crisis. On 1 May 1914 the King took the initiative in proposing a Speaker's conference to try to arrive at a compromise. Failure of the conference was soon overshadowed by the outbreak of World War One.

During the war George made several sacrifices including, making a gift of £100,000 to the Exchequer, adopting prohibition in the royal household in 1915, adhering to the new rationing regulations and changing the family name to Windsor in 1917.

In May 1923, when Bonar Law resigned through ill health and let it be known that he would prefer not to tender advice regarding his successor, the King might appear to have courted controversy in summoning Baldwin rather than Curzon but not only was this the clear preference of the senior figures consulted on the King's behalf but it could also be represented as the right choice in democratic terms as now that Labour was the official opposition it was even more important than hitherto that the prime minister should sit in the Commons.

Following the December 1923 election when Baldwin unsuccessfully sought a mandate for protection, George was in the unique position of there being three parties, each of which was prepared to form a government, whilst none commanded a Commons majority. The King sent for MacDonald following Baldwin's resignation and went out of his way to set his new ministers at ease. In so doing he helped make Labour respectable and divert it from the path of republicanism.

When the Campbell case led to MacDonald's request for a dissolution, George personally considered the affair insufficient in itself to justify a third general election within two years but appreciated that to deny the request could lead to accusations of partiality. George therefore granted the dissolution whilst recording his reservations in a memorandum to the prime minister.

The chief significance of Baldwin's Second Ministry (1924–29) for George lay in its redefinition of the relationship between Britain and the Dominions, set out in the Balfour definition of Dominion status in 1926 and embodied in the Statute of Westminster in 1931, whereby henceforth the King constituted the bond in a voluntary association of free peoples. This was a role which George was well suited to perform, assisted by his use of the relatively new medium of the wireless. The tradition of Christmas

Day broadcasts, which George began in 1932, helped crystallize the Crown's role as focus of the sentimental bonds uniting the Commonwealth.

George next played a major role in events when, on 23 August 1931, he urged MacDonald not to resign despite the fact that Henderson and many other cabinet members refused to accept the degree of public spending cuts which the prime minister and his chancellor, Snowden, considered necessary. Moreover, encouraged by his discussion with Herbert Samuel, the acting Liberal leader, regarding the merits of forming a national government under MacDonald's leadership, the King successfully persuaded Baldwin to accept this course. Thus when MacDonald sought to tender the resignation of the cabinet the King urged him to reconsider and successfully requested the three party leaders create a national government under MacDonald's leadership: a development which received the overwhelming endorsement of the electorate in the October 1931 general election.

George's silver jubilee celebrations on 6 May 1935 and his death on 20 January 1936 made him the focus of the nation's mood, first of gratitude then of grief.

George had had little expectation of becoming king until the age of twenty-six and this enabled him to pursue a naval career which not only made him one of the best-travelled of monarchs but also enabled him to see much more of the world and his fellow men than might otherwise have been the case. It is a tribute to George's common sense, concern for constitutional proprieties and ability to learn from experience that the Crown emerged not merely intact but strengthened, not least in its relationship to the Empire and Commonwealth, under his stewardship. As he showed over Ireland, the general strike, and the formation of the National Government, George's own preference was always for consensus and conciliation. This sailor king was beset by repeated storms and squalls but managed to keep the ship of state steered on an even keel.

George VI (Albert Frederick Arthur George) (14 December 1895–6 February 1952). Albert Frederick Arthur George was born the second of the five sons of the Duke and Duchess of York, afterwards George V and Queen Mary. Bertie, as he was known within the family, was a shy boy who coped less well than his siblings with his father's insensitive manner. He developed a stammer and became increasingly introspective, although prone to occasional outbursts of high emotion.

After private tuition Albert followed his older brother, the future Edward VIII, to Osborne naval college, which brought him somewhat out of his shell. After Osborne and Dartmouth, Albert was posted as a midshipman to HMS *Collingwood* in which he was to see action as a sub-lieutenant during the battle of Jutland (31 May 1916). However, his career in the forces was marred by poor health.

After the war Prince Albert qualified as a pilot, and received his commission as a squadron leader (July–August 1919). He then spent a year at Trinity College, Cambridge before taking up an increasing number of public engagements at home and abroad. His stammer and natural diffidence rendered these duties a great trial but he nevertheless became president of the Industrial Welfare Society and in 1921 founded the Duke of York's camps where boys from public schools and industry met and mixed annually (with one exception) until the outbreak of World War Two.

The Duke of York (as he was from 1920) married Lady Elizabeth Angela Marguerite Bowes-Lyon (the future Queen Elizabeth, the Queen Mother), on 26 April 1923. They were to have two daughters: Princess Elizabeth Alexandra Mary (later Elizabeth II) (21 April 1926) and Princess Margaret Rose (21 August 1930). The Duke and Duchess were a devoted couple and her strength of character and expertise in handling the media enormously assisted her husband in his public role. He was also better able to control his stammer after consulting a speech therapist in 1926.

The declining health and eventual death of King George V (on 20 January 1936) and the ensuing abdication crisis severely taxed the Duke's newfound equilibrium. Nevertheless, on 12 December 1936 he was proclaimed King, choosing George VI as his style and title, and was crowned on 12 May 1937. There were serious doubts whether George would be up to the job and whether the monarchy could survive. Whilst Queen Elizabeth clearly played a crucial role in steeling her husband, his own courage in adversity and sense of public duty should not be left out of account, although the strain resulted in occasional outbursts of ill temper out of the glare of the public spotlight and a recurrence of his stammer when in it.

Successful state visits to France (1938) and the United States and Canada (1939) assisted the diplomacy of the Chamberlain government, to which the King gave his public blessing by inviting the prime minister to share the balcony of Buckingham Palace with him following the signing of the Munich Agreement.

Given the King's partiality for the policy of appeasement and the fact that Churchill had opposed Edward VIII's abdication it is hardly surprising that George would have preferred Halifax as Chamberlain's successor in May 1940 but relations with his new prime minister gradually warmed into genuine friendship.

The war did more than anything else to cement the monarchy in general, and the King and Queen in particular, in the affections of the British people. It was the King's inspired idea in 1940 to create the George Cross and Medal, for civilian gallantry; and to award the Cross to Malta in 1942 for its collective heroism under siege. Most importantly, during the darkest days of the war when invasion had seemed likely, the royals did not leave the country or the capital (except to sleep at Windsor during the Blitz) but stayed to suffer something of the same danger and privations as their subjects: as symbolized by the fact that Buckingham Palace was hit nine times and the Duke of Kent, the King's younger brother, was killed whilst on active service in 1942. On VE and VJ Day, Buckingham Palace and the monarchy became a natural focus for popular rejoicing.

The King was able to witness the marriage of the Princess Elizabeth to Lieutenant Philip Mountbatten, R.N., the Duke of Edinburgh, in 1947, and to celebrate his silver wedding anniversary in 1948 but his health deteriorated markedly and he died on 6

February 1952. As a quiet, courageous family man who respected tradition without being hidebound he had earned the respect and then the love of his people.

Gladstone, William Ewart (29 December 1809–19 May 1898). William Ewart Gladstone was born in Liverpool on 29 December 1809, the fifth child and fourth son of Anne and John Gladstone. His father was a merchant of Scottish descent who had bought land and entered parliament as a supporter of Canning, who was MP for Liverpool and whom the infant Gladstone met and grew to admire. After Eton, William followed Canning's footsteps to Christ Church, Oxford where he not only became president of the Union but also took a Double First (in Literae Humaniores and Mathematics and Physics). He was also influenced by the Oxford Movement without wholly losing the evangelicalism which he had imbibed at home. Although persuaded by his father to consider public life rather than the Church, religion remained a dominant strand in Gladstone's personality and pronouncements for the rest of his life.

Gladstone's strictures against the Reform Bill in the Union so impressed his acquaintance, Lord Lincoln, that the latter persuaded his father, the Duke of Newcastle, to offer Gladstone his Newark pocket borough for which Gladstone was duly returned in the first elections of the reformed parliament.

Peel appointed Gladstone vice-president of the Board of Trade in 1841 and Gladstone soon moved closer to Peel both physically (entering the cabinet as president of the Board of Trade), and politically (assisting Peel in the formulation of the great free trade budgets of 1842 and 1845). Although he resigned over the Maynooth Grant in 1845 he actually voted for the measure, explaining his action by claiming that whilst he had privately changed his position since publication of *The State in its Relations with the Church* he had not made his change of mind public. This was a characteristically tortuous piece of reasoning by Gladstone and set the mark for many of his mysterious political moves of future years, which were similarly presented as prompted by conscience but which less subtle or more cynical observers interpret as more basely motivated. As Labouchère was later to remark, while he had no objection to Gladstone's habit of concealing the ace of trumps up his sleeve, he did object to his reiterated claim that it had been put there by Almighty God.

When Russell declined to accept the 'poisoned chalice' in December 1845 and Peel returned to office, Gladstone too returned, as colonial secretary. However, he felt obliged to resign his Newark seat in deference to Newcastle's protectionist sentiments, not returning to parliament again until December 1847 when elected as one of Oxford University's MPs. Gladstone could therefore witness Disraeli savaging his mentor but do nothing to shield him. His impotent rage at this condition goes a long way towards explaining his lifetime animosity towards Disraeli.

This personal animus and Disraeli's elevation within the ranks of the Conservatives constituted a major obstacle to Gladstone's rejoining the party even after Peel's death in 1850 and the Conservatives' quiet abandonment of protection in 1852. Gladstone took his revenge upon Disraeli by rubbishing his December 1852 budget and was thereby instrumental in bringing down the minority Derby–Disraeli government. Gladstone himself succeeded Disraeli as chancellor the same month under Aberdeen and showed himself to be as masterly in handling the national finances as he had shown Disraeli to be incompetent.

Gladstone's 1853 budget showed him to have assumed the fiscal mantle of Pitt and Peel by retaining income tax and freeing trade. This budget marked Gladstone's arrival upon the national scene as a future leader and confirmed that he had a viable substitute for his earlier High Tory faith in the Established Church as an instrument of moral progress. Henceforth fiscal probity became his moral touchstone.

At least as important in winning Gladstone friends amongst his new Whig, Liberal and Radical friends was his commitment to an ethical foreign policy, as signified by his condemnation of the Don Pacifico affair in 1850 and his 1851 *Letters to the Earl of Aberdeen* in which he condemned Bourbon rule in Naples.

The Crimean War upset Gladstone's plans in several respects. It resulted in the findings of the 1853 Northcote–Trevelyan Report being put on hold; it upset his fiscal plans to equalize the tax burden; and doubts regarding the wisdom of allowing Roebuck to get his Committee of Inquiry resulted in Gladstone and the Peelites Graham and Herbert leaving the government formed by Palmerston just two weeks after its birth.

Gladstone's acceptance of Derby's 1858 invitation to become High Commissioner Extraordinary for the Ionian Islands seems to have been motivated in part by the desire to re-think his future but Gladstone was back in parliament by 1859 when the second Derby–Disraeli ministry fell, whereupon he accepted Palmerston's invitation to serve as chancellor.

As chancellor from June 1859 to July 1866, Gladstone held the post for the longest continuous tenure between Vansittart and Lloyd George and implemented a very ambitious programme, the main features of which were retrenchment, repealing the 'taxes on knowledge', free trade and broadening the social basis of the income tax as part of a general scheme to balance direct and indirect taxation.

Gladstone found an ally in Cobden and the Manchester School in his efforts to promote peace and reduce defence spending through free trade. Gladstone also won praise from the radicals for his repeal of the duty on paper for when the Lords rejected a bill to this effect in 1860 Gladstone included the proposal in his 1861 budget. This measure also won Gladstone the gratitude of the press, which already had reason to feel benevolent towards him because the reduction of stamp duties, which he had begun in his 1853 budget, meant that newspapers had been completely relieved of this duty by June 1855.

Initially, Gladstone's pro-Confederate stance during the American Civil War seemed likely to alienate his recently made radical friends but Gladstone was moved by the display of dignified forbearance during the Lancashire Cotton Famine to speak out in favour of an extension of the franchise in 1864, when he stated that 'every man who is not presumably incapacitated by some consideration of personal unfitness or of political danger is morally entitled to come within the pale of the Constitution'. The expression of such sentiments helped ensure that he was elected for South Lancashire after being rejected by Oxford University in 1865.

On assuming his new seat Gladstone claimed himself 'unmuzzled' but although the Adullamites may have regarded his support for Russell's 1866 Reform Bill as signifying rabid radicalism the measure was far too moderate for genuine radicals with the result that Disraeli stole the Whigs' clothing, Derby approved a leap into the dark, and it was the Conservatives who passed the Second Reform Act.

However, Gladstone succeeded Russell as Liberal leader in December 1867 and reunited the party by means of his Irish Church Resolutions of March 1868, proposing Irish Church disestablishment. This tactic also helped Gladstone win the 1868 general election with a Liberal majority of 112, although it contributed to his defeat in South Lancashire (where his proposal was interpreted as pro-Catholic). However, he had taken the precaution of also standing for Greenwich, where he was duly elected.

As suggested in his 'Upas Tree' speech, Ireland was Gladstone's chief concern and he set about reforming the Anglican Church in Ireland, the land and education by means of disestablishment, the Irish Land Act (1870), and the Irish University Bill (1873) respectively. As the latter reference suggests, Gladstone's efforts with regard to Irish education did not bear legislative fruit, whilst his later ministries provide ample evidence that the legislation he did pass manifestly failed to pacify the Irish.

Gladstone's other major interests in government were foreign policy and finance. However, his capitulation, in the eyes of critics, to the Alabama award and Russia's repudiation of the Black Sea clauses of the Treaty of Paris allowed Disraeli to portray Gladstone's pacific policies as selling the pass and for himself to assume Palmerston's mantle as vigorous defender of Britain's interests.

Financial affairs provided little solace for Gladstone as he felt obliged to replace Lowe as chancellor with himself in 1873. He sought re-election in 1874 in vain on the basis of a promise to abolish income tax. In many respects he was the victim of his own success in financial matters, having already effectively fulfilled the Peelite fiscal programme.

Gladstone's First Ministry was, of course, characterized by a plethora of other reforms, of which the most notable were Forster's Education Act of 1870; Cardwell's army reforms; the Trade Union Act and repeal of the University Tests Act, both of 1871; and the Ballot Act and Bruce's Licensing Act, both of 1872. However, each of these reforms lost the Liberals as many friends as they gained and allowed Disraeli to create the impression that the administration was a whirlwind of misdirected activity which had blown itself out by 1873. The defeat of the Irish University Bill proved to be the Ministry's deathblow, although it limped on until defeated at the 1874 general election.

Gladstone made a comeback to the Liberal leadership via the Bulgarian atrocities agitation and was back in Downing Street in 1880 following his pioneering Midlothian campaigns. His Second Ministry was dominated by disturbances in South Africa, Egypt, Afghanistan and Ireland, and was dogged domestically by jockeying for the succession between Hartington (later Devonshire) on the right, and Chamberlain (most ostentatiously through his 1885 Unauthorized Programme) on the left. The Hawarden Kite wrong-footed both rivals and reaffirmed his leadership at the cost of splitting his party. His Third and Fourth Ministries (1886 and 1892–94 respectively) were dominated by Irish Home Rule and even in his nineties, after his final resignation from office, Gladstone showed that he retained the ability to shape the political agenda by intervening over Armenian atrocities.

Gladstone dominated nineteenth-century British politics by virtue of the quality of his intellect and character which, according to taste, was either intensely machiavellian or raised self-deception to the status of an art form.

Gladstone–MacDonald Pact, 1903. Herbert Gladstone as Liberal chief whip and Ramsay MacDonald as secretary of the recently formed Labour Representation Committee (1900) came to a secret understanding in 1903 whereby up to forty English and Welsh constituencies would be earmarked for Labour candidates.

The 1906 general election resulted in a Liberal landslide with 402 MPs. Although both the Scottish Labour MPs had defeated Liberals, in England and Wales the Pact worked much more successfully to maximize the prospects of both parties. Thus all but two of Labour's thirty MPs there were returned through active cooperation with the Liberals, compared with just two 'Labour' seats in 1900.

Goderich, Frederick John Robinson, 1st Viscount (Earl of Ripon) (30 October 1782–28 January 1859). Frederick John Robinson was the second son of the former Ambassador to Spain and Foreign Secretary Thomas Robinson, 2nd Baron Grantham.

Following Canning's death George IV invited Lord Goderich to form an administration. On the face of it, Goderich appeared to stand a good chance of reuniting the Tory party as it had been under Liverpool, given that he was widely respected as a man of integrity and administrative experience, having been continuously in office since 1809 (most notably at the Board of Trade, 1812–23, and as chancellor of the exchequer, 1823–27). He had also been both a protégé of Castlereagh and a close colleague of Canning (who had created him Viscount Goderich and appointed him colonial secretary and leader of the House of Lords upon becoming prime minister in 1827).

Goderich was expected to allow his colleagues considerable latitude. In the event, however, their bitter differences of opinion regarding policy and the disposal of patronage, and the King's rigid insistence that Catholic Emancipation remain an open question and the ministry be closed to new Whig recruits, put paid to Goderich's efforts to construct a majority in the Commons, and he resigned (on 8 January 1828) after just five months as premier without parliament even having met.

This failure has coloured assessments of Goderich's whole career, with George Wallace being credited as vice-president of the Board of Trade with the free trade successes formerly attributed to his departmental superior and Vansittart and Huskisson (respectively his predecessor at the Exchequer and successor at the Board of Trade) being said better to merit the applause which contemporaries accorded the fiscal policies of 'Prosperity' Robinson. However, when Goderich's failure to step into Liverpool's shoes is set against those of the much stronger personalities of Canning and Wellington the enormity of the task is better appreciated.

Although Goderich had been poorly treated by George IV he remained prepared to serve the Crown, and as 1st Earl of Ripon held office under both Grey and Peel.

Gold Standard, restoration of the, 1819. As a result of the French Revolutionary and Napoleonic Wars (1793–1815) Britain suspended cash payments in 1797 but in 1819 the Bullion or Currency Commission chaired by Peel recommended a phased return to the gold standard, which was due to take place by 1823 but was actually completed by 1821. In 1826 additional legislation forbade the English country banks from enlarging their note issue but allowed the circulation of small denomination notes already issued until April 1829.

Gold Standard, restoration of the, 1925. The gold standard had been formally suspended in March 1919 but this was done on the understanding that it would be reintroduced as soon as 'normal' conditions returned, not least in order to remove from politicians the temptation to manipulate monetary and fiscal policy for their own purposes. Thus informed opinion considered a return to the gold standard as both politically and economically desirable.

Moreover, conventional wisdom, as embodied by the City and the Treasury, took the view that sterling should be restored to its pre-war parity of \$4.86. John Maynard Keynes, Reginald McKenna and Lloyd George had reservations about this decision but none expressed outright opposition to the move. Thus Churchill as chancellor of the exchequer supervised the return to gold at the old parity in 1925. In late July, Keynes reworked a series of his *Evening Standard* articles to publish 'The economic consequences of Mr Churchill' in which he expressed the view that any return to gold should have occurred at a lower parity.

Indeed, it soon became the conventional wisdom that Britain had returned to gold at too high an exchange rate and economic historians have broadly seen this decision as contributing towards Britain's poor economic performance of the later 1920s (with unemployment never dropping below one million), by hobbling trade and fiscal policies so that it ultimately led the way to the financial crisis of 1931 during which the gold standard was finally abandoned (on 21 September 1931) in the wake of the Invergordon mutiny, and a floating exchange rate regime adopted (which resulted in a 30.6% devaluation of sterling against the dollar by the end of the year).

Good Friday Agreement, 1998. The Good Friday Agreement between Tony Blair and the Taoiseach Bertie Ahern, which emerged out of the peace process which was first manifest in the Hume–Adams talks, agreed to the formation in Ulster of a power-sharing devolved government with ministerial posts distributed according to party strength.

All parties save the Democratic Unionist Party of Ian Paisley approved the measure. The latter regarded it as even more invidious than the Sunningdale Agreement insofar as parties representing the paramilitaries including Sinn Féin (as well as the Ulster Democratic Party and the Progressive Unionist Party) would be admitted to the process, which would include the release of 'political prisoners', subject to a sustained period of ceasefire and decommissioning of weapons.

Referenda on the Agreement on 22 May 1998 were held in Ulster and the Republic (which forswore its constitutional aim of Irish integration), with 71.2% of the people of Northern Ireland and 94.39% in the Republic voting 'Yes' to accepting the Agreement.

In September 1998 an Assembly was elected in which the Ulster Unionists had 28 seats, whilst the SDLP took 24 and Sinn Féin 18.

David Trimble and John Hume, were awarded the Nobel Peace Prize for their role in securing the Good Friday Agreement although the path to lasting peace remains rocky with the Assembly already having been subject to suspension.

Government of India Act, 1935. The Government of India Act of 1935, promising ultimate Dominion status, had a stormy passage through parliament, with Churchill leading the opposition to its concessions, which predictably proved insufficient to satisfy Indian nationalist aspirations.

The 1937 provincial elections in India, the first to be held under the terms of the 1935 Act, greatly strengthened the cause of Muslim separatism and hence eventual partition because Congress rejected any prospect of power sharing with the Muslim League and swept to victory, with absolute majorities in six of the eleven provinces of British India and the largest single share of the vote in a further three.

Thus the 1935 Act, like its 1919 predecessor, provided increased scope for the manifestation of communal, provincial and ethnic rivalries and increased opportunities for the Raj to exploit these phenomena so as to divide and rule.

Government of Ireland Act, 1920. In 1920 the Lloyd George coalition passed the Government of Ireland Act which created devolved parliaments in Dublin and Belfast (covering the six counties of Northern Ireland), whilst both parts of Ireland were to send some members to the Westminster parliament.

Sinn Féin (whose elected representatives were already boycotting Westminster) rejected the scheme out of hand and continued to support the IRA in its guerrilla campaign, masterminded by Michael Collins, for a united Irish republic. The measure was thus stillborn and was soon superceded by the Anglo-Irish treaty.

Grand National Consolidated Trade Union (GNCTU) The Grand National Consolidated Trade Union was set up in 1834 as an industrial union of all trades. As such it offered the promise of maximizing industrial muscle and attracted perhaps half a million members, including previously unorganized groups. However, relatively few paid their subscriptions to the headquarters of this unwieldy organization which came to be presided over by Robert Owen.

Pseudo-Masonic ritual and terminology helped persuade the government that the organization was seditious: a fear exacerbated by the Captain Swing disturbances. Persecution by the authorities (symbolized by the Tolpuddle Martyrs incident) and by employers, worsening trade conditions, failure to provide adequate support for striking members, and the treasurer absconding with most of its remaining funds, all contributed to the GNCTU's collapse, in December 1834.

Great Depression The Great Depression suffered by the British economy from late 1929 until the outbreak of World War Two or even beyond (with particularly sharp downswings in 1929–30 and 1937–38) was part of a global phenomenon which is popularly regarded as having its origins in the Wall Street Crash of October 1929, although deflationary forces were in operation some months before the collapse in share prices. In Britain's case, the 1925 return to the gold standard at an overvalued exchange rate and the policy constraints arising from this had already ensured that the economy had largely failed to share in the recovery of world production and trade of the later 1920s. However, the decline in world trade hit Britain particularly harshly so that by 1931 the balance of payments current account was in deficit to the tune of £103m or 2.4% of Gross Domestic Product (GDP) despite first the progressive reduction of interest rates and then the abandonment of the gold standard in September of that year.

The British depression was milder than elsewhere as measured by the fall in GDP (4.9% in real terms, 1929–32) but this did not prevent unemployment from rising dramatically to 23% of the insured labour force or a little under 3 million people by January 1933. The nature and extent of inter-war unemployment is a major area of historical contention.

The impact of the Great Depression certainly varied enormously in regional, occupational and demographic terms. Thus whilst the North and West experienced great hardship, for example, the South and Midlands actually experienced a modest boom for part of this period. Two million dwellings were added to the total national housing stock during this period and the proportion of families owning their own homes doubled during the inter-war period.

Gender and age also had a marked influence upon experience of unemployment, with the rates almost twice as high for men as for women, and for males aged between 55 and 59 compared to those aged between 18 and 24.

Two distinct groups of those registered as unemployed need to be differentiated, namely, the core of long-term unemployed, often suffering the consequences of structural unemployment, who were mainly older men, and a larger number of those who moved into and out of unemployment (some of whom were cushioned or even encouraged in this movement by the benefits system), and who experienced only relatively short spells on the dole.

Nevertheless, the period is popularly remembered as one of great and unnecessary hardship epitomized by the Jarrow March. As such it acted as a major stimulus to the expansion of the welfare state, particularly after World War Two.

Great Exhibition, 1851. Inspired by the Paris Exhibition of 1849 the civil servant Henry Cole persuaded the

Prince Consort to work through the Royal Society of Arts (of which Albert was patron) and then through a royal commission to make London the home of a vast international exhibition showcasing 'the workshop of the world'.

Like the Millennium Dome, the Exhibition excited much ridicule regarding its rationale and site (in Hyde Park) but, unlike the Dome, proved to be an enormous success, with over six million visitors. The prize to design the Exhibition building was won by Joseph Paxton, in the face of over 250 rival submissions, and the prefabricated steel and glass structure, christened the 'Crystal Palace' by Douglas Jerrold, was essentially a magnified version of the Lily House conservatory at Chatsworth which Paxton had begun building as head-gardener to the Duke of Devonshire in 1837.

In 1854 the Palace was reconstructed, after the exhibition officially closed, on Sydenham Hill, only to be destroyed by fire on 30 November 1936.

It is fitting that the Great Exhibition, which began life as an assertion of national superiority masquerading as a celebration of international harmony, should have a Jekyll and Hyde legacy: in the rarefied atmosphere of South Kensington's museums (which grew out of its profits) and in the raucous celebration of South London football, where Crystal Palace perpetuates the name, and final resting-place, of Paxton's Palace.

Great Irish Famine, 1845–52. The Great Irish Famine is also known as the Irish potato famine as it was occasioned by the failure, through blight, of the potato crop which was the staple element in the diet of the rural masses. The disease (*Phytophtora infestans*) affected much of Europe but only in Ireland was its impact so lethal.

The Great Famine was great in comparison with previous crop failures in Ireland, in 1817, 1822 and 1831, because the failures occurred in consecutive years, 1845–47, affected more of the island of Ireland, and occurred at a time when alternative food sources were harder to find and prices higher because of the continental-wide nature of the blight.

The Irish population fell from an estimated 8.3 million in 1845 to 6.6 million in 1851 and less than 4.5 million by 1901 as a consequence of famine, famine-related disease, a decline in fertility and emigration (mostly to the US).

The famine did more than anything else to sour relations between the British and many of the Irish. The latter often felt that whilst the blight was a natural disaster, the famine arising from it was essentially man-made. *Laissez-faire* attitudes, Malthusian fears, the providentialist belief that the blight was sent by God as a punishment for the Maynooth Grant, and simple incompetence all conspired to ensure that British efforts at relief were woefully inadequate. The workhouses and special measures proved equally inadequate in relation to the size of the problem. It was not until 1847 that public works were abandoned in favour of direct relief in the form of food kitchens.

Great Reform Act, 7 June 1832. Wellington lost office in 1830 largely because unsympathetic to any reform of parliament. Earl Grey, who took his place as head of a Whig–Canningite–

Ultra coalition, was a long-term advocate of reform, although his motives were essentially conservative, seeking to defuse the extra-parliamentary agitation for reform which by this time was spearheaded by Attwood and the Birmingham Political Union. The passage of the Bill was tortuous, taking over two years and involving the judicious application of pressure upon both the Lords and William IV by playing up the threat of serious unrest in the country (notably during the Days of May). The Act that finally emerged was actually the third bill, although the final measure only differed substantially from the first by virtue of the Chandos amendment.

The Act removed some though by no means all the rotten and pocket boroughs; redistributed seats so as to take some account of demographic change and new forms of wealth; standardized the borough franchise (so as to apply to householders paying an annual rent of £10); and in the counties, enfranchised leaseholders alongside freeholders of land worth 40 shillings (£2) per annum.

The 1832 Reform Act came to be known as 'the Great Reform Act'. This epithet can be challenged on the grounds that only half a million were added to the electoral registers; some members of the working class in potwalloper boroughs ultimately lost their vote as a result of the reform; the social composition of the reformed parliament was not radically changed; and the reformed system continued to exhibit corruption and glaring anomalies, such as the over-representation of the South.

Of course, to claim that the Act failed to usher in democracy is to mistake the intentions of its architects. Nevertheless, the 1832 Reform Act still deserves to be termed 'great' because it set the decisive precedent for major constitutional change and in so doing helped ensure that change occurred through the constitution rather than, as on the continent, through convulsion.

Green Party Founded as the People's Party in 1973 and changing its name to the Ecology Party in 1975, it became the Green Party in September 1985. Whilst it has not yet achieved a seat at Westminster it has achieved seats in local government and the Scottish and European Parliaments. However, its greatest success has been in raising environmental awareness on the part of the general public and thus obliging the major parties to pay more attention to green issues.

Grenville, William Wyndham, Baron Grenville (24 October 1759–12 January 1834). William Wyndham Grenville was educated at Eton and Christ Church, Oxford. He entered the House of Commons as MP for Buckingham in 1782 and was created Baron Grenville in 1790. As leader of the 'Grenvilles' or 'Grenvillites', the last family connection to operate independently of party, comprising some thirty or so kinsmen and supporters, he disposed of a useful bloc of votes, not least when he entered into coalition with Fox and his supporters in March 1804. Indeed, at the time of the death of Pitt, in January 1806, this force was the largest single grouping in the Commons after the Pittites.

The Pittites were keen that Grenville should be invited to form a ministry as he appeared to them to represent the best insurance for the survival of Pittite policies, particularly in foreign policy, not least because of his long service under Pitt until 1801. However, although Grenville aimed at a comprehensive administration as prime minister 1806–7 the Pittites stayed out and the ministry was composed of Grenvillites (largely controlling domestic policy), Foxites (dominating foreign policy) and the followers of Sidmouth. It was thus a ministry of the talents but not a ministry of all the talents, as not only were the Pittites such as Perceval, Castlereagh and Canning excluded but leading Whigs such as Sheridan, Tierney and Whitbread were also denied high office.

Initial Pittite forbearance turned into active opposition which was not muted by the demise of Fox or the reshuffle attendant upon his death. Matters came to a head over Grenville's desire to add to the terms of the Irish Act of 1793 in a pro-Catholic manner which additionally alienated supporters such as Sidmouth and diluted, if it did not destroy, the confidence of the King. More fundamentally Grenville candidly recognized that 'I want one great and essential quality for my station … I am not competent to the management of men. I never was so naturally, and toil and anxiety more and more unfit me for it.' This political disability was to hamper his effectiveness as an opposition leader over the next decade, following his surrender of the seals of office on 25 March 1807.

Grenville and his followers (the Grenvillites) crossed the floor of the House in support of the ministry of Lord Liverpool between 1817 and 1821.

Grey, Charles, second Earl, Viscount Howick, and Baron Grey (13 March 1764–17 July 1845). After Eton and Trinity College, Cambridge, Grey was elected to parliament in a by-election for Northumberland, in which county the Greys had long had an interest, centred upon their estate at Howick. He was aged just twenty-two, and, as was not uncommon in the unreformed parliament, was elected in his absence (whilst still on his Grand Tour of the continent). On the death of his father in 1807 he moved from the Commons to the Lords as second Earl Grey.

A Foxite Whig, Grey was chiefly identified in the 1790s with the twin causes of maintaining peace with revolutionary France and reforming parliament, although the failure of the first entailed the delay, for the foreseeable future, of the latter. After a brief spell as First Lord of the Admiralty and then foreign secretary in the Ministry of All the Talents (February 1806 to March 1807), Grey was out of office and seemingly little interested in active politics, despite becoming leader of the Foxite Whigs in 1807 and overall Whig leader in 1807. However, he returned to government as prime minister in November 1830, in a coalition with the Huskissonites and with a mandate to reform parliament. This he proceeded to do, although the First Reform Act (1832) was actually the third of Grey's reform bills.

Grey inherited the problems of trade depression, cholera, agricultural unrest (in the shape of the Captain Swing riots) and a crisis in Belgium. Moreover, his attempts to reform parliament provoked a constitutional crisis and disorder in the country at large (most notably after the Lords rejected the second bill); Grey was disingenuous in claiming that 'We did not cause the excitement about Reform. We found it in full vigour when we came into office.'

According to Woodbridge, Grey wanted 'a Bill with the minimum that would satisfy the reform-demanding public and the maximum that would be acceptable to both Houses of Parliament and the King,' or as Greville put it, it was 'the least democratical bill it is possible to get the country to accept'. In the Whig interpretation of history (epitomized by Trevelyan), Grey occupies an exalted role as a far-sighted statesman who helped avert revolution and advance Britain along the path of peaceful constitutional development towards democracy. In the Tory interpretation of history (epitomized by Gash), Grey was a short-sighted party politician who for the sake of supposed electoral advantage and by the mode by which the Bill was secured as much as by its content, fatally compromised both the position of the Crown and the House of Lords relative to the House of Commons, and of members of parliament relative to their electorate.

Grey was nowhere near as closely involved in the legislation of the first reformed parliament (elected in December 1832) as he had been in the Reform Bill, and deprived of the latter as a unifying factor Grey found it increasingly difficult to keep his colleagues from openly bickering. Grey finally resigned on 9 July 1834 as a consequence of the cabinet divisions arising over clause 147 of the Irish Church Temporalities Bill.

In his political career's early years, as a follower of Fox, Grey preferred purity of principle to the prospect of office, and in its middle years, as Fox's successor, he preferred the homely comforts of Howick to London high society, but in its Indian summer he re-entered the political fray in order to reform parliament in such a way as to ensure the continued political dominance of his class until at least the end of the long reign of Queen Victoria.

Ground Game Act, 1880. The Ground Game Bill sought to give the occupier of land better protection against the ravages of hares and rabbits, and provide him with equal rights with the landlord to kill and take ground game. The measure was bitterly opposed by the Conservatives but was skilfully handled by the home secretary, Sir William Harcourt, and it went a long way towards reconciling farmers to the Game Laws.

Gulf War, 1991. On 2 August 1990 Saddam Hussein's Iraq invaded Kuwait. This act aroused fears that Saddam might attack Saudi Arabia. This clearly threatened western, including British, interests in the area. Thus in late August the UN imposed sanctions against Iraq and authorized armed forces to enforce them. A coalition of forces, including contingents from Arab states, assembled in the Gulf. Under Mrs Thatcher British forces in the Gulf rose to 45,000 servicemen under the command of General Sir Peter de la Billière.

On 30 November 1990 UN Security Council Resolution 678 set 15 January 1991 as the deadline for Iraqi withdrawal from Kuwait. On 15 January 1991 the government of John Major received overwhelming endorsement for this policy with 534 MPs supporting military action.

Operation Desert Storm for the liberation of Kuwait began the following day, with the bombing of Iraq's air defences. The US provided the largest force and played the leading role under General Norman Schwarzkopf but the role played by Britain at sea, in the air and on land was considerable.

After achieving air superiority the Allied air forces moved on to weakening ('degrading') Saddam's ground forces. Saddam responded with Scud missile attacks on Saudi Arabia and Israel but diplomatic efforts managed to persuade the Israelis not to retaliate, as this would jeopardize Arab membership of the coalition, whilst SAS units operating behind enemy lines did their best to locate and knock out Scud missile launchers. The ground attack began in earnest on 24 February and swiftly overcame Iraqi resistance. By 28 February a ceasefire had been signed, by which time Britain had suffered just 47 fatalities (9 of which were to 'friendly fire').

Both the Marsh Arabs in the south of Iraq and the Kurds in the north rose up against Saddam but he had not been sufficiently weakened for these risings to succeed and he crushed them with genocidal ferocity. Whether or not the Allies had directly encouraged the rebels they felt that they could not stand by and see them massacred and Britain took the initiative in creating 'no-fly' zones for the Iraqis in the north and south of their country and establishing 'safe havens' for the Kurds.

This was one reason why many commentators have claimed that the Allies should have driven on to Baghdad and toppled Saddam from power. However, such a course would not have been legitimated by UN resolution, would certainly have destroyed the unity of the coalition, would not necessarily have yielded a stable alternative to Saddam within Iraq, and would have decisively shifted the balance of power in the region to the equally anti-western Iran. The Gulf War thus resembles the Korean War insofar as UN-sponsored action by a US-led force in which Britain played a significant role secured the limited objective of successfully resisting aggression and liberating occupied territory without decisively defeating the enemy.

Habeas Corpus, suspension of, 1817–18. Habeas Corpus ensures freedom from arbitrary arrest by requiring that within a limited period of time those arrested are either released or charged and brought to trial. This safeguard of personal liberty was extended from criminal to other charges by the Habeas Corpus Act of 1816. In the following year, however, such was the perceived threat of unrest following the mobbing of the Prince Regent's coach, that the authorities suspended Habeas Corpus as well as passing the Seditious Meetings Act. In the event, the latter was allowed to lapse and the former was restored the following year, during which time just forty-four individuals had been imprisoned without trial.

Haldane army reforms These included the formation of the Officers' Training Corps (OTC) as a recruiting ground for officers from the secondary schools and universities; the creation of an expeditionary force and reserves; and the formation of an Imperial General Staff. They materially contributed to Britain's preparedness for World War One.

Hampden Clubs In the winter of 1816–17 Major Cartwright founded several dozen Hampden Clubs, particularly amongst the South Lancashire handloom weavers and East Midlands stocking-weavers. They took their name from John Hampden the seventeenth-century Buckingham squire who had resisted the 'tyrannical' ship tax.

The Hampden Clubs helped provide the radical movement with a degree of coherence which it would not otherwise have possessed, through such activities as sending out 'missionaries' to benighted parts of the country, organizing petitions to parliament and arranging a conference of deputies from petitioning bodies to meet in London in January 1817 to agree upon a plan of reform (which included a demand for universal suffrage). However, the Seditious Meetings Act and suspension of Habeas Corpus struck a blow at the movement from which it never fully recovered.

Hardie, James Keir (15 August 1856–26 September 1915). The illegitimate son of Mary Keir, with a step-father, David Hardie, who drove the family deeper into poverty through his intemperance, the young James Keir Hardie found solace first in the evangelical Scots Morrisonian Sect and later in socialism. A self-taught and self-made man, he was to rise from working in the Ayrshire and Lanarkshire pits at the age of ten to become a trade union leader, journalist and, by 1888, secretary of the Scottish Labour Party.

In 1892 he entered parliament as the MP for West Ham (South) and established himself as 'the man in the cloth cap' for his self-consciously proletarian image (although he actually wore a deerstalker), and as the 'member for the unemployed' for his efforts to raise the political profile of that group.

He played the dominant role in founding the Independent Labour Party (ILP) in 1893 and was its dominant figure as chairman 1894–1900 and 1900–15 (also occupying the role of chairman of the Labour Party 1906–8 and 1909–10).

Hardie never held public office and is thus revered by all members of the labour movement as an incorruptible idealist. He was in fact an outsider by temperament not only with regard to the establishment but also to the labour movement itself, despite having been identified in his youth with the new unionism in Scotland. As he himself said, towards the end of his life, 'Nature never intended me to be a leader. I find myself happier among the rank and file.'

This solitary figure embodied the ideal of independence for the labour movement, rejecting Lib–Labism, the Fabian Society and Marxist Social Democracy in favour of a mass, trade union-based independent labour party as an instrument of protest informed by ethical principle rather than economic doctrine or class consciousness.

He was not a good team player and found himself increasingly at odds with Ramsay MacDonald and MacDonald's policy of cooperation with the Liberals, which partly explains his increasing interest in international socialism and with a variety of progressive causes including Indian nationalism and women's suffrage (his interest in the latter cause being stimulated by his affair with Christabel Pankhurst).

He did not live long enough to see how World War One stimulated both women's suffrage and the movement for colonial freedom but saw only how socialist internationalism and its tactic of a general strike against war was swept away by a tide of patriotic nationalism.

Hartington, Marquis of See DEVONSHIRE, DUKE OF.

Hawarden Kite, December 1885. In December 1885 Herbert Gladstone revealed to the press that his father, William Gladstone, was a convert to the cause of Irish Home Rule. This disclosure occurred after the general election, in which Parnell and his Irish Nationalists had done well enough to hold the balance of power, but before Parliament had reassembled. It was called the Hawarden Kite because it was made at Gladstone's Flintshire country house and because, like a kite, it provided a means of assessing which way the wind was blowing.

In January 1886 Parnell joined with Gladstone's Liberals in defeating the Conservatives on an amendment to the address once Salisbury had made it clear that he would not make any concessions to the Irish but, on the contrary, intended fresh coercive measures. This cleared the path for Gladstone to form his Third Ministry which introduced his First Irish Home Rule Bill and, in so doing, split the Liberal Party.

Heath, Edward Richard George (9 July 1916–17 July 2005). Just as the arch-rivals Gladstone and Disraeli dominated the politics of the 1860s and 1870s, so the enmities of Ted Heath and Harold Wilson appeared to dominate British politics a century later.

As a deputy chairman of the Conservative Party W. F. Deedes voiced the opinion that 'The more I study

Harold Wilson's form, the more I favour contrast. It suits their book to have a gladiatorial contest. It does not suit ours.' However, this advice, given when Home was party leader and prime minister, could be represented as an attempt to make a virtue out of necessity. Once Home had lost the 1964 election, albeit by a very narrow margin, the party turned, through its new mechanism for electing a leader, to Heath who was in marked contrast to the three Old Etonians who preceded him, and who appeared, superficially at least, to be the closest thing to Wilson that could be found in the Conservative Party. Both men had been born in 1916 and both were grammar school and Oxford educated, Heath having attended Chatham House School in Ramsgate before winning an organ scholarship to Balliol College, Oxford. Both were also of lower-middle-class origins. Heath's father, Will, was a carpenter and later a builder, whilst his mother Edith, who doted on him, was a one-time domestic who had been the daughter of a farm worker. The comparisons don't end there: both served as civil servants and both were imbued with a modernizing, technocratic outlook.

At Oxford Heath made his mark in a number of ways, not least in the November 1938 by-election, during his first year, when he unsuccessfully campaigned with Harold Macmillan for A. D. (later Lord) Lindsay, the Master of Balliol, against the Conservative candidate, Quintin Hogg (later Lord Hailsham) because the latter was identified, in the wake of Munich, with the pro-appeasement policies of Neville Chamberlain.

Heath served with the Royal Artillery between 1940 and 1946 and after a brief spell as a civil servant in the Ministry of Aviation was adopted as prospective Conservative candidate for the marginal seat of Bexley in October 1947 (having been beaten at three seats previously) and in the February 1950 election was elected by a majority of 133.

In 1951 he joined the Whips' Office and in December 1955 succeeded to the post of chief whip, which was a more difficult post than usual at the time of Suez.

Heath, unlike fellow members of the 'One Nation' Group like Iain Macleod and Enoch Powell, favoured Macmillan rather than Butler to succeed Eden and was duly rewarded with first the Ministry of Labour (1959–60) and then, as Lord Privy Seal (1960–63), with the crucial job of negotiating Britain's application to join the EEC. The manner in which de Gaulle exercised his veto in January 1963 did nothing to diminish Heath's enhanced reputation.

By relatively quickly aligning himself with Home, the eventual (albeit caretaker) successor to Macmillan, Heath chose wisely and was rewarded with an enlarged Department of Industry (encompassing Industry, Trade and Regional Development), although the use to which he put this portfolio, in abolishing Resale Price Maintenance, was widely regarded as exhibiting his vigour rather than his tact (insofar as the measure was considered likely to damage 'corner shop' capitalism).

However, Maudling, his principal contender for the leadership once Home decided to step down in July 1965, had had an even more equivocal period as chancellor under Home, whilst his business interests after the Tories had lost office in 1964 provided a greater distraction than Heath's. These were the principal factors which resulted in Heath topping the poll in the leadership election, with 150 votes compared with Maudling's 133 and Powell's 15.

Despite losing the 1966 election and pushing Powell out of the shadow cabinet in 1968 after his 'rivers of blood' speech, Heath retained the leadership of the party because of the assiduous promotion of 'Heathmen', because the rank and file were unwilling to change leaders again so soon, and because he skilfully exploited the devaluation of November 1967 and associated economic problems which crowded in on Labour. Nevertheless, a resurgence in Labour's fortunes meant that few, other than Heath himself, was confident of victory in 1970. When the Conservatives won Heath's initial policies (including the winding down of the interventionist Industrial Reconstruction Corporation and the Prices and Incomes Board, announcement of arms sales to South Africa, and trimming government expenditure by such measures as stopping free school milk) were very pleasing to the right wing. All the greater was the sense of betrayal when Heath presided over a policy U-turn of epic proportions: restoring a prices and incomes policy; injecting £4,000m into the economy to 'pump-prime' it; nationalizing Rolls Royce and Upper Clyde Shipbuilders, and so on.

However, Heath threw away power by ignoring the advice of Macmillan in taking on the miners and ignoring the practice of Baldwin (later emulated by Thatcher) by taking them on without having first taken adequate precautions. The result was the Three-Day week and the weak appeal to the electorate in February 1974 on a 'Who governs Britain?' slogan. Sufficiently large numbers of people knew that the answer was not, and should not be, Heath, although the numbers switching from Conservative to Liberal meant that Labour lacked an overall majority. Heath vainly tried to cling to power by offering first a Speaker's Conference on electoral reform and a cabinet position to Jeremy Thorpe, and then the party whip to seven Ulster Unionists. Moreover, the October 1974 election saw Labour strengthen its hold on power by securing an overall majority, albeit a wafer-thin one of three.

Having now seen the Conservatives defeated in three out of the four elections which he had contested as leader there was as much dissatisfaction within Conservative ranks with Heath's leadership qualities as with 'the Grocer's' shop-soiled policies. He was to be replaced by a grocer's daughter but his enduring achievement – Britain's entry into the EEC in January 1973 – was to prove a thorn in her side.

Highland clearances As a result of the agricultural revolution many aristocratic landowners engaged in large-scale evictions or forcible relocations of their Scottish tenants between c.1770 and 1860. Men were moved to make way for sheep farming and/or to provide labour for crofting communities. The clearances of the Countess of Sutherland's estates c.1811–21 (involving perhaps as many as 10,000 people) and of Glengarry (1853) were amongst the more infamous examples of this practice which did much to stimulate emigration (initially to the Americas but later to Australasia) and anti-landlordism.

Hodgkinson's Amendment, 1867. The Reform Bill brought forward by Derby and Disraeli in 1867 was more radical than that of Russell and Gladstone in 1866, although it was not as radical as the eventual Act, not least because 400,000 'compounders' who paid their rates through their landlords were originally excluded from those to be enfranchised. However, Hodgkinson's Amendment proposed the abolition of compounding in parliamentary boroughs and was accepted by Disraeli as part of the price of keeping Gladstone wrong-footed. It thus added substantially to the impact of the 1867 Reform Act notwithstanding the fact that Disraeli limited the force of the amendment by allowing compounding to continue on an optional basis.

The Amendment, coming just eleven days after the Hyde Park riots, is viewed by Royden Harrison as symbolizing the effectiveness of extra-parliamentary agitation in broadening the scope of the Second Reform Act: a view effectively discredited by Maurice Cowling.

Home, Sir Alec Alexander Frederick Douglas, 14th Earl of Home (2 July 1903–9 October 1995). Although D. R. Thorpe's official biography has done much to rehabilitate Lord Home's memory, it was his fate during his lifetime to be consistently underrated. It was often assumed, for example, that the 14th Earl of Home's exquisite manners disadvantaged him in relation to Harold Wilson because the former peer lacked experience of the rough and tumble of Commons debate. Yet Home had actually spent sixteen years as an MP (1931–45 and 1950–51) before succeeding to his father's title. And when Churchill remarked that he had 'Never heard of him' when Home was recommended to him by the chief whip as minister of state in the Scottish Office in 1951, this is rather a reflection on Churchill's memory than on Home's profile, as the latter's talents had already marked him out as parliamentary private secretary to Prime Minister Neville Chamberlain as early as 1937.

Similarly, there were those who assumed that Macmillan made Home the foreign secretary in preference to Butler in 1960 less on his own merits than out of a desire to humiliate his rival and ensure that the post was not held by a potential challenger.

Home's eventual succession of Macmillan as leader can also be told in a disparaging way. Thus if Macmillan resigned, so the story goes, Heath would be the strongest amongst the younger generation of contenders for the leadership, so the Home camp persuaded Heath not to run as this would then inhibit Maudling and Macleod. Heath no doubt calculated that any self-denying ordinance would be rewarded by Home and that his day would come all the sooner if it was Home who succeeded Macmillan. Indeed Macmillan himself, having discovered that his condition was not terminal, may well, it is speculated, have decided to 'change peers in midstream' and back Home rather than Hailsham because the former was much more likely to prove to be a caretaker prime minister than the latter.

If these were the calculations that the likes of Macmillan and Heath made, it is amazing how close he came to throwing them out for not only did he block Butler but came within a hair's breadth of beating Labour at the 1964 election despite (or because of) the fact that he epitomized the old Etonian grousemoors image of Conservatism associated with Macmillan.

Macleod and Powell refused to serve under Home and tried in vain to persuade Butler to declare likewise. As it was Butler and Maudling agreed to serve if Hailsham did. If Butler had stayed out this would probably have been a terminal blow for Home who, anticipating trouble, had only asked the Queen to invite him to see if he could form an administration rather than directly appointing him prime minister. But the fight had gone out of Butler, if indeed one can say that the fight had ever been in him. He was simply unwilling to risk a further humiliation and the conspiracy accordingly came to naught.

For Home to limit Labour's overall majority to four against the background of a party that was not only manifestly disunited but which was also demoralized and lacking in moral authority (in the light of the Vassall and Profumo affairs) and stale (after thirteen years in office) was an amazing performance, particularly as he had been unable to prevent unpopular pre-election initiatives such as Ted Heath's Resale Price Maintenance Act and Beeching's proposed raising of rail fares, and was himself popularly depicted as an aristocratic throwback unable to match the nifty footwork of the meritocratic whizz-kid Wilson.

However, having done his duty and gone down fighting Home did the gentlemanly thing and moved aside to make way for men considered better able to take the fight to Labour, and he continued to serve the party without rancour and the nation with distinction as foreign secretary under Heath between 1970 and 1974.

Ironically, when it had appeared likely in 1970 that Heath would lose the election and Powell seemed likely to replace him as leader, Willie Whitelaw and Reginald Maudling conspired to bring back Home for a second stint as caretaker leader. In the event, of course, Heath won and this bizarre plan was never put to the test. It shows, however, that Home if never the favourite of historians or first past the post with the electorate was a dark horse, with influential backers who recognized the merits of a pedigree with the ability of coming through the middle. Home's diffident manner, which was part of that breeding, was responsible in large part for fostering the mistaken impression that he achieved little.

Home Rule All Round Home Rule All Round was the proposal, most popular in some Liberal circles, to enact devolution for all the constituent parts of the United Kingdom, or at least for all of England's Celtic peripheries.

Hooligans The Hooligans were also known as the 'Hughligans' as Lord Hugh Cecil was one of their leading lights. Winston Churchill was their driving force and he seems to have desired to recreate his father's Fourth Party antics, even at the cost of embarrassing his father's former colleague, now the party leader, Arthur Balfour. However, the chief target of the Hooligans' abuse was Balfour's secretary of state for war, St John Broderick.

The other factor uniting the Hooligans, which also included Lord Percy (the eldest son of the Duke of Northumberland), Arthur Stanley (the son of the 16th Earl Derby) and Ian Malcolm, was an admiration for Lord Rosebery.

Lord Hugh's penchant for rowdiness did not diminish with the passage of time and on Monday 24 July 1911 he and F. E. Smith played a leading role in orchestrating the howling down of the prime minister, Asquith, by Conservative MPs, which ultimately resulted in the Speaker adjourning the House on the grounds of grave disorder.

Hornby v. Close, 1867. The Hornby v. Close legal decision in the Court of Queen's Bench undermined the position of trade unions by declaring that although they were legal associations they acted 'in restraint of trade' and thus did not enjoy the ability to sue for the recovery of funds appropriated by dishonest officials. In other words, the judgement provided a charter for embezzling union treasurers.

Hotel Cecil The Conservative Party under Lord Salisbury was sometimes dubbed the Hotel Cecil given its leader's predisposition to bestow his patronage upon his relations. It was therefore entirely fitting that when he resigned as prime minister on the grounds of ill health in July 1902 he was succeeded by his nephew, Arthur Balfour. If Salisbury was guilty of nepotism at least he had talented relations.

Housing of the Working Classes Act, 1890. The 1890 Housing of the Working Classes Act codified earlier legislation allowing local authorities to provide housing for the masses and reformed the 1845 Land Clauses Consolidation Act so as to reduce the burden on local ratepayers of the compulsory acquisition of property for redevelopment.

Hume, John (18 January 1937–). A former teacher, who graduated from St Patrick's College, Maynooth, John Hume first rose to prominence in the province through the leading role he played in the civil rights movement in Derry in the late 1960s. In 1970 he helped to found the moderate nationalist Social Democratic and Labour Party (SDLP), served on the power sharing executive set up after the Sunningdale Agreement in December 1973, and succeeded Gerry (later Lord) Fitt as SDLP leader in 1979.

Hume helped shape the Anglo-Irish Agreement of 1985. This gave Dublin a limited say in the affairs of Ulster for the first time but failed to erode the Sinn Féin power base in the north. In 1988, however, Hume entered into private talks with the Sinn Féin president, Gerry Adams, and this Hume–Adams process, which became public knowledge in 1993, ultimately bore fruit in the form of the IRA ceasefire announced in 1994, the Downing Street Declaration and the Good Friday Agreement.

Hume worked tirelessly with his UUP opposite number, David Trimble, to campaign vigorously for a 'Yes' vote in the referendum on the agreement, and the two men were rewarded with a ringing endorsement of their efforts and being jointly awarded the 1998 Nobel Peace Prize. However, declining health meant that Hume first stood aside to allow his fellow SDLP member Seamus Mallon assume the role of deputy first minister to David Trimble in the new Northern Ireland Assembly, and then resigned his assembly seat in order to concentrate on his duties as a Westminster MP and as an MEP.

John Hume is a man of obvious integrity who has been prepared to endanger his health and his reputation in the search to bring peace to Northern Ireland. He has done much to enlist support for a solution of the Troubles both within Europe and North America and is as greatly respected abroad (especially in the States, where he has met every President from Jimmy Carter onwards) as he is by many of both sides of the sectarian divide within Northern Ireland.

Hume–Adams process See PEACE PROCESS.

Hunger Strikes, 1980–81. In Northern Ireland between 1972 and 1976 those who had been sentenced to more than nine months' imprisonment, who claimed political motivation and who were accepted as 'one of their own' by the paramilitary leaders within the gaols enjoyed 'special category' status, meaning that they were allowed to wear their own clothes, were exempted from work and had their own compounds. When these privileges were revoked a number of IRA prisoners in the Maze announced, on 10 October 1980, that they would begin a hunger strike on 27 October unless their demands were met.

The action was called off on 18 December after one of the hunger strikers began to lose consciousness and after two Catholic bishops announced (mistakenly) that they had won concessions from the government. It was resumed on 1 March 1981. The first strike had been timed to ensure that any deaths occurred at Christmas. The second was timed so that deaths would occur around Easter.

Gerry Adams had originally opposed the hunger strike strategy but was forced to acknowledge that it had mobilized popular support for the IRA not only amongst the Republican community but also within the wider Catholic community. This was graphically demonstrated when Bobby Sands, the IRA leader in the Maze and leading hunger striker, won the Fermanagh and South Tyrone by-election, and when 70,000 marched in protest on the day of his burial, following his death on 5 May.

Hunger strikes had, of course, been employed by the Women's Social and Political Union but Mrs Thatcher rejected the option of force-feeding or an updated version of the 'Cat and Mouse' Act. Instead, she allowed the next of kin to instruct the doctors to initiate feeding through a drip as soon as a hunger striker lapsed into unconsciousness. After ten prisoners had died, a group of families of those remaining announced that they would take such action to save their relatives and the strike was called off on 3 October 1981. Thereafter some small concessions on clothing, association and loss of remission were made.

The hunger strikes mark an important turning point in Northern Ireland politics. Although on the face of it the IRA had been forced to back down, the election of Bobby Sands to Westminster indicated the viability of an approach which, embracing the ballot box as well as the armalite, thereby strengthened the hand of Gerry Adams and those who thought like him within the IRA leadership, pointing the way forward, however crookedly, towards the 'peace process'.

'Hungry Forties' According to Norman Gash the phrase 'the Hungry Forties' appears to have been coined by Mrs Fisher Unwin (the daughter of Richard Cobden) in her 1904 book of that title designed to champion the merits of free trade in the face of the challenge mounted by Joseph Chamberlain in his tariff reform crusade. The implication of the phrase is that prior to the repeal of the Corn Laws in 1846 there was widespread and unnecessary hardship.

Huskissonites The Huskissonites were those 'left-wing' Tories including Palmerston, Grant, Dudley and Lamb (later Melbourne) who might previously have been referred to as 'Catholic Tories' or Canningites or (most misleadingly of all) exponents of Liberal Toryism. They joined the government of the Duke of Wellington in 1828 where they supported the modification of the Corn Laws and the Repeal of the Test and Corporation Acts. However, in May 1828 they fell out with him over the redistribution of the disfranchised corrupt boroughs of East Retford and Penrhyn. When Wellington refused to transfer these seats to the unrepresented cities of Manchester and Birmingham, Huskisson, Palmerston, Dudley and Grant resigned. Indeed, it was out of the need to replace Grant as president of the Board of Trade that the by-election was held in County Clare that resulted in the election of Daniel O'Connell and the passage, in 1829, of Catholic Emancipation.

The fact that this had occurred and alienated the Ultras suggests that Wellington might have sought to strengthen his ministry by persuading the Huskissonites to return, particularly after the death of Huskisson at the opening of the Liverpool to Manchester railway in September 1830 left them leaderless. Wellington did, in fact, approach Palmerston who agreed to rejoin the government if space could be made for a further two Huskissonites. However, Wellington considered this price too high, with the result that when Grey formed his government in November 1830, his cabinet contained four Huskissonites, of whom three were secretaries of state, namely, Melbourne at the Home Office, Palmerston at the Foreign Office and Ripon at War and the Colonies.

Hyde Park riots, July 1866. Karl Marx wrote that 'If the railings – and it was touch and go – had been used offensively and defensively against the police and about twenty of the latter had been knocked dead, the military would have had to "intervene" instead of only parading. And then there would have been some fun.'

In fact, the railings were not used in this way and had only become available for use as potential offensive weapons because they had given way under the weight of numbers when the Reform League organized a rally in Hyde Park in defiance of a ban by the home secretary.

The incident illustrates the mood of the extra-parliamentary agitation for parliamentary reform in the period immediately preceding the passage of the Reform Act of 1867: determined to stand up for perceived rights but not revolutionary and hence not instrumental in 'forcing' the government to accept Hodgkinson's Amendment.

I

In Place of Strife, January 1969. *In Place of Strife* was the White Paper on industrial relations published in January 1969 by Barbara Castle. At her husband's suggestion, the title had been chosen to echo Nye Bevan's *In Place of Fear* but it could have been called 'The Sermon on the Mount' for all the chance they had of its title endearing its contents to the unions. Indeed, *In Place of Strife* immediately generated enormous discord as organized labour strove to 'Kill the Bill' based upon its proposals. In early March 1969 57 Labour MPs voted against the government and another 30 or so abstained when the measure was debated in the Commons. Ultimately Castle's cabinet colleagues, with Jim Callaghan in the forefront, urged that the measure be dropped. This fatally compromised Castle's political career and Labour's credibility as a party prepared to reform the unions. Heath's 1971 Industrial Relations Act similarly fell foul of organized labour and it was left to Mrs Thatcher to impose discipline upon the trade union movement.

Income tax repeal, 1816. When the Younger Pitt introduced income tax in 1797 he did so as an emergency wartime measure. Liverpool and his chancellor of the exchequer, Vansittart, wished to retain the tax after the wars but the administration was outvoted on this issue by thirty-seven votes in the Commons. The contemporaneous repeal of the malt tax meant that the exchequer suffered a total loss of £17.5m per annum or about a quarter of the government's entire revenue.

Repeal meant that greater recourse had to be made to indirect taxation which pressed disproportionately heavily upon the poor and thus contributed to social unrest. It also delayed the return to the gold standard and to the policy of free trade which Pitt had had to abandon during the wars.

Income tax, reintroduction of, 1842. Peel reintroduced income tax in 1842 at the rate of 7d (3p) in the pound on incomes in excess of £150 per annum. He wished to do this in order to provide sufficient revenue in order to wipe out the deficit inherited from the Whigs and provide fiscal room for manoeuvre in order to return to the policy of free trade which the Liverpool government had pursued after 1820.

Peel also believed that Chartism would be weakened if it could be shown that the propertied political class was prepared to tax itself more highly for the common good. Chartist agitation also provided the atmosphere of national emergency and urgency which made it possible to overcome parliamentary resistance to the tax's reintroduction. Even so, the tax was originally only reintroduced for three years. However, it was renewed in 1845 and thereafter became a fiscal fixture despite Gladstone's 1874 pledge to repeal the tax if re-elected.

Independent Labour Party (ILP) The ILP was formed by Keir Hardie following a conference of various socialist groups in January 1893 in Bradford, including the Fabian Society and the Social Democratic Federation. In addition to campaigning for limited objectives such as the 8-hour working day, it aimed to secure the election of parliamentary representatives of organized labour who were independent of Liberal support. The ILP accordingly played a leading role in the formation in 1900 of the Labour Representation Committee, the forerunner of the Labour Party. The ILP effectively spelt the end of Lib–Labism, although ironically Labour's great breakthrough came as a consequence of the MacDonald–Gladstone Pact of 1903 and Labour remained in the shadow of the Liberal Party until the elections of 1910 rendered Labour and Irish seats crucial to the maintenance of the government's majority.

ILP pacifism during World War One and the adoption of more radical socialist policies associated with the Clydesiders thereafter marked an increasing divergence between the ILP and the Labour Party which culminated in the latter's refusal to endorse ILP candidates at the 1931 election, and ILP disaffiliation the following year. In 1935 four of the seventeen ILP candidates who contested the general election were returned (for Glasgow constituencies). The ILP presence in parliament shrank to just three by 1945, and they rejoined the Labour Party in 1947 following the death of the party's leader, James Maxton, in 1946.

Industrial Relations Act, 1971. Despite the Donovan Report coming out against a statutory framework for industrial relations and the fiasco surrounding *In Place of Strife*, the Conservative Party introduced its own Industrial Relations Bill, which became law in August 1971 after a particularly bitter passage through Parliament.

Robert Carr's legislation was designed to curb unofficial strikes by insisting that trade unions had to ballot their members before a strike. An Industrial Relations Commission and National Industrial Relations Court were set up to enforce the Act. The court could enforce a cooling-off period of up to 60 days in industries where industrial action could critically damage the economy or community.

Trade unionists repeatedly defied its provisions and it was repealed by the next Labour government.

International Monetary Fund (IMF) crisis, 1976. According to what proved to be exaggerated Treasury calculations there was a prospective deficit of £12 billion in 1976. The chancellor, Denis Healey, decided to cut public expenditure by £9 billion and apply to the IMF for assistance. During the forty-two days of the crisis, during which an uncontainable run on sterling was a real prospect, the cabinet held six special meetings which were mostly spent trying to decide what precisely should be done to meet IMF demands.

Initially ten to twelve cabinet ministers were opposed to the chancellor's proposed public expenditure cuts. However, the chief critics of the cuts, Crosland and Benn, failed to make common cause, some ministers were bought off by extra resources for their departments, and ultimately Callaghan threw his weight behind the plan.

Thus on 21 July 1976 the Labour cabinet accepted a package of severe public cuts as the price of securing the

IMF loan. This humiliation was followed by further cuts and the setting of monetary targets in the autumn.

Ultimately the IMF made available a loan of $3.9 billion in three instalments in return for cutting £1 billion in the public spending estimates for 1977–78 and a further £1.5 billion in 1978–79. In addition, a further £500m was to be raised by the sale of most British Petroleum shares.

This surrender of economic management to market forces marked a key point in the move from 'Butskellism' to Thatcherism.

Internment (Northern Ireland), August 1971–December 1975. As the Troubles escalated, the Heath government decided to suspend Habeas Corpus in Northern Ireland and introduce internment without trial. This move was principally directed against the IRA and meant that suspected terrorists (including Gerry Adams) were arrested and imprisoned without being charged or put on trial. Although in the short term such a policy may have eased the situation, in the longer term such a violation of civil rights was bound to prove counterproductive, increasing sympathy for the paramilitaries in the broader republican community both at home and abroad (notably in the United States): a process accentuated by Bloody Sunday and the imposition of direct rule (both 1972). Recognizing this fact, Labour ended internment in December 1975.

Invergordon Mutiny, September 1931. Most of the Royal Navy's capital ships were assembled at Invergordon when news of the National Government's emergency budget emerged. The mood amongst the lower ratings passed from sullen to boisterous to mutinous. Mountbatten subsequently suggested that the announcement went down so badly because hire purchase was just then becoming popular and that the cuts were about the same as many of the men were paying out each week for goods such as their furniture. He also pointed out that similar disturbances did not occur in the dispersed Mediterranean Fleet.

Although the mutiny was soon suppressed, it damaged confidence amongst foreign holders of sterling and thus contributed to the suspension of all sterling payments in gold on 21 September.

IRA The Irish Republican Army (IRA) emerged out of the Irish Volunteers in 1919 as an organization willing to use force to secure the creation of a united and republican Ireland. The Anglo-Irish Treaty and ensuing civil war represented the frustration of the IRA's aims but the advent of the Troubles created a new opportunity to pose as the defenders of the beleaguered Catholic minority in Northern Ireland and in 1968–69 the Provisional IRA was formed by Sean MacStiofain. Such was the success of the IRA's terrorist campaign and so evident was the failure of internment that the Heath government, in the shape of Willie Whitelaw, engaged in unofficial talks with representatives of the IRA but these came to naught.

In February 1993 the IRA responded to a statement by the Northern Ireland secretary, that Her Majesty's Government was willing to speak to anyone so long as they renounced violence by sending a message to John Major through a secret backchannel, stating that they wished to enter into peace talks but could not publicly renounce violence at present because this might be misunderstood by their members and might be crowed over by the media as a surrender. This change of tactics had been masterminded by Gerry Adams and Martin McGuinness once the hunger strikes had demonstrated the electoral appeal of Sinn Féin: the political wing of the IRA and the British had promised the release of political prisoners and a share in the new power sharing executive for all parties which sincerely entered the peace process.

The path to peace has not been straightforward. For example, the IRA ceasefire which began in 1994 was broken off on 9 February 1996 in order to explode a bomb at Canary Wharf which killed two and injured over 100. More fundamentally, dissident elements within the militant republican movement have created the Real IRA and the Continuity IRA in order to continue the armed struggle. Nevertheless, most of the IRA have backed the Sinn Féin line, with the result that it secured 15% of the vote in the elections to all-party talks and Sinn Féin ministers have subsequently taken their place in the Northern Ireland Assembly.

On 28 July 2005 the IRA publicly ordered its members to end their armed campaign in an effort to counteract the negative publicity after alleged IRA involvement in the theft of £26.5m from the Northern Bank in Belfast in December 2004 and the stabbing of Robert McCartney outside a Belfast pub in January 2005.

Irish Church Disestablishment, 1869. Gladstone used the disestablishment of the Established Anglican Church in Ireland as a means of discomfiting Disraeli, uniting the Liberal Party under his own leadership, and doing something to 'pacify Ireland' (appeasing moderate Catholic opinion and therefore isolating Fenianism). As a conservative statesman, moreover, Gladstone believed that the Anglican Church would be strengthened if its anomalous position in Ireland were brought to an end. With all major parties accepting the inevitability if not the desirability of Irish disestablishment, the key question was the extent to which the Irish Church was disendowed. Gladstone ensured that disendowment was partial, as he did not wish to see the Anglican Church gravely financially weakened as a consequence of its official connection with the state being sundered.

Irish disestablishment did something but not much to draw the poison from Irish politics as the issue was more symbolic than substantive, whilst encouraging the Liberation Society in its crusade to see the Anglican Church disestablished in all parts of the United Kingdom.

Irish Church Temporalities Act, 1833. The Irish Church Temporalities Act sought to rationalize the structure and finances of the Established Church in Ireland in the light of the fact that it appeared over-endowed and cumbersome given the size of the Anglican community in Ireland.

Clause 147 of the Bill which made possible the application of surplus Church revenues to secular purposes (the principle of lay appropriation) was so contentious within the Grey government that it had to be dropped (prompting Durham's resignation).

The Act as eventually passed reduced two archbishoprics to bishoprics, suppressed ten sees (out of a total of 22), reduced the revenues of the remainder and allocated surplus revenues (expected to amount to £150,000) to an Ecclesiastical Commission for ecclesiastical purposes such as repairing churches and supplementing low stipends.

Irish Home Rule Bill, the First, 1886. Gladstone proposed in his First Irish Home Rule Bill that Ireland would no longer be directly represented at Westminster. Given the success enjoyed by Parnell in pursuing the tactics of obstruction this was the most popular provision in the Bill amongst Liberals and Conservatives alike. However, it raised serious constitutional problems (of the nature later expressed as the West Lothian question) and it was a principle reversed with regard to the Second Irish Home Rule Bill of 1893.

The 1886 Home Rule Bill proposed the creation in Dublin of an Irish parliament comprising two 'orders'. This was not, strictly speaking, a bicameral body, although the two components could vote separately when they so desired and exercised a suspensory veto over measures put forward by the other. Although the Irish Executive was to be responsible to this legislature, the Imperial parliament at Westminster was to retain control over issues including the Crown, war and peace, defence, foreign and colonial relations, customs and excise, trade and navigation, postal affairs, coinage and legal tender.

One-fifteenth of the revenue raised in the United Kingdom budget for 'imperial purposes' was to be provided by Ireland, whilst any revenues in excess of this sum raised in Ireland were to be at the disposal of Irish parliament and government.

The Irish government would appoint and pay Irish judges, who would hold office on the same terms as their English counterparts but the Judicial Committee of the Privy Council would act as the court of appeal from the Irish courts as well as deciding whether any act of the Irish parliament or government exceeded its authority.

In June a combination of Conservatives and 93 Liberal Unionists (led by Hartington who had refused to serve under Gladstone and Joseph Chamberlain, who had resigned from the government in March) defeated the Bill in the Commons (by 343 to 313 votes) precipitating the fall of Gladstone's Third Ministry.

Irish Home Rule Bill, the Second, 1893. The Second Irish Home Rule Bill differed from its predecessor in two respects, one substantive, the other procedural. Firstly, it proposed that Ireland would continue to send some elected representatives to the imperial parliament at Westminster. Secondly, although Gladstone secured its passage through the Commons it was defeated in the House of Lords by 419 votes to 41.

Irish Land Acts of 1870 and 1881 Gladstone, having achieved Irish disestablishment in 1869, next sought to appease moderate Catholic opinion in Ireland by means of the Landlord and Tenant (Ireland) Bill. This was designed, in Gladstone's words, to allay 'the prevailing sense of instability in the tenure of the soil by those who cultivate it' by granting tenants security of tenure and compensating them for any improvements (such as fencing or drainage) which they had made to their holdings when their tenancy came to an end.

Gladstone drew up the Bill with his Irish secretary Chichester Fortescue and seized upon the proposal of the ex-Indian judge George Campbell that the measure should be based upon the tradition of Ulster tenant right, which conferred upon tenants the right to bestow or sell the right of occupancy, as this enabled him to reassure sceptical Whigs such as Argyll and Clarendon that the Bill did not provide a precedent for the reform of property rights on the mainland. However, Whig pressure within the cabinet ensured that the Bill merely took the form of giving statutory backing to the convention of Ulster tenant right and providing compensation for disturbance (eviction) elsewhere. Moreover, compensation did not apply in the event of eviction arising through non-payment of rent. This was enough to ensure that the Bill was fatally flawed as there was nothing to stop unscrupulous landlords from simply increasing rents to the point at which the tenant was unable to pay and then evicting them with impunity.

Gladstone sought to address this and other problems in his Irish Land Act of 1881. However, his strategy towards the Irish land question was fundamentally misconceived. No amount of tinkering with the contractual relations between Irish tenants and their often absentee landlords was likely to satisfy the former, whose real aim was to own the land they tilled. This alternative strategy of assisted land purchase so as to create a peasant proprietary, later associated with Jesse Collings and Joseph Chamberlain, was first proposed by the radical John Bright, and the so-called Bright clauses of the 1870 Irish Land Act were a faltering step in this direction. However, it was the Conservative Party which pursued this policy most vigorously and successfully through the Ashbourne Act (1885), Balfour's Act (of 1891) and Wyndham's Act (1903), although it is only fair to point out that the prospects of success were enhanced as land ownership became progressively less alluring to members of the aristocracy in the light of declining profits as a consequence of increasing Irish disorder and the impact of the Great Depression.

Irish Nationalist Party The Irish Nationalist Party evolved out of the Home Government Association founded by Isaac Butt in 1870. Under the leadership of Charles Stewart Parnell it adopted more militant tactics at Westminster (obstruction) and in Ireland (in association with the Land League as part of the New Departure). Neither coercion nor conciliation (the Kilmainham Treaty or measures such as the 1870 and 1881 Irish Land Acts) proved capable of drawing its sting. It reached its peak of influence in 1885–86, partly as a consequence of its pivotal importance to the parliamentary arithmetic of the time, and seemingly won its greatest prize when the Hawarden Kite announced the conversion of Gladstone to the cause of Irish Home Rule. The Liberal Party split over the first Irish Home Rule Bill and the consequent realignment of British politics effectively neutralized the Irish Nationalists and their Gladstonian Liberal allies: a position which contributed towards the adoption of the Newcastle programme and the emergence of the Liberal Imperialists. Moreover, the O'Shea divorce case not only strained cooperation with the Liberals but split the Irish Nationalists.

However, the fall out from the People's Budget left Asquith partly dependent upon Irish Nationalist (and Labour) votes and possessed of the means, in the form of the 1911 Parliament Act, to force Home Rule onto the statute book. World War One intervened and by 1918, partly as a consequence of the Easter Rising, Sinn Féin had replaced Redmond as the voice of Irish nationalism.

Irish Question Benjamin Disraeli offered a definition of the Irish Question in the House of Commons in 1844 which focused upon 'a starving population, an absentee aristocracy, ... an alien Church, and ... the weakest executive in the world'. The last point was clearly a Young England dig at Peel, whilst his claim that Ireland's 'teeming population' was living in 'extreme distress' overlooked both the work of improving landlords and the prosperity of the north-east of the island. Indeed, by the time Disraeli made this speech, Belfast had over 70,000 inhabitants and a booming economy based upon linen, shipbuilding and engineering.

However, as the Great Irish Famine was shortly to show, Disraeli was correct in warning that the bulk of the Irish were 'sustained ... upon the lowest conceivable diet [of potatoes], so that in the case of failure they have no other means of subsistence upon which they can fall back'. Nevertheless, it was Peel's disciple, Gladstone, rather than his critic, Disraeli, who took practical steps to address those dimensions of the Irish question relating to the established church and land.

Irish Volunteers, 1913–19. The Irish Volunteers were founded by Eoin MacNeil in 1913 as the nationalist counterpart of the loyalist Ulster Volunteer Force. By July 1914 it numbered 160,000 members.

Members of the Irish Republican Brotherhood took many of the key posts in the organization and in 1914 the Volunteers split, with those in favour of the policy of John Redmond of supporting the British war effort forming their own organization named the National Volunteers.

The Irish Volunteers were also divided over the advisability of the Easter Rising, with the IRB-dominated military council deciding to proceed with the doomed enterprise as a 'blood sacrifice' to the cause of Irish freedom.

In August 1919, in an abortive attempt to wrest control of the organization from Michael Collins, Cathal Brugha, the minister of defence in the first Dáil (parliament), had the Volunteers renamed as the Army of the Irish Republic.

J

Jarrow March, 1936. Jarrow on Tyneside was heavily dependent upon the shipbuilding industry and when this failed 8,000 men were made redundant and unemployment in the town rose to 67%. The Jarrow March or Jarrow Crusade was an attempt to bring this problem to parliament's attention by marching from Jarrow to Hyde Park. Thus two hundred volunteers headed by their local MP 'Red Ellen' Wilkinson emulated the example of the Blanketeers.

Baldwin refused to meet them on the grounds that the Communist Party had organized the march and on their return the Unemployment Assistance Board explained that they had not been available for work during their demonstration and cut their dole accordingly.

The quiet fortitude of the marchers and the mean-spirited action of the authorities helped to create a climate of opinion in the country that affairs should be better managed in future.

Jenkins, Roy Harris, Baron Jenkins of Hillhead (11 November 1920–25 January 2003). When Roy Jenkins entered parliament at the 1948 Southwark Central by-election one of his sponsors was the prime minister, Clement Attlee, as Jenkins's father had once been his parliamentary private secretary and the two families were very friendly.

Jenkins identified himself closely with Attlee's successor, Hugh Gaitskell, but ironically his death in 1963 accelerated Jenkins's political advancement because the new leader and, from 1964, the new prime minister, Harold Wilson, looked to Jenkins as a representative of the centre-right who might help balance his government, first as minister of aviation outside the cabinet, and then, in 1965, as home secretary, where he won a reputation as a liberal reformer through legislation (mostly initiated by private members) encouraging radical reform of the laws on homosexuality, censorship, divorce and abortion, and preparing legislation banning racial discrimination in housing and employment.

In 1967 Jenkins replaced Callaghan as chancellor of the exchequer following the latter's resignation over devaluation. Such was the prominence and success which Jenkins enjoyed that there were moves for him to displace Wilson when the latter ran into difficulties in 1968, just as there had been manoeuvres for Cripps to replace Attlee just over twenty years earlier. However, Jenkins refused, on his own account, to wield the knife because he feared that in so doing he might well undermine the government. Others argue that, like Rab Butler, Jenkins lacked a killer instinct.

In any event Wilson survived as party leader but lost office to Heath in June 1970. The somewhat surprising loss of this election has been attributed to Jenkins's failure as chancellor to deliver a 'giveaway' budget in April, although his admirers take this as proof not of political ineptitude but of political rectitude and financial prudence. Certainly alone amongst his colleagues he appeared to leave office with his reputation enhanced.

However, as deputy leader Jenkins was increasingly at odds with official party policy, most notably over Europe. Indeed, he led the sixty-nine Labour rebels who voted with the government on 28 October 1971 and thus allowed Heath to take Britain into the European Economic Community. However, the proposal, originating with Tony Benn, that there should be a referendum on Britain's membership of Europe proved too much for Jenkins when adopted as official Labour policy and he resigned as deputy leader on the morning of 10 April 1972 (and was followed by two other members of the shadow cabinet – George Thomson and Harold Lever – and by two junior spokesmen – Bill Rodgers and David Owen).

Jenkins didn't expect or really want Labour to win the 1974 election, believing it unfit to form a government and disagreeing with many of its policies. Nevertheless, when Wilson resigned in April 1976 Jenkins threw his hat into the ring to succeed him as both party leader and prime minister. However, victory went to Jim Callaghan who offered Tony Crosland rather than Jenkins the foreign secretaryship. Jenkins now left Westminster to take up the offer to be president of the European Commission. However, within three years his Dimbleby Lecture floated the idea of a new party which in due course materialized as the Social Democratic Party (SDP).

At the Warrington by-election in 1981 Jenkins failed to take the seat from Labour but polled respectably (with over twelve thousand and five hundred votes) and in March 1982 he was elected for Glasgow Hillhead and became leader of the Alliance. He campaigned alongside David Steel in the June 1983 general election as 'prime minister designate' but the Falklands Factor had turned the Alliance tide. Moreover, in the course of the campaign there were tensions between the Alliance partners centring upon Steel's determination to assume the leadership. Shortly after the election Jenkins stepped down as leader of the SDP but like many others, found it increasingly difficult to work with his successor, David Owen, and when he lost his seat in the 1987 election he accepted a peerage and the leadership of the Liberal Democrat peers. Tony Blair appointed him to chair a commission on proportional representation but ignored its report.

As well as contributing to the political history of his time one should also consider Jenkins's role as a historian, whose studies include Dilke, Gladstone, Asquith, Baldwin, Churchill and Truman. The assessment Churchill made of Rosebery (in his 'Great Contemporaries') might be applied with equal justice to Jenkins: 'He was one of those men of affairs who add to the unsure prestige of a minister and the fleeting successes of an orator the more enduring achievements of literature ... [having] enriched our language with a series of biographical studies, terse, pregnant and authoritative, which will long be read with pleasure and instruction on both sides of the Atlantic ... '

Like Rosebery, too, admirers of Jenkins see him as a figure too big for conventional party politics, though, again like Rosebery although not to the same extent, he ultimately succeeded in marginalizing himself rather than 'breaking the mould'.

Jewish Relief Act, 1858. The Jewish Relief Act enabled Jews to sit in the House of Commons without taking a Christian oath (as with Catholic Emancipation, Jews were explicitly debarred from holding certain offices). This meant that Lionel Nathan Rothschild, who had first been elected to Parliament in 1847, could now take his seat, although ironically he then proceeded to take no part in debates for the next fifteen years.

Jingoism A popular music-hall song by George Hunt at the time of the Russo-Turkish war of 1877–78 contained the chorus: 'We don't want to fight, but by jingo if we do, We've got the ships, we've got the men, and got the money too'.

'Jingoism' thus originally referred to sentiments of belligerence towards the Russian bear but came to be applied to any form of simple-minded chauvinism.

Joint Stock Companies Act, 1844. Under the terms of the 1844 Joint Stock Companies Act those enterprises with transferable shares and more than twenty-five members had to register with a new Registrar of Companies, who was also to examine regularly audited accounts. The measure created a safer environment for investors but not all were protected from rash speculation as those companies created under special Acts of Parliament, which included most railway companies, were specifically excluded from the terms of the Act. Thus the so-called railway mania continued unabated.

K

Keynes, John Maynard, Baron Keynes (5 July 1883–21 April 1946). Keynes was born in Cambridge, where his father, John Neville Keynes, was a university lecturer in political economy. After Eton and King's College, Cambridge, Keynes took the civil service exam. Working as a civil servant in the India Office (1906–8) he found intellectual stimulation and friendship in the Bloomsbury Group. In 1908 he returned to King's Cambridge as an economics lecturer and became editor of the *Economic Journal* and secretary of the Royal Economic Society.

In 1915 he joined the Treasury, working on overseas finances, and in 1919 became a member of the British delegation at Versailles. Disillusioned at what he regarded as the out-manoeuvring of Woodrow Wilson by Clemenceau and Lloyd George and regarding the prospect of heavy German reparations as a recipe for European political and economic disaster, he resigned and published *The Economic Consequences of the Peace* which turned him into an overnight celebrity.

Keynes later mended his fences with Lloyd George and championed his public works programmes of 1929 and 1935. However, this partnership worked to the former's disadvantage for such was the mistrust of Lloyd George within governing circles by this time that the association militated against acceptance of Keynes's other proposals.

In the 1920s and 1930s Keynes published a series of books, of which the most famous was *The General Theory of Employment, Interest and Money* (1936), which revolutionized economic thinking and sounded the death knell for neoclassical economic theory. Unfortunately the Treasury represented the last bastion of economic orthodoxy and it was only stormed once rearmament and World War Two apparently vindicated Keynes's view that instead of being concerned to balance the budget by cutting public spending in times of depression, governments should reflate the economy, if need be by borrowing, in order to stimulate aggregate demand and ensure full employment.

In 1940 Keynes became a special adviser to the chancellor and in 1942 he was created 1st Baron Keynes of Tilton. The man who had resigned from the British delegation in Paris was now chief negotiator at Bretton Woods (1944), in arranging Stage II of Lend-Lease (1944) and in arranging a vital US loan (1945). However, Keynes had been living on borrowed time since diagnosis of a heart condition in 1937 to which he finally succumbed in 1946.

Marx once denied that he was a Marxist. Doubtless had Keynes lived longer he would have found good reason to deny that he was a Keynesian. Nevertheless, what passed for Keynesian economics became an integral part of the post-war consensus commonly known as 'Butskellism', which prevailed in Britain until it met its nemesis in the form of Mrs Thatcher with her grocer's daughter's upbringing and housewife's understanding (buttressed by Friedmanite economics) that budgets have to be balanced and it does not pay to borrow.

Khaki election, October 1900. The general election of 1900 was termed the 'Khaki election' because it was held during the Boer War, because so many Conservatives canvassed in uniform and because it was fought almost exclusively on the Unionist record of having apparently won the war. In fact the war was to drag on until 1902 but not before Joseph Chamberlain had helped the Unionists to defeat the swing of the electoral pendulum and secure a majority of over one hundred seats. Crude jingoism characterized the electoral contest but in over a third of the seats there was no contest at all, with 22 Liberals and 163 Unionists elected unopposed. In this sense the first election of the twentieth century was also the last of the nineteenth century.

Kilmainham Treaty, 1882. The Kilmainham Treaty was the agreement arrived at between Charles Stewart Parnell and Joseph Chamberlain, acting on behalf of the Liberal government, whereby the former and two colleagues were released from Kilmainham Gaol in Dublin in return for a promise by Parnell to use his influence to discourage violence and secure cooperation with the Irish Land Act of the previous year, which was to be supplemented by an Arrears Act and to have its terms amended so that its fair rent clauses also applied to leaseholders.

Both sides kept to their bargain although Forster resigned as Irish chief secretary and Lord Cowper resigned as Viceroy because the deal had been done behind their backs; the legislation, even with the Arrears Act, failed to satisfy Irish tenants; and violence increased, in the short term at least, with the Phoenix Park murders occurring within a few days of Parnell's release.

Kinnock, Neil (28 March 1942–). Neil Kinnock was born the son of a miner, in Tredegar, Wales. He studied at University College, Cardiff, where he was active in student Labour politics. Following a postgraduate diploma in education he worked as a tutor and organizer in industrial policy and trade union studies for the Workers' Educational Association between 1966 and 1970, when he was elected MP for Bedwelty (which he represented until 1983 when it became Islwyn, for which he remained MP until 1995).

He became a member of the National Executive Committee in 1978 and joined the shadow cabinet as education spokesman in 1980. By the time Michael Foot resigned as leader, following Labour's disastrous showing in the 1983 election, the contenders to succeed him alongside Kinnock were Roy Hattersley, Peter Shore and Eric Heffer. The resultant elections produced the 'dream ticket' of Kinnock (representing the centre-left of the party) as leader, with Hattersley (representing the centre-right) as his deputy. Given that Kinnock looked back to Nye Bevan whilst Hattersley looked back to Hugh Gaitskell this pairing had the potential to balance the two strands within the party or produce friction. In fact, the two men worked harmoniously. The bonding process was assisted by their common detestation of an 'enemy within' in the shape of Militant, whom Kinnock attacked in his speech at the 1985 Bournemouth Party Conference. With the aid of Peter Mandelson, Labour was rebranded (with a red rose) and repackaged as a mainstream force only for this strategy to be jeopardized by the miners' strike. Thus Kinnock expressed sympathy with the striking miners but exasperation with their leadership and specifically with Arthur Scargill's failure to ballot for industrial action.

Kinnock could succeed Foot as leader and successfully reform and revive the party because he had not served as a minister under Callaghan (and was therefore not directly associated with the winter of discontent) and because as a unilateralist, distrustful of Europe and keen on wholesale nationalization, he appeared to lead from the left. However, precisely because he then converted to multilateralism, a mixed economy and a cautiously pro-European policy he could win seats for Labour but not enough to become prime minister because he was open to the charge of opportunism as well as inexperience.

Labour under Kinnock–Hattersley lost the 1987 and 1992 elections to the Conservatives under Thatcher and Major respectively. The second blow was especially bitter because the slick campaign had seemed to promise success until a triumphalist rally in Sheffield a few days before polling day when Kinnock confirmed the long-held suspicion that he lacked the gravitas to be prime minister by repeatedly punching the air and proclaiming 'Oh, yeah!'

Following this second defeat Kinnock resigned as Labour leader and John Smith was elected to succeed him. In 1995 Kinnock became European commissioner for transport, and vice-president in 1999 with the responsibility of overseeing internal reform. Following the forced resignation of the Santer commission in 1999, he was reappointed under president Romano Prodi.

Kinnock laid much of the groundwork for the later success of Tony Blair through reform of the Labour Party but the odds were always against the 'Welsh windbag' being personally embraced by the British public.

Korean War, 1950–53. In 1945 the former Japanese colony of Korea was divided at the 38th parallel, with the Soviet Union occupying Korea north of that line, and the United States occupying the area to the south. The Cold War resulted in this division becoming permanent so that by 1948 the US-backed Syngman Rhee was president of the new Republic of Korea, whilst the Democratic People's Republic of Korea was led by the Soviet-backed Kim Il Sung.

On 25 June 1950 North Korea invaded the South. This aggression was condemned by the UN Security Council, which the Soviets were temporarily boycotting. The Soviet failure to exercise its veto meant that the UN first called upon all member states to aid South Korea militarily and then voted for the dispatch of its own multinational force under a US supreme commander.

These moves were strongly backed by Britain which sent elements of the Far East Fleet into action along the North Korean coast, and dispatched two battalions to reinforce the Pusan Perimeter. Attlee flew out for urgent talks with Truman after the President had suggested a willingness to use the

Bomb, following Chinese intervention on the North Korean side. Attlee is sometimes credited with having made the President see sense but in fact Attlee discovered that there were no plans to use atomic weapons in Korea at that time and it was by hinting at a readiness to use nuclear weapons that President Eisenhower was eventually able to persuade the North Koreans to agree to an armistice.

When the ceasefire finally came into effect on 27 July 1953 South Korea had been saved from communism. Roughly 100,000 British servicemen and women served in the Japan–Korea theatre during the war, of whom 1,078 were killed in action, 2,674 wounded and 1,060 missing or taken prisoner.

Another casualty of the war was the Attlee government, as the prescription charges controversy which prompted Bevan's resignation and split the party arose from the need to find extra funding for increased defence spending. The long-term growth potential of the economy was adversely affected by heavy military expenditures (peaking at 12% of GNP in 1952) which overheated the economy.

L

Labour Exchange Act, 1909. Churchill replaced Lloyd George as president of the Board of Trade in 1908 as part of the reshuffle attendant upon Asquith replacing Campbell-Bannerman as prime minister.

Churchill was keen to introduce social reform in order to live up to his father's Tory Democratic reputation, in order to realize his own ambitions, in order that Britain be able to compete more effectively with Germany, and in order to pre-empt the advance of socialism by means of 'a sort of Germanized network of State intervention and regulation'.

Labour exchanges were intended to ease transitional unemployment and mitigate problems of casual labour. Churchill rejected Beveridge's proposal (based on the German experience) of labour exchanges operated by municipal authorities with grants-in-aid from the national government, in favour of a national system. Thus the 1909 Labour Exchange Act, which came into effect early in 1910, created 12 regional offices which operated over 400 exchanges by 1914.

The Act was flawed insofar as the labour exchanges were located so as to facilitate the anticipated needs of insurance processing rather than actual unemployment.

Labour Party In *The Future of Socialism* (1956) Tony Crosland identified twelve strands within the labour movement, including Owenite, Marxist socialist, municipal socialist, Morrisite, Fabian, and ILP influences. Even this list was not comprehensive as he omitted to mention such factors as Christian Socialism and corporatism. However, it is safe to say that whatever the intellectual influences, it has been the trade union movement which, since the 1900 formation of the Labour Representation Committee, has provided the core of the Labour Party in terms of finance and rationale: promoting the interests of organized labour in parliament. It is equally true to say that from the first the promotion of working-class interests has been leavened by middle-class members of the intelligentsia with various visions of remodelling society as a whole.

The balance between the two has sometimes been uneasy. Trade unions can be a very conservative force in society, whose leaders are more concerned to ensure a bigger slice of the capitalist cake for their members (or merely themselves) than to experiment with the nouvelle cuisine of public school philanthropists and self-appointed social engineers. The union of hand- and brain-workers was nevertheless confirmed by means of the 1918 Constitution (drawn up by Sidney Webb), Clause 4 of which committed the party to nationalization of key sectors of the economy.

Up until 1945 Labour had only succeeded in helping the Liberals to retain power after 1910 and holding office themselves in two minority governments: in 1924 (on Liberal sufferance) and in 1929–31. Both of these administrations were characterized by a timidity that goes beyond Labour's minority status and its perceived need not to frighten the electorate. The second Labour government ended in the 'betrayal' of Ramsay MacDonald and the party was only ultimately rescued from impotence by Hitler.

World War Two produced a radical change in the instincts and aspirations of the electorate, and Attlee and Labour emerged with a majority (of 147) for the first time in the 1945 general election, having secured 48.0% of the poll and 383 seats. Thus had it not been for the fuel and convertibility crises of 1947–48 and the outbreak of the Korean War in 1950 then Labour, rather than the Conservatives, might have become the natural party of government instead of trampling the electoral wilderness for the 'thirteen wasted years', 1951–64.

Harold Wilson looked capable for a time of capturing the electoral high ground (holding office in 1964–70 and 1974–76) by projecting an image of efficiency, dynamism and modernity but this was only an image and it rapidly appeared more dated than the grouse moors image of Conservatism with which it was meant to contrast. Callaghan (who took over from Wilson in 1976) not only mistimed his appeal to the country, falling foul of the 'winter of discontent' (1978–79), but had the misfortune of facing a sea-change in the popular mood comparable in intensity to that which swept Labour into office in 1945 but now moving in the opposite direction.

Tony Blair and New Labour have proved more adept than Foot, Kinnock and Smith in swimming with this new tide, not least by stealing much of the Conservative Party's swimwear to this end.

Labour Representation Committee (LRC) The Trades Union Congress established the Labour Representation Committee in February 1900 as an umbrella organization for those on the left who wished to create a political force independent of the Liberal Party. Numerous trade unions affiliated to the LRC (particularly in the wake of the 1901 Taff Vale judgement) as did the ILP, the Fabian Society and (more briefly) the Social Democratic Federation.

The LRC's first major success, which marked the death knell of the Lib–Labs, was the Gladstone–MacDonald Pact of 1903. In 1906 the LRC formally became the Labour Party.

Lancashire Cotton Famine, 1861–65. The Lancashire Cotton Famine arose from the fact that during the American Civil War (1861–65) the North or Union badly disrupted supplies of raw cotton to the mills of Lancashire by its blockade of the Southern or Confederate states. Yet despite the distress and hardship which this produced the Lancashire textile operatives remained supportive of the North, which they regarded as the democratic and morally superior side.

Gladstone, like many members of the British aristocracy, was initially sympathetic towards the Confederacy. However, not for the first time, Gladstone changed his mind and came to believe that the masses had shown greater perspicacity and integrity than the classes in their support for the North. He was particularly impressed by the fact that in the case of the Lancashire working class this stand had been taken despite the fact that it conflicted with their material self-interest. It thus provided evidence that at least a portion of the working class might be entrusted with the vote in the safe assurance that they would not use their new-found power to enrich themselves through redistributive taxation.

Land League The National Land League, to give it its full title, was launched in County Mayo in the spring of 1879 by Michael Davitt. It represented the organizational expression of the 'New Departure' in Irish politics whereby extremists like Davitt and John Devoy (both Fenians) joined hands with constitutionalists like Parnell in order to use the land issue in order to power the national issue.

Writing to Devoy on 16 December 1880, Davitt claimed that the Land League 'virtually rules the country' but expressed fears regarding coercion and the Government's Land Bill.

The Irish Land Act of 1881 indeed posed a dilemma for the Land League by offering the 3Fs (fair rent, free sale and fixity of tenure), to which the executive of the League, all either imprisoned or in exile, responded with the Manifesto of October 1881 which advocated the non-payment of rent supplemented by boycotting. The deadlock between the Land League and Gladstone's Second Government was only finally resolved by means of the Kilmainham Treaty.

Land War, 1879–82. The Land War was a campaign of protest which arose out of agricultural depression in Ireland and originally took the form of a demand for rent reductions. However, the Land League succeeded in radicalizing the tenantry so that they attacked the very institution of landlordism.

Unsympathetic landlords were confronted with a general refusal to pay rents followed by various obstructions to the eviction of tenants or their replacement. The best-known tactic employed in the Land War was boycotting. Increasingly, however, some of those engaged in the campaign stepped outside the law and committed violent crimes. This violence was so dramatic because up until this time there had been a steep decline in lawlessness since the Great Irish Famine. Thus in the quarter century 1852–78 there was a total of 6,915 agrarian outrages or an average of 256 per annum but in the years 1879–82 the figure rocketed to 11,325 or an average of 2,831 agrarian outrages each year.

The Second Gladstone government (1880–85) responded with a mixture of coercion and reform (the 1881 Irish Land Act and 1882 Arrears Act) which temporarily at least restored peace to the Irish countryside by 1882.

Lansbury, George (21 February 1859–7 May 1940). George Lansbury left school at the age of 14 to work on the railways and then in his father-in-law's lumber business. After briefly emigrating to Australia (1884–85) he returned to his native East End of London where he became immersed in turn in Christian socialism, Liberal politics (acting as Bow Liberal agent, 1886–92) and the Social Democratic Federation (SDF), under the auspices of which organization he was elected to the Poplar Board of Guardians from which he rose to become councillor, alderman and mayor (1919–20 and 1936–37) and achieved a certain degree of notoriety as a leading advocate of the radical confrontational tactic which came to be known as Poplarism (1919–25).

Having unsuccessfully contested Newington, Walworth in 1895 on behalf of the Social Democratic Federation and Bow as a Socialist in 1900, Lansbury eventually entered parliament by winning Bow and Bromley for Labour in the December 1910 general election, only to resign the seat two years later in order to fight an unsuccessful by-election in support of women's suffrage. This defeat resulted in his exclusion from parliament for a decade, during which time he made his mark in left-wing journalism whilst continuing his career in local government. In 1912 Ben Tillett invited him to join the newly formed *Daily Herald* committee, and in due course he went on to become chairman of the company which ran the paper (which came to enjoy a circulation of a quarter of a million) and, until 1922, its editor.

Lansbury's left-wing credentials were meanwhile affirmed by his pacifist campaigns against the Boer War and World War One, by his joining the Webbs in signing the Minority Report of the Royal Commission on the Poor Laws in 1909, by a well-publicized tour of the Soviet Union in 1920, and by imprisonment, alongside other Poplar councillors, in 1921 for refusing to pay the London County Council precept. In 1922 he returned to the Commons as MP for Bow and Bromley: a seat he was to hold until his death in 1940.

Lansbury turned down the offer of the Ministry of Transport in the first Labour government (1924) but served as First Commissioner of Works in the second Labour administration (1929–31) and was the most senior former minister who was not a member of the National Government to be returned at the 1931 general election. Thus as the most experienced survivor he became the leader of Labour's 46 MPs and leader of the opposition to the National Government.

In 1935 he resigned the leadership because his pacifist stance prevented him supporting even diluted sanctions against Italy over Abyssinia and this led to his being savaged by Bevin at the party conference who stated that, 'This conference ought to be influenced neither by sentiment nor personal attachment. We ought not to be put in a position of watching Lansbury cart his conscience round from conference to conference asking to be told what to do with it.'

Bevin was right. Lansbury may as an individual have merited respect but Christian pacifism was never more of a luxury than in the 1930s when Britain was faced by the rise of the aggressive dictators. Passive resistance might work against Britain in India but it would hardly work for Britain in the Europe of Mussolini's Italy and Hitler's Germany so Lansbury was right to throw in the towel.

Law, Andrew Bonar (16 September 1858–30 October 1923). Andrew Bonar Law was always something of an outsider, having been born and received his earliest education in Canada. However, his Presbyterian upbringing meant that he transferred quite readily to Glasgow where he completed his education at the High School before entering business. Fifteen years later he entered parliament as a Conservative MP for Glasgow (Blackfriars) and two years later (in 1902) he moved off the backbenches to become parliamentary secretary to the Board of Trade. By 1911, when the divisions within the party over protection, the People's Budget and the Parliament Act and the defeats of 1906 and January and December 1910 had created the 'Balfour Must Go' movement, it was Bonar Law to whom the party turned for reassurance and wholehearted resistance to the New Liberalism, after Austen Chamberlain's and Walter Long's candidacies cancelled each other out.

Bonar Law gave the party a sense of unity and purpose by championing the resistance of Ulster to the policy of Irish Home Rule which the Parliament Act had made practicable and imminent. In so doing he consolidated his reputation for tough speaking and tough-mindedness as he came close to condoning civil war, although behind the scenes he worked for some compromise. He served in the Asquith coalition government as colonial secretary, 1915–16, and was chancellor of the exchequer, leader of the House of Commons and de facto deputy prime minister to Lloyd George, 1916–18, and then Lord Privy Seal in the post-war period of the coalition, 1919–21, resigning for reasons of ill health.

He therefore provided a natural rallying point for disaffected Conservatives in the last eighteen months of the coalition. He was persuaded by Beaverbrook to overcome his friendship for Austen Chamberlain (his loyal deputy for many years) and attend the Carlton Club revolt which brought down the coalition and paved the way for his becoming prime minister on 23 October 1922, which he followed three days later by announcing a general election.

Jibes regarding 'second-class brains' and the 'second eleven' by the likes of Birkenhead to describe the men promoted by Law to replace the more experienced coalitionist ministers (like himself, Austen Chamberlain, Horne, Worthington-Evans, Balfour and Churchill) were probably counter-productive as the electorate was as tired as the rank and file of the Conservative Party with men of 'genius' who, like Lloyd George, offered 'movement' but appeared to have misplaced their moral compass. Certainly the Conservatives achieved their first electoral victory since 1900.

Law's tenure of the highest office was, however, to be short-lived (just 219 days) as ill health obliged his resignation on 20 May 1923. It was not the poor state of his health so much as his concern for the paramountcy of party unity that led to Law accepting the US debt settlement terms in 1923 although he disagreed with the entire cabinet on the issue. He similarly displayed his pragmatism by refusing to attempt to go back on the Anglo-Irish Treaty and by continuing the cabinet secretariat whilst jettisoning Lloyd George's style of political management.

Not the least valuable legacy which Law passed on to the party was Stanley Baldwin, who had been his parliamentary private secretary in 1916, who had stood shoulder to shoulder with him at the Carlton Club meeting that brought down the coalition and whom Law had promoted to the chancellorship after little over a year in the cabinet. Law's support for Baldwin as his successor was not expressed formally – out of deference to the feelings of Lord Curzon who had been the most prominent of the coalition Conservatives to come over to the rebels – but it was not the less wholehearted, as Baldwin embraced, embodied and projected the values of common-sense and decency which Law enshrined.

The title of Blake's biography of Bonar Law perpetuates the witticism ascribed to Asquith that he was 'the

Unknown Prime Minister' but the contents amply explain why this often enigmatic figure who occupied the summit of British politics for over a decade deserves to be better known.

Left Book Club, 1936–48. The left-wing publisher, Victor Gollancz, had the idea of offering a series of inexpensive uniform books on left-wing topics, with low prices guaranteed through subscription to a book club. For 2/6 (12.5p) each month, subscribers received the monthly magazine (produced by Gollancz, John Strachey and Harold Laski) as well as that month's book.

The Club proved to be enormously popular, particularly amongst the Labour Party's white-collar and professional middle-class constituency activists, with the result that at its peak, in April 1939, the Club numbered nearly 60,000 subscribers, with 1,200 affiliated study and discussion groups.

Less eligibility principle The Royal Commission report upon which the 1834 Poor Law Amendment Act was based stated that 'Every penny bestowed, that tends to render the condition of the pauper more eligible than that of the independent labourer, is a bounty on indolence and vice ... nothing is necessary to arrest the progress of pauperism, except that all who receive relief from the parish should work for the parish exclusively, as hard and for less wages than independent labourers work for individual employers.'

In other words, in order to deter scroungers or able-bodied undeserving poor from abusing poor relief, outdoor relief would end and conditions in the workhouses should be made less eligible or desirable than those of the lowest-paid labourer outside. As the Poor Law Commission report put it, 'The first and most essential of all conditions is that the pauper's situation, on the whole, should not be made really or apparently so eligible as the situation of the independent labourer of the lower class'. Unfortunately, the standard of living enjoyed by independent labourers of the lower class was so meagre that undercutting that standard produced workhouse conditions which were inhumane.

The less eligibility principle derived from the thought of Jeremy Bentham (in his writings on the 'Panopticon') and chiefly influenced the Poor Law report and legislation through the medium of his follower Edwin Chadwick. The latter claimed to have 'been the first to demonstrate ... that which had not been seen by Mr Ricardo, Dr Malthus, or any other political economists ... that the condition of the recipient should not on the whole be more eligible than that of any labourer living on the fruits of his own industry ... '

The principle provides a classic example of the way in which the road to hell is paved by good intentions.

Liberal Anglican Whigs The liberal Anglican Whigs were deeply impressed by evangelicalism and sought to attract moderate non-conformists and Catholics to the standard of the Whig party by sponsoring reforms such as the appropriation of the surplus revenues of the Anglican Church in Ireland, which would assist the transformation of the British state from one in which Anglicanism enjoyed a privileged position to one which was Christian but non-sectarian.

Their numbers included Hobhouse, Spring Rice, Morpeth, Mulgrave, Howick, Thomson and Lord John Russell, under whose leadership they became the dominant force in the 1830s, particularly after the retirement of Grey in 1834 and the withdrawal from government of the High Churchmen, Richmond, Ripon, Derby and Graham. Richard Brent stresses the influence of the liberal Anglican Whigs by referring to their role in achieving reforms such as the Tithe Commutation Act, Dissenters' Marriage Act and Civil Registration Act (all of 1836).

Liberal Democrat Party The Liberal Democrat Party came into existence in 1988 as a result of the merger between the Liberal Party and the Social Democratic Party. Its first leader, Paddy Ashdown, had to contend in its earliest days with many Liberals unhappy with their change of name. The party nevertheless retained the Liberal Party's post-Grimond strategy of simultaneously presenting itself as both a centre party and a progressive party to the left of Labour. Under Ashdown and Charles Kennedy (who was elected to the leadership in 1999) it is otherwise distinguished from the two other main parties by its unabashed pro-European stance and by its willingness to advocate an increase in income tax (to fund higher spending on the social services).

In line with Paddy Ashdown's 'project' the Liberal Democrats have cooperated with New Labour over constitutional reform and been rewarded with seats in a cabinet committee and partnership in the Scottish parliament whilst being denied the real prize of proportional representation. The Tories' disastrous performance in the June 2001 general election and consequent leadership election have meanwhile enabled the Liberal Democrats to pose as the 'real' opposition to Labour.

Liberal Imperialists The leading Liberal Imperialists were Asquith, Grey and Haldane and they all drew inspiration from Rosebery. When it became clear that Rosebery had ruled himself out from ever returning to leadership of the Liberal Party they planned to hijack it for themselves through the Relugas Compact. Although they failed to prevent Campbell-Bannerman from becoming prime minister (in 1905) they found his leadership surprisingly tolerable, not least because they enjoyed high office and influence under his easy-going regime.

Historians differ as to the significance of the Liberal Imperialists. H. C. G. Matthew, for example, has devoted a book of over three hundred pages to them whilst Peter Clarke has dismissed them in less than thirty words, writing that, 'Liberal Imperialism ... never amounted to much more than a readiness to look further than the Gladstonian agenda in domestic policy as much as in foreign policy.'

Liberal League, 1902–10. The Liberal League was the successor of the Liberal Imperial League and its main lines were drawn up by Rosebery, Grey, Haldane and Robert Perks in order, in the words of Asquith, 'to press forward Liberal work in the country on the lines and in the spirit of Chesterfield': a reference to Rosebery's Chesterfield speech of 16 December 1901 in which he chiefly appealed for a 'clean slate' (dropping the Gladstonian commitment to Irish

Home Rule in order to enable the Liberal Party to identify itself with imperialist sentiment and social reform).

The Liberal League was initially very well funded and attracted the support of Fabian and Fabian-minded MPs, wealthy landowning and more traditionally minded Liberals, non-conformists and certain journalists. However, such a disparate alliance was unlikely to hold together even had Rosebery been a less volatile leader.

Liberal National Party The 23 Liberals led by Sir John Simon formed in 1931 to support the Conservative-dominated National Government were termed Liberal Nationals. In the 1931 general election they were opposed by Liberals but not by Conservatives and won 35 of the 41 seats they fought. In 1932 the Liberals split between the 'Simonites', like Hore-Belisha, who continued to support the National government, and the 'Samuelites' who followed Herbert Samuel in rejecting the government because of its abandonment of free trade through the Ottawa Agreements.

By 1947 the Liberal Nationals had shrunk to thirteen MPs and they began to be absorbed (as National Liberals) into the Conservative Party.

Liberal Party The Liberal Party effectively came to an end in 1988 when it merged with the Social Democratic Party (SDP) to form the Social and Liberal Democrat Party, later the Liberal Democrat Party. However, it is much more difficult to state when the Liberal Party emerged as a result of the fusion of Whigs, Peelites and Radicals. Ideologically it could be said to date from as early as 1846. Organizationally it could be said to date from as late as 1868. However, most historians would be willing to accept that a good case can be made for the meeting in Willis's Rooms in 1859 as marking the origins of the party as a significant parliamentary force.

Gladstone split the party over Irish Home Rule in 1886 but the tariff reform controversy of 1903 helped produce a Liberal landslide in 1906, and the so-called 'New Liberalism' seems to some historians (notably P. F. Clarke) to have held out the promise of the party entrenching itself as the natural party of government, whilst others view Liberalism as doomed to suffer a fatal attrition as it was ground down by the upper and nether mill-stones of conservatism and socialism respectively. In any case, the strains of total war (notably the issue of conscription) and the rivalries of Asquith and Lloyd George sapped Liberal strength to such an extent that after 1923 the party appeared to be in terminal decline. Excepting participation in the national governments of the thirties and the wartime coalition, the Liberals remained out of power and with no prospect, short of the introduction of proportional representation, of attaining power.

Under the leadership of Joe Grimond and Jeremy Thorpe the party won some spectacular by-election victories and appeared to exercise an influence upon political debate out of all proportion to their numbers. It thus appeared the senior partner when it merged with the SDP.

Liberal Toryism The fashion is now for historians to deny the claims of their predecessors that the ministry of Lord Liverpool (1812–27) can be neatly divided into two phases with the changes of key cabinet personnel of 1821–23 signifying the shift from a reactionary and repressive Toryism (associated with the likes of Sidmouth, Eldon, Castlereagh and Wellington) towards a more progressive, enlightened, reform-minded or liberal Toryism.

W. R. Brock coined the term 'Liberal Tory' in his 1941 book *Lord Liverpool and Liberal Toryism* to apply to those Tories on the left of the party. The leading Liberal Tories were supposedly Canning, Huskisson, Robinson and Peel. In fact, contemporaries would merely refer to individuals being more or less liberal on specific issues. There was nothing approximating to a distinct Liberal Tory ideology. Thus whilst all those mentioned above were liberal with regard to commercial matters (as supporters of free trade) Peel was illiberal compared with the others with regard to Catholic Emancipation. Moreover, some allegedly Liberal Tory policies appear, on closer inspection, to be anything but liberal. For example, Peel relaxed the severity of the penal code, radically commuting the number of capital offences not because he was 'soft' on crime or criminals but rather because he was frustrated by the way in which hitherto juries were inclined to acquit those who were blatantly guilty because they considered the punishment too severe in relation to the crime. That is to say, Peel reduced the severity of sentences in order to ensure a higher rate of conviction in order to combat the rising crime wave more effectively, not because he was a liberal or humanitarian.

Liberal Unionists Liberal Unionists were those members of the Liberal Party who objected so strongly to the Irish Home Rule policy pursued by Gladstone in 1886 that they voted with the Conservatives to maintain the Act of Union and subsequently, given the failure of the Round Table Conference, coalesced with the Conservatives to form the Conservative and Unionist Party in 1912.

The Liberal Unionists basically comprised Whigs who acknowledged the leadership of Hartington (later Duke of Devonshire) and Radical followers of Joseph Chamberlain.

Lib–Labs The Lib–Labs were those Liberal MPs of working-class origins such as Thomas Burt and Henry Broadhurst who were endorsed by local Liberal organizations and took the Liberal whip in parliament but who represented the interests of organized labour.

At first they were mostly representatives of craft unions. After the Third Reform Act of 1884 their numbers included more miners. However, Lib–Labism was ultimately marginalized by the creation of the Labour Representation Committee in 1900 and the Gladstone–MacDonald Pact in 1903.

Lib–Lab Pact, 1977–78. Although Labour had transformed itself from a minority to a majority administration thanks to Wilson's success in the October 1974 general election, this position was technically reversed by a series of by-election losses, whilst the government's authority was seriously undermined by the 1976 IMF crisis. In March–April 1977 Jim Callaghan for Labour and David Steel for the Liberals agreed to the Lib–Lab Pact, whereby the latter agreed to use their twelve votes to help keep the former in office so long as their policies were not left wing.

The Pact enabled Labour to hang on to office (also assisted by the tacit support of the Ulster Unionist Party) in the vain hope that an improvement in the economy might secure its re-election with a workable majority. For their part the Liberals got the shadow of power: exercising a veto over socialist policies which were no longer on the table whilst incurring the odium of sustaining in power an increasingly discredited and unpopular administration.

The economy, cushioned by the advent of North Sea oil and gas, did show signs of improvement, with the 30% inflation of 1975 down to under 10% by 1978. However, Callaghan missed the opportunity of going to the country in the autumn of that year and the ensuing winter of discontent blighted the electoral prospects of both pact partners for more than a decade.

Lichfield House Compact, 1835. Following Melbourne's dismissal by William IV, Peel formed his First Ministry in December 1834. In February and March 1835 a series of meetings were held at Lord Lichfield's house between the Whigs and the Irish, which resulted in February 1835 in the so-called Lichfield House Compact, whereby Lord John Russell was promised Irish support by O'Connell in return for the Whigs promising to return to the task of reforming Ireland which they had begun with the Irish Church Temporalities Act of 1833. This understanding sounded the death knell of Peel's minority administration which duly resigned after defeat over the question of Irish Church revenues.

Melbourne returned to office but the Lichfield House Compact played into the hands of the Conservatives in the long term insofar as they could plausibly claim that the Whig dog was wagged by its Irish tail.

Liverpool, Robert Banks Jenkinson, second Earl of (7 June 1770–4 December 1828). Robert Banks Jenkinson was the eldest son of Charles Jenkinson who became first Baron Hawkesbury and then the first Earl of Liverpool. After Charterhouse and Christ Church, Oxford (where he began his close friendship with George Canning), Robert entered parliament. Not only did he arrive young he also rose fast, serving as a commissioner at the Board of Control (1793); master of the Mint (1796); foreign secretary (1801–3); home secretary (1804–9, with a brief hiatus in 1806–7); and secretary for war and the colonies (1809–12). Moreover, from 1802 he was Tory leader in the House of Lords, where his capacity for closely reasoned argument greatly strengthened the government's debating team against Lord Grenville. He was therefore very experienced when Spencer Perceval was assassinated in May 1812, and the Prince Regent (later George IV) prevailed upon him to form a government.

Lord Liverpool (as he had by then become) faced a formidable and unprecedented range of problems arising from the dislocation caused by dramatic population growth and the impact of the agricultural, industrial and French revolutions. Not only were the French Revolutionary and Napoleonic wars in full flight but Britain was soon at war with the United States in the War of 1812. The coming of peace in 1815 merely brought new problems including a post-war slump affecting both agriculture and industry, a massive debt burden (with 80% of government expenditure required merely to service the National Debt), and a monarchy in disrepute, particularly in the light of the Queen Caroline affair, 1820–21.

Derided as 'rulers who neither see nor feel nor know' Liverpool's government was most immediately agitated by a series of disorders, including Luddism, the Corn Bill riots, the Ely and Littleport rising, Spa Fields, the mobbing of the Prince Regent's coach and the March of the Blanketeers, which may appear relatively trifling in retrospect but at the time may genuinely have seemed to presage a revolution to men who, like Liverpool himself, had witnessed the fall of the Bastille, who lacked a large standing army and modern police force and who were obliged to rely upon agents provocateurs. The Cato Street conspiracy of 1820 provides a reminder that there were genuine revolutionaries intent upon destroying the fabric of society. Nevertheless 'Peterloo', and the Six Acts in particular, have resulted in the administration unjustly becoming a byword for mindless reaction, as when Michael Foot speaking about the Heath administration of 1970–74 claimed 'We're being governed by the most reactionary government since Lord Liverpool'.

Liverpool undoubtedly made mistakes but he was far from being the 'Arch-Mediocrity' that Disraeli described him as being. Indeed Gladstone was much closer to the truth when he declared his belief that 'England was never better governed than between the years 1822 and 1830'. Not that one should write off the decade prior to the alleged watershed between reaction and Liberal Toryism. In the first place, apart from the diplomatic and military successes of the earlier period there were reforms, including the 1818 grant of £1m for the construction of new Anglican churches, the 1819 Factory Act and the first post-war steps towards free trade. More could have been accomplished earlier in the direction of the last point had not Liverpool and his chancellor, Vansittart, been defeated by the Commons in their desire to defeat the repeal of income tax in 1816. The resumption of cash payments by the Bank of England in line with the recommendations of the committee chaired by Peel may have aggravated distress in the short term by deflating the economy but in the longer term helped ensure that stability of currency which was a precondition of growth in the longer term, whilst 'Peterloo' occurred because the local magistrates ignored rather than followed the advice of Sidmouth at the Home Office, and Liverpool was one of those privately critical of the way in which the affair was mishandled, although he felt obliged to stand by them publicly, as was later the case with George IV and the Bill of Pains and Penalties.

Last but not least, the fact that Liverpool retained the highest office for fifteen years despite all the trials and tribulations listed above, whilst managing a talented but quarrelsome team (containing at different times six future prime ministers), is testament to his ability and his personal qualities, including integrity, courage, realism and the ability to reduce the political temperature by calming words. So far from being the 'Arch-Mediocrity' he was the 'Arch-mediator' and his presence was soon sorely missed after a stroke in February 1827 obliged his leaving office. The premiership of his successor, Canning, had already come to end before Liverpool himself died on 4 December 1828.

Lloyd George, David, first Earl Lloyd George of Dwyfor (17 January 1863–26 March 1945). The 'Welsh Wizard' was actually born in Manchester but both his parents were Welsh. His schoolmaster father, William George, died in 1864, whereupon his mother, Elizabeth Lloyd, brought her family back to her home in North Wales. They lived with her bachelor brother Richard, a master cobbler, in the small village of Llanystumdwy, Caernarvonshire. 'Uncle Lloyd' as Richard Lloyd was known was also an unpaid minister of the Baptist sect known as Disciples of Christ and as such he was a conduit of the cultural revival experienced by Wales at that time.

After leaving the village Anglican school David Lloyd George (as he became known in deference to Uncle Lloyd's role in his upbringing) became an articled clerk to a firm of Portmadoc solicitors. After establishing an independent practice he installed his younger brother, William, as a partner who took the lion's share of the work in order to allow David to pursue his political ambitions.

Returned to Westminster as a Gladstonian Liberal in the 1890 Caernarvonshire Boroughs by-election, Lloyd George made his mark in his maiden speech by eschewing convention and using the occasion to attack two parliamentary giants: Joseph Chamberlain and Lord Randolph Churchill. He thereafter concentrated upon the affairs of the Principality and became in the process the unofficial leader of the Welsh MPs.

It was the outbreak of the Second Boer War in 1899 that made him a politician of national note or rather of national notoriety as he was a leading 'pro-Boer' who risked his life in espousing his cause in the lion's den of the Birmingham Town Hall, in the heart of Chamberlain's fiefdom, on 18 December 1901, where he had to disguise himself as a policeman in order to escape the violent attentions of the Unionist mob (who injured many and killed two).

Opposition to the 1902 Balfour Education Act, when he led the 'revolt' of the Welsh county councils, provided him with a further opportunity to consolidate his claims to office and in 1905 he was duly appointed president of the Board of Trade. His gifts as a legislator (passing a Merchant Shipping Act, a Patents Act and creating a single Port of London Authority) and as an industrial conciliator (notably in ending the 1907 railway dispute) were such that in 1908 he was promoted to become chancellor of the exchequer when Asquith moved from that post to succeed Sir Henry Campbell-Bannerman as prime minister.

1908 also marks Lloyd George's transformation from 'Old' to 'New' Liberal, as his visit to Germany in the summer of that year turned the rural radical who hitherto possessed a scant understanding of the problems of urban society and a predominantly Gladstonian agenda, comprising issues such as disestablishment, temperance and land reform, into an enthusiast for old age pensions, labour exchanges, and health and unemployment insurance schemes.

With Asquith, Lloyd George deserves the credit for creating the modern welfare state, with the introduction of old age pensions in 1908, whilst his 'People's Budget' of 1909 may be regarded as the first redistributive budget and as such provoked a constitutional crisis with the House of Lords which resulted in their powers being clipped by the 1911 Parliament Act. In the same year the National Insurance Act provided health and unemployment insurance. The land campaign of 1913–14, cut short by the outbreak of World War One, sought, not altogether successfully, to marry traditional and New Liberal attitudes towards the subject, dealing with the depredations of pheasants as much as slum clearance.

When Britain entered World War One Lloyd George supported its vigorous prosecution and in May 1915 became the first minister of munitions to address the desperate shortage of shells. As secretary for war, following the death of Lord Kitchener, he lost confidence in both the tactics of the high command and the leadership of the coalition government, and thus at the end of 1916, with Conservative support, displaced Asquith as prime minister: a fact which soured relations between the two men and their supporters so deeply and for so long that it inflicted irreparable damage upon the long-term electoral prospects of the Liberal Party.

Nevertheless, Lloyd George's unconventional approach to decision-making helped galvanize the war effort and provide the basis for post-war reconstruction, with the development of new ministries for Labour, Housing, Health, Transport and Pensions. Nor were Lloyd George's methods entirely informal as his premiership was also marked by the creation of the cabinet secretariat under Hankey.

Lloyd George may not have been able to avert the carnage on the Western Front but his insistence on the introduction of the convoy system did much to ensure that the war was not lost at sea. In 1918 he was certainly seen as the man who had won the war and he exploited this fact to hold a 'Khaki election' although the 1918 election became known as the coupon election because candidates supportive of the Lloyd George coalition were identified in this fashion and won an overwhelming victory.

At the Paris Peace Conference Lloyd George occupied an intermediate position on many issues between those of Woodrow Wilson and Georges Clemenceau and thus ensured, for example, that Germany was not treated so leniently that she might soon pose a threat to France, whilst ensuring that her debilitation was not carried so far that she might herself succumb to Bolshevism. In certain respects he was even more conciliatory towards Germany than Wilson, for example, prevailing over the President over the issue of the plebiscite for Upper Silesia.

However, the Lloyd George coalition came unstuck as increasing numbers of Conservatives, who provided the bulk of coalition MPs became disillusioned over a number of issues, including the brutality of the campaign of counter-terror in Ireland associated with the Black and Tans; the Anglo-Irish Treaty of 1921; the honours scandal; and the Chanak crisis of 1922. Matters came to a head with the Carlton Club revolt on 19 October 1922 when Baldwin and

Bonar Law secured a majority of votes amongst Conservative MPs in favour of leaving the coalition, thus precipitating Lloyd George's resignation and ending, as it turned out, his career in office.

His years in the wilderness witnessed an uneasy rapprochement with the Asquithian Liberals in November 1923 and the development, with Keynes, of far-sighted plans for regenerating the British economy in the 1930s (notably through the *Yellow Book*) but Baldwin and MacDonald between them effectively kept him and the Liberal Party marginalized. Churchill offered him work when World War One ended his own wilderness years (despite Lloyd George's ill-advised tributes to Hitler on his return from Berchtesgaden in the summer of 1936) but by then Lloyd George realized that age made him unequal to the task. He married Frances Stevenson, his mistress of thirty years, in 1943, after the death of his first wife, and shortly before his death on 26 March 1945 to please her took the title of Earl Lloyd George of Dwyfor.

That the champion of the common people should end up an earl is just one of the many paradoxes presented by Lloyd George's personality and career. He was both parliamentary spokesman of the non-conformist conscience and 'the Goat'; both pro-Boer Little Englander and the man who presided over the expansion of empire to its greatest extent; both Old and New Liberal; both confrontational partisan and coalitionist; both 'rooted in nothing' (according to Keynes) and rooted in the populist radicalism of late-nineteenth-century rural Wales (according to K. O. Morgan).

Given these contradictions it is not surprising that the literature on Lloyd George should present conflicting pictures of the man. Nevertheless, K. O. Morgan has distinguished three broad phases in the treatment of Lloyd George. Firstly, prior to his fall from office, Lloyd George was generally depicted hagiographically, as a self-made superman, which is hardly surprising given that most of his biographers were Liberal, radical and Welsh. From 1922 until roughly 1966, however, with notable exceptions (the most notable of which being Morgan himself), reverence gave way to denigration as Asquithian Liberals dominated the literature and portrayed Lloyd George as almost single-handedly responsible for the decline of the Liberal Party, public morality and liberal values. Since then a more balanced and sympathetic picture has emerged, partly as a response to the availability of new sources and partly because the loose-living, anti-establishment Lloyd George is more appealing – or at least less shocking – to those living through or after the sixties. More specifically, Morgan has convincingly made out the case for the administration of 1918–22 as the last stand of the New Liberalism, with Lloyd George less the prisoner of the Tories than vice versa. By focusing upon Lloyd George's later collaboration with Keynes, Robert Skidelsky has also done much to rehabilitate Lloyd George's reputation and to suggest that his absence from office after 1922 was a tragedy not only of personal but also of national dimensions. John Grigg's (sadly incomplete) biography presents a fully rounded picture of Lloyd George which does this remarkable man justice.

Local Government Act, 1888. The 1888 Local Government Act created elected county councils, whilst major towns became county boroughs. Major towns were defined as those with a population in excess of 50,000, excepting the metropolis, which was dealt with separately, by the creation of the London County Council.

Local Government Act, 1894. The 1894 Local Government Act created urban district councils, rural district council and parish councils within the counties, which had received elected councils under the 1888 Local Government Act.

The Act established annually elected parish councils in every parish, consisting of a chairman and between 5 and 15 councillors, with powers over such matters as allotments, recreation grounds and public walks.

London Dock Strike, 1889. John Burns, Ben Tillett and Tom Mann led a five-week strike in London's docklands, which secured a guaranteed wage of 6d (2.5p) per hour: the 'docker's tanner'. The dockers won public sympathy, financial support from Australian trade unionists and the mediation of Cardinal Manning (the head of the Catholic Church in England) and the Lord Mayor of London.

This victory led to the creation of the dockers' union (which soon numbered 30,000) and was a milestone in the development of the New Unionism.

London Government Act, 1899. The 1899 London Government Act created twenty-eight new metropolitan boroughs which received powers formerly exercised by the London County Council (LCC), which had been created in 1888. This devolution of power occurred because the Unionist government disliked the radicals' hold over the LCC and because separate borough status provided an opportunity for ratepayers in the wealthier London districts, such as Westminster and Kensington, to escape from an overall London valuation of 1894 which forced them to subsidize poorer districts such as Deptford and Poplar.

London Working Men's Association (LWMA) The London Working Men's Association was founded in June 1836 by Henry Hetherington and William Lovett who became respectively the body's treasurer and secretary. The LWMA at no time exceeded more than roughly one hundred working-class members and thirty-five honorary members, including Place, Owen, Oastler, O'Connor and O'Brien. However, its influence was extended by means of pamphleteering and by sending out 'missionaries' into the provinces.

It was conceived of as a ginger group for radical ideas and is chiefly remembered for having acted as midwife to the People's Charter (published on 8 May 1838) and as typifying moral force Chartism with its emphasis upon extending equal political rights by all lawful means.

Luddism and **Luddites**, 1811–17. West Riding croppers, Lancashire cotton workers and Midlands framework knitters were amongst those who turned to machine-breaking or Luddism between 1811 and 1817. These activities took their name from Nedd Ludd, their mythical leader.

The disturbances are popularly associated with technological unemployment: new machinery rendering traditional skills – and skilled workers – redundant. However, in some instances, machines were broken simply because this provided the best available means of protesting against other grievances, including wage cuts, the employment of un-apprenticed workmen and the production of shoddy goods. Thus Hobsbawm described Luddism as a species of 'collective bargaining by riot' in the absence of legal trade unions as a result of the Combination Laws.

In February 1812 the Perceval administration responded to the Luddite threat by passing the Frame-breaking and Watch and Ward Acts. These failed to act as an effective deterrent. Indeed, Luddite activity escalated with the attack on William Cartwright's Rawfolds Mill in April 1812, and the murder of the mill owner William Horsfall, for which the Luddites Mellor, Thorpe and Smith were hanged in January 1813.

M

Maastricht, Treaty of (1992). The Maastricht Treaty envisaged three stages to economic and monetary union within the European Community, namely, linking the currencies of member states through the Exchange Rate Mechanism; the managed convergence of the economies of member states, bringing them into line on inflation, interest rates and government borrowing (to begin in earnest in 1994); and acceptance of a single currency issued through an independent central bank which would also control interest rates and borrowing. The third stage was set to occur on 1 January 1999 unless an alternative date had been agreed upon by the end of 1996.

At Maastricht John Major secured an 'opt out' for Britain from the latter, reserving the right of the Westminster parliament to decide to enter the single currency later, if it considered such a move to be in the national interest. He also secured an 'opt out' from the Social Chapter, which would extend common European rules on social security, employment law and issues such as the minimum wage. These 'opt outs' nevertheless failed to satisfy the critics of Maastricht, not least those 'Eurosceptic' Conservatives, who believed that even with these 'opt outs' Maastricht represented an unacceptable reduction in Britain's economic sovereignty which would lead to a further diminution in Britain's political sovereignty.

The legislation needed to bring the treaty into law – the European Communities (Amendment) Bill – was first delayed by the May 1992 general election and then brought into doubt by the slimness of Major's majority (just 21) and increasing Euroscepticism, resulting in open rebellion on the Conservative backbenches fanned by a Danish referendum rejecting the Treaty, Black Wednesday, and by Margaret Thatcher and Norman Tebbit. The Treaty was only finally ratified in July 1993 when John Major reversed a government defeat by tabling an emergency Motion of Confidence in the government and making it clear that he had advised Her Majesty to dissolve parliament and call a general election in the event of defeat.

The Maastricht Treaty thus exposed to prolonged public scrutiny the extent of the divisions within the Conservative Party and thereby contributed to its massive defeat in the May 1997 general election at the hands of Tony Blair and New Labour.

MacDonald, James Ramsay (12 October 1886–9 November 1937). Ramsay MacDonald was the illegitimate offspring of a ploughman and a serving-girl. He thus experienced both poverty and social stigma during his upbringing at Lossiemouth in the north of Scotland. His education had not progressed beyond board school before he set off to England to make his living, although he continued his own studies in the evenings after clerical and journalistic work.

MacDonald's interest in politics led to his acting as private secretary to a Liberal candidate before, in 1894, joining the ILP. He became a member of the ILP's national council and then, in 1900, unpaid secretary of the newly formed Labour Representation Committee. In this capacity he attracted trade union support, in the wake of the Taff Vale judgement, and negotiated the secret Gladstone–MacDonald electoral pact of 1903, which ensured that so far as possible the two 'progressive' parties would not stand against one another in national elections south of the border: an agreement which assisted MacDonald's own election at Leicester in 1906.

When Asquith became dependent upon Labour and Irish support in 1910, MacDonald was instrumental in ensuring that the government ceded payment of MPs in 1911 in return for support of what became the Insurance Act, despite the reservations of Snowden, Lansbury and the Webbs. This relieved the problems caused by the Osborne judgement until its reversal by means of the 1913 Trade Union Act. Labour thus appeared relatively well placed until split by the outbreak of World War One, when MacDonald found himself in the pacifist minority (although Robbins, amongst others, disputes whether 'pacifism' provides an entirely accurate representation of MacDonald's position).

He resigned the party's chairmanship (which he had held since 1911), although remaining as Treasurer. In September 1914 he joined the Union of Democratic Control which was to provide a bridge whereby a number of Liberals would enter the Labour Party.

Labour's wartime divisions were much more easily healed than those within the Liberal Party and Labour emerged as the Opposition after the coupon election, although MacDonald lost his seat. He returned to parliament and the party chairmanship in 1922, in which year the title of 'leader' was also formally adopted. As such MacDonald was ideally placed to appeal to both former Liberals and traditional ILP socialists. Following the 1923 election called by Baldwin on the issue of Protection, MacDonald formed Labour's first (minority) administration in 1924. MacDonald, as his own foreign secretary, chiefly occupied himself with foreign affairs, not only because this was what most interested him but because it also seemed to him to offer the best prospect of Labour appearing 'safe' and competent in the eyes of the electorate. Wheatley's Housing Act represented modest social reform.

In the event, the international stage offered scope for MacDonald to make statesmanlike gestures, including a London conference which led to the 1924 Dawes Plan, and the Geneva Protocol. However, his recognition of the USSR enabled the Conservatives to exploit anti-Soviet feelings over the Campbell case and through the Zinoviev letter. The net result was that although Labour increased its vote by 500,000 in 1924 it lost forty seats and its tenuous hold on office.

MacDonald's rejection of class warfare in preference to 'organic evolution' not only survived but was also strengthened by the experience of the general strike. The real test for his vision came during his second minority administration which came to power in June 1929 because Labour, in the wake of the Wall St Crash, appeared to be presiding over the collapse of capitalism with no clear idea of what to put in its place. Mosley, who did have clear ideas of how to tackle rising unemployment, was forced to resign and MacDonald clung to the Gladstonian orthodoxies of his chancellor of the exchequer, Snowden. When the cabinet was split almost exactly down the middle over cuts, MacDonald's ministers followed his advice in tendering their resignations only to be told the next day that he had accepted the King's invitation to head a 'National' Government, which would include Baldwin and Samuel.

It was anticipated that the National Government would be short-lived as it would only be required to pass an emergency budget to achieve the (supposedly complementary) aims of saving sterling and balancing the budget. However, the crisis and the coalition continued because the currency did not so much float as sink. MacDonald (along with Snowden, Thomas and Sankey) had cut himself adrift from the bulk of his party and was now execrated as a traitor to the Labour movement because duped by a bankers' ramp and dazzled by high society. Certainly there is a much stronger case to be made in favour of the proposition that MacDonald became a prisoner of the Conservatives than either Joseph Chamberlain from 1895 or Lloyd George between 1916 and 1922.

MacDonald remained prime minister until he exchanged places with Baldwin in 1935 and became Lord President of the Council until the two men resigned in 1937, but whereas Baldwin left office in full possession of his faculties and at the height of his powers, MacDonald, who died later the same year, had long appeared to be a shadow of his former self.

The Labour Party owes MacDonald an enormous debt as his brand of ethical evolutionary socialism made it respectable and electable. However, his more immediate legacy has been to breed distrust of the leadership and its potential vulnerability to the charms of Society and the wiles of the City.

Macmillan, Maurice Harold, first Earl of Stockton, Viscount Macmillan of Ovenden (10 February 1894–29 February 1986). Harold Macmillan was the youngest of the three sons of Maurice Crawford Macmillan and an American mother, Helen Macmillan (née Belles). The Macmillans were of Scottish crofting ancestry but Harold's grandfather and great uncle had founded the family fortune through setting up the publishing house of Macmillan. Harold joined the family business in 1920 after Eton; Balliol College, Oxford; service with the Grenadier Guards, 1914–18 (during which he was twice wounded); and a spell as ADC to the governor-general in Canada (during which he became engaged to his future wife, Lady Dorothy Cavendish, the daughter of the ninth Duke of Devonshire).

He stood unsuccessfully for Stockton-on-Tees in the December 1923 general election but won the seat for the Conservatives in the October 1924 general election. He went on to represent the constituency until defeated in the July 1945 election, with the exception of the period May 1929 to October 1931.

The comradeship of the trenches and the spectacle of mass unemployment in Stockton-on-Tees acted on Macmillan to make him an advocate of social reform and a planned economy, notably in a series of books and pamphlets such as *The Middle Way* (1938). This put him on the left of the party and helped keep him out of office.

Like Churchill and Eden, Macmillan was also one of those Conservatives who distanced himself from the appeasement policies of the Baldwin and Chamberlain governments, whereas his arch-rival Butler, like his successor as prime minister, Douglas-Home, was irrevocably identified with 'The Guilty Men'. However, Macmillan's dissent had carried him even further than Churchill's or Eden's, so that he had defied a three-line whip in 1936 to vote with the Labour Opposition in condemnation of the Chamberlain government's recognition of Italy's conquest of Abyssinia and resigned the party whip shortly afterwards, sitting as an Independent Conservative until 27 July 1937, when he successfully applied to Chamberlain for readmission to the whip. He nevertheless supported A. D. Lindsay against the official Conservative candidate, Quintin Hogg (later Lord Hailsham), in the October 1938 Oxford by-election, which was effectively a referendum on Munich.

Macmillan's chance for office came when Churchill replaced Chamberlain as prime minister. He was made parliamentary secretary to the Ministry of Supply, 1940–42; parliamentary under-secretary at the Colonial Office, February–December 1942; and a member of the cabinet and minister resident at Allied Force Headquarters in north-west Africa in December 1942. As the allied armies advanced Macmillan's portfolio expanded until by May 1945 he was British resident minister in the Mediterranean, political adviser to the supreme allied commander, and acting president of the allied commission for Italy. These Mediterranean duties exhibited to the full Macmillan's ability to pick his way through the potential minefield of overlapping jurisdictions, conflicting priorities and multifarious nationalities. However, after two months as secretary for air in Churchill's caretaker government Macmillan suffered both the loss of office and his seat, although his success in the Bromley by-election saw him return to parliament in November 1945.

As minister of housing, 1951–54, Macmillan won a reputation in the national eye as 'a man who got things done' as his 'Great Housing Crusade' met the 1950 Tory party conference target of 300,000 houses built each year, although most of the actual work was done by his deputy, the self-made practising engineer (with a partnership in Marples Ridgeway) and MP for Wallasey, Ernest Marples. As Macmillan later admitted, 'Marples made me PM: I was never heard of before housing'.

318,000 houses were built in 1953 and in 1954 a further 357,000 were built. Macmillan's success was not, however, without a price. In addition to relaxing controls on the private sector he cut standards. Thus the quality of housing declined both in terms of erosion of the minimum size of council housing and in terms of materials (reinforced concrete and steel-reinforced lintels increasingly replacing timber and steel). He may not be, as his detractors would have us believe, the patron saint of the sink estate and the tower block but Macmillan certainly paved the way for these blots on the landscape.

Eden miscalculated in moving Macmillan from Defence (which he had held for just six months) to the Foreign Office in April 1955, as he renewed his international contacts and enhanced his reputation for gravitas.

Moreover, when it was considered necessary for him to replace Butler at the Treasury he was in a strong enough position to lay down preconditions for accepting the post which further strengthened his ultimate claims to the succession, namely, that he be 'undisputed head of the Home Front'; have the firm support of the prime minister at all times; and that Butler (now Leader of the House and Lord Privy Seal) not be designated 'deputy' prime minister.

Macmillan soon flexed his muscles as chancellor, succeeding where Butler had failed by insisting (through threat of resignation) that food subsidies be cut, although nominal support remained for each item so that Eden was not left with egg on his face. His 'common touch' was also evident in the introduction of premium bonds in what proved to be his one and only budget as chancellor in April 1956. This was presented in a populist speech which effectively rendered him heir apparent in the eyes of most Conservative MPs, particularly when they contrasted this barnstorming performance with Rab Butler's unpopular last budget of the previous October.

Having encouraged the Suez expedition Macmillan then sabotaged it by grotesquely exaggerating the run on the pound and by refusing to defuse the situation by floating it. Eden resigned shortly afterwards and his successor was chosen by the cabinet who were interviewed individually by the senior cabinet minister Lord Salisbury (the Lord President of the Council) and Lord Kilmuir (the Lord Chancellor), being invited on 9 January, 1957 to state a preference for Macmillan or Butler (with Salisbury famously asking, 'Is it Wab or Hawold?'). Backbench opinion was less than scientifically sounded by Salisbury and Kilmuir quizzing the chairman of the 1922 Committee, the chairman of the Conservative Party, and the chief whip, Edward Heath.

Butler had already been outflanked by Macmillan in appealing to the backbenchers when he not only allowed Macmillan to accompany him to the post-Suez 1922 Committee meeting on 22 November 1956, but allowed him to speak last. Butler, having shouldered the burdens of office as deputy during Eden's illness, and having already been on his feet in the House for almost three hours, turned in a downbeat lacklustre performance whilst Macmillan pulled out all the stops in a performance which 'verged upon the disgusting' to Enoch Powell but which had the rank and file eating out of his hand.

Those cabinet members suspected of voting for Butler (Gwilym Lloyd George, Patrick Buchan-Hepburn, Walter Monckton and James Stuart) were purged on Macmillan becoming prime minister. Rab himself wanted the Foreign Office but had to make do with the Home Office.

Whatever the views of the cabinet – as the Queen's private secretary, Sir Michael Adeane, discovered – the die had effectively been cast by Macmillan's bravura performance before the 1922 Committee that Thursday evening in November.

As premier, Macmillan succeeded in reuniting the party, restoring confidence in the government and repairing Britain's international reputation (not least with the United States through the Bermuda conference) to such an extent that by October 1959 he was able to win a general election with an increased majority.

It was not all plain sailing, however. Although he brushed it off, the resignation of Macmillan's entire Treasury team on the eve of his departure for his first Commonwealth tour in January 1958 might well have fatally undermined confidence in his leadership rather than adding to his reputation for unflappability. Moreover, the threat of rising inflation to which the erstwhile Treasury ministers had pointed, and to which Macmillan himself had repeatedly alluded in his 'never had it so good' remarks, was a real one and by 1961 there was a 'pay pause', a credit squeeze and rising unemployment. The prospect (however illusory) of curing Britain's economic ills through entry into the Common Market was removed in January 1963 by de Gaulle's use of the French veto and in the meantime Macmillan had overreacted to the gloomy situation by the 'Night of the Long Knives' of July 1962 when he butchered his cabinet in order to give his government an infusion of new blood. Significantly, it was Lord Home who, as president of the National Union of Conservative Associations, came to the 1963 Party Conference at Blackpool to read out the resignation letter from the hospitalized prime minister. However, even before ill health forced this move and catapulted the conference into an unseemly scramble for the succession, Macmillan's premiership had become mired in sexual scandal through the Vassall and Profumo affairs and the knives were out.

Historians are divided regarding Macmillan's conduct regarding his succession, with Anthony Howard and Ben Pimlott accusing him of acting deviously and unconstitutionally to block Butler from succeeding (and taking up and then ditching Hailsham), whilst Alistair Horne and D. R. Thorpe deny the charge.

Macmillan's claims to statesmanship rest not only on his work in reviving the 'special relationship' and reducing Cold War tensions (culminating in the 1963 Test Ban Treaty) but also in his acknowledgement of the 'wind of change' of national consciousness blowing through Africa. However, it is as a consummate political showman stage-managing national decline that 'Supermac' best deserves to be remembered.

There was an Indian summer in Macmillan's political career in his nineties, when he accepted the title of Earl of Stockton and urbanely twisted the knife into Mrs Thatcher, for example characterizing her policy of privatization as tantamount to 'selling off the family silver'.

Major, John (29 March 1943–). John Major was the son of Abraham Thomas Ball (whose stage name was Tom Major) and his wife, Gwen, who were music hall artistes and founder members of the Variety Artistes Federation. They were elderly parents – Tom Major being 63 and Gwen being 37 – when John was born, so that his father's days as an acrobat and trapeze artist were long departed and he had moved into the business of producing garden ornaments. Shortly after John began attending Rutlish grammar school a sharp downturn in the family's fortunes resulted in the family moving from a bungalow in Worcester Park to two rooms in Brixton.

John Major was largely self-educated because he made little effort to work at school, leaving with just three 'O' Levels. Thereafter he used correspondence courses to improve his tally of 'O' Levels and to secure a Banking Diploma, a profession which he entered in May 1965 after spells as a clerk at an insurance-broking office; making garden ornaments; unemployed (during which period he was turned down as a bus conductor) and working for the London Electricity Board. He also took the first steps in his political career: joining the Young Conservatives in 1959 and unsuccessfully contesting the Lambeth Council elections in 1964.

A serious car crash in Nigeria (where he was working for the Standard Bank Group) in 1967 resulted in a long period of convalescence and left his left leg so badly damaged that thereafter he walked with a slight limp. The following year he was elected a councillor for Lambeth largely on the back of the Enoch Powell 'Rivers of Blood' speech (although he personally disagreed with Powell's analysis) which was made three weeks prior to the local government elections and which helped turn a drift towards the Conservatives into a landslide (winning 57 of Lambeth's 60 seats). He served on Lambeth's Finance and Housing Committees, rising to become chairman of the latter (a post in which he was succeeded in 1971 by Ken Livingstone).

Moving from local to national politics, he stood unsuccessfully for St Pancras North in both the February and October 1974 elections before being selected as candidate for the safe Conservative seat of Huntingdonshire, for which he was returned as MP in the 1979 general election. After serving as parliamentary private secretary to both Patrick Mayhew and Timothy Raison (when they were both ministers of state in the Home Office), Major joined the Whips' Office in January 1983, gaining his first ministerial experience at Social Security (under Norman Fowler), becoming parliamentary undersecretary there in 1985 and minister of state for social security (with special responsibility for the disabled) in 1986. Following her third consecutive general election success, in 1987, Mrs Thatcher promoted Major to a seat in the cabinet as chief secretary to the Treasury. During his two years in this post he showed his emollient efficiency in eyeball-to-eyeball negotiations by conducting the spending surveys without recourse to 'Star Chamber' (the body which adjudicates disputes between ministers and the chief secretary). He also assumed some of the responsibilities of Willie Whitelaw when he resigned as deputy prime minister in January 1988.

Few, however, could have anticipated Major's next leap up the ministerial ladder, when he was made foreign secretary in July 1989. This massive promotion may have indicated that he was being groomed for the succession but more probably indicates Mrs Thatcher's desire to have a more biddable colleague at the Foreign Office than Geoffrey Howe had latterly proved to be (for example having conspired with Nigel Lawson at Madrid in June 1989 to force Mrs Thatcher into publicly accepting the case in principle for British membership of the Exchange Rate Mechanism).

If Major's elevation to the Foreign Office was unpredictable so was the brevity of his tenure of that office: a mere 94 days. This was so because Lawson resigned as chancellor of the exchequer on 26 October 1989 (because Mrs Thatcher wouldn't sack her economic adviser, Alan Walters) and Thatcher turned to Major to fill the gap. Major similarly had little time to make his mark, or blot his copybook, at the Treasury, before Geoffrey Howe's resignation from the cabinet precipitated the leadership challenge which resulted in Mrs Thatcher being forced from office. He did, however, have the chance to introduce one budget in which the most eye-catching innovation was the creation of TESSAs (Tax Exempt Special Savings Accounts) to encourage small savers. More importantly, in conjunction with Douglas Hurd, he somewhat improved relations with Europe by floating the idea of the hard Ecu (allowing Ecu notes to circulate as a common currency alongside national currencies) as an alternative to the abrupt adoption of a single European currency (in line with the Delors plan for monetary union) and managed to persuade Mrs Thatcher of the political and economic desirability of Britain entering the Exchange Rate Mechanism, which took place on 5 October 1990: a decision which was to haunt him later on 'Black Wednesday'.

When Geoffrey Howe's resignation speech precipitated a leadership election in which Mrs Thatcher was mortally wounded in the first round and eventually withdrew, Major entered the second round against Hurd and Heseltine. Like Thatcher he was 2 votes short of an outright win, with Hurd securing 56 votes and Heseltine 131 to his 185 (49.7% of the vote). However, they then conceded and Major became party leader and prime minister.

Major's campaign had been 'prolier than thou', contrasting his Brixton background, grammar school education and non-attendance at any university with his rivals' privileged backgrounds (Heseltine having gone from Shrewsbury to Oxford to the Guards and Hurd from Eton to Cambridge to the Diplomatic corps). In some respects Major was, indeed, a throwback to the One Nation Tory tradition of Macmillan, Macleod and Butler who could speak, without any sense of irony, of wishing to build a classless society and a country 'at ease with itself'. However, the reasons why he won in 1990 were rather less philosophical. Firstly, he had just enough experience to appear to be a serious contender without ever having been long enough in a cabinet post to have suffered any serious setbacks. He thus appeared to offer a safe pair of hands. Secondly, he represented the best means of halting the Heseltine bandwagon and a more voter-friendly face for the Conservative Party than Mrs Thatcher's had latterly become. He thus appeared not only as Mrs Thatcher's chosen successor but also as someone much less strident in tone, dogmatic in ideology and autocratic in decision-making.

Major inherited a situation in the Middle East which shortly led to the Gulf War (January–February 1991) in which Britain played a major role in partnership with its allies, of which President Bush's America was the most important. This conflict accomplished its principal objective of evicting Saddam Hussein's forces from Kuwait, thereby punishing aggression and protecting British interests in the region but in retrospect many condemned the 'failure' to push on to Baghdad and overthrow Saddam. However, this was not authorized by the United Nations and would have resulted in the withdrawal of the Arab contingent from the Allied coalition. The plight of the Kurds, who were targeted by Saddam when they, like the Marsh Arabs in the south, vainly tried to overthrow him, excited concerns voiced by Mrs Thatcher which Major dispelled by organizing 'safe havens' for Kurdish refugees in northern Iraq protected by British, American and French forces.

One domestic legacy of the war which emerged shortly afterwards was Gulf war syndrome, which the Major government, on expert advice, largely discountenanced. With the return of peace Major was able to turn his thoughts to domestic policy prior to the general election campaign (having discounted any thoughts of a 'Khaki election' in the Spring of 1991) and launched the Citizen's Charter in a bid to improve the quality of public services: a noble aim but one that was poorly managed in terms of governmental presentation.

Major did, however, win plaudits from both the press and his party for his handling of the negotiations on the Maastricht Treaty as he managed to secure opt-outs for Britain from both the single currency (EMU) and the Social Chapter, whilst Heseltine, as environment secretary, managed to substitute the council tax for the hated poll tax. Nevertheless, the prospects of a fourth consecutive Conservative election victory in April 1992 were not good, not least because of the poor state of the economy. However, the Tories were returned with an overall majority of 21, partly because people found Major on a soapbox shouting down hecklers through a loudspeaker more appealing than the vacuities of a prematurely triumphalist Neil Kinnock at Labour's Sheffield rally but more fundamentally because the Conservatives were able persuasively to portray the 'shadow budget' presented by John Smith as a recipe for higher taxation.

In the event it was Major's government, with Norman Lamont once again serving as chancellor until he was replaced by Ken Clarke in July 1993, which was obliged to put up taxes as well as suffering a series of humiliations and reversals including Black Wednesday, the unpopular coal mine closure programme, damaging splits over Maastricht ratification, BSE and the 'Back to Basics' campaign being undermined by repeated allegations of sleaze. Major's overall majority was whittled away by by-election defeats, defections and disciplining the most extreme Eurosceptic rebels in relation to the European Communities (Finance) Act by temporarily withdrawing the party whip. Moreover, Mrs Thatcher continued to cast a long shadow and there was a whispering campaign against Major from right wingers within the cabinet.

In 1995 Major called the latter's bluff, resigning the leadership and encouraging his critics to 'put up or shut up'. John Redwood resigned as Welsh secretary in order to challenge for the leadership but merely won a moral victory over those like Portillo who decided not to enter the ring at this point. However, Major's reward was to lead the Conservative Party to the 1997 general election when its worst electoral defeat since 1906 (or 1832, according to some calculations).

Major's tenancy of Number 10 Downing Street from November 1990 to May 1997 saw real achievements, of which the most notable was the advance in the peace process but this counted for little in the eyes of the electorate compared with Tory sleaze (such as 'cash for questions' and arms to Iraq), New Labour 'spin' and Black Wednesday destroying the Conservatives' reputation for financial competence.

Manchester School The Manchester School is the name given to the mid-Victorian school of thought propagating the advantages of *laissez-faire* in general and free trade in particular. Its foremost representatives were Richard Cobden and John Bright. It was identified with Manchester because Manchester's wealth was mostly derived from cotton which flourished under free trade conditions, because Manchester was the home of the Anti-Corn Law League, and because Bright represented Manchester between 1847 and 1857.

Cobden and Bright advocated freer trade, lower taxation and a cheaper foreign policy which would avoid acquiring colonial possessions. In the eyes of the Manchester School colonies were a burden to the taxpayer and a potential source of international tension which were maintained partly as a form of outdoor relief for the sons of the aristocracy.

The success of free trade would lead, according to its advocates, to a state of heaven upon earth. Thus Cobden, speaking in the Free Trade Hall, Manchester on 15 July 1846 claimed that the Free Trade principle could act on the moral world like the principle of gravitation in the physical world, 'drawing men together, thrusting aside the antagonism of race, and creed, and language, and uniting us in the bonds of eternal peace ... '.

The repeal of the Corn Laws might have led contemporaries to suppose that the future lay with the Manchester School. This was, however, to misread how repeal came about. Moreover, the invasion scares of 1852 and 1859 helped marginalize the Cobdenite radicals because their identification with the cause of peace was ill suited to a period characterized by anxiety about national security, and made it easy for their critics to brand them as placing commercial considerations above patriotism.

The Manchester School nevertheless profoundly influenced reform politics from the 1840s until the 1860s when it was displaced in this role by the Birmingham of Joseph Chamberlain with his collectivist creed of civic pride.

Marconi scandal, 1913. In March 1910 Herbert Samuel, as postmaster-general in the Asquith government, entered into talks with the English Marconi Company with a view to setting up a chain of wireless stations connecting areas of strategic importance for imperial defence. These negotiations resulted in a contract for this work being submitted to the cabinet and to Parliament. However, rumours began to circulate to the effect that Godfrey Isaacs, the managing director of the company, had sold shares in the Marconi Company of America to his brother, the Attorney General, Sir Rufus Isaacs, and to the chancellor of the exchequer, David Lloyd George. In other words, these two appeared to be standing to profit from privileged information, insofar as the contract awarded to the English Marconi Company would probably produce an increase in the share price of its American mother company. In February 1913 *Le Matin*, broke the story and additionally accused Samuel of being implicated in what it described as a Jewish intrigue. Indeed, much of the criticism of these transactions possessed an anti-Semitic flavour. However, Samuel successfully sued the French newspaper and Asquith stood by his colleagues who had not done anything technically illegal, although they had undoubtedly acted very imprudently.

Married Women's Act, 1882. The 1882 Married Women's Act allowed wives to claim maintenance on the grounds of desertion.

Married Women's Property Act, 1870. One year after the publication of the *Subjection of Women* by John Stuart Mill, the First Gladstone government passed the Married Women's Property Act which recognized the principle that henceforth a married women was entitled to her own property in certain circumstances, namely, when it was inherited, invested, or derived (up to a sum of £200) from paid employment distinct from her husband.

It was an important milestone on the road to the legal recognition of sexual equality although it was not until the 1884 Married Women's Property Act that parity was established in this area.

Married Women's Property Act, 1884. The 1884 Married Women's Property Act repealed the 1870 Act (and amending legislation of 1874) and asserted the principle that married women should enjoy the same property rights as unmarried women. Thus they could keep all the personal property that they brought to a marriage or acquired during its course (rather than this automatically becoming the property of their husbands), and could sue and be sued in their own names in the civil courts.

The Married Women's Property Committee was sufficiently satisfied by the law to wind itself up.

Master and Servant Act, 1867. The Master and Servant Act of 1867 amended existing legislation so as to ensure that strikers could now only be prosecuted for breach of contract. The trade unions remained dissatisfied, however, not only by the language of the Act but because it was still possible for criminal proceedings to take place on the grounds of 'aggravated causes'.

The Master and Servant Act was accordingly repealed by the 1875 Employers and Workmen Act.

Matrimonial Causes Acts Under the terms of the 1857 Matrimonial Causes Act a divorced woman could apply to a magistrate for an order to protect her earnings against the husband who had deserted her or his creditors, and those women officially recognized as separated or divorced acquired the same rights in their own property as unmarried women, enabling them to inherit or bequeath property in their own right. A man could also be ordered by a court to pay maintenance to his divorced or estranged wife.

The Act also established secular divorce in England. Hitherto divorce had only been possible by a private Act of Parliament: a procedure so prohibitively expensive as effectively to place it beyond the reach of the overwhelming majority of the population. Indeed, prior to 1857 only four women had obtained a divorce by this means.

However, the 1857 Act was manifestly biased towards men in one important respect. A husband was able to divorce his wife for adultery but a wife had to prove adultery and either bestiality, bigamy, cruelty, sodomy or long-term desertion: a neat illustration of the sexual double standards of the time.

The 1878 Matrimonial Causes Act empowered magistrates to provide protection orders to wives whose husbands had been convicted of aggravated assault, and enabled women to secure a separation on the grounds of cruelty, as well as entitling them to claim maintenance and custody of any children.

Prior to the 1884 Matrimonial Causes Act, a wife deserted by an adulterous husband had to wait two years before petitioning for a divorce. Henceforth she could begin divorce proceedings immediately. The Act also denied husbands the right to confine their wives if they refused to have sex: a legal position reinforced in 1891 by the Court of Appeal ruling on the Jackson case.

The 1923 Matrimonial Causes Act addressed the double standards in the 1857 Matrimonial Causes Act by stating that adultery provided grounds for divorce for wives as well as husbands. Under the 1969 Matrimonial Causes Act, divorce could now be secured if the 'irretrievable breakdown' of the marriage was established, as indicated by separation of the partners for two years.

Maynooth Grant, 1845. As part of his policy of conciliating moderate Catholic opinion in Ireland in general and the highly influential priesthood in particular, Peel proposed in 1845 to increase the annual grant to the seminary at Maynooth (from £9,000 to £26,000); to make the grant permanent; and to make a special one-off grant of £30,000 for building.

This policy offended a large section of the British public. Thus 1,039 delegates attended an anti-Maynooth Conference in London and 8,922 petitions against the Bill were presented to Parliament. Moreover, it enraged the right-wing Conservatives who regarded it as another betrayal, comparable to Catholic Emancipation, by the one-time 'Orange' Peel. Thus on the Third Reading of the Bill 149 Conservatives voted against the measure and 148 for: the first time a majority of Conservative MPs voted against Peel. Gladstone voted for the measure but quixotically resigned from the government because such a policy ran counter to his published views (in *The State in its Relations with the Church*, 1839) which he had not publicly recanted.

The rebellion within Conservative ranks was insufficient to block the passage of the legislation but helps explain the growing disillusionment with Peel which culminated in the following year with the revolt over the repeal of the Corn Laws and Peel's eventually being forced to resign.

Maurice Debate, 9 May 1918. On 7 May 1918 General (Sir) Frederick Maurice, recently retired from the War Office as director of military operations, Imperial General Staff, wrote to the press alleging that the Commons had been misled at the time of Ludendorff's Spring offensive by statements from Bonar Law regarding extension of the British front and Lloyd George regarding manpower.

The government proposed a confidential judicial inquiry undertaken by three judges but Asquith demanded a Select Committee of the House of Commons, whereupon the government withdrew the offer of an inquiry and decided to treat Asquith's motion as one of confidence, winning the vote by 293 votes to 106.

A few days after the debate Lloyd George's secretaries discovered, in a hitherto unopened red box, conclusive proof that Maurice's claims were correct.

McKenna Duties In 1915 the coalition chancellor, Reginald McKenna, introduced a levy on a number of luxury imports in order to combat excess demand arising from over-full employment, raise revenue and improve the exchange rate of the pound relative to the dollar. This was symbolically significant as marking the first move away from free trade and towards protection since the heyday of Gladstonian finance.

Presented as a temporary wartime expedient (rather like income tax during the French Revolutionary and Napoleonic wars) the duties were removed in 1925 only to be almost immediately reintroduced by Churchill in order to facilitate the reintroduction of the gold standard.

Means-Test The means-test most famously assessed a person's entitlement to unemployment benefit by taking their income into consideration.

In 1929 the Poor Law guardians were replaced by Public Assistance Committees (PACs), who assumed the responsibility for administering relief to the unemployed. However, the perceived need to cut public spending radically at this time meant that these committees used their powers to target the most needy by applying an especially rigorous household or family means-test. This meant that all sources of income within the family were taken into account from an aged parent's pension to a child's paper round earnings.

There were enormous regional variations in the scale and conditions of benefits but universal revulsion at the inquisitorial methods of the means-test men. The transfer of responsibility for the means-test from the Public Assistance Committees of local authorities to a national Unemployment Assistance Board in 1934 addressed the former problem but not the latter. This means-test was discontinued in 1942.

Melbourne, William Lamb, second Viscount (15 March 1779–24 November 1848). As the second son of Peniston Lamb, the 1st Viscount Melbourne, William Lamb was not intended for a political career and was called to the Bar in 1804 after Eton and Trinity College, Cambridge. However, the death of his elder brother in the following year made him heir to the title and in 1806 he entered the House of Commons as MP for Leominster.

It also had the effect of making him an eligible match for Lady Caroline Ponsonby (the only daughter of the 3rd Earl of Bessborough), who became Lady Caroline Lamb in 1805. William and Caroline's personalities can be regarded as respectively embodying the classical and romantic temperaments. Certainly the marriage was soon in difficulties with Caroline's indiscretions (most notably with Lord Byron) making her the talk of Society and the embarrassment of her husband.

It is impossible to gauge the precise extent that William's private difficulties impinged upon his public career but it was not until 1827 that an offer from Canning enabled him to take office as secretary for Ireland. As an advocate of Catholic Emancipation Melbourne (as he became on his father's death in 1828) commended himself to the mass of the Irish people but the feeling was not reciprocated when the granting of Catholic Emancipation in 1829 failed to pacify the Irish and Melbourne increasingly came to regard the intractable nature of the Irish Question as having its roots in 'the natural disposition of the people'.

Melbourne, unlike fellow Canningites such as Grant and Palmerston, did not serve even briefly in the administration of the Duke of Wellington (1828–30) but like them joined the predominantly Whig administration of Earl Grey in 1830, as home secretary. In this role he oversaw the suppression of the Captain Swing rioters in 1830–31 and showed no greater clemency towards the Tolpuddle martyrs in 1834.

When the party fell into disarray over lay appropriation and Grey resigned in 1834, it was Melbourne whom William IV invited to take his place as prime minister. Melbourne regarded this as a duty rather than a pleasure but managed to hold the administration together so that apart from a few months in the winter of 1834–35 he held office for the next seven years.

Melbourne was a Whig by tradition but deeply conservative by temperament as shown by his statement that 'I am for holding the ground already taken but not for occupying new ground rashly'. It would therefore be pointless to anticipate that his administration would be characterized by massive innovation, and Melbourne's refusal to reappoint the reforming Brougham or Durham in 1835 indicated his preference for doing little or nothing. There were some reforms of note but these were mostly the work of the liberal Anglican Whigs. Melbourne chiefly concerned himself after 1837 with acting as mentor to the young Queen Victoria.

Ironically, the increasing dependence of the Whigs upon Radical and Irish support (as advertised by the Lichfield House compact), through the departure of the Derby Dilly and losses at the 1835 and 1837 general elections, gave increasing credibility to Conservative claims that the Whigs were a dog wagged by a Radical-Irish tail, which further alienated moderate Whigs and hastened the decline of Melbourne's parliamentary majority until Peel won the chance of forming a minority administration in 1839, at the time of the Bedchamber crisis, and eventually succeeded in winning a majority at the 1841 general election.

Melbourne left the country in economic depression, threatened by Chartism and with the national finances in disorder (1841 being the fifth successive year of government deficit). His legacy with regards to training Victoria were more ambiguous. In some respects he schooled her in the ways of constitutional monarchy, in others he may be said to have confirmed or even bred in her a spirit of partisanship which ran directly contrary to her constitutional role. He was not the last prime minister to have been born in the eighteenth century but he may be regarded as the last prime minister whose outlook was almost entirely shaped by that time.

Merchant Shipping Act, 1876. The Merchant Shipping Act began life as a private member's bill sponsored by the Liberal MP for Derby, Samuel Plimsoll. It addressed the problem caused by unscrupulous shipping companies routinely overloading their ships. Disraeli originally mis-read the public mood and opposed the measure but was eventually persuaded of the merits of marking ships with a line (which came to be called the Plimsoll Line), which would indicate to the port authorities if a ship was overloaded (although it was not until 1890 that the legislation was tightened so as to take the placing of the Plimsoll Line out of the hands of the ship owner).

Metropolitan Police Act, 1829. In 1829 Robert Peel as home secretary created the first standing police force on mainland Britain in order to combat the rising crime wave in the metropolis. He drew upon his experiences as Irish chief secretary in passing the 1814 Peace Preservation Act. Partly to allay fears of a threat to civil liberties, and to enlist the cooperation of the citizenry, the police were armed with nothing more than a truncheon and were given a uniform which more closely resembled civilian than military dress.

The 1829 Metropolitan Police Act applied only to the metropolis, excluding the City of London. The force was financed through local rates levied by the overseers of the poor. Two Commissioners with headquarters at Scotland Yard had operational responsibility, whilst the home secretary had overall direction of the force and was answerable to parliament.

Midlothian campaigns, 1879–80 See GLADSTONE.

Militant/Militant Tendency Militant or the Revolutionary Socialist League was a Trotskyite group associated with the *Militant Tendency* newspaper, which gained entry to the Labour Party in order to render its members more electable and push Labour policy sharply leftwards. Assisted by Bennite reforms of the party's organization such as enhanced powers for deselecting MPs, it also experienced considerable success in the realms of local government, most notably under Derek Hatton on Merseyside. However, Neil Kinnock effectively declared war on *Militant Tendency* at the 1985 Labour Party Conference and its power diminished as most of its members were expelled from the Labour Party.

Mines and Collieries Act, 1842. The 1842 Mines Act prohibited the employment of females and boys under the age of ten underground, and specified that winding gear was only to be operated by those over the age of fifteen. Opposition from mine owners in the House of Lords was, however, successful in removing clauses relating to reports on the safety of mines and machinery, which were not made law until the 1850 Mines Act was placed on the statute book.

Mines Regulation Act, 1872. The 1872 Mines Regulation Act prohibited the full-time employment of boys under the age of twelve in coal mines and specified that those aged between ten and thirteen had to attend school on one half-day each week. This represented the first significant reduction in the employment of young children in mines.

Mosley, Sir Oswald Ernald, sixth baronet (16 November 1896–3 December 1980). Oswald Ernald Mosley (who became known as 'Tom' to his intimates) was the eldest of the three sons of Oswald Mosley, who was in turn the eldest son of Sir Oswald Mosley, the fourth baronet of Rolleston Hall, Burton-on-Trent. The family was an old landed Staffordshire one. Mosley's parents separated when he was five and he spent much time thereafter with his mother and his paternal grandfather.

Educated at West Down and Winchester, Mosley developed into a fine athlete, winning the public schools championship at sabre and foil at the age of fifteen. In January 1914 he entered Sandhurst and shortly after the outbreak of World War One was commissioned into the 16th Lancers. Joining the Royal Flying Corps, he acted as an observer with the 6th Squadron from December 1914 to April 1915 but broke his ankle in the course of trying to obtain his pilot's licence. He returned to the trenches but his injury worsened to such a point that in March 1916 he was invalided out of the service with a severe and permanent limp.

He spent some time working in the Ministry of Munitions and in the Foreign Office but also became well known in high society and was encouraged by F. E. Smith (later Earl of Birkenhead) and Sir George Younger (later Viscount Younger of Leckie) to contest the Harrow Division of Middlesex in the Conservative interest in the coupon election of 1918. He won the seat, becoming the youngest member of the House, and further enhanced his political prospects by winning the hand of Lady Cynthia Blanche, second daughter of the Conservative grandee and then foreign secretary, Lord Curzon. They married on 11 May 1920 and became the toast of high society.

Mosley became an ardent champion of the League of Nations. However, it was opposition to the coalition government's Irish policy in general, and the operations of the Black and Tans in particular, which led, in late 1920, to his taking the dramatic action of crossing the floor of the House and sitting on the opposition benches. In the 1922 general election he was returned for his old seat as an independent. The whole affair illustrated Mosley's scorn for conventional party divisions and confidence in his own abilities: features that remained constant throughout his turbulent political career.

In March 1924, two months after Ramsay MacDonald formed the first (minority) Labour government, Mosley joined the Labour Party, and became a member of the ILP. He narrowly failed to defeat Neville Chamberlain at Birmingham Ladywood later that year but won the December 1926 Smethwick by-election. In the meantime he had shored up his grass roots support by active work on behalf of the striking miners whilst investing much emotional and intellectual capital (alongside John Strachey) into developing what were then highly unconventional economic policies much influenced by the thought of John Maynard Keynes.

In 1928 he succeeded to the baronetcy and the following year became Chancellor of the Duchy of Lancaster in MacDonald's second administration, with the brief of assisting J. H. Thomas, the Lord Privy Seal, in addressing the unemployment problem. The latter, however, like the chancellor, Snowden, and indeed most men in public life at the time favoured classical political economy. The Mosley memorandum of 1930 accordingly advocated extensive public works as part of a programme of state intervention to assist economic recovery, and was rejected by the Cabinet. Mosley responded by resigning on 20 May 1930 and on 1 March 1931 launched the New Party. Mosley and four other MPs (including his wife, who had been elected in 1929) remained in Parliament under the new banner but in the October 1931 elections all twenty-four candidates were defeated and in October 1932, following a visit to Mussolini's Italy, Mosley launched the British Union of Fascists.

With the fallout from the Wall St Crash making capitalism appear a busted flush and with confidence in his own charismatic appeal and a growing detestation of conventional party politics, Mosley persuaded himself that he could seize control of the levers of power and rescue Britain from its current economic and political malaise. Nor was he alone in this vision, with the likes of Lords Morris and Rothermere prepared to give the movement their blessing and backing. However, the violence at the great Olympia meeting in June 1934 and the adoption of increasingly overt anti-Semitism alienated more than it attracted, particularly amongst the respectable middle classes. By turning to the streets Mosley increasingly occupied the gutter and by 1936 the renamed 'British Union of Fascists and National Socialists' was, as its name suggests, increasingly influenced by Nazism. Lady Cynthia Mosley had died of peritonitis in 1933 and Hitler attended the wedding, at Berlin in October 1936, of Mosley to the Hon. Mrs Diana Guinness, one of the Mitford sisters.

From that year the BUF warned of the approaching war between Nazi Germany and Britain as a national tragedy engineered by the Jews: a viewpoint which, together with the initial threat of Nazi invasion, earned Mosley and his new wife detention from May 1940 until November 1943, when they were released into house arrest, the threat of invasion having disappeared and Mosley's health having declined.

From 1948 to 1966 Mosley led the Union Movement, which advocated European unity on racial grounds, and sought to exculpate his pre-war politics. He was encouraged by the Notting Hill race riots to contest North Kensington in 1959 but lost his deposit and was similarly unsuccessful at Shoreditch in 1966. He died at his home in France in 1980.

Mosley was a young man in a hurry, whose arrogance and impatience habitually frustrated his ambition. He was thus a 'coming man' who never arrived.

Mundella Education Act, 1880. The Foster Education Act of 1870 had empowered school boards to compel attendance by elementary schoolchildren and by 1876 half of the school population of five to twelve year olds were thus obliged to attend board schools. The Mundella Education Act, recognizing the increasing desirability of providing an elementary education if Britain was to compete effectively with rivals such as Germany, made school compulsory for all five to ten year olds.

Municipal Corporations Act, 1835. The Great Reform Act of 1832 stimulated local government reform insofar as it appeared anomalous that some of those now able to exercise a vote nationally should be denied that privilege locally, and it was widely felt that reform of corrupt corporations was required in the interests of national as well as local politics. Thus in July 1833 a Royal Commission was established to examine the question.

The Commission's secretary, Joseph Parkes, one of the Philosophic Radicals, played a major role alongside J. R. Drinkwater in drafting the ensuing legislation, which was introduced to parliament by Lord John Russell. Moreover, Peel worked with Melbourne to negotiate a compromise which ensured that the Act represented a landmark in local government reform.

The principal features of the Act, which affected 178 corporations in England and Wales, were that town councillors were henceforth to be elected for three-year terms by all male ratepayers of three years' residence; one-third of the council was to be elected annually after the council was first elected; the councillors elected one-third of their number to be aldermen to serve six-year terms; and councillors and aldermen collectively elected a mayor each year. All debates were to be open and all accounts publicly audited. Councils were obliged to form a watch committee and create a borough police force and were empowered to levy a rate for purposes such as street paving and refuse collection.

Those urban centres, which were not directly affected by the Act because not incorporated, could apply for incorporation. In the course of the next twenty years twenty-two were incorporated, including Manchester and Birmingham in 1838.

In total it is estimated that the Municipal Corporations Act enfranchised 20–25% more people than the 1832 Reform Act. This extension of democracy particularly benefited the urban Dissenting middle class at the expense of the old, predominantly Tory, self-perpetuating oligarchies.

Murder (Abolition of Death Penalty) Act, 1965. The Murder (Abolition of Death Penalty) Bill, which began life as a Private Member's Bill from Labour backbencher Sydney Silverman, proposed a trial abolition of the death penalty.

Amendments to retain hanging for crimes such as a second murder or the murder of a policeman or prison officer failed. However, two safeguards were introduced which went some way towards satisfying critics. The first required both Houses of Parliament to declare that the Act be extended by affirmative resolution before 31 July 1970 (which was done in December 1969), whilst the second empowered judges to recommend a minimum period before a convicted murderer could be released.

N

National Convention (4 February 1839–6 September 1839). The 'National Convention of the Industrious Classes' was a body consisting of elected delegates, who met to decide upon the best means of implementing the People's Charter. It ran parallel to the Westminster Parliament and as the delegates considered their body to be the more genuinely representative of the two, some of them proudly placed the letters 'NC' after their names.

The Convention initially met in London, the birthplace of the Charter, but soon adjourned to Birmingham, which Thomas Attwood and the Birmingham Political Union had turned into a provincial stronghold of the movement. However, the Convention reflected the deep divisions within the movement, particularly over what tactics to adopt in response to parliament's rejection of the first Chartist petition, which duly occurred on 12 July 1839.

On 1 July the Convention adjourned and called upon the localities to make their preferred chose of tactics known to their delegates. Back in Birmingham on 4 July there were disturbances in the Bull Ring, which were suppressed by troops and it dissolved in confusion on 6 September.

National Front (NF) The National Front was formed in 1967 out of a merger between A. K. Chesterton's League of Empire Loyalists, the British National Party and members of the Racial Preservation Society, and was joined shortly afterwards by the Greater Britain Movement. Its high point was in the early 1970s. Thereafter its influence has waned not least because of disagreements among its leaders, notably Martin Webster and John Tyndall, the latter leaving to set up what became the British National Party.

National Health Service charges In 1951 Hugh Gaitskell proposed small NHS charges to help towards the £4,700m rearmament budget for 1951–54 which had effectively been forced upon the Attlee government as the price of involvement in the Korean War and an American pledge to consult its allies on the use of nuclear weapons. However, Bevan was opposed to this proposal on principle whilst the fact that he had been passed over as chancellor by Gaitskell, who was his junior, in October 1950 added an element of frustrated ambition to the clash.

In March 1951 the ailing Bevin persuaded Gaitskell to abandon prescription charges in return for increased dental and ophthalmic charges and in April Morrison, acting as prime minister whilst Attlee was indisposed, got Gaitskell to concede further that the charges would not be levied immediately and would only last for a year in the first instance.

These concessions were sufficient to mollify most of the cabinet but Bevan was not in a mood to be reconciled and duly resigned on 20 April. His departure marked a rift in Labour ranks which was only patched up in the aftermath of Suez and which helped the Conservatives to victory in the 1951 and 1955 general elections.

National Health Service creation, 1948. The National Health Service (NHS) was set up by Aneurin Bevan in 1948 to deliver universal medical care free at the point of need. Bevan was without ministerial experience but had the example of the Emergency Medical Service (set up in the aftermath of Munich) to show how a national health service could be run.

Municipal and voluntary hospitals were both taken into public ownership and administered through regional health boards (despite a rearguard action in cabinet by Chuter Ede and Herbert Morrison in favour of the policy of municipalization).

The NHS was only created after bitter disputes with the British Medical Association and other professional bodies which bitterly resented the idea of general practitioners becoming full-time salaried civil servants or consultants being denied the opportunity to engage in private practice. Sir Alfred (later Lord) Webb-Johnson and Lord Moran, respectively the Royal College presidents for the surgeons and physicians, helped arrange a compromise and Bevan ultimately succeeded in pacifying the medical profession with merit awards for doctors, on top of the basic salary, and by allowing part-time consultants to continue to treat private patients in NHS 'pay beds'. Thus five weeks from the launch of the NHS the doctors formally agreed to take part.

Bevan's brainchild boldly broke with the insurance principle, whereby entitlement followed contribution and instead was largely tax-financed. However, the consequence of this has been that NHS finances have always been problematical, so that NHS charges were introduced as early as 1951 and radical restructuring to break the monolithic structure of health care provision was attempted under Mrs Thatcher (although the impetus came from Nigel Lawson). These reforms included the 'contracting out' of certain services (such as cleaning and laundering); the creation of the 'internal market' (so that money followed patients even if they sought treatment outside their own health authority); allowing hospitals to become self-governing; the creation of GP (General Practitioner) fund-holding (giving practices control over their own budgets); and the compilation and publication of lists for waiting times.

National Insurance Act, 1911. The 1911 National Insurance Act was principally the work of three men: Winston Churchill, David Lloyd George and William Beveridge. It involved the world's first statutory insurance scheme against unemployment and the first state-backed health insurance scheme in Britain.

At first the unemployment scheme ran out after fifteen weeks and covered only about a sixth of the workforce, namely, those workmen in industries such as iron and steel and shipbuilding where there was a high risk of cyclical unemployment.

The health scheme, by contrast, covered all male workers earning below £160 per annum but there was no cover for wives or children other than a maternity grant. Under the so-called tripartite system workers, employers and taxpayers all had to contribute to the insurance fund, with the workers' fourpence per week matched by threepence from the employer and twopence from the state. Lloyd George thus represented this as 'Ninepence for Fourpence' (or just over 3.5p for just under 2p).

'Approved societies' administered the scheme and provided the services of a 'panel' family doctor. Sick pay was at the rate of ten shillings (50p) per week.

Daniel Benjamin and Levis Kochin claim that the generous provision of benefit under the 1911 National Insurance Act effectively subsidized inter-war unemployment to the tune of five to eight percentage points. Their estimates have been disputed, although most historians of the period are prepared to admit that the insurance system contributed to the phenomenon whereby a relatively large number repeatedly moved into and out of the unemployment pool, experiencing relatively short spells on the dole. This is not, however, to deny the existence of a substantial number of long-term unemployed, comprising many, like those who engaged on the Jarrow March, who were the victims of structural unemployment.

National Insurance Act, 5 July 1946. The 1946 National Insurance Act was inspired by the 1942 Beveridge Report, although there were some departures from its recommendations. For example, Beveridge had suggested that instead of unemployment benefit being paid for the first six months it should be provided indefinitely (subject to attendance at a work or training centre after a specified period). However, the Attlee government rejected this proposal in favour of a limit of twelve months.

National Liberal Federation (NLF) In a move widely condemned by contemporaries as 'caucus politics' or the 'Americanization' of British politics, Joseph Chamberlain created the National Liberal Federation (popularly known as 'the Caucus') in Birmingham in 1877. This body united local Liberal Associations with a view to counteracting Whig influence within the party, placing more radical policies higher up the political agenda and promoting Chamberlain's own profile. The NLF succeeded in all these aims to a certain extent, although when the Liberal Party split over Irish Home Rule in 1886 it backed Gladstone (who had attended its first meeting) rather than Chamberlain, and relocated to London.

The NLF's radical credentials were reaffirmed in 1891 when its conference adopted the Newcastle Programme.

National Service, 1948–63. Ernest Bevin was strongly in favour of retaining conscription after the war in order to enable Britain to meet its global defence commitments. The need for men was certainly pressing because in addition to the responsibilities of the largest empire the world had ever seen, the British were also contributing substantial forces to the occupation of Austria and Germany.

National service was based upon the principle of equality of sacrifice and the 1948 National Service Act made every male citizen aged between 18 and 26, who was not declared medically incapable, liable to 18 months' compulsory active military service, with 4 years in the reserve. In 1950 this changed to 2 years service with three and a half years in the reserve. For every National Service sailor, there were 12 airmen and 33 soldiers.

The medically unfit and certain skilled workers were exempt from service, whilst apprentices and university students could defer. Conscientious objectors could also escape service, although the numbers who did so were very small (4 in every 1,000 on average).

After 8 weeks' basic training recruits could apply for officer selection. Between 1949 and 1963, 395 officers and men were killed in action, mostly in Malaya, Cyprus, Kenya and Korea, where National Servicemen comprised 10% of the British contingent.

The 1957 Defence White Paper presented by defence secretary Duncan Sandys announced a scaling down of conventional forces in favour of increasing reliance upon nuclear weapons. National Service recruitment accordingly ended on 31 December 1960 and the last group of conscripts were demobilized in May 1963.

National Society The National Society's full name was the National Society for Promoting the Education of the Poor in the Principles of the Established Church and was founded in 1811 to provide an Anglican education in church schools. It emerged in response to the creation of the nonconformist British and Foreign Schools Society in the previous year and their rivalry plagued religious education until the 1944 Butler Education Act.

New Departure, 1879. It was Fintan Lalor who first prophesied that the land question would be the engine that would pull the national question in its train but it was Michael Davitt who gave practical impetus to this insight by means of the so-called 'New Departure'.

This consisted in Fenianism (represented by Davitt in Ireland and John Devoy and the Clan Na Gael organization in the United States) joining hands with the constitutional movement (represented at Westminster by Charles Stewart Parnell) mobilizing the Catholic Irish tenantry through the Land League in order to challenge the Protestant Ascendancy.

The New Departure was timely because economic conditions conspired to threaten the already precarious situation of those engaged on the land in Ireland. Agriculture throughout the British Isles was hit by foreign competition, particularly from America, arising from improvements in shipping. This agricultural depression not only hit the Irish directly but also meant that there were reduced opportunities for seasonal migrant labour to supplement their wages on the mainland. The final straws comprised poor harvests in 1877 and 1878 and the failure of the potato crop in 1879. The net result was that many tenants found themselves unable to repay loans or meet rent payments.

New Journalism Matthew Arnold coined the term 'The New Journalism' to apply to the work of William Thomas Stead and George Newnes which wrapped sensationalism in a social conscience. The *Pall Mall Gazette*, which Stead edited from 1880, also acted as a prototype for the popular press in a number of presentational innovations including strong cross-headlines, the use of maps and diagrams, interviews, gossip columns and a stop press section.

New Labour Just as Peel sought to re-label and repackage the Tory party as the Conservative Party in the 1830s because it had become unable to form a viable administration under Wellington, so Tony Blair re-branded the Labour Party as New Labour in the 1990s in the belief (vindicated on 1 May 1997) that this would render it re-electable after its wilderness years following the 'winter of discontent', the embarrassments of the 'loony left', and the defection of the Social Democrats.

New Liberalism The New Liberalism emerged in the late nineteenth century and had its heyday in the Edwardian period. It was associated with intellectuals such as John Hobson, Lionel Hobhouse and Graham Wallas, and politicians such as David Lloyd George, Charles Masterman and Winston Churchill.

Whereas hitherto the Liberal Party had chiefly concerned itself with extending the liberties of the individual, the New Liberals were critical of a *laissez-faire* approach and sought instead to create the rudiments of a welfare state to provide a safety net or lifebelt for the more vulnerable members of society. In practice this meant that whereas Gladstonian Liberalism was orientated towards the middle class, the New Liberalism was orientated towards the working class (and those members of the middle classes sensitive to their needs).

This clearly made sense in view of the progressive extension of the franchise and has led some historians, such as P. F. Clarke, to argue that the New Liberalism offered a viable means of the Liberal Party escaping the fate of being squeezed out of existence between the Labour and Conservative parties. The question turns upon the strength of the Asquith government prior to the outbreak of World War One and whether the People's Budget, with its taxation of land values, is regarded as ushering in a new style of politics or whether the Parliament Act opened the door to a reversion to Gladstonian politics by making Irish Home Rule a real possibility.

New Model unionism In the 1850s and 1860s a new type of trade union and a new breed of trade unionist emerged. The latter ultimately became known as 'the Junta' and the unions such as the Amalgamated Society of Engineers (founded 1851) and the Amalgamated Society of Carpenters and Joiners (founded 1860), which they served as full-time, paid, London-based secretaries, were amalgamated unions of highly-skilled, relatively well-paid and respectable craftsmen who had turned their backs upon the old secretive union clubs whose strong-arm tactics were on the margins of legality when they weren't downright criminal.

Under the inspired leadership of such men as William Allen (secretary of the ASE) and Robert Applegarth (secretary of the ASCJ) the new model trade unions favoured argument and arbitration rather than industrial or criminal action and were thus able to distance themselves from those responsible for the Sheffield outrages and persuade three sympathetic members of the 1867 commission of inquiry (Robert Hughes, Frederic Harrison and the Earl of Lichfield) to publish a minority report which provided the basis for the 1871 Trade Union Act which gave unions legal protection against embezzlement of their funds.

New Poor Law See POOR LAW AMENDMENT ACT, 1834.

New Unionism The 'New Unionism' of 1888–90 was characterized by a greater militancy by those groups of unskilled or semi-skilled workers (such as dockers and gas workers) who were hitherto poorly organized or whose unions were not recognized by employers and by the formulation of national rather than local agreements.

The New Unionism helps to account for the rapid expansion of the trade union movement (doubling its numbers, 1889–91) and for several major strikes, including the 1889 London Dock Strike.

Newcastle programme, 1891. On 2 October 1891 Gladstone gave his blessing to the Newcastle programme, which was formulated by the National Liberal Federation in an attempt to rally those elements in the party who felt that their pet subjects for reform were being marginalized by the commitment to Ireland. Thus alongside a commitment to Irish Home Rule the programme's proposals included Welsh Disestablishment, land law reform, the ending or mending of the House of Lords, local control of liquor traffic, the payment of MPs, and local government reform.

Adoption of the programme enabled Gladstone to rally the party but allowed the Unionists to claim that the Liberal Party had succumbed to collectivism and socialism. It signified the extent to which the 1886 split over Irish Home Rule had moved the Gladstonian Liberal Party to the left as a result of the departure of the Whigs and provided an early indication of frustration with the millstone of Irish Home Rule which was later expressed by the Liberal Imperialists on the right of the party.

Newport rising, 3 November 1839. The Newport rising was the last act of insurrection on mainland Britain and the last full-blown manifestation of physical force Chartism. The rising's immediate aim was to free Chartist colleagues held prisoner in the Westgate Hotel in Newport (then in Monmouthshire and now in the county of Gwent). Success would then act, it was hoped, as a signal for a national uprising. However, only two of the three columns converging on Newport met at the assembly point. Thus they arrived later than planned in Newport, drenched by heavy rain, and obliged to attack in daylight rather than at night. Moreover, the authorities had not only sworn in special constables but also drafted in a company of the 45th Regiment. At least ten Chartists were shot dead and roughly two hundred were subsequently arrested. The three ringleaders – John Frost, Zephaniah Williams and William Jones – were convicted of high treason, but their sentence was then commuted to transportation for life. In March 1854 they were pardoned conditionally, and in 1855 unconditionally. Both Jones and Williams remained in Australia but John Frost returned home to a hero's welcome in 1856.

Nightingale, Florence (12 May 1820–13 August 1910). Florence Nightingale was the eldest daughter of parents who were well connected with both the aristocracy and the liberal-intellectual bourgeoisie. She showed in 1844 that she had a mind of her own when she decided to dedicate her life to nursing – a profession then held in very low regard – and managed, in 1852, to persuade her father to grant her an allowance of £500 per annum and to allow her to become the Superintendent of the Harley Street Hospital for Gentlewomen.

She made her mark on the national stage in 1854 when the Crimean War broke out and she persuaded her friend, the secretary at war, Sidney Herbert, to send her to the Scutari military hospital to tend to the wounded and ill there. She transformed conditions at the hospital in the face of incompetence and hostility from the Army's Chief of Medical Staff, Dr Hall and the legend of 'The Lady with the Lamp' was born.

In 1856 she returned to Britain so exhausted that she was henceforth effectively an invalid. Her spirit, however, was undaunted whilst the enormous prestige that she enjoyed gave her considerable influence. £45,000 was subscribed to a Florence Nightingale Fund which enabled her to establish both St Thomas's Hospital and a Training School for Nurses in London (entrants to the profession also being fortified by her 'Notes on Nursing').

She continued to push for reforms, securing a Royal Commission on Army Medical Organization which successfully recommended reforms in the construction and superintendence of barracks and military hospitals, the establishment of an Army Medical School and the creation of a Statistical Branch to provide the data to establish the need for further improvements.

She was also the prime mover behind the Royal Commission on the Health of the Army in India, which proposed far-reaching sanitary reform but which was not implemented because of the fall of the Liberals in 1866. It nevertheless became the convention for Indian Viceroys to seek an audience with her before taking up their post.

A legend in her own lifetime, she became the first woman to receive the Order of Merit, in 1907. Shortly after her death, Lytton Strachey sought to debunk that legend and pour ridicule on her achievements in his *Eminent Victorians.* He was not entirely successful, although he has inspired a series of more scholarly imitators, the most distinguished of whom is F. B. Smith. His misreading of Nightingale, or at least of the primary sources relating to her work, has been exposed by the editor of the *Collected Works of Florence Nightingale*, Lynn McDonald.

'Non-conformist conscience' Whilst the Anglican Church was traditionally referred to as the Tory party at prayer, non-conformity (or non-Anglican Protestantism) was particularly associated with the Liberal Party and the non-conformist conscience which publicly moralized from this perspective affected both the style and substance of Liberal politics. Cobden, Bright and Joseph Chamberlain all sought to present themselves at various times as articulating the non-conformist conscience but no one exploited it to better effect than Gladstone, notably through his great moral crusades such as the Bulgarian atrocities agitation.

'Non-conformist revolt', 1874. The 'non-conformist conscience' was certainly vexed by Forster's Education Act of 1870 and by the Irish University Bill presented to parliament by Gladstone in 1873. The former agitated the Education League, which particularly disliked Clause 25, whilst the latter was defeated by three votes as the result of a backbench rebellion. However, some claimed that non-conformist disaffection with Gladstonian Liberalism ran so deep that their revolt effectively cost him the 1874 election. Certainly, party divisions led to unauthorized Liberals standing for 34 seats, whilst Francis Adams, the historian of the Education League, estimated that non-conformist abstentions at the polls cost the Liberals about 20 seats. However, the causes of Gladstone's defeat run much wider, whilst Arthur Peel, the Liberal chief whip, estimated that only 13 seats were lost due to interventions by unauthorized candidates and H. J. Hanham has also qualified the significance of any non-conformist revolt by pointing out that non-conformist voters tended to be concentrated in the under-represented cities of the Midlands and North.

'No Rent Manifesto', 1881. William O'Brien, the editor of the *United Ireland* newspaper (which appealed to the more extremist supporters of Charles Stewart Parnell by its denunciations of both the coercive and reformist legislation of the Second Gladstone government), drafted the 'No Rent Manifesto' and persuaded the mostly imprisoned leaders of the Land League to sign it. The document called for the non-payment of rent by tenants 'until the Government relinquishes the existing system of terrorism and restores the constitutional rights of the people'. This appeal was sufficiently effective for it to help persuade the government to negotiate the Kilmainham Treaty with Parnell, although not before the government had suppressed the Land League and seen it succeeded by more extreme organizations, such as the Ladies' Land League.

Northcote–Trevelyan Report, 1853
See COMPETITIVE EXAMINATIONS FOR THE CIVIL SERVICE.

O

Obscene Publications Act, 1959. In 1959 Roy Jenkins guided the Obscene Publications Bill through parliament. The Act allowed the publication of material hitherto considered obscene if it could be shown to possess 'redeeming social merit'.

The first real test of the new legislation came with Penguin's 1960 paperback edition of D. H. Lawrence's *Lady Chatterley's Lover.* Mervyn Griffith-Jones for the prosecution famously inquired of the jury, 'Is this a book that you would ... wish your wife or your servants to read?' Having heard all the evidence, the jury answered in the affirmative and *Lady Chatterley* went on to sell 2 million copies for Penguin in the next two years, spearheading the 'Paperback Revolution' whereby the book-reading public bought rather than borrowed their reading matter.

O'Connell, Daniel (6 August 1775–15 May 1847). Daniel O'Connell's family came from old Gaelic West Kerry landowning stock, although his father, Morgan O'Connell, was a general storekeeper, farmer and businessman. The oldest of 10 children, Daniel (and his brother, Maurice) was adopted by his uncle Maurice (who was nicknamed Hunting Cap) at the age of 4. After preparatory school at St Omer in France he moved on to the English College at Douai but it was decided to cut short his education there, after just 5 months, following the execution of Louis XVI.

In 1794 Daniel enrolled in Lincoln's Inn, returning to Dublin in December 1796 in order to keep terms at King's Inn so as to be called to the Irish Bar, which duly occurred in 1798. At this stage in his life O'Connell was a deist (returning to Catholicism in 1809) but tolerant of those with religious faith and a radical but one who favoured moral force rather than violence. He was accordingly critical of the rebellion by the United Irishmen in 1798 and Robert Emmet's Dublin insurrection of 1803.

His increasingly prosperous legal career also encouraged him to rebel against his family, secretly marrying his penniless distant cousin, Mary O'Connell, in 1802, and rejecting their pro-Union politics. He moved into politics himself in 1804, serving as a member of the committee preparing Lord Fingall's petition to parliament for full or unqualified Catholic Emancipation. The petition failed but it initiated a campaign in which O'Connell was finally, in 1815, successful both in persuading the Catholic Church in Ireland to enter secular politics in support of full Emancipation and in establishing himself in the public eye as leader of the popular wing of the Irish Catholic movement. O'Connell's personal courage was revealed and his popularity enhanced in February 1815, when he duelled with John D'Esterre, a crack shot and member of the Dublin Corporation, an Orange stronghold, whom he managed to hit. He was later prevented by the authorities from a similar duel with 'Orange' Peel. However, he managed to inflict a lasting wound by describing Peel's smile as like the gleam of silver plate on a coffin lid.

O'Connell proceeded to pioneer mass constitutional politics through the medium of the Catholic Association. His legal training proved invaluable in enabling him to antagonize the authorities without making it easy for them to arrest him. The Association was extremely successful in recruiting members, in raising funds (through the Catholic Rent) and in publicizing its cause.

O'Connell's tactics were twofold, arising from the fact that he was addressing two distinct audiences. The Catholic Irish were roused by appeals to natural justice, whilst the British or English were left in no doubt that civil unrest or even repeal of the Union would be the consequence of ignoring legitimate Irish claims and refusing concessions.

The 'Bolívar' speech of 1824 illustrated O'Connell's use of sedition by innuendo, stating his hope that if Ireland 'were driven mad by persecution he wished that a new Bolívar may be found … and that the spirit of the Greeks and of the South Americans may animate the people of Ireland'. The authorities put O'Connell on trial for sedition after this speech was reported only to see their case collapse when the journalist upon whose published account the government had based its case, swore on oath that in fact he'd been asleep during the proceedings.

However, the authorities did make life more difficult for O'Connell in the following year by taking steps to outlaw the Catholic Association (and all political associations of more than 14 days' duration). This forced the Association into a pre-emptive dissolution and meant that the Catholic Rent went uncollected between March 1825 and June 1826, when the Association was reconstituted under a slightly different banner ('the Order of Liberators').

June 1826 was also significant because the general election of that month allowed O'Connell to appreciate the willingness of the 40s (£2) freeholders to stand up to their landlords: a willingness which O'Connell utilized in the 1828 County Clare by-election in order to defeat the popular Protestant landlord and incumbent MP, Vesey Fitzgerald, by 2,057 votes to 982. This victory persuaded Wellington and Peel to concede Catholic Emancipation, albeit with the greatest reluctance. The suppression of the Catholic Association and the raising of the Irish county franchise from 40s to £10 per annum, which accompanied the measure, appeared to be a small price to pay for this achievement.

One by-product of the Great Reform Act was the creation of an 'Irish Party' under O'Connell, numbering about forty-five of the 105 Irish members. This bloc was sufficiently powerful to persuade Melbourne to woo O'Connell by means of the 'Lichfield House Compact', whereby the Whigs, Irish and Radicals agreed to cooperate against Peel's Conservatives. In practical terms this meant that O'Connell secured concessions such as the 1836 Tithe Act. However, alliance with the Irish added to Melbourne's unpopularity on the mainland and was instrumental in bringing about Peel's return to the premiership in 1841.

O'Connell launched a series of 'monster meetings' to press the case for repeal of the Union. However, the banning of the proposed meeting at Clontarf in 1843 and his imprisonment for fourteen weeks for conspiracy, prior to the House of Lords reversing the verdict in September 1844, allowed the militants of 'Young Ireland' to enter the political scene and outflank O'Connell. His health also failed him and he was en route to Rome when he died at Genoa on 15 May 1847. His heart completed the journey, being taken to Rome and buried in St Agathe's.

In his lifetime O'Connell had won the epithet of 'the Liberator' but he had freed his fellow Irishmen from the worst excesses of feudalism rather than the Union. He had not inflicted a mortal wound on the Protestant Ascendancy but merely dented it because he believed, in the last resort, that 'human blood is no cement for the temple of liberty'. Moreover, whilst appealing in his youth for a non-sectarian Irish nationalism (a sort of pacific counterpart to the United Irishmen movement), the Liberator had himself become imprisoned in an increasingly partisan Catholic party spirit.

O'Connor, Feargus Edward (18 July 1794–30 August 1855). Feargus O'Connor was born at Connorville, County Cork and claimed descent from the ancient kings of Ireland. After studying law at Trinity College, Dublin he was called to the Irish Bar and practised law until 1832 when he was returned to parliament for County Cork as a follower of Daniel O'Connell. Losing his seat in 1835 because he failed to meet the property qualification for MPs, O'Connor became involved in Chartism and soon emerged as the movement's leading publicist, through his demagogic performances as a public speaker ('the Lion of Freedom') and the popularity of his Leeds-based journal, the *Northern Star* (founded in 1837). However, O'Connor's advocacy of physical force and his Land Plan (for resettling industrial workers as smallholders on Chartist settlements) alienated the likes of Francis Place and William Lovett.

In 1840 he was imprisoned for a year for seditious libel, arguing the right of every man to bear arms in the defence of justice, but emerged from jail as the movement's undisputed leader. He was returned to parliament for Nottingham in 1847 but the fiasco surrounding the third petition, which he presented to parliament in the following year, marked the end of Chartism as a mass movement and the end of O'Connor's role as a national figure. Increasingly deranged, O'Connor was declared insane in 1852 and died three years later.

Official Secrets Act, 1911. Haldane as secretary of state for war introduced the 1911 Official Secrets Bill into the House of Lords on 25 July. This was shortly after the Agadir crisis and the legislation was presented as a measure of national security. As such it enjoyed an exceptionally rapid passage through parliament, attracting a second reading after just four speeches in the Lords and going through all its stages in the Commons in just forty minutes on 18 August. Although presented by the Asquith government as marking no change in principle to the 1889 Act, its Section 2, covering the unauthorized communication and receipt of all official information (not just classified or secret information) by a Crown servant, radically extended the government of the day's powers to restrict access of information about matters of legitimate public concern, such as corruption.

Oil crisis See OPEC I and OPEC II.

Old Age Pensions Joseph Chamberlain had publicly flirted with the idea of old age pensions funded out of the proceeds of tariff reform but it was Lloyd George who introduced the first old age pensions through his 1908 budget (which had been largely prepared by Asquith before he succeeded Campbell-Bannerman as premier). These payments were non-contributory but hardly generous as single persons aged 70 or over with an annual income of less than £26 would be entitled to receive a pension of five shillings (25p) a week, whilst married couples would receive double. Roughly 500,000 proved initially eligible. Nevertheless, this measure contributed substantially to reducing pauperism and the threat of the workhouse amongst the aged and was understandably popular.

In 1925 Neville Chamberlain as minister of health introduced contributory pensions (funded from insurance contributions rather than through taxation) for those aged 65 and over.

In 1940 the age at which women qualified for their pension was reduced to 60, as part of a series of measures which successfully tried to lure more women into the workplace.

OPEC I, 1973. The quadrupling of oil prices in 1973 following the outbreak of the Yom Kippur War in early October, created severe economic problems for all oil-importing countries, including Great Britain, halting a long phase of growth for the OECD economies, fuelling inflation and accentuating current account problems with the balance of payments (initially accounting for nearly 3 percentage points of GDP on the visible balance). Moreover, this oil crisis (which came to be called OPEC I after the Organization of Petroleum Exporting Countries who controlled world prices of crude oil) coincided with, and then accelerated, the breakdown of the Bretton Woods fixed exchange rate system, thereby creating even greater economic instability.

In the short term the quadrupling in the price of oil helped bring the Heath government to its knees, or rather it delivered the death blow, as it was already facing growing opposition to phase III of its Prices and Incomes Policy which culminated in the second national miners' strike it had had to face, which was due to begin on 9 February 1974. The oil crisis and the growing shortage of coal combined to produce a record trade-deficit figure of £383m and a record balance-of-payments deficit of £1.5 billion in early February 1973.

However, in the long term the rise in oil prices rendered the development of North Sea oil and gas viable and once it came on stream from the mid-1970s transformed Britain's economic prospects.

OPEC II, 1979. OPEC II, like OPEC I, raised the price of oil but OPEC I enabled Britain to become a producer and, by 1981, a net exporter of North Sea oil and gas. Thus whilst the extractive sector accounted for only 0.01% of GDP in 1975, this figure rose to 4.4% by 1980 and 6.2% by 1985, after which time oil revenues passed their peak. North Sea oil added an estimated 6–7% to GDP. However,

Britain's economic growth remained disappointing compared with its OECD rivals because North Sea oil inflated the value of sterling whilst its revenues were frittered away. The net impact of North Sea oil and gas was thus to reduce the rate rather than reverse the trend of Britain's relative economic decline.

Orsini affair See PALMERSTON.

Osborne Judgement, 1909. In 1909 the House of Lords found in favour of W. V. Osborne, a Liberal, who objected to the political levy (a proportion of his union subscription going to fund the Labour Party).

The Osborne Judgement outlawed a compulsory political levy on the part of trade unions and thus, like the Taff Vale judgement, represented a serious threat to the Labour movement. Moreover, the Labour Party's finances were soon put under enormous strain by the fact that there were two general elections in 1910: one in January on the People's Budget, and a second in December on curbing the powers of the House of Lords. However, these elections reduced the Liberal government from a position of having a comfortable majority to being dependent upon its Labour and Irish allies, so in this respect it was easier for Labour to secure redress.

Thus the effects of the Osborne Judgement were partly mitigated by the introduction of the payment of MPs in 1911 and completely removed by the 1913 Trade Union Act (until it, in its turn, was undone by the 1927 Trade Disputes Act).

Owen, David Anthony Llewellyn, Baron Owen (2 July 1938–). David Owen came from a medical background as his father was a doctor and his mother was a dentist. After school at Bradfield he read Medicine at Sidney Sussex, Cambridge, completing his medical training at St Thomas's Hospital, London. In 1966 he was elected Labour MP for the Sutton division of Plymouth (where his father had practised) and identified with that part of the party that looked to Crosland and Jenkins. Appointed under-secretary for the Navy by Wilson in 1968, he resigned from the opposition front bench in 1972 and helped organize the rebellion of 69 Labour MPs who defied the party whip in voting to join the European Economic Community.

In the second Wilson government he served at Health and Social Security under Castle and as minister of state at the Foreign Office under Crosland. In 1977, at the age of just 38, he was chosen by Callaghan to become foreign secretary, in which capacity he worked towards a settlement of the Rhodesian problem (which eventually bore fruit under Mrs Thatcher). However, discontent with the direction the Labour Party was taking led to his becoming one of the Gang of Four and thus one of the founder members of the SDP.

Owen's profile soared with the Falklands War as he convincingly supported military action yet criticized government negligence in allowing the Argentinians to invade and in 1983 was unanimously elected leader of the six SDP MPs following the resignation of Roy Jenkins. Relations with the Liberal Party became more strained than hitherto as the SDP under Owen moved closer to the Conservatives on some policies, notably defence, than his partners. He also opposed moves towards joint selection of candidates in favour of preserving the SDP's distinctive image. Thus the 1987 election saw Owen moving to the right whilst Steel inclined leftwards. Such visible disunity damaged the electoral performance of the Alliance, which in turn pushed Steel to push for a merger of the parties shortly after the election. Owen felt that he was being steamrollered and resigned the leadership in August 1987 after a national ballot of SDP members saw a majority vote in favour of merger. The Owenite rump SDP finally disbanded in 1989 after humiliation in local government elections. Owen left the Commons in 1992 but went on to become a crossbench peer in the Lords. Two issues in particular exercised him in the 1990s, namely, opposition to British membership of the Euro and the search for a settlement in Bosnia (including the failed Vance–Owen plan).

So far from Owen breaking the mould of British politics it would be truer to say that it broke him but it would only be fair to add that despite his professed love of cricket, Owen was never a good team player himself and was always likely to up stumps when the going got tough.

Oxford Movement, 1833–c.1845. The Oxford Movement was an Oxford-based movement of reform within the Church of England. Its focus was initially church–state relations, asserting that the secular or temporal authority should not interfere in the religious or spiritual authority: an issue that centred upon protest at the 1833 Irish Church Temporalities Act. However, its leading lights, Newman, Keble, Pusey and Froude, also known as the 'Tractarians' (because their ideas were propagated through a series of *Tracts for the Times*), moved increasingly and even more controversially into the broader doctrinal realm, stressing the catholicity of the Anglican communion and suggesting that the Church might best be regenerated by rediscovering the teaching and practices of early Christianity.

Evangelical concerns that the Oxford Movement's emphasis upon Catholic tradition was deeply subversive seemed vindicated by Newman's conversion to Rome in 1845. His defection also marked the effective end of the Oxford Movement although its legacy continued within the Church of England in the form of Anglo-Catholicism. Memories of the movement also helped fuel later manifestations of anti-Catholic and anti-High Church sentiments such as the Ecclesiastical Titles Act and the Public Worship Regulation Act respectively.

P

Pains and Penalties, Bill of, 1820. The Bill of Pains and Penalties was George IV's preferred method of obtaining divorce from Queen Caroline: depriving her of her royal title and rights without providing her with an opportunity to submit evidence relating to his shortcomings as a spouse.

Paisley, Ian Richard Kyle (6 April 1926–). Ian Paisley's father was an Armagh Baptist minister. Educated at Ballymena Model School, Ballymena Technical High School, the South Wales Bible College, and the Reformed Presbyterian Theological College, Belfast he was ordained on 1 August 1946. He founded and became Moderator of the Free Presbyterian Church of Ulster in 1951. His brand of Christianity is vociferously anti-Catholic to the extent that he protested when Belfast City Hall flew its flag at half-mast when the Pope died.

Embodying the inextricable intertwining of religion and politics in Northern Ireland, from 1963 Paisley embarked upon a political career which ran in tandem with his ministry, being eventually elected in turn to the Northern Ireland Parliament (1970), the Westminster Parliament (1974), the European Parliament (1979) and the Northern Ireland Assembly (1998). In 1971 he founded the Democratic Unionist Party (DUP) and became its leader.

His power base is North Antrim and his niche in Northern Ireland politics is as the abominable 'no man', roundly condemning the Ulster Unionist Party for betraying the Unionist cause and denouncing every political initiative to introduce power sharing. Thus he opposed the Sunningdale Agreement in 1973, the Anglo-Irish Agreement in 1985 (in a pact with the UUP) and the Good Friday Agreement in 1998. He has also repeatedly condemned sectarian violence whilst flirting with the Loyalist paramilitaries.

Paisley's pessimism regarding the peace process (which his critics would claim to be self-fulfilling) paid dividends in the 2005 general election when Paisley's DUP humbled Trimble's UUP to become the dominant voice of Ulster unionism. As Paisley entered his seventies his voice was less booming and his once commanding presence was noticeably frailer but neither his attitudes nor his language had mellowed. He remained intransigent in his opposition to Rome, Dublin and those whom he considers to be serving their ends. To his critics he epitomizes religious bigotry and political negativity. To his admirers – and there are many – he is the archetypal conviction politician who can be relied upon not only never to surrender the cause but also never to put it at risk through compromise.

Palmerston, Henry John Temple, third Viscount Palmerston in the Irish peerage (20 October 1784–18 October 1865). Henry John Temple was born into the Irish peerage and was hence eligible to stand for election to the House of Commons. He was educated at Harrow, Edinburgh and St John's College, Cambridge. On his fourth attempt he entered the Commons in June 1807 as a Pittite Tory for the pocket borough of Newport on the Isle of Wight. Both his parents having died before he reached the then age of majority (21), a board of trustees had been created to protect his interests and he was indebted in his early political career to the patronage of one of these in particular, namely, the First Earl of Malmesbury, who helped secure Palmerston's appointment as one of the Junior Lords of the Admiralty. In 1809 Spencer Perceval offered him the post of chancellor of the exchequer but he preferred to remain outside the cabinet in the relatively junior office of secretary at war (dealing with army finances). As prime ministers, Liverpool, Canning and Goderich all offered Palmerston promotion but their blandishments were unable to detach him from his post at the War Office, although he did enter the cabinet in 1827.

In May 1828 he finally resigned this post when he joined with the other 'Canningites' in resigning from the government of the Duke of Wellington in protest at the latter's refusal to reassign the disfranchised seats of East Retford and Penrhyn to the unrepresented cities of Manchester and Leeds. He also followed the other Canningites in November 1830 in joining the predominantly Whig administration of Earl Grey, becoming foreign secretary. Grey (a former foreign secretary himself) played a significant role in determining foreign policy until he resigned in 1834. Palmerston enjoyed a freer hand under Melbourne, who became his brother-in-law in 1839 when Palmerston's long-standing affair with Lady Cowper was legitimized following her husband's death.

The first major issue with which Palmerston had to deal at the Foreign Office was the nationalist revolt of the Belgians (August 1830) against Dutch rule, where his policy was to prevent the French from exploiting the situation and restore the balance of power. This was successfully achieved by supporting the Anglophile Leopold of Saxe-Coburg (the widower of the daughter of George IV) for the Belgian throne in 1831 and by sponsoring the Treaty of London in 1839.

Prior to accepting the Foreign Office Palmerston had identified himself with the Greek rebels and the constitutionalists in Portugal and between 1832 and 1834 he had the opportunity to provide diplomatic support for Pedro (King of Brazil until forced to abdicate in 1831), when he intervened in Portugal to restore his daughter Donna Maria to the throne from which she'd been deposed by Dom Miguel. Britain's support for the cause of constitutionalism throughout the Iberian Peninsula was formalized by the creation in April 1834 of the Quadruple Alliance with Portugal, Spain and France.

Over Belgium and the Iberian Peninsula Palmerston had managed to work with France but in dealing with the Eastern Question in the 1830s he found himself at variance with the French because they backed the Egyptian, Mehemet Ali, in his challenges to the integrity of the Ottoman Empire of 1831–33 and 1839–41. On the first occasion Palmerston was tardy in responding to the Sultan's appeal for help and it was Russia who reaped the benefits in the 1833 Treaty of Unkiar-Skelessi (whereby the Sultan secretly agreed to close the Straits of the Dardanelles to all foreign warships if St Petersburg requested this). However, British intervention in 1840 under the Convention for the Pacification of the Levant resulted in Unkiar-Skelessi being replaced by the much more favourable Straits Convention of 1841, whereby the Straits were closed to all foreign warships whilst the Ottoman Empire was at peace.

Palmerston was not responsible for the outbreak of hostilities which became known as the Opium War (1839–42) but he fully supported the efforts to use force to open China to British trade. The success of the Conservatives in the 1841 election meant that it was left to the new foreign secretary, Lord Aberdeen, to conclude the Treaty of Nanking.

In turn, when Palmerston returned to the Foreign Office in 1846 he inherited from Aberdeen problems in both Spain (the Spanish marriages affair) and Portugal (where Palmerston secured Maria on the throne but exerted pressure to persuade her to restore the liberal constitution which she had annulled in 1845).

Palmerston's relations with Queen Victoria were often strained and the visits of two dignitaries in 1850–51 highlighted their differences. In 1850 the Austrian General Haynau who had been involved in the brutal suppression of internal unrest in 1848–49 was jostled by draymen when he visited Barclay's Brewery in Southwark. Palmerston refused to issue what the Queen regarded as an adequate apology because he obviously sympathized with the rough treatment meted out to the general. Conversely, when Louis Kossuth, the hero of the Hungarian revolt, visited Britain in 1851 he was widely fêted, despite the reservations of the Peace Society and Queen Victoria. She was successful in prohibiting Palmerston from receiving Kossuth but he managed to publicize this injunction, thereby reinforcing his reputation as a supporter of nationalist rebels, winning the support of many Radicals and further taxing the patience of Lord John Russell.

Palmerston's populism and gunboat diplomacy reached new heights with the Don Pacifico affair in 1850 when his strenuous support for the dubious claims of a Portuguese Jew born in Gibraltar saw him emerge triumphant despite exciting censure from Cobden, Peel and Gladstone amongst others. However, over-cordial relations with Britain's traditional enemy across the Channel were shortly afterwards to bring down Palmerston, at least temporarily.

Already, in 1848, he had been too quick for Queen Victoria's liking, in recognizing the Second Republic. Then, on 3 December 1851, he told Walewski, the French Ambassador to London, that he was pleased by Louis Napoleon's action of the previous day in dissolving the National Assembly and ending the Second Republic. When news of this approval of the coup leaked out Russell asked for his resignation. Palmerston was to gain his 'tit-for-tat' revenge in February 1852 when the government's defeat on an amendment which he proposed to their Bill to set up a county militia forced Russell's resignation.

Palmerston was soon back in office under Aberdeen, after a brief Derby–Disraeli minority government, but at the Home rather than the Foreign Office. However, not only did his appointment as home secretary enable him to implement valuable penal, factory and public health reforms, it also meant that he was not held responsible for the mistakes of the ministry in drifting into the Crimean war and failing to prosecute it effectively. Thus he finally attained the premiership in 1855 after his defence of Aberdeen's administration from the charges of John Arthur Roebuck had proved insufficient to save the government, and both Russell and Derby had proved incapable of forming a ministry.

Disraeli was characteristically less than charitable in his estimation of the new prime minister, writing to a friend that 'Palmerston is really an impostor, utterly exhausted, and at the best only ginger-beer, and not champagne, and now an old painted Pantaloon, very deaf, very blind, and with false teeth, which would fall out of his mouth when speaking, if he did not hesitate so in his talk'. However, even Victoria accepted Palmerston as inevitable, given his undoubted popularity in the country, his almost unrivalled experience of parliament, and his supposed special relationship with Britain's French ally, Napoleon III.

Palmerston's reshuffling of ministers and promise of reforms proved insufficient to persuade Roebuck to abandon his demand for a committee of inquiry and the premier's position appeared to be weakened by his initial attempts to block the committee, the resignation of the Peelites Graham, Gladstone and Herbert, which its creation provoked, and the resignation, in July 1855 (in advance of a vote of censure), of Russell as Palmerston's envoy at the peace talks in Vienna. In reality, however, these events served merely to emphasize Palmerston's indispensability and the 1857 general election was little more than a vote of confidence in Palmerston remaining as prime minister.

The Orsini affair in 1858 was characteristic insofar as the Conspiracy to Murder Bill showed Palmerston solicitous towards Napoleon III (bringing forward legislation to prevent assassination being plotted in Britain) but was uncharacteristic insofar as he badly misjudged the mood of the electorate and Parliament, allowing Derby to form his second minority government. He was, however, back in office at the head of what most would regard as the first recognizably Liberal administration by the end of 1859. The remaining years of his life, until his death in 1865, are traditionally represented as a sad swan song to his long career. This period was characterized by the souring of Anglo-American relations by the Alabama and Trent affairs and by Schleswig–Holstein, which had been the scene of diplomatic success in 1852 (when the succession to the Duchies was settled in a manner which avoided war between Denmark and other interested parties), becoming the source of humiliation in 1864, when Bismarck called his bluff and Palmerston backed down rather than risk war with Prussia and Austria. It was also a period of stagnation at home, although Salisbury, for one, regarded the lack of reform in a positive light, praising Palmerston for succeeding 'in doing that which is most difficult and most salutary for a parliament to do: nothing'.

Palmerston appreciated, long before the advent of 'spin', that the best way of ensuring a good press consists of producing your own. Thus he built up a close relationship with the press in the 1840s – particularly the *Globe*, the *Morning Chronicle* (until 1848 when it was acquired by Peelites) and the *Morning Post* – and even became an accomplished leader writer. However, when he wasn't writing his own notices he was producing good copy by virtue of his increasingly flamboyant behaviour, which culminated in the Don Pacifico affair. By presenting himself as the champion of liberalism (notably in supporting the cause of Italian unification) Palmerston simultaneously appealed over the heads of the great Whig families to the increasingly important middle-class electorate and silenced the charge of radical critics (such as the Chartist George Julian Harney) that he tended to side with the forces of reaction. Thus between 1848 and 1850 Palmerston tapped into a rich seam of domestic support 'by speaking forcefully even when he could not act forcefully' (M. E. Chamberlain): offering the comforting illusion of British influence or even dominance in world affairs. Palmerston may have engaged in bluff and his bluff may finally have been called but he played the game in his public, as in his private life, with such roguish charm and panache that it is impossible to dislike him.

Pankhursts, the: Emmeline (4 July 1858–14 June 1928); **Dame Christabel Harriette** (22 September 1880–13 February 1958); and **Estelle Sylvia** (5 May 1882–27 September 1960). Emmeline Pankhurst, the daughter of Manchester middle-class radicals Robert Goulden and Sophia Crane, was born in Manchester on 4 July 1858. Notwithstanding their politics, her parents possessed conventional views regarding upbringing and the young Emmeline concluded her education at a Parisian finishing school.

In 1879 Emmeline married the lawyer Richard Marsden Pankhurst, whose views were even more progressive than her parents'. Their union produced several children, two of whom – Christabel and Sylvia – were to join their mother in the suffragette campaign.

Richard Pankhurst died in 1898 but Emmeline continued her political activity, founding the Women's Social and Political Union in October 1903. It made headlines two years later when Mrs Pankhurst decided that the issue of women's suffrage would only command attention if the campaign embraced militancy. Thus on 13 October 1905, Christabel Pankhurst and Annie Kenney heckled a meeting addressed by Sir Edward Grey, and then assaulted the policeman charged with evicting them. When they refused to pay the fine they were sent to prison: the beginning of a prolonged campaign of civil disobedience which took many forms including arson, assault and hunger strikes.

From 1909, however, the WSPU was in decline as a consequence of the 'Cat and Mouse' Act saving the government from the bad publicity arising from force feeding of hunger-striking suffragettes; a series of debilitating splits within the movement; and the eclipse of the campaign by labour troubles and the Ulster crisis. War arrested this process as Mrs Pankhurst announced the suspension of all suffragette activity for the duration on 4 August 1914. The government announced the release of all suffragettes from prison and the WSPU threw itself into the war effort.

After the War and the concession of the vote to all women over the age of 30 in 1918, the suspension of militancy for the duration allowing the concession to be granted without losing face,

Emmeline spent several years in the USA and Canada lecturing on behalf of the National Council for Combating Venereal Disease. Her political odyssey was completed when, on her return to Britain in 1926, she joined the Conservative Party and was adopted as their candidate for Whitechapel. However, she died in 1928 before contesting the seat.

Mrs Pankhurst was clearly a remarkable women, not least for the ruthlessness with which she pushed herself and others, although some would claim that it was actually Christabel who focused her mother's attention upon the suffragette campaign and steeled her to embrace militant tactics. Christabel generally took little direct part in militant actions but was arrested and imprisoned in 1908 for joining her mother in appealing to the public to help the suffragettes rush the House of Commons. When threatened, in 1912, with arrest on a charge of conspiracy, Christabel fled to Paris where she edited *The Suffragette* and continued to plan the campaign until the outbreak of the war.

Whereas Sylvia opposed the war, Christabel herself returned home to join her mother in assisting the government's recruiting campaign. Peace and the passage of the Fourth Reform Act left Christabel at something of a loose end, eventually joining her mother in Canada. She was appointed DBE in 1936 and settled in the United States in 1940.

Christabel was neither as radical nor brave as her sister Sylvia but she shared in full with her and their mother the ability to inspire and the willingness to serve a cause at considerable personal cost.

Sylvia left her artist's studio in Chelsea in order to work for the WSPU when it transferred from Manchester to London in 1905. She campaigned, particularly in the East End, not only for extending the vote to women but also for improved welfare provision. Her interest in the needs of working-class women, encouraged by her friend and mentor, Keir Hardie, led to a growing estrangement with her mother and older sister which finally resulted in her East London Federation of Suffragettes breaking away from the WSPU.

Sylvia was bitterly opposed to Britain's intervention in World War One and passionately enthusiastic for the Russian Revolution. Indeed, the ELFS was gradually transformed into the first Communist party in Great Britain.

In 1920 she attended the second congress of the Third International in Moscow, only to be imprisoned on her return for sedition because of articles published in her newspaper during her absence. On her release she was expelled from the party for refusing to hand over control of the paper to her comrades. In addition to campaigning for women's rights she embraced a variety of other causes, notably condemnation of the rise of fascism in Italy. She was encouraged in this by a left-wing Italian journalist, Silvio Erasmus Corio, who became her lover and the father of her only child.

Italy's 1935 invasion of Abyssinia sparked an interest in Ethiopian affairs which lasted the rest of her life. In May 1936 she began *New Times and Ethiopia News*, a weekly journal which she was to edit for twenty years, and she died in Addis Ababa in 1960, having received the Queen of Sheba decoration, first class, from Emperor

Haile Selassie for her various contributions to the welfare of his country.

Sylvia was arguably the most extraordinary member of an extraordinary family. She showed great personal courage and a willingness to make sacrifices not only in her refusals of food, drink and sleep when imprisoned as a suffragette but also in turning her back upon her mother and her art in her efforts to do good for the downtrodden, first of the East End and then of Ethiopia.

Parliament Act, 1911. Following rejection of the People's Budget by the Lords in 1909 (by 350 votes to 75) the momentum for reform of the upper house increased and a mandate for such change was delivered by the elections of January and December 1910. Thus in 1911 the Liberals (backed by their Labour and Irish allies) introduced a Parliament Bill to reduce the Lords' powers. It was intended that this would be complemented by legislation reforming the composition of the second chamber but this failed to materialize.

The Parliament Bill was only passed, like the 1832 Reform Act, under the threat of the creation of a sufficiently large number of government peers to swamp the Tory majority in the Lords.

Under the terms of the Act the maximum life of a parliament was reduced from seven years to five; the Lords lost the right to revise money bills; and other public legislation (excepting bills to extend the life of parliament) were to receive the Royal Assent without the consent of the Lords if passed by the Commons in three successive sessions, providing two years elapsed between the first Second Reading and final passage in the Commons, and if sent up to the Lords at least one month before the end of each of the three sessions.

Thus the Lords effectively lost its power of veto and its powers of delay were reduced to two years, making even the most contentious legislation, such as Irish home rule legislation, feasible.

Parliament Act, 1949. Under the terms of the 1911 Parliament Act the Attlee government's Parliament Bill became law in 1949. It amended the 1911 Act so as to reduce the delaying power of the Lords in respect of public bills other than money bills to two sessions and one year respectively. This was done because the Attlee government wished to nationalize the iron and steel industries but realized that they had left it too late to accomplish this in the lifetime of the 1945 government using the machinery of the 1911 Act. As with the earlier legislation, it was intended that this reform would be accompanied by a reform of the composition of the Lords but once again this did not occur.

Parnell, Charles Stewart (27 July 1846–6 October 1891). A half-American Protestant member of the Wicklow squirearchy, Charles Stewart Parnell failed to take his degree at Cambridge but entered the House of Commons in 1875 as an Irish Home Ruler and within three years had displaced Isaac Butt (becoming the president of the Home Rule Confederation of Great Britain) by virtue of his tactical grasp of the situation. Whereas many Irishmen have got themselves elected to the House of Commons only to refuse to sit there,

Parnell was assiduous in his attendance of the Westminster parliament but always used the floor of the House as a platform for his audience in Ireland and amongst the Irish community in the United States (which he also addressed directly – including once before Congress itself – in the winter of 1879–80).

Although himself a landlord, Parnell allied himself and his party with Davitt's Land League (becoming president of the League in October 1880) as part of the 'New Departure': an effort to use the land issue to promote nationalism. Following the rejection of the Compensation for Disturbance Bill by the Lords in 1880, the Gladstone government came round to the idea of a Land Bill, which would address the Irish land question in a much more radical manner than the 1870 Irish Land Act. However, Parnell decided in advance that this measure would not suffice and urged Land League members to respond to any effort to bid for the farms of evicted tenants by treating the offending parties as pariahs. The government responded to this boycotting, as it came to be known, with coercion.

After the failure of an attempt to have the Land League leaders convicted in the Dublin courts on a charge of conspiracy to prevent the payment of rent, a Coercion Bill was introduced at the beginning of the 1881 parliamentary session to equip the Irish chief secretary with special powers to deal with agrarian violence. Parliamentary procedure had to be radically modified – by the introduction of the closure of debate – in order to overcome Parnellite obstruction to the Bill, and shortly after it became law the Government's announcement of its intention to arrest Davitt and others provoked such disorder amongst the Irish members that thirty-six of them, including Parnell himself, were ejected from the House.

The 1881 Irish Land Act represented a problem for Parnell insofar as tenants were likely to be attracted by the promise of the 3Fs (fair rent, free sale and fixity of tenure), and specifically by the opportunity of availing themselves of judicially fixed – and in all probability reduced – rents. The Act therefore raised the spectre of the bulk of rank and file Land League members accepting the protection offered by the Westminster parliament. Parnell therefore trod very carefully. For example, whilst abstaining on the Bill's First and Third Readings he reserved the right to press constructive amendments at the committee stage. Similarly, he urged the Land League to approach the legislation cautiously by means of taking certain test cases into the land courts.

Simultaneously, he attempted to appease his extremist left wing by successfully courting a second suspension from parliament and by attacking the Act through a series of speeches in Ireland and through the newly launched *United Ireland* newspaper. The British government responded to this baiting by interning Parnell in Kilmainham Jail, which secretly gratified him as his political martyrdom strengthened the movement at a time when it was under considerable pressure, as the Land League was proscribed following its issuing of the 'No Rent Manifesto'.

The Kilmainham Treaty, arrived at between Joseph Chamberlain, acting for the government, and Parnell, arranged for the latter's release on condition that he used his influence against lawlessness, whilst the Liberals, for their part, agreed to amend the Land Act in a manner desired by Parnell and supplement it with legislation relating to rent arrears. Parnell's rejection of extremism in favour of the path of moderation (symbolized by his destruction of the Ladies' Land League and creation of the Irish National League) was largely obscured, at least temporarily, by the Phoenix Park murders and Parnell's opposition to the ensuing Coercion Bill.

On 8 June 1885 the Parnellites joined with the Conservatives in bringing down the Liberal government. Parnell was unimpressed by Chamberlain's central board scheme and alienated by Gladstone's intention of passing a new Coercion Bill, whilst the Conservatives, through Lord Randolph Churchill, were hinting to him that were they in office then coercion legislation might not be renewed. Lord Salisbury duly formed a caretaker administration until a general election could be held on the basis of the 1884–85 parliamentary reform and in the meantime coercion was allowed to lapse and the new Lord Lieutenant in Ireland, Lord Carnarvon, discreetly investigated the prospects of some longer-term understanding between the Conservatives and the Parnellites. These negotiations went well enough for Parnell to advise Irish voters in Britain to vote against the 'perfidious, treacherous, and incompetent' Liberals.

This fact, the support of the Irish hierarchy and the terms of the Fourth Reform Act in 1884 and the 1885 Redistribution all helped to produce the situation whereby the 86 Irish Nationalist MPs held the balance of power at Westminster following the 1885 general election. When Carnarvon's feelers were withdrawn, Salisbury announced that new coercive legislation was being contemplated, and Herbert Gladstone flew the Hawarden Kite, signifying Gladstone's sympathy with the cause of Irish Home Rule, Parnell duly shifted his weight to side with the Liberals in forcing the defeat and resignation of the Conservatives in January 1886. However, the Liberal Unionists who were opposed to the First Irish Home Rule Bill, and who included in their ranks John Bright, Joseph Chamberlain and Hartington, outnumbered the Parnellites and thus ensured that the Bill was defeated by 40 votes on its Second Reading, and Salisbury returned to the premiership.

Renewed agricultural depression resulted in the implementation in the countryside of the Plan of Campaign to which Balfour, the new Irish chief secretary, responded with a new 'perpetual' coercion act, so called because it did not require regular renewal. Parnell tried to reassure his Liberal allies that he had taken steps to ensure that the Plan was not too closely identified with either the Irish National League or the Irish Nationalist party. However, a more direct threat to his reputation for moderation appeared in the form of a series of articles in *The Times* newspaper entitled 'Parnellism and Crime', in which it was alleged that Parnell had sponsored terrorist outrages and secretly sympathized with the perpetration of the Phoenix Park murders.

Parnell was vindicated by the Parnell Commission, which began its deliberations in September 1888 but only reported in February 1890. However, in December 1889, after having turned a blind eye for several years to his wife's adulterous relationship with Parnell, Captain William O'Shea had filed for divorce from his wife Katharine (or Kittie) and named Parnell as co-respondent. The divorce, which was granted on 17 November 1890, neither Parnell nor Mrs O'Shea defending the case, ruined Parnell's political career because it offended the 'non-conformist conscience' which provided the moral backbone of the Gladstonian Liberal Party and the Roman Catholic church which comprised the core of the Irish nationalist community. Thus on 24 November 1890 Gladstone saw Justin McCarthy, the vice-chairman of the Irish Nationalists, to impress upon him the need for Parnell to retire and on the following day made public a letter to John Morley stating the view that Parnell's continued leadership of the Irish Nationalists would hold back the cause of Home Rule and render his own leadership of the Liberals 'almost a nullity'.

Parnell refused to retire, despite the fact that he had lost the support of the Catholic Church and many of the leading members of the Irish American community. Thus between 1 and 6 December 1890 the Irish Nationalist party debated his fate in Committee Room 15 of the House of Commons. The outcome was a debilitating split with the majority, led by Justin McCarthy, repudiating Parnell's leadership. Moreover, the embittered rump of Parnellite loyalists were left leaderless after Parnell failed to win three by-elections and then died in the arms of his new bride in Brighton in October 1891.

It is easy to regard Parnell as a tragic hero insofar as Irish Home Rule appeared in some respects to be a more distant prospect when he died than was previously the case. His tragic credentials are enhanced by the facts that his enterprise appeared doomed from the beginning (a somewhat withdrawn Protestant landlord appearing triply disqualified from successfully uniting Ireland), whilst Parnell found himself opposed by gigantic forces (including Ulster sentiment and hypocritical social convention) as well as exhibiting flawed judgement (entering into his relationship with Kittie O'Shea in 1880 and refusing to resign in 1890). However, his legacy is more ambiguous. By skilfully straddling the extremist and moderate positions (notably through the New Departure), by trading his influence over the men of violence (the Kilmainham Treaty) and by mobilizing the Irish vote inside and outside parliament, he was able to achieve practical concessions (such as the 1882 Arrears Act) and place Home Rule at the top of the political agenda but ultimately his loyalty to the path of constitutionalism (rejecting withdrawal from Westminster in 1881 and 1890–91), his dependence upon Gladstone (after 1886) and his loyalty to Kittie fatally restricted his room for manoeuvre.

Payment by results, 1862. Payment by results was the most notorious aspect of the revised code of education introduced by Robert Lowe as vice-president of the Education Department of the Privy Council in 1862.

Believing that examination provided a more efficient test of good school management than the reports of school inspectors, grants to elementary schools with more than 100 pupils were henceforth to be made only if the children passed an examination in the three R's: reading, writing and arithmetic. In Lowe's formulation, 'If education is not cheap it should be efficient: if it is not efficient it should be cheap'. The predictable practical consequence of payment by results is that many teachers focused on parrot-fashion rote learning (supplemented by corporal punishment) so as to provide a veneer of learning which was not allied with genuine understanding.

Peace Preservation Act, 1814. In 1814 Peel, as Irish chief secretary, took steps to deal with any agitation inspired by O'Connell following dissolution of the 'Catholic Board' by renewing the Insurrection Act and passing the Peace Preservation Act. Under this legislation the Lord Lieutenant was entitled to 'proclaim' a disturbed district and to appoint to it a salaried superintending magistrate in charge of a body of up to fifty special constables which would reinforce the local county police.

This professional police force – the first in the United Kingdom – ultimately became the Royal Irish (and later, Ulster) Constabulary. It helped to contain but not eradicate violence. Hence periodic recourse to measures of coercion. Nevertheless, the success of the Irish Constabulary provided a model for Peel's 1829 Metropolilitan Police Act.

Peace Process, in Northern Ireland. The peace process in Northern Ireland began with the realization on the part of men like Gerry Adams that the military campaign of the IRA was getting nowhere; that Sinn Féin could garner significant electoral support in Ulster (as shown by the response to the Hunger strikes campaign); and that concessions could be won from the British government if Sinn Féin suggested that the IRA might be willing to renounce terrorism: a development hinted at in the Hume–Adams talks.

The British government responded in 1990 by reopening a backchannel line of communication to the IRA and by publicly stating, in November of that year, that it had 'no selfish strategic or economic interest in Northern Ireland'. In other words, Britain would not maintain the current status of the Province within the United Kingdom if a majority of its inhabitants clearly consented to some change in that status.

A framework for examining that status was initiated in 1991 when talks were arranged between the four 'constitutional' parties, namely, Jim Molyneaux's Ulster Unionist Party (UUP), the Democratic Unionist Party (DUP) led by Ian Paisley, John Alderdice's Alliance Party and the Social Democratic and Labour Party led by John Hume. Their talks had three interlocking strands so that agreement on all was required for progress to be made. The first strand related to the internal political development of Northern Ireland and focused upon the Unionist desire to end direct rule and restore some form of Northern Ireland Assembly. The second strand dealt with relations between the North and South of Ireland, whilst the third involved relations between the United Kingdom as a whole and the Republic.

This process led to the Downing Street Declaration of 15 December 1993, comprising a joint statement of principles by John Major and the Irish Taoiseach (Prime Minister), Albert Reynolds, on behalf of their respective governments.

Fearing their possible marginalization, the paramilitaries on both sides implemented a ceasefire in 1994 as the price of entry to the talks, although whether the renunciation of violence was permanent or temporary was fudged. Just over a fortnight after the IRA declared a 'complete cessation of military operations' John Major responded by relaxing some security measures and by lifting the ban on broadcasting the voices of paramilitaries, although the Unionist majority was simultaneously reassured by being told a referendum would be held in the Province on the outcome of any constitutional talks.

Subsequently, political prisoners have been released, decommissioning of (some) weapons has taken place, referenda have been held on the peace process both north and south of the border, and a power-sharing executive has been created. In short, the peace process has made considerable progress despite efforts to derail it, such as the Omagh bombing, by those opposed to the whole idea, and notwithstanding ongoing friction between and within the various parties who have signed up to the package.

The IRA ordering all its units 'to dump arms' and all volunteers 'to assist the development of purely political and democratic programmes through exclusively peaceful means' has been widely hailed as a landmark in the peace process. Ironically the announcement was delayed until 28 July 2005 for fear that the news would be submerged by the Al-Qaeda-inspired terrorist attacks on London of 7 and 14 July.

Peel, Sir Robert (5 February 1788–2 July 1850). Robert Peel was born on 5 February 1788, the third child and eldest son of a wealthy cotton manufacturer turned Tory MP, Robert Peel (1750–1830), who was made a baronet by Pitt the Younger and who went on to be the author of the 1819 Factory Act.

After a distinguished academic career at Harrow and Christ Church, Oxford, Peel entered parliament in 1809 as MP for the rotten borough of Cashel City, County Tipperary, thanks to the patronage of his father and Arthur Wellesley (the future Duke of Wellington). Promotion quickly followed, with appointment as under-secretary for war and the colonies in the government of Spencer Perceval. In this department he served under Liverpool who was so impressed by his intellect and administrative ability that when he became prime minister in 1812 Peel was appointed chief secretary for Ireland. An additional reason for this appointment was that Peel's views on Ireland were identical to his chief's, particularly in his hostility to Catholic Emancipation. Indeed, such was Peel's eloquence on this topic in speaking against Henry Grattan's motion for Emancipation in 1817 that he became the darling of the Ultras and won the honour of representing Oxford University.

During his six years as Irish chief secretary Peel combined firmness in dealing with the threat posed by O'Connell (for example, passing the Peace Preservation and Insurrection Acts in 1814) yet also displayed flexibility and compassion (for example, organizing relief when failure of the potato crop threatened famine in 1816). At the time of the 1818 general election Peel relinquished the post because bored by it. His six-year stint was three times longer than any of his predecessors and longer than that of his nineteenth-century successors. Peel was not out of the limelight for long, however, chairing the Bullion Committee or Currency Commission which in 1819 recommended the phased restoration of the gold standard.

In 1822 Peel entered the cabinet when he replaced Sidmouth at the Home Office. He refused to serve under Canning or Goderich because they were Catholic Tories but returned to the Home Office during the premiership of the Duke of Wellington (1828–30). Peel was a reforming home secretary in four areas: prisons (the Gaols Acts of 1823–24), juries (the 1825 Jury Act), policing (the 1829 Metropolitan Police Act) and the penal code (an example being the 1830 Forgery Act).

Peel faced a personal and political crisis in passing Catholic Emancipation in 1829. He was only persuaded to overcome his long-standing opposition to this measure and work for its passage through parliament because his experience of Ireland persuaded him that it was the lesser of two evils (the alternative being civil war in Ireland) and Wellington persuaded him that the measure would not pass through the House of Commons without his support. Realizing that this would be seen by the Ultras as a betrayal, notwithstanding the anti-Catholic measures which accompanied Emancipation (such as raising the Irish county franchise), Peel resigned his seat at Oxford University in an effort to explain his apparent betrayal to his constituents. However, this plan backfired and he was defeated. He thus had to resort to re-entering parliament through the pocket borough of Westbury.

Peel's personal experience of the benefits of pocket and rotten boroughs partly explains his opposition to parliamentary reform. However, he refused to serve under Wellington in May 1832 to pass even a moderate Bill not so much because his opposition was total as because he calculated that he could not afford to be seen to be performing another U-turn so soon after Catholic Emancipation.

Despite having stymied the desire of William IV for a Tory administration in May 1832, Peel was the monarch's choice as prime minister after he dismissed Melbourne in 1834. This led to Peel's First Ministry which lasted roughly 100 days over the winter of 1834–35. Although Peel's supporters gained about 100 seats in the 1835 general election this remained a minority government and as such was vulnerable to the concerted opposition of his enemies, which was formalized through the Lichfield House Compact and resulted in the Whigs returning to power, 1835–41.

However, the period 1834–35 was crucial in transforming the Tory party into the Conservative Party and in radically improving Peel's electoral prospects. The Tamworth Manifesto allegedly shows Peel reaching out to the newly enfranchised middle class insofar as he now accepted the Great Reform Act. However, much more significant, especially in the short term, were his overtures to those High Anglican Whigs who were increasingly worried that Melbourne would be unable to dampen down the reforming demands of the liberal Anglican Whigs (led by Lord John Russell), the Irish (led by Daniel O'Connell) and the Philosophic Radicals. Moreover, Peel's creation of the Ecclesiastical

Duties and Revenue Commission provided concrete proof of his ability to pass reforms which epitomized his aim of strengthening traditional institutions (in this case the Established Church). If F. R. Bonham, the party agent, largely deserves the credit for reforming party organization to accommodate and exploit the changes wrought by the 1832 Reform Act, Peel at least deserves the credit for backing Bonham.

The fruits of all these changes, combined with increasing dissatisfaction with the performance of the Melbourne government, is shown by the fact that the Conservatives (as they were now increasingly called) improved their position in the 1837 and 1841 elections, winning a comfortable majority in the latter. Indeed, had it not been for the Bedchamber Incident (when Peel insisted that Queen Victoria should replace her Whig ladies of the Bedchamber with Conservative ones) he could have formed his second minority government in 1839.

Peel's Second Ministry of 1841–46 was marked by a sustained attempt to pacify Ireland by means of a judicious mixture of coercion (for example banning the 'monster meeting' which O'Connell proposed holding at Clontarf in 1843) and conciliatory reforms (such as the 1843 Devon Commission Report, 1844 Charitable Bequests Act and 1845 Maynooth Grant). It also witnessed a series of measures which showed a sympathetic appreciation of the needs of industry, finance and commerce, including the great free trade budgets of 1842 and 1845, the 1844 Bank Charter Act and the Railway Acts of 1842 and 1844. However, the Repeal of the Corn Laws in 1846, which theoretically united these two themes, irrevocably split the party and resulted in Peel's losing office. He was never to hold it again, dying in 1850 from the effects of a horseriding accident. In his resignation speech to the House of Commons on 29 June 1846 Peel had expressed the hope that he might leave a name 'sometimes remembered with expressions of good will in the abodes of those whose lot it is to labour' and his death prompted a genuine outpouring of grief on the part of the masses which took the form of many successful subscriptions for monuments honouring his political life.

Peel's gifts as a politician were considerable. He was an extremely able parliamentary debater and a skilled administrator with experience of some of the most demanding posts. He understood economics better than most and theoretically possessed the ability to appeal to all shades of opinion in the party, being liberal on trade but akin to an Ultra on religious affairs. However, he also suffered from considerable drawbacks.

As the son of a cotton manufacturer who retained a Bury accent he was an 'outsider' who lacked the redeeming exoticism of a Disraeli. This was made worse by the fact that he was not 'clubbable', finding it difficult to mix with his foot soldiers partly because of the aforementioned difference in background, partly because of his fastidious temperament and partly because there was no fund of common experience because he had spent so little time on the backbenches himself. He managed to transform the Tory party by giving it a new name and a new image designed to broaden its appeal but in the nature of such makeovers much of this metamorphosis was only skin deep. One did not need to scratch the Peelite Conservative Party very deep to reveal raw and unreconstructed Tory attitudes. This is hardly surprising when one remembers that his success in 1841 consisted of winning back traditional supporters as a result of Whig mistakes and improved organization rather than attracting new ones.

Nor could Peel reinvent himself anew. He carried an enormous amount of baggage, not least from his time as Wellington's loyal lieutenant, and the ability of his followers to forget or forgive his 'betrayal' over Catholic Emancipation, if it existed at all, was placed under intolerable strain by his willingness to pursue other policies susceptible to a similar interpretation. The problem was not that Peel lacked principles or exhibited inconsistency in his principles. He was firm in the defence of traditional Tory principles such as upholding the Crown, the Established Church, the aristocratic order and the unity of the British Isles. The problem was rather that, notwithstanding the Tamworth Manifesto, he failed to recognize the need to explain how his policies served those principles to those most requiring reassurance along these lines. Peel was a great statesman but a poor politician if by this is meant someone who sees the big picture at the neglect of the small one.

Peerage Act, 1963. The 1963 Peerage Act made it possible to disclaim an hereditary peerage for life, thus rendering the individual concerned entitled to vote in parliamentary elections and eligible for election to the Commons. Tony Benn had campaigned for the latter right since 1960. Passage of the Act allowed both Hailsham and Home to throw their hats into the ring to succeed Macmillan.

The Act also admitted to the House hereditary peeresses and all Scottish peers (the system of Scottish representative peers having been abolished).

People's Budget At his Mansion House speech in July 1908 Lloyd George referred to the likelihood of his having to face 'a stunning deficit, a falling revenue and depressed trade' and that autumn it appeared doubtful whether his cabinet colleagues would sanction the far-reaching budget he had in mind. However, on 11 December 1908 Asquith made a speech that was widely interpreted as signifying his personal commitment to a radical budget. Fiscal radicalism was required not only to meet a deficit inflated by the recent introduction of old age pensions and increased naval estimates but also to give the party direction and passion and to demonstrate the vitality of free trade finance to those urging tariff reform as the way forward.

Critics were to claim that Lloyd George deliberately overestimated expenditure and underestimated revenue in order to justify the land taxes which constituted the most radical part of the people's budget, or alternatively that Lloyd George included the land taxes in the budget as this provided the justification for including land valuation in the budget, which if it were the subject of a separate bill would almost certainly be blocked by the Lords.

Alternatively it is argued that land valuation and taxes were included in the Finance Bill so as to provoke the Unionist-dominated House of Lords into blocking the budget, thereby provoking a constitutional crisis in which the veto of the upper house itself might be challenged. The Liberals were certainly frustrated with the policy of 'filling the cup' as the rejection of measures such as the 1908 Licensing Bill seemed more likely to win the Lords' favour than unpopularity with the bulk of the electorate.

The 1909 budget increased existing taxes such as income tax and death duties and introduced a new super-tax on incomes over £5,000 per annum. However, it was the proposed land taxes and accompanying valuation which occasioned the greatest anger.

These land taxes were four in number, namely, an 'unearned' increment value duty of 20% on all increments accruing after the date of valuation (30 April 1909); a reversion duty of 10% on the value accruing to a lessor from the determination of a lease; an annual tax of 1/2d (roughly 6p) in the pound on unexploited minerals; and an annual duty of 1/2d in the pound on the capital value of undeveloped land (that is, land suitable for building yet not built upon and excluding all agricultural land).

Whether or not Lloyd George framed these taxes and the budget in general to challenge the Lords' power of veto or to circumvent it (as Gladstone had done over the paper duties), his rhetoric certainly inflamed the situation and the Lords rejected the budget, with the result that two general elections were held in 1910 on the issue of 'the peers versus the people', the Liberals retained power but only with the assistance of the Irish and Labour, and the 1911 Parliament Act cleared the way for Irish Home Rule and other radical measures, by restricting the powers of the Lords.

Perceval, Spencer (1 November 1762–11 May 1812). The second son of the second marriage of the second Earl of Egmont, one might be forgiven for thinking that Spencer Perceval was fated to be one of life's also-rans. However, after Harrow and Trinity College, Cambridge he entered Lincoln's Inn and embarked upon a successful career as a barrister before being invited to stand for parliament as a Tory candidate in 1796. In 1801 he became solicitor-general under Addington, and in the following year became Attorney General: a post which he continued to hold under Pitt, until the latter's death in 1806.

Joyce Marlow argues that whilst Perceval was a man of the eighteenth century in his political ideas (such as his attachment to the Crown and the Established Church) he was a man of the nineteenth century in his professional approach to the business of government (being industrious, earnest and incorruptible). Both these facets of his character recommended him to the King when the administration of the Duke of Portland foundered in the early autumn of 1809. However, denied support by the followers of Canning, Castelereagh, Sidmouth (as Addington had now become) and the Whigs Grenville and Grey, the prospects of Perceval presiding over anything more than a caretaker ministry initially appeared negligible.

However, Perceval not only survived the immediate problems of constructing an administration but also surmounted numerous difficulties including the emergence of the Regency and of Luddism in 1811, the resignation of his foreign secretary, Lord Wellesley (older brother of the future Duke of Wellington), and the dislocation of trade caused by the continental system, the retaliatory Orders-in-Council, and the consequent falling out with the United States (which degenerated into the War of 1812). Perceval's response to such problems such as passing the Framebreaking Act and saturating the troublespots with troops was hardly imaginative but was the most that could be expected in the context of the times and at least prevented the problem from getting out of hand.

When the madman John Bellingham fired at Perceval at point-blank range in the lobby of the House of Commons on 11 May 1812 he snuffed out the life of a politician who lacked genius but who demanded respect for his integrity, commitment and resilience.

'Peterloo', 16 August 1819. The so-called 'Peterloo Massacre' occurred at St Peter's Fields, Manchester, after a crowd estimated at roughly 60,000 assembled to hear Henry 'Orator' Hunt. As the Liverpool government had allowed the Seditious Meetings Act to lapse, this was a lawful gathering, and the home secretary, Lord Sidmouth, advised the local magistrates not to intervene unless the crowd rioted or acted feloniously.

However, disregarding these wise words, the Manchester magistrates sent fifty men of the local yeomanry into the sea of humanity in order to arrest Hunt. They were soon engulfed, whereupon the regulars of the 15th Hussars were sent in to rescue them, with sabres drawn. In the ensuing mêlée eleven were killed and possibly as many as four hundred, including women and children, wounded.

Feeling obliged to stand by the local representatives of law and order, the government applauded the magistracy and the military for their prompt action. However, many referred to the incident as 'Peterloo', in ironic reference to Waterloo.

'Peterloo' has been seized on by left-wing historians who wish to depict the Liverpool government, at least prior to its alleged liberal Tory facelift, as reactionary or even tyrannical, when a cursory consideration of the facts reveals that the fault lay with the men on the spot and that had they followed the wishes of central government there would have been no 'massacre'.

Philosophic Radicals According to historians such as Dicey, Halévy and Finer the Philosophic Radicals (otherwise known as the Benthamites or Utilitarians because followers of the teachings of Jeremy Bentham) exercised an influence out of all proportion to their numbers in the 1830s and 1840s because of their ability to mould the intellectual climate through the world of letters and work on several of the Royal Commissions which issued in important legislation such as Edwin Chadwick and the 1834 Poor Law Amendment Act and Joseph Parkes and the 1835 Municipal Corporations Act.

Other leading philosophic radicals included James Mill, John Stuart Mill, George Grote, Charles Austin, Joseph Hume, Francis Place and John Arthur Roebuck.

The trend has been for more recent historians than those mentioned above, such as MacDonagh and Brent, to downplay the influence of the Philosophic Radicals, in Brent's case in relation to that of the liberal Anglican Whigs.

Phoenix Park Murders, 6 May 1882. Lord Frederick Cavendish was appointed Irish chief secretary by

Gladstone after Forster resigned in pique at the Kilmainham Treaty having been concluded behind his back.

Cavendish was strolling in Phoenix Park, Dublin, with his undersecretary, Thomas Henry Burke, when the two men were set upon and stabbed to death by a group using surgical knives and calling themselves 'the Invincibles'.

Pitt ('the Younger'), William (28 May 1759–23 January 1806). William Pitt is popularly known as William Pitt 'the Younger' in order to differentiate him from his father, William Pitt 'the Elder' (1708–78), who was created Earl of Chatham in 1766. Following a private education and his graduation at Pembroke College, Cambridge the young Pitt, his father's second son, entered Lincoln's Inn in 1778 and was called to the bar in 1780. In the same year he came bottom of the poll at his old university but the following year entered the House of Commons as Sir James Lowther's nominee for the pocket borough of Appleby.

When Shelburne, his father's disciple, was appointed prime minister in 1783, Pitt was appointed chancellor of the exchequer. When Shelburne fell later in the year, Pitt twice refused an invitation to form a ministry (as this would have depended upon Lord North's goodwill) but once Fox brought down the Portland administration through his India Bill, Pitt became prime minister, on 19 December 1783, at the age of twenty-four. In addition to the confidence of the King, Pitt won a considerable victory at the 1784 general election. In the event he was to hold the office of prime minister for the next seventeen years.

Pitt's premiership prior to 1793 was marked by settlement of the government of India (establishing the system of dual Westminster and Company control which lasted until the Indian Mutiny) and of Canada (until the Durham Report); free trade; and the reform of the nation's finances (notably by sweeping away sinecures and setting up the Sinking Fund to reduce the National Debt). The only threat to continued sound government was the illness of George III and the threat of a regency in late 1788. The King, however, recovered and as late as 1792 Pitt looked forward to fifteen years of peace and using that time to pay off a further £25m of the National Debt: a dream rudely shattered by the French declaration of war in the following year.

The French Revolutionary and Napoleonic wars not only ruined Pitt's plans for further reform but resulted in measures restricting personal liberty and the freedom of the press. Although such actions confirmed Fox in his view of Pitt as an enemy of liberty, many Whigs were persuaded by the French threat and incidents such as naval mutiny to take a contrary view, and moved into support of Pitt.

The Irish rebellion of 1798 persuaded Pitt of the importance of securing the union of the two countries, which was achieved by the 1800 Act of Union. However, George would not accept Catholic Emancipation, although Pitt considered this an essential corollary to the enterprise. This, and the strains of prosecuting the war, led to his resignation and replacement by Addington (later Viscount Sidmouth) in early 1801.

Pitt returned to head a ministry which included Addington in 1804 but could not succeed in reconstructing the coalition of forces which he had previously led (Grenville, for example, staying out). Strains between Sidmouth and Canning led to the former and his followers resigning, whilst the war was going from bad to worse, following Spain's entering into hostilities with Britain. When Pitt died on 23 January 1806, Trafalgar had ensured that Britain was safe from invasion but Austerlitz had brought the Third Coalition to an end and ensured that there was no foreseeable prospect of French arms being defeated on the continent.

Pitt was unable to give his country victory but he had made Britain better able to withstand the vicissitudes of war, so that Britain was able to emerge from the loss of the American colonies with the potential to consolidate her colonies and ultimately expand her empire.

It is a measure of Pitt's greatness that so many of his contemporaries claimed to be 'Pittites' even after his death. His career had been both reforming in the 1780s and repressive in the 1790s and thus allowed conflicting inspirations to be drawn from his record.

Plaid Cymru (the Welsh National Party) Plaid Cymru was formed by John Saunders Lewis in 1925 to campaign for an independent Wales. Its chief source of support is Welsh-speaking rural central and northern Wales.

The 1966 by-election victory at Camarthen of its president, Gwynfor Evans, marked a turning point in its fortunes and by the February 1974 general election it had three seats. Support fell back in the late seventies, with only 20% registering their support for devolution in the 1979 referendum. However, by 1992 Plaid Cymru had four MPs and in the first elections to the Welsh Assembly in Cardiff became the main opposition to Labour.

Plan of Campaign, 1886. On 17 October 1886, following the failure of the First Irish Home Rule Bill, the Plan of Campaign was announced at Woodford, on Lord Clanricarde's Galway estate, where the tenants were being threatened with eviction for non-payment of rent. On 23 October the Plan was published in *United Ireland*. It consisted of the election on each estate, where the Irish National League had influence, of a committee which would offer the landlord what was considered a just half-year's rent for the entire tenantry and, should he refuse it, that fund (supplemented, if need be, from National League funds) would be used to support those evicted. Any landlord evicting in such circumstances would be subjected to a complete rent strike and anyone engaged in the process of eviction or attempting to move on to the property of an evicted tenant would be subject to boycotting.

The movement eventually foundered as a consequence of Papal disapproval, governmental coercion and the financial strains arising from support of evicted tenants.

Pluralities Act, 1838. Although in exceptional cases bishops might issue licences permitting non-residence, the purpose of the Act was to clamp down on pluralism wherever possible. Thus no one holding two benefices, for example, could hold a third or any cathedral preferment, and preferments could not be held in more than one cathedral, with certain exceptions for archdeacons. Concentrating clerical minds on matters spiritual rather than material was also facilitated by ensuring that clergy could not engage directly in trade or farm more than eighty acres of land without their bishop's consent.

Pocket borough A pocket borough was so-called because it was a constituency said to be in the pocket of a particular individual. That is to say, a dominant figure, usually a landowner, controlled a majority of the votes and could thus effectively choose the MP or MPs. An example of such a pocket or nomination borough was Newark, which was controlled by the Duke of Newcastle, enabling him to ease the entry of the young Gladstone into the House of Commons in December 1832. Although such boroughs were clearly undemocratic they did allow able men who were not necessarily well suited to electioneering to begin a parliamentary career at a very early age.

Poll Tax, 1989–92. The poll tax is the popular name – or rather the deeply unpopular name – for the community charge which was introduced by Margaret Thatcher, against the advice of Nigel Lawson, and which did more than any other domestic issue to contribute to her downfall.

Prior to the poll tax, local government was funded locally out of the rates, which took into account the size, standard and use of properties but not the number of occupants or the use they made of local authority services. Thus a minority of property owners paid for local government services from which the entire community benefited. Periodic revaluation of rateable liability (pushing the rates upwards) merely compounded this injustice and added to the demand for the reform of local government finance.

Instead of opting for local income tax (the Liberal solution), Kenneth Baker, as environment secretary, proposed to replace the rates with a universal flat-level community charge (with rebates for the less well-off). In addition a Uniform Business Rate, set nationally and inflation-indexed, would replace the non-domestic rate. This new system of local government finance would ostensibly have two advantages over the rating system: it would be more equitable as every adult would pay something towards the cost of services that everyone used, and higher-spending (Labour) local authorities would now theoretically be subject to the discipline of the ballot box so that local government expenditure would be constrained. Moreover, those who defaulted on their community charge payments – who might be considered more likely to vote Labour – would ultimately be removed from the electoral register and thus be disfranchised. However, local authorities took the opportunity to raise local government spending by setting much higher than anticipated community charges, secure in the knowledge that central government and not themselves would be blamed.

Rather than phasing in the new system it was decided to transfer to the poll tax as quickly as possible with Scotland in the vanguard because there revaluation of rateable liability had enhanced the demand for abolition of the rates. However, once the practical disadvantages of the poll tax became apparent this fact became a source of grievance north of the border that strengthened the demands for devolution. On 31 March 1990, the day before the poll tax was due to come into effect in England and Wales, there were riots in Trafalgar Square and the local election results in May more quietly but even more persuasively demonstrated to the government that the poll tax was a dreadful political liability.

Two steps were taken as an exercise in damage limitation: limits were placed on the community charges which local authorities could set and the Exchequer increased grants to local government so that the taxpayer provided relief to the poll taxpayer. These measures proved inadequate, however, to stem the tide of criticism to which the poll tax was subjected.

Michael Heseltine made abolition of the poll tax a major plank in his bid for the Tory leadership and when John Major won he sent him to the Ministry of the Environment to clear up the mess, which he did (at least temporarily) in 1991 by replacing poll tax with council tax: a banded property tax, taking account of both size of property and number of occupants, with discounts for single-person households.

Poor Employment Act, 1817. The 1817 Poor Employment Act was a very forward-looking measure passed by the Liverpool government to relieve or forestall economic distress by making available state loans totalling £500,000 for mainland Britain and £250,000 for Ireland in order to encourage fisheries and other public works undertaken by the local authorities.

Poor Law Act, 1847. In the light of criticism arising from incidents such as the 1845 Andover Workhouse scandal, the 1847 Poor Law Act amended the 1834 Poor Law Amendment Act by replacing the Poor Law Commission (of which Chadwick was secretary) with a Poor Law Board, headed by a president, who would be a member of the government and usually of the Cabinet. This reform thus ensured greater accountability to parliament of those engaged in administering the New Poor Law.

Poor Law Amendment Act, 1834. In 1832 the Whig government led by Earl Grey responded to the rocketing costs of local taxation to cover poor relief by setting up a Royal Commission, chaired by the Bishop of London, to look into the deficiencies of the Speenhamland system and what more generally came to be called the Old Poor Law.

The Commission's Report was largely the work of its Philosophic Radical secretary, Edwin Chadwick, whose Benthamite beliefs were reflected in the 'less eligibility' principle, which was enshrined in the legislation arising from acceptance of the Report's findings by the Melbourne government: the 1834 Poor Law Amendment Act.

Parishes were grouped together into Poor Law Unions, each of which was large enough to build and run a workhouse where those desirous of assistance had to become inmates. In other words, the New Poor Law abolished outdoor relief in favour of indoor relief. Moreover, the principle of less eligibility was designed to discourage scroungers and thus entry into the workhouse not only meant surrendering one's liberty but also one's dignity as inmates were obliged to accept a dehumanizing regime in which families were broken up, the sexes separated, harsh discipline enforced, poor food dispensed and hard monotonous labour undertaken in order to contribute to one's upkeep. The advocates of a free market cost-cutting approach triumphed over those whose outlook was shaped by evangelical or humanitarian considerations. The cost of local taxation diminished but at a terrible price in human terms.

Centralized regulation of the poor law administration was undertaken by means of a three-man Poor Law Commission, with Chadwick serving as its secretary. In the localities Assistant Commissioners supervised the implementation of the New Poor Law, with day-to-day administration performed by Poor Law Guardians elected by ratepayers.

The New Poor Law soon proved itself to be clearly unfitted to deal with mass urban unemployment so that its writ never ran over large parts of the country including South Wales, the Midlands and the North, so that 84% of those receiving relief in 1844 still received it in the form of outdoor relief.

The Andover Workhouse scandal of 1845 showed that the new system of poor relief was subject to just as bad, if not worse, abuses as the old system and contributed to an overhauling of the administrative structure so as to ensure greater parliamentary scrutiny through the 1847 Poor Law Act.

Poor Law Report, 1909. The creation of the Royal Commission on the Poor Laws was one of the last measures taken by Balfour before resigning office in 1905.

The majority of Commission members supported the principles of the 1834 Poor Law Amendment Act and sought merely to improve its operation by means of various modifications, whereas the authors of the Minority Report advocated abolition of the existing Poor Law organization and the farming out of its functions to other bodies already dealing with specific groups of disadvantaged people including the ill, the old, the mentally deficient, the unemployed and deprived children.

The Minority Report was so influential because it not only provided a blueprint for the modern welfare state but also anticipated the 1944 Employment Policy White Paper, calling for the state to stimulate aggregate demand through public works 'in the lean years of the trade cycle'.

The difference in attitude between the authors of the Majority Report and Minority Report was ably summed up by Beatrice Webb when she said that the former approached the poor like a man drowning in a swamp to whom they would throw a lifeline, whereas the latter not only wished to pull him out but then to drain the swamp.

Portland (William Henry Cavendish Bentinck), third Duke of (14 April 1738–29 October 1809). William Henry Cavendish Bentinck was the eldest son of the 2nd Duke of Portland. After Westminster School and Christ Church, Oxford he began a political career in the Whig interest which culminated in his twice holding the highest office of state, separated by a gap of twenty-four years.

On both occasions he was effectively the 'frontman' for more assertive colleagues who could agree on little more than their willingness to serve under him. On the first occasion, in 1783, he was the nominal head of the Fox–North Coalition who was pushed into office by Fox and Burke whilst on the second occasion, 1807–9, it was the Pittites Perceval, Castlereagh and Canning who provided the necessary initial impetus (Portland having abandoned his opposition to Pitt in 1792 and joined him in 1794).

However, the contrasts between the two premierships are at least as marked as the similarities. Portland's first ministry early came to grief because Fox needlessly antagonized the King over the finances of the Prince of Wales and the government of India, whereas his second ministry fell prey to internal squabbles, with Canning feuding first with Perceval and then with Castlereagh.

A more substantial difference is that on the first occasion Portland's triumph over Shelburne represented an assertion of the Whiggish principle that the will of the Commons should prevail over that of the King (George III), whereas on the second occasion he assumed the traditional Tory role of defending royal prerogative by acting with the King to displace the Ministry of All the Talents after George quarrelled with Grenville over Catholic Emancipation.

Portland's career thus illustrates the fact that a title was at least as valuable a political commodity as a reputation for integrity but that both still paled into insignificance compared with royal favour.

Powell, John Enoch (16 June 1912–18 February 1998). John Enoch Powell was born in Birmingham in 1912. Both his parents were schoolteachers. The young Enoch was imbued with a love of learning and soon distinguished himself as a brilliant classicist. He won a scholarship to King Edward's Birmingham and then a scholarship to Trinity College, Cambridge. At the age of twenty-five he became Professor of Greek at Sydney University, emulating the precocity of one of his idols of that time, Friedrich Nietzsche (who had become Professor of Classical Philology at Basel aged just twenty-four).

When the war, which he felt was inevitable, finally broke out, he volunteered and became a private in the Royal Warwickshire Regiment. His talents were soon recognized and he entered the Intelligence Corps, ending the war as a brigadier. His experience of India resulted in his falling in love with the Raj and deciding to enter politics after the war in order to sustain the imperial dream.

Rab Butler recognized his talents and employed Powell alongside Reginald Maudling and Iain Macleod in the Conservative Research Department. Powell was also eventually chosen as the Conservative candidate for Wolverhampton, South West, after presenting himself at nineteen other constituencies. In 1950 he entered parliament and immediately fell under the spell of Westminster. Less precipitately but no less deeply or enduringly, he fell in love with his secretary, Pamela Wilson, whom he married and who was to bear him two daughters.

In 1958 Powell resigned as financial secretary to the Treasury along with Nigel Birch, the economic secretary, and the chancellor of the exchequer, Peter Thorneycroft, because the cabinet would not accept their recommended level of public expenditure cuts and proposed curbing of the money supply. It was this embarrassing loss of his entire Treasury team which Macmillan memorably dismissed as a 'little local difficulty'. This incident showed that Powell anticipated Thatcherism in identifying money supply as the primary cause of inflation. It proved only a minor setback in his ministerial career as he was back as health minister within two years, where he enthusiastically increased his department's spending as the economy boomed.

When Macmillan stepped down in 1963 Powell caballed for Butler to succeed him. He claimed to have put a loaded gun in Butler's hand but Butler was too squeamish to pull the trigger, with the result that Home became prime minister. Powell (and Macleod) refused to serve under him and when Home himself stepped down, in 1965, threw his own hat into the ring. Heath won and Powell entered his Shadow Cabinet, only to be dismissed as shadow defence spokesman for his 'Rivers of Blood' speech in April 1968, which Heath branded as 'racialist in tone'. The speech undoubtedly aroused fear and anger amongst many blacks and Asians living in Britain but it equally articulated the feelings of many Britons who felt that Powell had shown enormous courage in speaking out on the hitherto taboo subject of race.

Powell claimed that his 1970 campaign put Heath into office, just as his 1974 decision not to stand for parliament and advice to his supporters to vote Labour put Heath out of office. There is no way of knowing for sure just how great his influence was but both elections were close enough for the claim to appear credible, especially given the fact that national trends appeared to be magnified in the Powellite heartlands of the West Midlands. Powell had already chosen internal exile and the path of the prophet but if he was to play the part of John the Baptist to Mrs Thatcher it was Heath's head that he was determined should be served up on a platter.

Europe proved to be the final issue which marked the parting of the ways between Heath and Powell, with the latter announcing that he would not stand at the next election and urging the country to vote for Labour because at least Wilson offered the prospect of a referendum on Britain's continued membership of the Common Market. Powell had his revenge on Heath insofar as he lost office never to hold it again. Powell's prospects of resuming his ministerial career had likewise been dashed but the Royal Warwickshire kingmaker had one last card to play and by the end of 1974 had returned to Parliament as an Ulster Unionist. This seemingly bizarre move was actually consistent with his career hitherto since he was resolutely opposed to the surrender of British sovereignty and the supremacy of the House of Commons whether it was justified in terms of the special relationship, European integration or the peace process in Ireland.

Equally revered and reviled, Powell can be seen as either a self-promoting demagogue who made racism seem respectable and who manoeuvred to succeed Heath if he lost the 1970 election, or as a statesman who had the courage to sacrifice his chance of office because he consistently uttered the most unpalatable of truths in the most lucid of language, not just about immigration but about the British economy and Britain's pretensions to continued great power status.

Prevention of Terrorism Act, 1973. The Prevention of Terrorism Act of 1973 gave the police special powers to stop, search, arrest and detain terrorist suspects, and had to be renewed each year. It was introduced partly in response to protests from foreign governments that Britain was being used as a sanctuary for various groups planning violence in their countries of origin. The legislation was obviously also of assistance in combating domestic terrorist groups, of which the most notable was the IRA (internment having failed to solve the problem).

The Prevention of Terrorism legislation was superseded by the Terrorism Act passed by Parliament on 20 July 2000 (which came into force on 19 February 2001) and the anti-Terrorism, Crime and Security Act which was passed in the immediate aftermath of the 11 September attacks in 2001.

Primrose League The Primrose League was dedicated to the memory of Benjamin Disraeli, in the mistaken belief that the primrose was his favourite flower. By 1900 the League numbered 1.5 million members, of whom half were women and a great number, possibly a majority, were working class. Thus Richard Shannon describes the Primrose League as 'the greatest organization ever created in popular politics dedicated to the cult of an individual leader'. He also suggests that the League may have been developed by the party hierarchy as a means of undermining the pretensions of the National Union to dictate policy and elect the leader. The League was certainly a more genuine expression of Tory Democracy, although it was again wrong about Disraeli in regarding him as the patron of Tory Democratic politics.

Profumo affair, 1963. The Profumo affair gravely damaged Macmillan and the Conservative Party for two reasons. Firstly, Profumo, the secretary of state for war, brazenly and repeatedly denied an affair with Christine Keeler before eventually coming clean. Secondly, the fact that Keeler had also shared her favours with the Soviet military attaché, Captain Ivanov, apparently gave the affair a security dimension and made it appear the latest in a series of security scandals.

'Protestant Tories' The 'Protestant Tories' or Ultras were those Tories such as the Marquis of Winchilsea and the Duke of Richmond whose devotion to the cause of maintaining the privileged position of the Established or Anglican Church rendered them most bitterly opposed to Catholic Emancipation and to those 'Catholic Tories' who advocated that step.

The 'Protestant Tories' refused to serve under Canning as prime minister in 1827 and their disagreements with the 'Catholic Tories' helped ensure the collapse of the Goderich administration (the 'Protestant' Tory chancellor of the exchequer, Herries, threatening to resign if Althorp was appointed chairman of a key financial committee, whilst the 'Catholic Tory' Huskisson threatened to resign if Althorp was not appointed).

The 'Protestant Tories' turned their ire upon Wellington and Peel for what they regarded was their betrayal in passing Catholic Emancipation in 1829.

Public Health Act, 1848. The 1848 Public Health Act was the result of the work of Edwin Chadwick, notably through his 1842 Sanitary Report on the Condition of the Labouring Poor and the 1844 and 1845 reports of the 1844 Royal Commission on the Health of Towns.

The 1848 Act established a Central Board of Health answerable to Parliament, which was loosely modelled on the Poor Law Commission. Local boards of health, answerable to the Central Board, together with medical officers and Inspectors of Nuisances, were mandatory where the death rate exceeded 23 per thousand (compared with the national average of 21 per thousand) and were otherwise permitted where at least 10% of ratepayers expressed a desire for them.

Those authorities which had their own arrangements under separate legislation (including London and Scotland) were not subject to central inspection.

In its first six years the Central Board of Health supervised the implementation of local boards in roughly 300 towns containing, in all, about 2 million people or about 16% of the population.

Public Health Act, 1875. In requiring local authorities to provide adequate sewage, drainage and water supply; remove nuisances; provide notification of infectious diseases; and dispose of contaminated food, the 1875 Public Health Act consolidated earlier legislation (notably the 1871 Local Government Act and 1872 Sanitary Act). It also empowered the new sanitary authorities to provide hospitals out of the rates.

Whilst retrospectively considered a landmark in public health legislation, Sir John Simon, the pioneering medical reformer, was so disillusioned with recent developments that he resigned as Medical Officer of the Board of Health in 1876.

Public Worship Regulation Act, 1874. Tait, the Archbishop of Canterbury, originally put forward the measure which became the Public Worship Regulation Act as a private member's bill. The measure sought to strengthen the disciplinary powers of diocesan bishops over their clergy so as to facilitate a clamp down on 'popish' or 'ritualistic' practices. Despite the misgivings of senior colleagues including Salisbury, Disraeli effectively adopted the measure in order to curry favour with Victoria, exploit Liberal divisions and pre-empt an unholy alliance of Anglo-Catholics and radical non-conformists.

The 1874 session of parliament was dominated by consideration of the Bill which merely created several martyrs to the cause of ritualism and alienated support for the Conservative Party in High Church quarters.

R

Race Relations legislation The 1965 Race Relations Act criminalized discrimination in public places through 'race, colour, ethnic or national origin'. A Race Relations Board (and later the Community Relations Commission) answerable to the home secretary was set up to investigate complaints under the Act.

The 1968 Race Relations Act extended the scope of the 1965 Act to cover areas such as housing and employment. It granted power to bring prosecutions and established the Community Relations Commission to improve race relations.

The Act specifically mentioned the Queen and thereby included her as an employer within its provisions.

The 1976 Race Relations Act sought to address shortcomings in the 1965 and 1968 Acts by covering indirect discrimination and acts of private discrimination. 'Incitement to racial hatred' was made a criminal offence and the Commission for Racial Equality (CRE) was established to promote equal opportunities.

Radical Programme, 1885. See UNAUTHORIZED PROGRAMME.

Railway Act, 1844. The 1844 Railway Act had two particularly far-sighted provisions. Firstly, it obliged the railway companies to run at least one train each day which would stop at each station on the line at a charge of no more than 1d per mile for adults and half this price for children under the age of twelve. This so-called 'parliamentary train' placed rail travel within the means of all but the very poorest members of society and thus ensured that rail transport became a medium of mass transportation.

Secondly, the Act provided the state with the option of purchasing those railways constructed in or after 1844 after twenty-one years if they made what were judged to be excessive profits. In the event, however, it was left to the Attlee Labour government to implement railway nationalization in 1946.

Real IRA The so-called Real IRA broke away from the Irish Republican Army (IRA) and its political wing Sinn Féin in late 1997 following the latter's decision to participate in the peace process. In other words, it is a hardline terrorist republican organization.

Politically the group has been linked to the 32 County Sovereignty Committee, which was set up to challenge Sinn Féin's peace strategy under the leadership of Bernadette Sands-McKevitt, the sister of the IRA hunger striker Bobby Sands, and partner of Michael McKevitt.

The 1998 Omagh bombing, which killed 28, including an 18-month-old infant, saw the Real IRA subjected to such condemnation even in Republican circles that it briefly suspended its 'military operations'.

Rebecca riots, 1842–43. The Rebecca riots were a series of attacks initially directed against toll gates in West Wales in protest against high turnpike tolls and tithes paid to the Established Church (the Anglican Church in Wales). Later workhouses were attacked and the Poor Law Commissioners.

The protesters disguised their identity by blackening their faces and dressing as women. They took their name from the Biblical text which states that 'the seed of Rebecca shall possess the gates of her enemies' (Genesis 24: 60). The authorities used troops, spies and police to suppress the disorders but more effective in restoring order in the long term was an Act of 1844 to reduce tolls.

'Red Clydeside' Glasgow's Clydeside was the centre of revolutionary socialism in Edwardian Britain and hence 'red'. However, the extent to which Clydeside posed a genuine threat of revolution remains disputed.

Wartime rent increases provoked a campaign against the landlords which united 'progressive' employers, 'official' Labour bodies such as the ILP, as well as the British Socialist Party and the Socialist Labour Party. Clydeside's women played a leading role in the campaign at grass roots level.

In February 1915, one of Glasgow's leading industrialists started importing non-union American labour onto Clydeside, thereby exacerbating industrial relations. A strike by engineering workers was only averted after a deal negotiated by the Admiralty. However, the 1915 Munitions Act triggered a new wave of trade union unrest which the government only dispelled through a twin track policy of concessions and a move, in the spring of 1916, to arrest, on sedition charges, those Clydeside leaders like John Maclean, who continued to advocate industrial action.

To justify the latter, the authorities alleged that Clydeside was subject to 'a systematic and sinister plan' on the part of revolutionary socialists to undermine the war effort and overthrow the state. The outbreak of the Russian revolution in 1917 and the presence on Clydeside of the Russian revolutionary agitator Peter Petroff added to the authorities' alarm, not least because he and Maclean sought to reorganize the British Socialist Party along Bolshevik lines and convert the Clyde Workers Committee to an anti-war policy.

The Armistice brought some relief but the transition to a peacetime economy introduced new tensions. More specifically, the workers were alarmed lest demobilization produce a return to high unemployment. To prevent this happening, the unions secured an immediate reduction in the basic working week from 54 to 47 hours, to come into effect from 1 January 1919. However, this was considered insufficient by socialists who persuaded the rank and file to embark upon a Forty-Hours strike campaign. 70,000 workers were idle by 28 January and the 'Riot of George Square' (a clash between strikers and police) took place on 31 January.

Iain Maclean considers the very concept of 'Red Clydeside' to be a myth on the grounds that bodies such as the Clyde Workers Committee were unrepresentative of the workforce as a whole, revolutionaries such as John Maclean were ineffectual, and the government exaggerated the threat of revolution on Clydeside by taking the revolutionaries at their own estimation. However, in 1922 the ILP won 10 out of the 15 parliamentary constituencies in Glasgow, whilst the

Communist party took Motherwell and came within 800 votes of winning both Greenock and Paisley. Nevertheless, in parliament the Red Clydesiders were effectively muzzled despite, or because of, the fact that some of their number, including John Wheatley and Emmanuel Shinwell, joined Labour in office.

Redistribution, June 1885. Salisbury recognized that if the agricultural labourers were enfranchised along the lines suggested by Gladstone (by extending household suffrage to the counties) the consequence would be an erosion of Conservative influence in the county seats. He therefore insisted that parliamentary reform be counterbalanced by a radical redistribution of seats: a compromise agreed through the Arlington Street compact.

Henceforth most constituencies (647 seats out of a total of 670) became single-member seats with pretty well equal numbers of voters in each (thereby meeting one of the six demands of the People's Charter). Salisbury recognized the party political advantage to be gained from redistributing voters from the small boroughs (where the Liberals were making inroads) to suburbia.

Under the terms of the redistribution boroughs with a population of less than 15,000 lost their separate parliamentary representation by being merged with the surrounding counties; boroughs with a population of less than 50,000 lost one of their two MPs; and cities henceforth had one constituency for every 50,000 people. The division of cities allowed villa Toryism to flourish in the leafier suburbs so that the Conservatives started to do well in places like Sheffield, Leeds and London (winning 36 of the 62 seats there post-redistribution compared to none in 1865). In short, the Conservatives did best out of redistribution.

Redmond, John Edward (1 September 1856–6 March 1918). John Edward Redmond was born into the Catholic gentry of County Wexford, the eldest son of William Archer Redmond, MP, a supporter of the Irish Home Rule policy of Isaac Butt. Educated by the Jesuits at Clongowes and then at Trinity College, Dublin, in 1880 he became a clerk in the House of Commons where he was increasingly drawn to Parnell and he was elected unopposed in the Parnellite cause in January 1881 for the borough of New Ross in his home county. Thus he arrived in Westminster when Parnellite tactics of obstruction were at their height, delivering a maiden speech comprising a single sentence before he was removed by the sergeant at arms, Speaker Brand having suspended all Irish members for refusal to obey the rules of the House.

Redmond's oratory was more fully tested in his 1882 mission to Australia to shore up support for the nationalist cause in the wake of the Phoenix Park murders. Having collected £15,000 and married, Redmond proceeded to the States where he raised a comparable sum. In 1886 he was called to the bar and in 1888 served five weeks' imprisonment on a charge of intimidation.

However, it was not until 1890 when Parnell was cited as co-respondent in the O'Shea divorce case that Redmond began to make his mark on national politics. He played the leading role in mobilizing continued support of Parnell despite the 25 November 1890 publication of Gladstone's letter declaring him a liability to the Home Rule cause and it was Redmond who led the Parnellite rump of 9 MPs returned after the June 1892 general election.

When the Second Boer War reunited the Irish Nationalists in 1900 Redmond was chosen as their chairman and steadily assumed the role of leader of the movement. Rejection of the People's Budget by the Lords in 1909 gave Redmond the chance he was looking for to clear a way for Home Rule by challenging the peers' veto, whilst the outcome of the 1910 elections rendered Asquith more amenable to Irish nationalist influence. Redmond was, however, slow to recognize the threat of armed resistance from Ulster, only backing the Irish Volunteer movement after the Curragh mutiny and Larne gun-running in 1914, by which time the volunteer organization was largely controlled by those with a more radical agenda than his own.

When Britain declared war on Germany Redmond magnanimously declared – without consulting his colleagues – that 'the armed Catholics in the south will be only too glad to join arms with the armed Protestant Ulstermen' in guarding Ireland so as to release Crown forces for service elsewhere. However, Kitchener blocked any official recognition of the volunteers and even rejected the formation of a Catholic Division. Redmond nevertheless successfully promoted enlistment in Ireland and was offered but declined a post in the coalition cabinet formed in May 1915. When conscription was finally introduced in 1916, Redmond was instrumental in persuading Bonar Law and Carson to accept the exclusion of Ireland from the first National Service Bill.

Nevertheless, disaffection in Ireland was growing and culminated in the Easter Rising. The suggestion that the Home Rule Bill, which had been suspended for the duration, would immediately come into force but that the six Ulster counties would be excluded until the end of the war, came to nothing and Sinn Féin exploited the backlash provoked by the executions following the Rising, thereby outflanking the Irish Nationalists in the affections of the Irish nationalist electorate.

Redmond died unexpectedly on 6 March 1918 as his life's work lay in ruins. Thus in the Coupon election the Irish Nationalists won just seven seats compared to the Sinn Féiners' 73.

Redmond was a man of principle whose steadfast aim was the peaceful achievement of a free Ireland within the Empire. During his leadership and largely thanks to his moderation, dignity, courage and sincerity, the Irish nationalists moved a long way towards this goal, achieving control of local government, the ownership of the land, and the creation of an Irish parliament with an executive responsible to it. However, Redmond was unable or unwilling to exert pressure to force the pace of events and younger more militant men marginalized him.

Referendum on continued membership of the Common Market, 5 June 1975. In its successful 1974 election manifesto Labour promised renegotiation of the terms of Britain's membership of the European Economic Community (EEC). At a summit in Dublin in March 1975 a formula was arrived at to reduce Britain's budgetary contribution. Thus the process of renegotiation produced enough concessions to allow foreign secretary, Jim Callaghan, to recommend that Britain stayed in.

However, a substantial number within, and outside, the Labour Party begged to differ and a special Labour conference decisively supported withdrawal. With Labour split it was decided that the people would adjudicate by means of a referendum held on 5 June 1975. During the campaign the Cabinet's collective responsibility was suspended, with each minister enjoying a free vote.

The 'Yes' camp included Roy Jenkins, Shirley Williams, Harold Wilson, Edward Heath, Jeremy Thorpe and the bulk of industry, finance and the press, whilst the 'No' camp included Michael Foot, Tony Benn, Barbara Castle, Enoch Powell, the SNP and many trade union leaders. The former successfully depicted themselves as representing modernity, enterprise, dynamism, internationalism, and the future, whilst portraying their enemies as backward looking 'little Englanders'.

At 64%, the turnout was low (compared with 73% in the October 1974 election), despite £125,000 having been provided out of public funds to finance both the pro- and anti-market campaigns, and the fact that the former spent a further £1.5m.

There was an overwhelming majority in favour of remaining in the Community: with 67.2% voting 'Yes' and 32.8% voting 'No', and with no significant variations of response in the constituent parts of the UK.

The whole affair illustrates Wilson's willingness to subordinate constitutional convention to party political pragmatism.

Reform Act, 1832 See GREAT REFORM ACT.

Reform Act, the Second, 1867. As Chartism declined, a growing section of the governing class came to believe that a section of the working class could be trusted with the vote: a belief strengthened by the development of craft unions and by the passive popular reaction to the Lancashire Cotton Famine. Moreover, the death of Palmerston in 1865 removed a formidable obstacle to parliamentary reform. Thus Russell sought to cap his career by bringing forward a bill promising a very limited extension of the franchise in 1866. Despite the best efforts of Gladstone in framing and presenting the bill it was, however, too strong for many Liberals to stomach and Robert Lowe led the Adullamites in joining with the Conservatives in voting for an amendment which brought down both the bill and the government.

A third Derby–Disraeli minority government came into being and the latter decided to 'steal the Whigs'' clothing and introduce his own Reform Bill, as this promised to embarrass Gladstone (who succeeded Russell as Liberal leader); keep the Liberals divided; show the electorate that the Conservatives were capable of passing major legislation; perpetuate Conservative government; and give the Conservatives some scope to extract party advantage from framing the terms of the new measure. Such a plan was not to the liking of all Conservatives and Carnarvon (the colonial secretary), General Peel (the war secretary) and Cranborne (the India secretary and future Lord Salisbury) all resigned from the government. Their fears regarding Derby's 'leap in the dark' were well founded insofar as the bill became progressively more radical as a result of amendments during its passage through parliament, so that what was finally passed into law was decidedly more sweeping than the 1866 Liberal bill which the Conservatives had helped to kill.

Royden Harrison regards the timing and extent of the legislation as determined by socio-economic forces, specifically the development in size and political consciousness of the urban working class, as symbolized by the Reform League. More specifically, it is claimed that the May 1867 Hyde Park riot was the direct cause of Disraeli surrendering over Hodgkinson's amendment, which abolished compounding and thus added another 400,000 to the borough electorate. However, Maurice Cowling shows that the passage and terms of the Bill, which ended up enfranchising men in the boroughs renting or owning property valued over £10, together with some males holding long leases in the counties, owed more to high political manoeuvring than to extra-parliamentary agitation.

Compared with the Great Reform Act, the electorate rose by 80%, to just under 2.5 million adult males out of a population of over 30 million. However, these global figures mask considerable national and regional variations. In Ireland, excepting Belfast, for example, the change was slight, whereas an increase of nearly 180% took place in the Scottish boroughs.

The landed aristocracy continued to dominate government but they were increasingly joined in parliament by representatives of industrial, commercial and financial wealth.

Reform Act, the Third, 1884. The Second Reform Act of 1867 was open to criticism in several respects. For example, there were regional imbalances in the distribution of seats and the denial of household suffrage in the counties appeared anomalous after it had been conceded in the boroughs. Moreover, both the Liberals and the Conservatives were looking to ways of extracting party political advantage from any change.

As extending the franchise to the agricultural labourers appeared likely to favour Gladstone, Salisbury insisted that parliamentary reform would have to be complemented, or rather counteracted, by a redistribution of seats. This, together with much of the detail, is what was agreed between the two men and their lieutenants by the Arlington Street compact.

The Reform Act (which unlike its predecessors applied to the United Kingdom as a whole) created a uniform franchise and enfranchised all male householders who paid rates and had lived in the house for at least one year; all male lodgers who occupied lodgings worth £10 a year and who had lived there for at least one year; and all those who had land or property worth £10 a year. Plural voting was not addressed by the Act.

The number eligible to vote thus rose from 3.3 million to 5.7 million, meaning that 2 in 3 adult men could vote, rather than one in three. Out of a population of 34.9 million, the electorate rose from 8% to 18%.

The Third Reform Act and the accompanying redistribution of 1885 is viewed by David Cannadine, for example, as a critical milestone in the decline of aristocratic power, whilst F. M. L. Thompson prefers to view the 1867 Reform Act as decisive.

Reform Act, the Fourth (the Representation of the People Act), 1918. The Representation of the People Act which became law on

5 February 1918 is popularly known as the Fourth Reform Act. It enfranchised all men over the age of twenty-one and all women over the age of thirty who were on the local government register or who were married to men on it. The difference in the ages of male and female voters is explained by the fact that parity would have meant substantially more women than men in the electorate, given the numbers of men who had been killed in the war, and that such a state of affairs was unacceptable to many MPs, even if a majority had now put aside most of their reservations regarding the suffragette cause.

The creation of manhood suffrage added 5 million male voters to the existing figure of 8 million, whilst the partial enfranchisement of women added a further 8.4 million to the electorate. Thus the total electorate more than trebled, increasing from 8 million to 21.4 million.

The Act also restricted polling to a single day, restricted plural voting to a single extra vote (either for occupation of business premises or possession of a university degree) and involved a major redistribution, which benefited the Conservatives by an estimated thirty seats.

World War One had played a role in hastening parliamentary reform in two respects. Firstly, the fact that World War One had been a total war strengthened the claim that those who survived deserved the right to vote. Indeed, the Act marked the final transition from the view that the vote was a privilege to the view that it was a right of every man (and many women). Secondly, and more mundanely, if reform did not occur then many demobilized servicemen would effectively be disfranchised by the residence qualifications then in place.

Reform League In February 1865 the Reform League was set up with the barrister Edmund Beales as its president and the former bricklayer, George Howell, as its secretary: a function which he already performed for the TUC. The League had its origins in frustration with the action of the authorities in breaking up a meeting of the Working Men's Garibaldi Committee to protest against curtailment of the Italian patriot's visit to Britain.

The League agitated for what became the Reform Act of 1867, declaring its willingness, in 1866, to agitate on the basis of household suffrage – as proposed by its provincial rival, the Reform Union – rather than hold out for universal adult manhood suffrage.

Historians dispute the extent to which extra-parliamentary agitation in general, and the Hyde Park riot in particular, influenced the passage of the Second Reform Act. To refer to the incident as a riot is, however, somewhat misleading, for whilst the League ignored a ban to use the park and the weight of the demonstrators' numbers (estimated at between one and two hundred thousand people) resulted in the park railings giving way on the night of 23 July 1866, the demonstration then passed off peacefully.

Reform Union The Reform Union was set up in Manchester in 1865 to agitate for household suffrage, reflecting its largely middle-class membership as heir tactically and, to a certain extent, in terms of personnel of the

Anti-Corn Law League. Dominating the reform campaign in the North and Midlands, the Union persuaded the Reform League to moderate its demand for universal adult manhood suffrage to the more realistic one of household suffrage in 1866, which became the basis for the 1867 Reform Act.

Relugas Compact, 1905. The Relugas Compact was the abortive plan of Asquith, Haldane and Grey, hatched at the latter's Scottish fishing lodge, to ensure that a future Liberal government followed the policies of the Liberal Imperialists, by kicking Campbell-Bannerman upstairs to the Lords, whilst ensuring that Asquith was the leader in the Commons and Haldane became Lord Chancellor.

Repeal of the Combination Laws, 1824–25. The repeal of the Combination Laws of 1799–1800 legalized trade unions and has traditionally been viewed as a prime example of liberal Toryism in action. In fact, it was the Radical MP Joseph Hume who succeeded in obtaining a select committee to investigate the laws and who worked with Francis Place to obtain a favourable report. Hume then secured the passage of the legislation with such little fanfare that his triumph escaped the notice of Hansard. This was the first time any state conferred official recognition on trade unions. However, the Liverpool government only sat up and took notice when the 1824 boom stimulated a wave of wage demands pressed home by strikes.

In 1825 another select committee was appointed, this time chaired by Thomas Wallace (former vice-president of the Board of Trade), which did not re-criminalize trade unions but which did limit their room for manoeuvre by making illegal all combinations except those to fix wages and hours, and by conferring upon magistrates summary powers to punish anyone using force to compel membership of an association or participation in industrial action.

Repeal of the Contagious Diseases Acts, 1886. The Contagious Diseases Acts of 1864, 1866, and 1869 arose out of concern that the incidence of VD was undermining the efficiency of the armed forces, and double standards regarding prostitutes and the men who consort with them. Thus the legislation licensed brothels and prostitutes in eighteen seaports and garrison towns, so that regular inspection could ensure the cleanliness of the girls.

In 1869, however, the Ladies' National Association for Repeal was formed, with Josephine Butler as honorary secretary, to further the agitation for repeal of the Acts which had been begun by Daniel Cooper, as secretary of the Rescue Society. Mrs Butler argued that the Acts were an alien system (long established in France and Prussia) for legislating on behalf of vice (by condoning prostitution) and against women (insofar as their sex alone paid a penalty). She thereby succeeded in mobilizing support from the likes of Florence Nightingale, Harriet Martineau, and Victor Hugo, and in embarrassing the government, for example at the 1870 Colchester by-election. In 1871 the home secretary introduced a bill that substituted for the Acts provisions under the Vagrancy Act. This failed to satisfy Mrs Butler or her supporters who continued their campaign until the Acts were partially repealed in 1883, and wholly repealed in 1886.

Repeal of the Corn Laws, 1846. Robert Peel may have been converted to the cause of free trade as a student in Oxford. He certainly supported the free trade measures of the Liverpool administration in which he served as Irish chief secretary and then home secretary.

By the time he entered into his Second Ministry in 1841 there were only two major exceptions to what had become the orthodoxy of free trade, namely, the Navigation Laws and the Corn Laws, and even the latter had been modified in 1822 and 1828: a process which Peel himself carried forward in 1842. In other words, Peel regarded agricultural protection as increasingly anomalous so that the repeal of the Corn Laws in 1846 can be seen as the logical culmination of the policy which he had first supported and then himself carried forward through measures such as his 1842 and 1845 free trade budgets.

Moreover, he came to regard the Corn Laws as economically indefensible, believing that repeal would benefit the economy because it would stimulate aggregate demand and promote greater stability in food prices, trade and the pound.

However, whilst all this may explain a predisposition on Peel's part to look favourably upon repeal it is insufficient to explain why he would embark upon a policy which he must have known would stretch loyalty to him and the unity of the party to breaking point. It was because repeal promised political benefits that matched or even exceeded the economic ones that Peel embraced the policy.

The Anti-Corn Law League (ACLL) claimed that the landed interest opposed repeal because agricultural protection artificially inflated their profits by keeping the price of bread artificially high. Thus Cobden and Bright argued that if this economic prop were removed the aristocratic order's political and social dominance would also be undermined. Peel, by contrast, believed that, as has been argued above, the landed interest would be at least no worse off financially if agricultural protection disappeared whilst politically the position of the aristocracy would be strengthened if it no longer had to face the charge of sheltering behind self-interested legislation. In other words, Peel wished to call the ACLL's bluff, superficially accepting its economic arguments in order to expose its political agenda as based upon false assumptions.

The repeal of the Corn Laws was irrelevant to Ireland insofar as free trade in corn did nothing in itself to relieve suffering. Indeed, the role of the Great Irish Famine in all this was not to persuade Peel of the desirability of repeal but merely to encourage him to move towards repeal sooner than might otherwise have been the case, believing that the British taxpayer could not realistically be asked to spend large sums on famine relief in Ireland whilst paying more than he need for his own food as a consequence of the Corn Laws. Thus instead of attempting to educate his party in favour of repeal in time for the 1847 election he first proposed the immediate suspension of the Corn Laws in November 1845, the month after the potato blight struck Ireland. Russell sought to outbid him by announcing his conversion to total repeal in his Edinburgh Letter of 22 November and Peel responded by renouncing suspension in favour of a phased elimination of the Corn Laws as part of a general package of tariff reform to be completed by 1849. This was too much for Stanley (the colonial secretary) and Buccleuch (the Lord Privy Seal) to swallow so Peel resigned on 5 December 1845 and gave Russell the opportunity to form a Whig administration to pass repeal. Russell 'passed the poisoned chalice back to Peel' who duly resumed office on 20 December.

Repeal passed the Commons on 15 May 1846 but although 112 Conservatives (mostly ministerialists) voted for it, 241 voted against, including 86% of those Conservatives representing the counties and universities and 63% of those who represented the smaller, more rural, boroughs. The party was thus even more out of sympathy with the leadership over Repeal of the Corn Laws than it had been over issues such as Maynooth. Thus on the same day (26 June 1846) that Repeal passed the Lords by 47 votes, Peel was defeated in the Commons over his Irish Coercion Bill by a combination of Whigs, Radicals, Irish and Protectionist Conservatives, despite about one-third of those who had voted against repeal having returned to the fold by this time.

The Repeal of the Corn Laws did not damage British agriculture or the aristocracy as predicted by an unholy alliance of protectionists and the Manchester School. On the contrary, both entered a golden age which lasted until he agricultural depression of the 1870s. However, the damage to the Conservative Party lasted at least as long.

Repeal of the Test and Corporation Acts, 1828. The Test and Corporation Acts dated from the reign of Charles II and discriminated against non-conformists by insisting that they must receive holy communion according to the rites of the Church of England in order to become eligible to hold public office. Although the passage of an annual indemnity bill removed the practical inconvenience of conforming to this legislation, its continuance on the statute book was resented as symbolizing the second-class status of non-conformists.

On 26 February 1828, in line with his liberal Anglican Whig beliefs, Lord John Russell moved for the repeal of the Test and Corporation Acts and his bill was accepted by the Tory party after Peel inserted an amendment whereby an oath was substituted for the sacramental test, which was compulsory for non-conformists holding offices in corporations and at the Crown's discretion for those holding civil offices, and under which office holders declared that they would not abuse their position so as 'to injure or weaken the ... Church'.

The Ultras disliked this concession as they correctly saw that it would render resistance to Catholic Emancipation more difficult. In retrospect, as J. C. D. Clark has argued, the repeal of the Test and Corporation Acts marked the first, fatal breach in the *ancien regime*

Representation of the People Act, 1918 See REFORM ACT, THE FOURTH.

Representation of the People Act, 1948. The 1948 Representation of the People Act abolished plural voting and the university seats, and removed the requirement of a period of residency in order to get on the electoral register.

Representation of the People Act, 1969. The 1969 Representation of the People Act reduced the minimum voting age from 21 to 18.

Retrenchment Retrenchment was part of the trinity of 'Peace, Retrenchment and Reform' which was associated with the Liberal Party under Gladstone. It consisted of cutting back public expenditure so as to keep taxation low and the state small. Gladstone followed Peel in aiming to balance the budget at the lowest possible level and finance public spending out of taxation rather than borrowing.

Thus notwithstanding the heavy costs of the Crimean War (1854–56), Gladstone, who presented thirteen budgets between 1853 and 1882, managed by vigorous retrenchment to reduce annual government spending from £73m in the 1860s to £66m by the end of his First Ministry in 1874.

Even the advent of compulsory, free state education with Mundella's Education Act in 1883 did not prevent public spending falling as a percentage of GNP from 16.5% in 1830 to just under 9% in 1890.

Indeed, it was only war and the threat of war (as signified by increased defence spending) towards the end of the century that sounded the death knell for cheap government and a minimal state even before that prospect was destroyed forever by the advent of the welfare state.

Robbins Report, 23 October 1963. In 1960 Harold Macmillan appointed Lord Robbins (a London University Economics Professor) to chair a committee to inquire into higher education in Great Britain. The Report's major recommendations included the immediate creation of six new universities, the large-scale expansion of existing universities, and the progressive raising to university status of many other higher education institutions, so that the number of students receiving higher education would increase from 216,000 to 560,000 by the academic year 1980–81. New institutions would include five 'special institutions for scientific and technological education and research' comparable to the Massachusetts Institute of Technology.

By 1966 seven new universities had been opened (Sussex, East Anglia, York, Kent, Warwick, Essex and Lancaster) and the ten Colleges of Advanced Technology founded since 1956 also received increased funding and new status as university institutions. The Wilson government also set up the Open University, which began teaching in 1971.

'ROBOT', 1952. Robot is an acronym for the three Treasury civil servants – Sir Leslie Rowan, Sir George Bolton, and Sir Richard 'Otto' Clarke – who vainly suggested a policy of convertibility or freeing the exchange rate (floating the pound and blocking overseas sterling balances) in early 1952.

Although Butler himself gave serious consideration to the idea of 'setting the pound free' this was the only serious intellectual challenge to 'Butskellism' before the mid-seventies and it fell foul of the fear that it might result in unemployment topping one million and the fact that it would annoy the US as contrary to the Bretton Woods Agreement. Indeed, it was Eden as foreign secretary who played a decisive role in persuading cabinet to reject the proposal, which is richly ironic as the consequences of that decision were to undermine Eden's own premiership four years later when the United States revealed the limits of the 'special relationship' by scuppering the Suez expedition by selling sterling short.

Rosebery (Archibald Philip Primrose), fifth Earl of (7 May 1847–21 May 1929). Archibald Philip Primrose was the eldest son of Archibald, Lord Dalmeny, the heir to the Rosebery title and estates. In January 1851, when he was just three and a half years old, his father died and Archibald succeeded to his father's title. He succeeded to his grandfather's title in 1868, by which time he had attended Eton and become an undergraduate at Christ Church, Oxford. His Oxford career was terminated the following year when, faced with a choice between selling his racehorse (which was entered for the Derby), or going down before taking his degree, he chose the latter course. Given that he was thought likely to win a first and that his horse, in the event, finished last, this was the first of many poor decisions taken by the future prime minister.

Rosebery identified himself with Gladstonian Liberalism to the extent of stage-managing the Midlothian campaigns of 1879 and 1880. On the fourth offer of office from Gladstone, Rosebery became an undersecretary at the Home Office in July 1881, with special responsibilities for Scotland, but relations between the two men deteriorated to such an extent that Rosebery resigned in 1883.

Rosebery's world voyage in the winter of 1883–84 did much to kindle his interest in, and commitment to, imperialism, so that he became a strong supporter of the Imperial Federation League on his return. He rejoined the government as First Commissioner of Works and Lord Privy Seal with a seat in the cabinet in February 1885, when Gladstone's government was under severe pressure following the failure of the relief expedition to reach Khartoum before the death of Gordon. This was to be a brief and disillusioning spell as a cabinet minister as the government fell in June 1885.

The Irish Home Rule split, however, provided Rosebery with the opportunity for promotion as he was one of the few Whigs to remain loyal to Gladstone and in Gladstone's Third Ministry he served as foreign secretary, February–June 1886. His handling of a potentially grave situation in the Balkans won the plaudits of both Gladstone and the Queen, whilst his popularity with the general public was marked by his election to the newly created London Council in 1889 and subsequent election as its first chairman.

Rosebery returned to the Foreign Office in Gladstone's Fourth Ministry in 1892. Gladstone did not wish Rosebery to succeed him when he resigned in March 1894, not least because Rosebery's policies with regard to Uganda and Egypt differed from Gladstone's own. However, Victoria wanted Rosebery and a majority of the cabinet did not want Harcourt, so he became prime minister in March 1894. As prime minister he won the Derby twice (with Ladas and Sir Visto), thereby offending the non-conformist conscience. He was to last just fifteen months in the post, resigning in June

1895, following defeat in a snap vote in the Commons on the supply of cordite to the army. For more than a year following the humiliating Liberal defeat, Rosebery remained as leader, taking the opportunity to resign when Gladstone launched his crusade against the Armenian atrocities. The experience of leading a dispirited and bitterly divided party had proved so demoralizing that Rosebery never sought or held public office again.

However, Rosebery remained a political force with devoted and influential followers including the Liberal Imperialists Wolverhampton, Asquith, Grey and Haldane, and admirers amongst the Conservatives including the Hooligans Lord Hugh Cecil and Winston Churchill. All hope of his returning to active politics was only ended in late 1905 when he cut himself off from Campbell-Bannerman over Home Rule.

Schoolmasters are not always noted for their prescience in writing reports, yet Rosebery's tutor at Eton is widely thought to have hit the nail firmly on the head when he expressed the view that his young charge 'sought the palm without the dust'. Rosebery was too sensitive and too highly-strung to cope with the bruising world of inter- and intra-party politics. In Churchill's analysis, 'He would not stoop; he did not conquer'. Rosebery bore no grudge against his alma mater, asking for the Eton Boating Song to be played on a gramophone as he died.

Rotten borough A rotten borough is a corrupt constituency, usually with very few voters. They were sometimes also pocket or nomination boroughs because controlled by a single powerful patron.

Royal Titles Act, 1876. The Royal Titles Act conferred upon Queen Victoria the title of 'Empress of India'. It was justified as providing the generality of the people of the Indian subcontinent with a form of governance more suited to their traditions and understanding than references to the English crown. However, many Britons felt that in bowing to the queen's wish in this matter Disraeli was, not for the first time, adopting vulgar, alien ways and subverting constitutional tradition.

Rural Police Act, 1839. At the insistence of Chadwick, Melbourne's government established a Royal Commission in 1836 to consider 'the means of *preventing* crime within the rural districts *especially* by the agency of a paid constabulary force or police'. Chadwick was also chief author of the report that in due course led to the passage of the Rural Police Act: a permissive measure which authorized the appointment of constabulary forces by the county magistrates, where it did not interfere with the corporate towns. The principle of local control was retained except that the home secretary might draw up rules relating to discipline and pay.

Less than half the counties had police forces by 1853 but the measure nevertheless ensured that the country was better prepared than would otherwise have been the case to face disorder such as Chartism and the Rebecca riots.

Russell, Lord John, first Earl Russell (18 August 1792–28 May 1878). Diminutive, prickly and financially incompetent, Lord John Russell according to A. J. P. Taylor was 'the last great Whig' and 'the first Liberal ... belonging to the old order by birth' (as the younger son of the 6th Duke of Bedford) and to the new 'by his ideas', which were those of traditional Whiggism, which he inherited, and those of the Scottish Enlightenment, which he imbibed during his time at Edinburgh University.

He entered the House of Commons as a Whig in 1813. He was instrumental in securing the 1828 Repeal of the Test and Corporation Acts and supported Catholic Emancipation in 1829. As a junior minister (Paymaster General) without a cabinet seat Russell was one of the three-man committee who in 1831 drafted the bill that was eventually to become the Reform Act of 1832, and it was he who introduced it into the Commons. Thus Taylor describes Russell rather than Grey as 'the principal architect of the Reform Bill', although both men believed that the passage of the Bill would establish the moral fitness of the aristocracy to continue to dominate government. After earning the nickname 'Finality Jack' for his assertion of 1837 that the 1832 Reform Act represented a final settlement, Russell came to recognize the desirability of a further instalment of parliamentary reform and was the prime mover behind the abortive Liberal Reform Bill of 1866.

Russell was a liberal Anglican Whig whose guiding principle was 'the cause of civil and religious liberty'. Thus he championed a range of causes designed to appeal to moderate nonconformists, including repeal of the Test and Corporation Acts (1828) and appropriation of the surplus revenues of the Irish Church. His attempt to commit the government to the latter in 1834 precipitated the resignations of Ripon, Stanley, Graham and Richmond, and when Melbourne wished to appoint him as leader of the House of Commons to succeed Althorp later in the year (following the latter's elevation to the Lords as Earl Spencer), William IV reacted by dismissing the Whigs and inviting Peel to form an administration. Having inadvertently done much to weaken fatally the coalition welded by Grey in 1830 and inherited by Melbourne in 1834, Russell's Edinburgh Letter of November 1845 did much to render Peel's position as prime minister untenable. It was with the support of Russell's followers that Peel was able to repeal the Corn Laws and when Russell formed his First Ministry (1846–52) the Peelites returned the compliment by supporting Whig measures which furthered free trade (notably the repeal of the Navigation Laws, 1849). He was unable, however, to accomplish a more permanent realignment of parties which might have imparted greater political stability to the period 1846–68. The more pressing problem which he failed to address adequately was famine relief in Ireland, in part because of an inflexible attachment to the doctrine of *laissez-faire.* Generally Russell gave the impression of being at the mercy of events rather than controlling them. Thus the Public Health Act (1848), Encumbered Estates Act (1849) and repeal of the Navigation Laws (1849) were all second attempts at legislation in these fields.

Russell's First Ministry was a minority administration and a weak regime needs the appearance of a strong enemy. Russell only recovered some of his grip upon the public affection by an attack upon the Catholic Church in his open letter to the Bishop of Durham and the Ecclesiastical Titles Act of 1851 that forbade Catholic bishops from taking territorial titles of places in England. However, by alienating both the Catholic Irish and the Peelites Russell put paid for all time to the possibility of his leading a reconstructed centre-left coalition.

Russell thus sought to facilitate this end by means of moving the constitutional goalposts, specifically creating life peers and passing a second Reform Bill. However, Russell was not a good team player, as shown by his dismissal of Palmerston in 1851 over the latter's endorsement of Louis Napoleon's coup in France. Russell's unilateral initiative in the area of parliamentary reform provided Palmerston with the opportunity to exact a speedy revenge for his recent humiliation by bringing down the government in 1852.

The realignment which Russell craved was achieved, depending upon your point of view, under either Aberdeen (under whom Russell served, 1852–55) or Palmerston. However, the consequence of the outbreak of the Crimean War and the ascendancy of Palmerson placed obstacles in the path of parliamentary reform which were only removed by the death of Palmerston in 1865 (Russell having served under him as foreign secretary, 1859–65) and Russell's formation of his Second Ministry in October 1865. However, the rebellion of the Adullamites ensured that Russell would not preside over the Second Reform Act, despite the conversion of Gladstone to the cause in 1864, and Russell resigned in 1866 a mere eight months after embarking upon his second premiership.

Prest makes out the case that although Russell may have failed to achieve strong government himself he at least diagnosed what was wrong and anticipated the means whereby others successfully addressed the problem.

Peel and Russell can both be portrayed as disastrous party leaders with the former trying to kill off Toryism by name in the 1830s before his administration of 1841–46 inadvertently destroyed the Conservative Party's prospects of a parliamentary majority for over a quarter of a century, whereas Russell's ministry of 1846–52 killed off the Whigs as a party of government, whilst his second ministry of 1865–66 came close to being both the first and last Liberal administration. Both men can, however, equally be portrayed as statesmen who masterminded peaceful change and extended the lifetime of the aristocratic order by timely concessions, of which the 1832 Reform Act and the 1846 Repeal of the Corn Laws were the greatest. It is only relatively recently, however, with the work of Jonathan Parry that Russell has found an historical champion comparable to Peel's Gash.

S

Sale of Food and Drugs Act, 1875. The 1875 Sale of Food and Drugs Act sought to discourage adulteration by appointing public analysts to test for the purity of food and drugs. However, the appointment of such analysts by local authorities was not made compulsory until 1879.

Sale of honours scandal Honours had been sold before Lloyd George but he was more systematic and unprecedentedly brazen in his exploitation of the system, soliciting funds from would-be recipients, with the asking price ranging from £100 for an OBE (founded by George V in 1917) to up to £120,000 for a viscountcy. Thus by 1922 when he resigned as prime minister he is estimated to have made over £1.5m from his trade in honours.

Salisbury (Robert Arthur Talbot Gascoyne-Cecil), third Marquis of Salisbury (3 February 1830–22 August 1903). The future Lord Salisbury was the second son of the 2nd Marquis and was thus not in line to inherit his father's title or the family estates. He was withdrawn from Eton to avoid bullying, in favour of private tuition at Hatfield. However, he suffered a nervous breakdown at Christ Church, Oxford and left the university with a fourth class degree in Mathematics. His mental equilibrium was restored in the course of a voyage around the world, 1851–53, which encompassed visits to many outposts of empire, and on his return home he was elected unopposed in the Conservative interest at Stamford.

Marriage in 1857 to the elder daughter of the judge Sir Edward Hall Alderson produced a contraction in his social circle and financial difficulties. The latter was addressed by means of political journalism, notably contributions to the *Quarterly Review*. These pieces on domestic politics and international diplomacy trenchantly demonstrated Lord Robert's independence of thought. He already aimed at a reconstruction of party politics along class lines, with the Whigs being detached from the Liberal alliance so that the propertied stood foursquare behind the Conservative Party.

The prospect of needing to live by his pen was removed in 1865 when he succeeded his brother as Lord Cranborne, and it was under this title that he entered the administration of Lord Derby as secretary of state for India in 1866. However, together with Carnarvon and General Peel, he resigned in February 1867 in protest at the extension of the franchise proposed by Disraeli. The two men could hardly have been more dissimilar in terms of personality or political philosophy but when the latter invited Salisbury (as he had become on his father's death) to return to the India Office in 1874 he returned to the political stage, and moved closer to its centre when he was appointed foreign secretary in 1878. As such he played a pivotal role with Beaconsfield (as Disraeli had become) in bringing back 'peace with honour' from the Congress of Berlin later that year. Equally, the Treaty of Berlin played a pivotal role in establishing Salisbury as a strong contender to succeed Beaconsfield.

Salisbury was duly invited by Victoria to form a caretaker administration in 1885 when Gladstone was defeated on the budget. This minority government lasted just seven months but following Gladstone's return to office and embracing of Irish Home Rule, the Liberal Party split and Salisbury's Conservatives (greatly assisted by the skills of Captain Middleton as Chief Agent) became the natural party of government for the next two decades.

The challenge to Salisbury and his profoundly pessimistic yet intellectually attractive conception of politics posed by Randolph Churchill and his more obviously populist conception of Tory Democracy was surmounted, not least thanks to the latter's capacity for self-destruction, but Salisbury showed consummate skill in consolidating the alliance with the Liberal Unionists and ultimately assisting in their assimilation into the party by means of cautious domestic reform (including free elementary education) and imperial expansion (including Kenya, Uganda, Nigeria and Rhodesia).

Foreign and imperial affairs remained Salisbury's first love and for more than eleven of his almost fourteen years as prime minister he was also his own foreign secretary. Although popularly identified with the policy of 'Splendid Isolation', Salisbury's diplomacy was supremely flexible. However, his success in facing down the French over the Fashoda incident in 1898 was not matched in his dealings with the Boers, where Chamberlain and Milner between them managed to push Britain into a war the following year which was to expose not only Britain's military unpreparedness but the limitations of isolationism. In 1900 he handed over the Foreign Office to Lansdowne and in 1902 he finally stepped down as prime minister in favour of his nephew, Arthur Balfour, only to die a year later.

Salisbury was a curious amalgam of seemingly contradictory characteristics: a patrician prepared to stump the country and appeal to 'Villa Toryism' and a profound Christian pessimist who was nevertheless prepared to embrace reform. He was the intellectual equal of Gladstone and anticipated Baldwin in shaping a fundamental realignment of politics that secured the dominance of the Conservative Party.

Sandon Education Act, 1876. The 1876 Education Act or Elementary Schools Act is better known as the Sandon Education Act, after its author. The measure imposed upon parents the responsibility of sending their children to school between the ages of 5 and 10, and set up school attendance committees in areas where no school boards existed in order to ensure that children received 'efficient instruction in reading, writing and arithmetic'. An amendment expressed overt hostility to board schools by authorizing their dissolution where it could be shown that they had 'originated from merely party motives'. Less obviously the measure sought to undermine the board school system by strengthening the voluntary system, particularly in rural areas.

Sanitary Report, 1842 See CHADWICK, SIR EDWIN.

Scot and lot boroughs In scot and lot boroughs the ability to pay certain local taxes conferred the right to vote. Prior to the Great Reform Act 59 of the 203 English parliamentary boroughs were of this type.

Scottish National Party (SNP) The Scottish National Party (SNP) was created in 1934 from the merger of the Scottish party and the National Party of Scotland but did not win a seat in parliament until Robert D. McIntyre won the Motherwell by-election in 1945, only to lose it again in the general election three months later. By-election victories of Winifred Ewing at Hamilton in 1967 and Margot Macdonald at Glasgow Govan in 1973 and the general election victory of Donald Stewart in the Western Isles in 1970 were the only successes until seven seats were won in the February 1974 general election and a further four seats in the October 1974 election. The relative failure of the 1979 referendum on devolution depressed SNP spirits and it was not until the late 1980s that its fortunes revived with another Glasgow Govan by-election win in November 1988 pointing the way forward to its becoming the main opposition party to the Labour–Liberal Democrat government in the Scottish parliament.

Seditious Meetings Act, 1817. Liverpool quickly pushed through the suspension of Habeas Corpus and a Seditious Meetings Act after the mobbing of the Prince Regent's coach on the day of the state opening of Parliament: 28 January 1817.

The terms of the new legislation were studiously moderate, laying down that, with certain exceptions, meetings of fifty or more could not take place until a magistrate had granted permission. However, this law was allowed to lapse in 1818 so that the crowds which assembled at St Peter's Fields in 1819, and who were to become the victims of the Peterloo massacre, had assembled legally.

Sex Discrimination Act, 1975. The 1975 Sex Discrimination Act outlawed discrimination on the grounds of sex or marital status, with the Equal Opportunities Commission (EOC) enforcing the legislation by taking action in the courts itself or by supporting individuals taking such action. Whilst the 1970 Equal Pay Act dealt with the issue of sex discrimination with regard to contractual employment, the 1975 legislation covered non-contractual employment as well as the letting of accommodation and financial and other services. As is customary with such legislation, certain explicit exemptions were written into the Act.

Sexual Offences Act, 1967. The Sexual Offences Act was one of a series of liberal measures enacted by Roy Jenkins as home secretary. It decriminalized homosexual acts performed in private between consenting males (the original legislation not having applied to women because allegedly Queen Victoria could not conceive of lesbianism).

Sidmouth (Henry Addington), first Viscount (30 May 1757–15 February 1844). Henry Addington was the son of Dr Anthony Addington, a physician who specialized in insanity and whose lucrative practice enabled him to purchase a small estate in Oxfordshire. In the fullness of time the young Addington did more than most to establish the notion of 'the old school tie' as something which offered an easy road to preferment as four of the members of his first administration (including Vansittart) had been playmates at his preparatory school (Mr Gilpin's academy at Cheam), whilst a further two were former school friends at Winchester: the core of a loyal interest group.

After Brasenose, Oxford, Henry was admitted to Lincoln's Inn and read for the bar. He entered parliament as MP for Devizes in 1784, where he renewed his childhood friendship with Pitt (which stemmed from the time when his father was physician to Chatham), and in 1789 Pitt ensured that he succeeded Grenville as Speaker of the House of Commons. He was to hold the post for twelve years until late 1801 when both George III and Pitt asked him to form an administration after the former withdrew his confidence in the latter because of his support for Catholic Emancipation. Pitt also supported Addington in his search for a truce with France, which was accomplished by the 1802 Treaty of Amiens. With the return of war (in May 1803) and the withdrawal of Pitt's goodwill, Addington's days as prime minister were numbered. 'The Doctor', as Addington was nicknamed, was presiding over a moribund administration, albeit one which reintroduced the income tax in a more efficient form. The deathblow was effectively administered when the Lord Chancellor, Eldon, entered into private negotiations with Pitt.

Addington resigned in 1804 and was created Viscount Sidmouth the following year. He served as Lord Privy Seal in the Ministry of All the Talents, 1806–7, and as president of the Council under Spencer Perceval in 1812. However, it was as home secretary under Liverpool, 1812–21, that Sidmouth was demonized by those on the left.

Sidmouth was associated in the popular mind with reaction and repression ranging from the Seditious Meetings Act of 1817, via Peterloo, to the Six Acts of 1819. Whereas Ziegler considers it inevitable that Sidmouth 'would gain – and indeed largely earn – the label of diehard reactionary', Gash is amongst those historians who have rehabilitated Sidmouth by pointing to the essentially moderate nature of the actions which he took, given the nature of the threat to law and order and the poverty of the means at his disposal for ensuring the public peace.

Although he resigned as home secretary in December 1821, Sidmouth remained in the cabinet as minister without Portfolio until December 1824, when he resigned in protest at the policy of recognizing the new Latin American republics.

Sidmouth deserves to be remembered as the minister who advised the Manchester magistrates not to intervene at St Peter's Field in 1819 unless the crowd rioted or committed felonies. Unfortunately, he tends to be remembered either for the doggerel of Canning that, 'Pitt is to Addington as London is to Paddington' or for the better verse but even worse judgements of Byron and Shelley.

Single European Act (SEA) Ironically it was Mrs Thatcher, the doyenne of Euro-sceptics, who signed the Single European Act in February

1986, allowing the European Community to override the national veto in numerous areas by extending qualified majority voting.

Following ratification by all the member states it came into force in July 1987 and the 'internal market' was formally completed on 31 December 1992.

Sinn Féin In 1905 Arthur Griffiths formed Sinn Féin (Gaelic for 'ourselves alone'), which absorbed other Irish nationalist groups to become the Sinn Féin League in 1907–8. In the 1918 election its 73 MPs boycotted Westminster in favour of their own Dublin parliament.

The modern party dates from 1970 when Provisional Sinn Féin split from Official Sinn Féin: a split reflected in that between the IRA's Official and Provisional wings. As the political wing of the IRA, Provisional Sinn Féin put up hunger strikers as candidates for both the Dáil and the Westminster parliament and their success helped to persuade Gerry Adams to argue in favour of serious political engagement, culminating in its 1986 decision to take any seats which it won in the Dáil, and in the Hume–Adams talks of 1988 which can be said to mark the beginning of the peace process. This approach has paid dividends in helping to secure gains on both sides of the border, with Sinn Féin winning 17.6% of the votes and 18 seats in the 1998 Northern Ireland Assembly elections, and ministerial positions in the power sharing executive.

Six Acts, 1819. The so-called Six Acts, which were passed by the Liverpool government in the aftermath of 'Peterloo', have traditionally – but wrongly – been depicted as reactionary or repressive.

The Seizure of Arms Act permitted the seizure of weapons deemed 'dangerous to the Public Peace' whilst the Training Prevention Act banned paramilitary training. So far from infringing civil liberties such acts were conducive to the maintenance of law and order.

The Seditious Meetings Act, like its 1817 namesake, sought to prevent any abuse of the right of assembly (such as had occurred at Spa Fields in December 1817) by requiring those organizing meetings to consider 'any public Grievance or any Matter on Church and State' to give the local magistrates notice of the time and place at which such meetings would be held, which they might then alter.

The Misdemeanours Act speeded up the judicial process, so that those accused would experience greater difficulty than hitherto in causing or exploiting delays and getting themselves released on bail.

The Blasphemous and Seditious Libels Act strengthened existing legislation, making banishment or transportation for fourteen years the maximum penalty for a second conviction, and giving magistrates the right to search for and confiscate libellous material.

The Newspaper Stamp Duties Act obliged publishers and printers to be more responsible regarding what they disseminated by requiring them to provide sureties of their good behaviour in the form of guarantees of payment if found guilty of libel, and by increasing the penalties for libel. Moreover, if they appeared at least once every twenty-six days, and retailed for sixpence (2.5p) or less, then newspapers became liable to the stamp duty of four pence that Vansittart had originally levied in 1815.

Two of the Six Acts (the Seizure of Arms and Seditious Meetings Acts) were temporary measures which were allowed to lapse, three more (relating to Misdemeanours, Newspaper Stamp Duties and Blasphemous and Seditious Libels) were largely designed to plug loopholes in existing laws, whilst the remaining measure (the Training Prevention Act) was a sensible precaution which appeared more than justified in the eyes of many contemporaries given recent disorders. Considered dispassionately, therefore, the Six Acts hardly presaged the creation of a police state.

Slave trade, abolition, 1807. Quakers and evangelical Anglicans such as William Wilberforce led the campaign to abolish the slave trade. This eventually became law with the passage of the Abolition of the Slave Trade Bill in 1807 (with Grenville persuading the House of Lords to accept the measure by 41 votes to 20). With effect from 1 January 1808 any British subject engaged in dealing or trading in slaves faced a £100 fine and the forfeiture of his ship to the Crown.

Under the terms of the new law, British captains caught continuing the trade were liable to be fined £100 for every slave found on board. This was, however, insufficient to prevent the trade completely and provided an incentive for those captains facing capture to throw slaves overboard as a means of reducing their fines. In 1811 slave trading was made a felony punishable by transportation, and in 1824 it was reclassified as a form of piracy, punishable by death.

Thomas Fowell Buxton was one of those who recognized that the suffering would only cease once slavery itself was abolished and those, like Wilberforce, who initially resisted this conclusion were eventually brought round. It was not, however, until 1833 that parliament legislated to end slavery within the British Empire and even then the slaves were not freed overnight.

In the meantime Britain also played a leading role internationally in attempting to end the slave trade. Castlereagh worked hard at the Congress of Vienna in 1815 to persuade the other powers present to follow Britain's example. Thus Britain and France by a separate article of the First Peace of Paris (of 30 May 1814) agreed to work together 'at the approaching Congress, to induce all the Powers of Christendom to decree the abolition of the Slave Trade' and on 8 February 1815 the representatives of Great Britain, France, Austria, Portugal, Prussia, Russia, Spain and Sweden signed a Declaration stating their general commitment to the principle of abolishing the trade, although conceding that their individual timetables for achieving this was subject to 'the interests, the habits, and even the prejudices of their subjects'.

Nevertheless, by the time that Palmerston addressed the Commons on the question on 16 July 1844 he was able to report that Britain had concluded treaties to that effect with France, Spain, Portugal, the Netherlands, Sweden, Denmark, the ports of the Hanseatic League, Sardinia, Tuscany, Naples, Brazil, Buenos Aires, Venezuela and Haiti. The most prominent and prized exception from this list was, of course, the United States and slavery was to blight Anglo-American relations until the American Civil War (1861–65) resulted in the abolition of slavery there.

Thomas Fowell Buxton, who succeeded Wilberforce as the leading British critic of slavery, argued that Christianity and Commerce were together required to bring an end to the trade in Africa, which Livingstone said 'pressed into the very centre of the continent from both sides' and much exploration and exploitation of the 'dark continent' was justified in terms of substituting the trade in human flesh with trade in such items as wax, ivory and ostrich feathers.

Continuing British anxiety about the slave trade was decisive in persuading the powers assembled for the Berlin Congress to declare (on 26 February 1885) that 'the territories forming the Conventional basin of the Congo … may not serve as a market or means of transit for the trade in slaves'.

Slavery, abolished in the British Empire (Bill passed 28 August 1833, outlawing slavery from 1 August 1834). The campaign to abolish slavery intensified following the outbreak of a slave rebellion in Jamaica in the late winter of 1831 because until that time, and despite the slave revolt of 1823 in Demerara (later part of British Guiana), it had been felt by reformers such as William Wilberforce that slave owners would be obliged to take better care of their assets once the chance of replenishing their stocks by traditional means disappeared with the abolition of the slave trade in 1807.

In the first elections for the reformed parliament in December 1832, the two leading abolitionist pressure groups – the Agency Committee and the Anti-Slavery Society – managed to extract pledges to support immediate abolition from 104 candidates who were returned to parliament. Conversely the abolition of many rotten boroughs under the terms of the 1832 Reform Act and the defeat of sixteen sitting 'West Indians' helped to ensure that the latter were outnumbered roughly three to one in the new parliament. Thus the act to abolish slavery that was passed in the first session of the new parliament 'was a rare instance of the direct influence of the reform act on the substance of British politics' (Stewart).

However, the passage of the bill was not quite as straightforward as the above might suggest. The King's Speech had made no mention of the reform and when the cabinet refused to endorse the scheme put forward by the son of Earl Grey, the colonial secretary, Viscount Howick, resigned from the government in order to campaign for change from the backbenches. Indeed, it was only after Fowell Buxton gave notice of his intention to introduce a motion for the abolition of slavery that Stanley, the new colonial secretary, introduced a government bill.

The abolitionist pressure groups had not been consulted over the drawing up of this bill and they were dismayed by the proposal that the freed slaves should serve lengthy 'apprenticeships' and that their former owners should receive a loan of £15m to enable them to adjust to their new circumstances. Their criticism of these aspects of the bill had mixed results: the period of apprenticeship was reduced (to 7 years for slaves who worked on plantations and 5 years for the rest) but the £15m loan was converted into

£20m compensation to the planters for the loss of their property.

The measure remained deeply flawed insofar as local legislatures, such as the Jamaica Assembly, were entrusted with the responsibility for drawing up and administering the apprenticeship terms, subject to Colonial Office approval. This was a recipe for conflict which flared up in 1839 and would have seen the Melbourne administration supplanted by a minority Conservative administration under Peel had it not been for the Bedchamber Incident.

The Slavery Abolition Act also strained relations between the imperial parliament and another of the colonies. The fact that the Cape Colony was not exempted from its terms (unlike India and St Helena, which received their own legislation in 1843) increased the sense of frustration which the Boers felt with British rule, leading to some 14,000 of them migrating eastwards and northwards, in a migration known as the Great Trek of 1837–44, which ultimately led to the creation of the Boer republics of the Transvaal and the Orange Free State.

Smith, John (13 September 1938–12 May 1994). Born in western Scotland at Dalmally (Argyll and Bute), John Smith was educated at school in Dunoon before studying law at Glasgow University (where he also established himself as a first-class debater). He practised successfully as a barrister before being elected as Labour MP for Lanarkshire North (which later became Monklands East) in 1970. He was a strong advocate of devolution and was frustrated by the 'no' vote in the referendum of 1979. In the previous year he had entered the cabinet as secretary of state for trade under Callaghan and subsequently served as Opposition spokesperson on a number of economic and industrial issues, acting as shadow chancellor under Kinnock from 1987.

Despite a serious heart attack in 1988 and the fact that his shadow budget was widely credited with having contributed to Labour's defeat at the polls in April 1992, Smith emerged as the only serious contender for the Labour leadership after Kinnock's resignation and on 18 July he was elected leader by 91.02% of votes cast by 1,500 delegates at a meeting of the party's electoral college.

Smith carried on the reform of the party begun by Kinnock, abolishing the trade union block vote at Labour Party conferences, and replacing it with 'one member one vote'. Under his leadership Labour gained a significant lead in the polls over the Conservatives, chiefly by exploiting dissatisfaction with the government rather than by winning public support with detailed policies or promises (although he did commit a future Labour government to establishing a Scottish Parliament).

Thus Smith was widely expected to be the next prime minister when he died suddenly after suffering a heart attack at his flat in central London on 12 May 1994. Campaigning for the elections to the European parliament and five by-elections (due to take place on 9 June) was suspended by all major parties until after Smith's funeral on 20 May. He was buried on the holy island of Iona.

Margaret Beckett, Labour's deputy leader, assumed the leadership on an interim basis on 12 May but it was

Smith's shadow home secretary, Tony Blair, who was ultimately elected Labour leader and, on 1 May 1997, became prime minister.

John Smith played a pivotal role in Labour's long march back to power not only by virtue of his reforms of the Labour Party, which weakened its left wing and held the unions at arm's length, but because he himself appeared to be a leader of integrity, intelligence and humanity. His untimely death was a source of genuine and widespread grief.

Social and Liberal Democrats (SLD) When the Alliance ended in the merger of the Liberal and Social Democratic parties the resulting party was initially known as the Social and Liberal Democrats until this unwieldy name gave way to the party becoming known as the Liberal Democrats.

Social Democratic and Labour Party (SDLP) The Social Democratic and Labour Party is a moderate Catholic or Nationalist party that emerged in 1970 out of the civil rights movement in Northern Ireland. In 1983 John Hume succeeded Gerry Fitt as leader whose efforts to bring peace to the province by engaging in dialogue with Sinn Féin have rendered the SDLP constituency increasingly vulnerable to Sinn Féin penetration.

Social Democratic Federation (SDF) The Social Democratic Federation had started life as the Democratic Federation in 1881, the change of name in 1884 signifying a more explicitly socialist, indeed Marxist, commitment. Early members included William Morris, George Lansbury, Ben Tillett, Edward Aveling and Eleanor Marx. The leader, H. M. Hyndman, was increasingly regarded by some, especially those in the ILP, as too dogmatic and autocratic, whilst his willingness to accept Tory money in an attempt to split the Liberal vote in Hampstead and Kensington in the 1885 general election tainted him in the eyes of many. The violence of 'Bloody Sunday' (13 November 1887) alienated others.

Despite defections the SDF played a role in forming the Labour Representation Committee in 1900 but in 1901 the SDF disaffiliated from the Labour Party and Hyndman himself eventually established a new group, the British Socialist Party (BSP), which had even less influence than the SDF.

Social Democratic Party (SDP) Following his resignation as deputy leader of the Labour Party in April 1972 over opposition to a referendum on continued membership of the Common Market, Roy Jenkins made a number of speeches in the country, one of which (to the Oxford Labour Club in March 1973) reads very ironically in the light of later events. In it he stated:

> There's been a lot of talk about the possible formation of a new centre party. Some people have even been kind enough to suggest I might lead it. I find this idea profoundly unattractive. I believe that the most likely effect of such an ill-considered grouping would be to destroy the prospect of an effective alternative government to the Conservatives.

In 1981 Jenkins as leader of the Gang of Four (together with David Owen,

Bill Rodgers and Shirley Williams) created the Social Democratic Party. This new centre party indeed helped to ensure that there was no practical alternative to Mrs Thatcher for most of that decade.

In the short term it briefly looked as if the SDP might succeed in breaking the electoral mould with Shirley Williams winning the Crosby by-election in 1981 and Jenkins winning Glasgow Hillhead in 1982. However, the bulk of SDP MPs were Labour defectors motivated by principle (because disillusioned by Labour's increasing extremism) and/or self-interest (fearing deselection and being optimistic regarding the prospects of the SDP bandwagon). They resolutely refused to give their constituents the opportunity to register their views by resigning their seats and standing under their new colours and in the 1983 general election, the SDP returned only six MPs. In the meantime they had formed the Alliance but the Falklands had done a great deal to restore public approval of the Conservative government. David Owen succeeded Jenkins as leader only to fall out with his Alliance partners over defence policy and see the SDP reduced to five MPs at the 1987 general election, with Owen the only survivor of the Gang of Four. He resigned the leadership and was replaced by Robert Maclennan when a majority of SDP members voted in favour of entering into merger talks with the Liberals. The creation of the Social and Liberal Democratic Party, shortly afterwards known as the Liberal Democrats, was finally approved by the SDP membership in March 1988 (with Owen's efforts to maintain a rump SDP even less successful than Michael Meadowcroft's efforts to maintain a traditional Liberal Party).

Socialist League Just as military defeat is often the midwife of revolution, so electoral defeat is often the midwife of ideological extremism, as the defeated party lurches further from the centre.

So it was for the Labour Party after the humiliation of 1931, when just 46 MPs were returned to oppose the National Government. The Socialist League, led by Cripps within parliament and by Laski outside it, sought to regain the moral high ground after the betrayal of socialist principles by Ramsay MacDonald by moving the party substantially to the left (which later involved campaigning for a popular front against fascism). However, this pressure was successfully resisted by, among others, Attlee, Bevin, Morrison and Dalton, who had the 'big battalions' and block votes of the trade unions on their side.

Spa Fields, 1816. A public meeting was arranged at Spa Fields in November 1816 in support of the presentation of a petition to the Prince Regent. This meeting was well attended and peaceful. However, when a second meeting was called for 2 December 1816 to receive the Prince Regent's response, a group of Spenceans decided to use the occasion to foment revolution. A large crowd assembled to hear Henry 'Orator' Hunt but before he appeared several hundred, some of whom had been drinking heavily, were incited by Spencean rhetoric to emulate the storming of the Bastille by marching on the Tower of London and the Bank of England. Several shops were looted, including gunsmiths' and at least two were shot. However, the authorities quelled the disorder relatively easily.

Five Spenceans were nevertheless charged with high treason but after Dr Watson was found 'not guilty' by the jury, the Crown decided to abandon the other prosecutions. The Spenceans thus survived to plot the Cato St conspiracy.

Speenhamland system See POOR LAW AMENDMENT ACT.

Steel, David Martin Scott, Baron Steel (31 March 1938–). David Steel was the eldest of five children, and son of a Church of Scotland minister (and later moderator of the General Assembly). His father's ministry meant that part of his childhood was spent in Kenya, attending the Prince of Wales School in Nairobi, before returning to Scotland and attending George Watson's College in Edinburgh.

He received a law degree from Edinburgh University in 1962 although his studies took second place to his involvement in student politics, which included a successful campaign to make Jo Grimond the university rector. Between 1962 and 1964 Steel worked for the Scottish Liberal Party and the BBC.

In March 1965 he became the youngest member of the House of Commons after winning the border seat of Roxburgh, Selkirk and Peebles in a by-election (having previously failed to win it at the 1964 general election). He made his mark nationally and gained valuable experience by piloting through parliament the 1967 Abortion Act. He also raised his profile through his presidency of the British Anti-Apartheid Movement, 1966–67.

Following Jeremy Thorpe's resignation, Steel beat John Pardoe to replace him as party leader in 1975 and asserted his strategic vision over doubters in the party (notably the Young Liberals) when a Joint Assembly in 1976 accepted in principle the idea of coalition. Steel was therefore not hamstrung in the way Thorpe had been when approached by Heath in 1974. This policy was put into practice with the Lib–Lab Pact of 1977–78. It is commonly accepted that the Callaghan government got the better part of this deal but at least when Steel withdrew his support in May 1978 he had the satisfaction of knowing that he had given the Liberal Party its first taste of national power and responsibility since World War Two. However, in the 1979 general election the voters were apparently willing to blame the Liberals as much as Labour for the 'winter of discontent' and their vote dropped by 1 million (from 18.3% to 13.8%) whilst their MPs fell from 13 to 11.

However, Steel's grand scheme for a realignment of politics bore fruit as disillusion mounted within certain sections of the Labour Party. It was Steel who in 1981 was chiefly responsible for persuading Jenkins not to defect to the Liberals immediately but rather create a social democratic centre party. Steel then worked with the 'Gang of Four' to create the Liberal–SDP Alliance. For one brief moment it really looked as though the mould of two-party politics might be broken but the Falklands conflict effectively put paid to that dream.

Jenkins was the Alliance's premier designate in the 1983 general election but Steel spearheaded the campaigning. The result highlighted Liberal

SDP complaints regarding the first past the post electoral system, with the Alliance vote just 2% below Labour's but only securing one-tenth of Labour's seats. When David Owen replaced Jenkins as SDP leader, problems over policy and the selection of candidates greatly intensified. The Owen–Steel double act during the 1987 election didn't work very well, with Steel seemingly obliged to make most concessions.

The Alliance vote fell from 7.7 to 7.4 million and from 25.4% of the vote to 22.6%. Overall the Alliance lost one MP as three SDP MPs (including Jenkins) lost their seats whilst the Liberals gained two in Scotland. The increasingly frustrated Steel called for a merger of the two parties within days of the result. This action was precipitate, pre-empting a move along these lines by Jenkins and allowing Owen to portray the move as a hostile takeover. To make matters worse, Steel failed to get involved in the detailed negotiations after securing his party's approval for the move at a special conference at Blackpool in 1988.

When the SDP's Robert Maclennan published the draft of the initial policy declaration for the merged party it was clearly unacceptable to the Liberal wing and Steel was obliged to have the worst of both worlds: accepting joint responsibility for the document's formulation but agreeing that it would have to be redrafted.

Once the Liberal and SDP parties merged, Steel did not contest the leadership, which was won by Paddy Ashdown. Instead, he focused his energies on the international and Scottish stages, standing for the European Parliament in Italy and accepting the joint chairmanship of the Scottish Constitutional Convention in 1989; serving as president of Liberal International, 1994–96; and serving as presiding officer (or speaker) for the new Scottish parliament in 1999. In 1997 he became Baron Steel of Aikwood, of Ettick Forest in the Scottish Borders, and deputy leader of the Lib Dems in the Lords.

There have been few perorations inviting bathos more than David Steel's rallying cry for the faithful at the 1985 Liberal Party conference to 'Go back to your constituencies and prepare for government!' By reaching for government rather than the role of intellectual powerhouse Steel did not so much break the mould of politics as destroy the historic Liberal Party. But if British politics remained essentially a two-horse race it is worth remembering the time when Steel, albeit briefly, played a pivotal role in raising serious doubts whether that would continue to be the case. The boy David ultimately failed in his bid to slay Goliath but managed to deliver some telling blows before the slings of fortune told against him.

Suez Crisis, 1956. In July 1952 King Farouk of Egypt was deposed in a military coup, from which Gamal Abdel Nasser soon emerged as the dominant figure. Initially, Britain was conciliatory towards the new regime. However, Eden interpreted King Hussein's dismissal of General Sir John Glubb ('Glubb Pasha') in February 1956 as inspired by Nasser and urged Anglo-US moves against the Egyptian government, including the withdrawal of financial aid for the planned Aswan Dam. The US supported the latter move upon discovering that Egypt had bought large supplies of arms from behind the Iron Curtain, to which Nasser responded by announcing nationalization of the Suez Canal (25 July 1956).

Although London hosted a conference of Canal Users to resolve the crisis, Anglo-French military preparations proceeded concurrently and secret negotiations were entered into with the Israeli government so as to provide a 'justification' for intervention. Thus Israel attacked Egypt, and British and French forces were sent in to 'protect' the Canal Zone.

The military operation was misconceived and was effectively sabotaged by Eisenhower's America encouraging a run on the pound. Faced with an outflow of $300m of gold and dollar reserves in November, the chancellor, Macmillan, who had been a leading 'hawk', now advised disengagement and the rest of the cabinet, more or less, reluctantly agreed.

Suez resulted in a loss of confidence within the Conservative government and in the Conservative government by the nation at large. Butler was nominally in charge whilst Eden retired from the field of combat but when his ill health resulted in Eden's permanent retirement from the political fray it was Macmillan who emerged as his successor.

Sunningdale Agreement, December 1973. In December 1973 at Sunningdale in Berkshire a conference of British and Irish politicians, including Brian Faulkner, the leader of the Unionists and Gerry Fitt, the leader of the SDLP, agreed to create a power sharing Executive for Northern Ireland in which Faulkner would be leader and Fitt his deputy. Moreover, a Council of Ireland in which the Republic of Ireland was represented would hold discussions on cross-border issues.

All of this was too much for many in Northern Ireland, notably Ian Paisley and the DUP. The Ulster Unionist Council rejected the Sunningdale Agreement, and in the general election of 28 February 1974, 11 of the 12 MPs elected for Northern Ireland were opponents of power sharing. However, what finally killed off the Agreement was a strike by Protestant workers, particularly power workers, which paralysed the province.

Direct rule returned and it was not until the Good Friday Agreement that power sharing got a second chance.

T

Taff Vale judgement, 1900–1901. In 1901 the House of Lords ruled in favour of the Taff Vale Railway Company which had sued the Amalgamated Society of Railway Servants for losses incurred during a strike. The judgement, by thus placing union funds in jeopardy, enabled Ramsay MacDonald to persuade unions to affiliate to the Labour Representation Committee, of which he was secretary, which had been set up in the previous year in order to create an independent Labour force in parliament. By failing to introduce legislation to reverse the judgement the Conservatives alienated the working-class vote in the 1906 general election. Conversely, the Campbell-Bannerman government helped cement its cordial relations with organized labour by means of the 1906 Trade Disputes Act.

Tamworth Manifesto, 18 December 1834. On 14 November 1834 William IV dismissed Melbourne's government – the last occasion in which the royal prerogative was used in this way – and invited Peel to form a minority Conservative administration.

The convention was that officers of the Crown had to resign their seats and stand for re-election. Peel thus issued an address to his Tamworth constituents on 18 December 1834 but the intended audience of this so-called Tamworth Manifesto was the entire political nation, making it the first party political manifesto.

Peel used the Manifesto to offer a 'middle way' between Wellingtonian reaction on the one hand (as symbolized by his initial opposition to Catholic Emancipation and parliamentary reform) and alleged Whig appeasement of the Irish and Radicals on the other (as symbolized by the Irish Church Temporalities Act of 1833). Thus Peel accepted both the Great Reform Act as 'a final and irrevocable settlement of a great Constitutional question' and the need for 'a careful review of institutions, civil and ecclesiastical ... combining, with the firm maintenance of established rights, the correction of proved abuses and the redress of real grievances'.

Historians such as Blake and Gash present Peel as using such language as part of a strategy to widen the social basis of support for traditional Toryism by appealing to those members of the middle class who were newly enfranchised in 1832. It is however easy to exaggerate the numbers and political influence of this class and makes more sense to regard Peel's more immediate concern as one of building a bridge to those on the right wing of the Whig coalition, like Stanley and Graham, who were increasingly alarmed by the prominence given to Russell and issues such as appropriation.

The Manifesto was successful insofar as the Conservatives gained roughly 100 seats in the 1835 general election, although this was still not enough to give them a majority in the Commons against the combined forces of the Lichfield House Compact.

Tariff Reform League The Tariff Reform League was set up by Joseph

Chamberlain to promote protectionism after he left government in 1903 to mount his tariff reform crusade.

The Tariff Reform League set the standard for pressure-group campaigning in the Edwardian period, pioneering the use of motion pictures and gramophone records in much the same way as the Anti-Corn Law League provided the model for mid-Victorian campaigning by its pioneering use of the penny post and paid lecturers.

Temperance movement Temperance began as a working-class movement to reduce liquor consumption but developed into a movement encouraging teetotalism or complete abstinence from alcohol. Organizations such as the British Association for the Promotion of Temperance, the British Women's Temperance Association, the Band of Hope, and the United Kingdom Alliance grew up to provide support for those who had signed the pledge and to exert pressure upon parliament to remove the source of temptation by restrictive licensing legislation.

Non-conformists were active in the temperance movement through bodies such as the National Temperance Federation and became identified with the Liberal Party, whilst the drink trade had powerful friends in the Conservative Party, leading Gladstone to attribute electoral defeat in 1874 to the adverse effects of Bruce's Licensing Act and Lloyd George to lament the malign influence of the 'beerage' in blocking the 1908 Licensing Bill.

Ten Hours Act, 1847. The Ten Hours Movement was a pressure group of the 1830s and 1840s, which combined paternalistic Tory evangelicals with working-class radicals in a campaign to reduce the working day in factories to a maximum of ten hours. The 1847 Factory Act – popularly known as the Ten Hours Act – appeared to mark the success of their campaign insofar as women and youths aged between thirteen and eighteen working in textile factories had their working day limited to 10.5 hours a day (with a maximum of 58 hours per week). However, adult male textile workers had to wait until 1853 before they received this concession.

Ten-Year Rule, 1919. The Ten-Year Rule was a running assumption in all matters of military equipment and supply procurement, that a major war was unlikely for at least ten years. This made sense at the end of World War One and chimed with the popular feeling enshrined in the League of Nations Union in favour of universal disarmament. However, it made less sense with the passage of time, given the emergence of aggressively nationalistic regimes. The rule was formally abandoned in 1932, following the 1931 Manchurian Incident.

The Ten-Year Rule nevertheless helped underpin appeasement of Hitler's Germany insofar as military unpreparedness and/or the need to buy time to rearm by making concessions helped to justify this policy.

Thatcher, Margaret Hilda, Baroness Thatcher (13 October 1925–). Mrs Thatcher was born Margaret Hilda Roberts at Grantham in Lincolnshire. Like Harold Wilson she came from a Methodist background. Her father was Alfred Roberts, a local grocer who went on to become a Conservative councillor and mayor of the town. Although educated at Grantham High School and Somerville College, Oxford (where she became president of the Oxford University Conservative Association and graduated in chemistry), she claimed that the most important lessons she learnt had been taught by her father including the 'Victorian values' of hard work and thrift, and the importance of not compromising in her beliefs.

After Oxford she worked in the research department of a plastics factory and at Jo Lyons food company before standing unsuccessfully as Conservative candidate in a strong Labour seat in the 1950 general election. In the course of this adventure she met Denis Thatcher, who ran a family paint and chemical company, and they married the following year.

She embarked upon a second career and was called to the Bar, specializing in patents and tax. Elected to Parliament in 1959, she was parliamentary secretary, Ministry of Pensions and National Insurance, from 1961 to 1964, and during the Labour Governments of 1964–70 was Opposition spokesman successively on transport, power, Treasury matters, housing, pensions and education, joining the shadow cabinet in 1967.

With Ted Heath as prime minister, Mrs Thatcher served as secretary of state for education and science 1970–74, during which time she rejected only 115, or less than 4%, of the 2,700 proposals which she received for comprehensivization, thereby winning the dubious distinction – at least for a Conservative – of having closed more grammar schools than any other education secretary. She also received unfavourable national publicity as 'Mrs Thatcher, Milk snatcher' for discontinuing free school milk.

When the Tories lost office, Mrs Thatcher became first Opposition spokesman on financial affairs and public expenditure and then, in October 1974, was chief spokesman on the environment. However, by this time, chiefly through the tutelage of Keith Joseph and the Institute of Economic Affairs, through whom she read Hayek, Mrs Thatcher broke with Heathite conservatism and decided to challenge him for the leadership herself, once Joseph's blunt speech to Birmingham Conservatives regarding the desirability of limiting procreation amongst the lower orders effectively ended his hopes of leading the party.

Although Ted Heath represented the grammar school meritocracy, his leadership of the party did not significantly displace or greatly displease the grandees. Retrospectively Mrs Thatcher's replacement of him, when she secured 53% of the vote in the 1975 leadership election, witnessed a 'Peasants' revolt' whereby 'wets' – patrician exponents of one-nation Toryism like Gilmour, Carrington and Pym – were ultimately replaced by men like Tebbit, Fowler and Moore who, like Thatcher herself, had their roots in suburbia and embodied lower-middle-class aspirations.

A decade younger than Heath, Mrs Thatcher did not share his sentimental attachment to the post-war settlement. She was prepared to ditch 'Butskellism' as soon as it was seen as having failed to deliver the goods.

Although obliged to honour the recommendations of the Clegg commission for enormous pay increases to public-sector workers, Mrs Thatcher otherwise dug her heels in regarding pay demands and progressively emasculated the trade unions by means of a series of industrial relations Acts. Her government signified its attachment to the principles of monetarism by setting targets for monetary growth but in the short term the impact of Clegg and OPEC II was to stoke inflation, whilst unemployment continued to rise, provoking inner-city riots and rendering Mrs Thatcher (with 23% support) the most unpopular prime minister since polling began. Many 'wets' in her own cabinet, where true believers were currently in the minority, advised a change of course but she characteristically announced to the 1980 Conservative Party conference that 'The lady's not for turning'.

The turnaround in her political fortunes came with victory in the Falklands War, which acted like a mirror image of the Suez Crisis, with the 'Falklands factor' paving the way for the 1983 general election landslide of a 144-seat majority: the largest since that of the Attlee Labour government in the summer of 1945.

The National Union of Mineworkers, the elite troops of the trade unionist 'enemy within', who had brought down the Heath government a decade earlier, began industrial action in March 1984 to halt the government's programme of pit closures. Many ordinary miners were fighting to preserve their jobs and their communities. Arthur Scargill and the militant leadership of the NUM were, however, fighting a class war to topple Mrs Thatcher and the forces of capitalism she represented. Conversely, she was fighting to preserve the changes which she had already made and for the opportunity to press further ahead with the Thatcherite revolution, which was increasingly identified with privatization.

More fundamentally Mrs Thatcher had taken the precaution of building up large stockpiles of coal whereas Scargill, in failing to ballot his membership (in line with the requirements of Thatcherite industrial relations legislation), appeared to act undemocratically; an image which was hardly dispelled when it was revealed that the NUM was soliciting financial support from Britain's 'enemies without', including Libya's Colonel Gaddafi and the 'trade unions' of Soviet-controlled Afghanistan. More and more men returned to the pits, notably under the aegis of the Nottingham-based breakaway Democratic Union of Mineworkers, until the NUM eventually capitulated, about twelve months after the strike had begun.

Mrs Thatcher's third election victory in 1987 showed that she still enjoyed much support, although her radical right agenda made her as many enemies amongst the old establishment as it did on the left. As Julian Critchley, one of the few openly dissident Tories of the time, once wryly remarked, she couldn't see an institution without taking her handbag to it. The Stock Exchange, the BBC, the Arts Council, the medical and legal professions, and the universities were amongst those institutions affected.

To her critics she was a brutally self-confident philistine suburbanite: a puritanical provincial populist. They also liked to point out that she was a populist who was not really popular: her electoral successes were built upon the divisions of her opponents rather than a majority of the electorate endorsing her vision. These critics portray her later well-publicized expressions of concern over the depletion of the ozone layer not as an instance of statesmanlike vision but rather as a green herring, designed to divert attention from the fact that she presided over a marked deterioration in the immediate physical environment, notably in Britain's inner cities.

However, Mrs Thatcher became a figure on the world stage who epitomized the anti-collectivist counter-revolution and who enabled Britain to punch above its weight. This was so for a number of reasons. Firstly, Mrs Thatcher was easily comprehensible to foreigners, with a series of simple messages delivered simply. Secondly, the Soviets enhanced her standing in the West by branding her the 'Iron Lady': a sobriquet which was a gift to Saatchi and Saatchi and Conservative Central Office as it ideally synthesized the two contradictory images which her gender and policies engendered: fluffy and toughie. Thirdly, the 'special relationship' never seemed stronger than in the hands of Thatcher and Reagan. Fourthly, success in the Falklands War seemed all the greater when contrasted with the Suez Crisis or the post-imperial imbroglios of other nations such as the French in Vietnam and Algeria, or the Belgians in the Congo. Last but not least, Mrs Thatcher's central position in the formal photography and film of international summits, which perhaps originally had more to do with considerations of aesthetics or gallantry, was increasingly conceded in acknowledgement of her continuing electoral success and sheer longevity.

Ultimately Mrs Thatcher's longevity, combined with her imperious temperament, caused problems. A combination of purges and 'natural wastage' meant that by the time Willie Whitelaw departed from government in January 1988 there was really no one to offer her countervailing advice to which she was prepared to listen. As Mrs Thatcher herself said, 'Every prime minister needs a Willie'. Geoffrey Howe and Nigel Lawson tried and failed to take his place.

Hence, in part, the debacle of the poll tax and her increasingly shrill response to Europe. Having signed the Solemn declaration of Stuttgart (1983) and pushed the Single European Act (1986) through both cabinet and the House of Commons, Mrs Thatcher's fears regarding Europe were first fully voiced in her 1988 Bruges speech and culminated on her return from a Rome summit in her triple negative in the House of Commons to the aspirations of Jacques Delors (president of the Commission), which provoked the resignation of Geoffrey Howe as deputy leader and whose resignation speech on 13 November precipitated the fateful leadership election.

On the first ballot Mrs Thatcher scored 204 votes. This represented 55% of the vote, given that Heseltine (who had nearly brought her down over the Westland affair) scored 152 and there were 16 abstentions. Under the arcane rules then prevailing this meant that Mrs Thatcher was just 2 votes short of a win. Even so, she had done better than in 1975 when she first won the leadership, and scored more than 5% more than John Major did to win in the second ballot. Thatcher had initially decided to fight on but had withdrawn after Ken Clarke and a succession of cabinet colleagues had told her face to face that they would vote for her but considered her cause doomed and the executive of the 1922 Committee had called for a wider field.

Mrs Thatcher's final failure was grooming a successor or rather, from her perspective, grooming a reliable successor. John Major had received her seal of approval in the second ballot for the leadership but once he took the reins of power seemed to be a profound disappointment. Once her attempts at 'backseat driving' were discountenanced Mrs Thatcher championed the cause of the Kurds but Major's policy of safe havens for them also provided him with a safe haven from her, insofar as her intervention more closely resembled Gladstone and the Armenian atrocities agitation of 1895–96 than Gladstone and the Bulgarian atrocities agitation of 1876: a plaintive voice from a bygone age rather than a clarion call announcing a return to centre stage.

Thatcherism If one can speak of Thatcherism as a coherent philosophy or political programme (a subject much disputed) its main features were a rejection of the principal features of the post-World War Two settlement for which the term 'Butskellism' provides a (similarly controversial) shorthand, namely, Keynesian demand management to preserve full employment, a mixed economy and the welfare state. These were rejected in favour of the supposed 'Victorian values' of patriotism, unfettered enterprise, living within one's means and low inflation. The instruments by which these ideals were to be achieved included trade union reform, privatization and control of the money supply. The price of these policies included the Falklands conflict, strained relations within the European Community and the Commonwealth, mass unemployment, the growth of the yuppie culture, the erosion of Britain's manufacturing base, and the widening of the divisions between North and South and between the rich and poor.

Thus although Mrs Thatcher invoked the spirit of St Francis of Assisi before entering Number 10 for the first time as prime minister, Thatcherism came to be more closely associated with ambition, acquisition and abrasion than the qualities of consensus, cooperation and compassion. K. O. Morgan relates this to the fact that Thatcherite values were not rooted in the 'One Nation' patrician values of the shire grandees, or the manufacturing Tories beloved of the vision of Tory Democracy associated with Disraeli, or even the villa or suburban Toryism nurtured by Salisbury and consolidated by Baldwin and Chamberlain but rather with the acquisitive culture of provincial business.

Notwithstanding this fact, Thatcherism provided a sense of purpose and pride even when it failed to offer material rewards and this, together with the weakness of the opposition, enabled Mrs Thatcher to become Britain's most successful twentieth-century prime minister, whilst its shift of emphasis from state to individual responsibility, and from wealth redistribution to wealth creation, has inspired conservatives throughout the developed world.

Theatres Act, **1968**. The right of the Lord Chamberlain to censor plays (dating from the 1737 Licensing Act) was abolished by the 1968 Theatres Act.

Three-Day Week, 31 December 1972–21 February 1973. The Three-Day Week was imposed from 31 December 1972 by the government of Edward Heath in order to conserve energy, in the light of the miners' strike for higher pay which was due to begin on 9 January 1972.

It was called off on 21 February 1973 after adding £116–17m to the bill for coal, with the average miner's earnings rising by 24%. Other unions sought similar settlements and when talks with the TUC for a voluntary policy of pay restraint broke down the government announced the return to a formal, statutory prices-and-incomes policy in early November 1973.

Tithe Commutation Act, 1836. The 1836 Tithe Commutation Act helped end the tithe war by commuting tithes to cash payments. The measure was one of a series supported by the liberal Anglican Whigs as a means of satisfying moderate non-conformist demands.

Tolpuddle Martyrs, 1834. The Tolpuddle Martyrs were six agricultural labourers from the Dorsetshire village of Tolpuddle who were sentenced in March 1834 to the maximum penalty of seven years' transportation for the 'administering or taking of unlawful oaths' for seditious purposes. This was a crime under a law of 1797 originally devised to suppress the Nore mutiny that these labourers fell foul of in the course of trying to set up a friendly society or trade union to resist wage cutting. Indeed, this appears to have been their real 'crime'.

Melbourne, as home secretary, refused to show clemency and the episode helped confirm the view of many members of the working class that there was a sustained governmental campaign against their interests.

However, the men were pardoned in 1836 and repatriated in 1838, following the public outcry on their behalf.

Tory Democracy The term 'Tory Democracy' was popularized by Lord Randolph Churchill. Disraeli was credited with having acted as John the Baptist to Churchill's Christ by passing the 1867 Reform Act (which created virtual household suffrage); creating the National Union in the same year (to organize the new mass electorate in the Conservative interest); and by passing the social reforms of 1874–80 (which cemented the new working-class constituency to the party).

In fact, Disraeli's role in these three developments was much more problematical than Primrose League hagiography suggests. Firstly, Disraeli's primary interest in taking up parliamentary reform in 1867 was not so much to enfranchise potential Conservative supporters amongst the working class as to keep Gladstone embarrassed, the Liberal Party disunited, and control of the terms of reform in his own hands so as to be able to show the world that the Conservative Party was capable of passing major legislation and otherwise to reap whatever party political advantage he could from the proceedings. However, even these limited aims were compromised by the minority status of the Derby administration, with the result that radical amendments (notably Hodgkinson's amendment) rendered the final Act much more sweeping than Disraeli had originally envisaged.

Secondly, so far from creating the National Union, Disraeli opposed the idea and actually boycotted the

Union's first meeting. The man who actually deserves the credit for this innovation was William Nevill, Lord Nevill, and later Lord Abergavenny.

Thirdly, it is similarly misleading to credit Disraeli with the social reforms of 1874–80. Disraeli was lacking in inspiration and frequently ill. The initiative for reform came from others, notably his home secretary, Richard Cross. Insofar as Disraeli promoted social reform it was for no more lofty motive than giving the Commons something uncontroversial and vaguely worthwhile to keep them occupied.

If Disraeli has any claim to have laid the foundations for Tory Democracy it was rather through identifying himself and his party with the Crown, for example through the Royal Titles Act of 1876, and with foreign and imperial policies reminiscent of Palmerston. Thus jingoism rather than slum clearance proved to be the way to the hearts of working-class Conservatives.

Toryism, One-Nation *Sybil*, published in 1845, is the second of the Young England trilogy of novels by Benjamin Disraeli (the others being *Coningsby* and *Tancred*). *Sybil or The Two Nations* provides the formal inspiration for one-nation Toryism.

Chapter 5 of Book II provides the most famous passage:

> Two nations: between whom there is no intercourse and no sympathy; who are as ignorant of each other's habits, thoughts, and feelings, as if they were dwellers in different zones, or inhabitants of different planets; who are formed by a different breeding, are fed by a different food, are ordered by different manners, and are not governed by the same laws.
>
> "You speak of" said Egremont hesitatingly, "the rich and the poor?"

One-nation Toryism thus involved the attempt to promote social harmony by such means as paternalistic legislation, pride in the Empire or respect for the Crown.

Rab Butler appreciated that the experiences of wartime and particularly of evacuation enhanced the public's realization of the continuing relevance of Disraeli's analysis or perhaps it would be more accurate to say that One-Nation Toryism became transmuted over time from a paternalist to a classless ideal.

Butler's protégé Iain Macleod was an original member of the One-Nation Group and a One-Nation Tory, whose death in 1970 removed a stabilizing influence from the Heath government, which had veered to the right in the guise of 'Selsdon man' but which somersaulted in the opposite direction after a series of well-publicized U-turns. The 1968 rebellion of Macleod and fourteen other Conservatives over Labour's Commonwealth Immigrants Bill shows that some Tories defined 'One-Nation' so comprehensively as to include former Commonwealth citizens.

In the Thatcher years One-Nation Toryism was a coded means whereby 'wets' distanced themselves from the allegedly divisive policies pursued by the government that had become the new orthodoxy. Thus Chris Patten's non-Thatcherite publication *The Tory Case*, for example, advertised itself as containing 'a few ideas which may one day return to fashion'. However, even the famous 'One Nation' pamphlet of

1950 that endorsed the welfare state contained important qualifications, which is hardly surprising given that its contributors included Angus Maude and Enoch Powell.

Tory party (Tories, Toryism) In the late seventeenth century there were moves to exclude the Catholic James, Duke of York, from succeeding his brother, Charles II, to the English throne. The Tory party emerged as a group opposed to exclusion not because they were pro-Catholic but because they believed that he was the legitimate heir. The name – like 'Whig' – was originally a term of abuse, referring to Irish bandits.

The modern Tory party emerged in opposition to the French Revolution of 1789. Although Pitt the Younger did not describe himself as a Tory, he inspired politicians like Liverpool and Canning who were known by this label. The Tory party was typically the party of the squirearchy and the parson and its members sought to maintain the privileges and prerogatives of the Crown, the Established or Anglican Church, and (like their Whig rivals) the landed interest.

Wellington managed to alienate both the party's Huskissonite left wing (chiefly over parliamentary reform in 1828) and its Ultra right wing (over Catholic Emancipation in 1829). Indeed, Repeal of the Test and Corporation Acts (1828), Catholic Emancipation (1829) and the Great Reform Act (1832) represent a triple blow from which Toryism never fully recovered.

Indeed, Peel is generally credited with the process of repackaging the Tory party in the aftermath of the loss of office in 1830, with the Tamworth Manifesto representing a key moment in the party's transformation into the Conservative Party. However, an unreconstructed Toryism lurked beneath the Peelite Conservative Party which mounted a series of rebellions culminating in massive protests against the Maynooth Grant (1845) and the Repeal of the Corn Laws (1846), which split the party. The Peelites ultimately coalesced with the Whigs and Radicals to form the Liberal Party and it was left to Disraeli to remould the rump of protectionist Conservatives so as to render them once more electable.

Nowadays Tory and Conservative are interchangeable terms.

Tractarianism See OXFORD MOVEMENT.

Trade Boards Act, 1909. As president of the Board of Trade, Churchill was responsible for the 1909 Trade Boards Act which established boards of employers and workers to fix minimum wages for about 500,000 labourers in the mostly un-unionized 'sweated trades' such as tailoring.

Trade Disputes Act, 1906. The Trade Disputes Act reversed the Taff Vale judgement by making trade unions immune from legal action for damages incurred during strikes.

Trade Disputes Act, 1927. Having persuaded the TUC General Council to call off the General Strike in part by hinting that the strike might render void the protection afforded to unions by the 1906 Trade Disputes Act, the Baldwin government nevertheless proceeded with legislation in May 1927 to outlaw any strike defined by the courts as 'designed or calculated to coerce the government', to ban sympathetic strike action and to prevent civil servants from belonging to any union affiliated to the Trades Union Congress.

The Act did turn back the clock insofar as it reversed the 1913 Trade Union Act (which had itself reversed the Osborne judgement of 1909). Thus henceforth, instead of the political levy being raised unless trade unionists contracted out, they now had explicitly to 'contract in'. This was clearly a device to damage the finances of the Labour Party, which repealed the measure in May 1946.

Trade Duties Reciprocity Act, 1823. The Trade Duties Reciprocity Act of 1823 involved the repeal of roughly 300 ancient statutes so as to allow Britain to abolish or reduce duties on goods imported from those countries which made reciprocal arrangements regarding British imports to their shores. The Navigation Laws were modified so as to allow free intercourse between the colonies and foreign countries, although trade between the colonies and the mother country were still confined to British ships until 1849.

Trade Union Act, 1871. The 1871 Trade Union Act sought to protect union members and their funds from the threat of prosecution for restraining trade.

Trade Union Act, 1913. The 1913 Trade Union Act repaired the damage done to the Labour Party by the 1909 Osborne Judgement by permitting trade unions to establish political levies so long as this was supported in a secret ballot by a majority of the members, and those individuals who objected retained the right to 'contract out': a principle reversed in the aftermath of the general strike by the 1927 Trade Disputes Act.

Trade Union Act, 1980. Jim Prior's Trade Union Act of 1980 outlawed secondary picketing, made closed shops more difficult and provided public money for ballots on strikes and leadership elections.

Trade Union Act, 1982. Norman Tebbit's Trade Union Act of 1982 fined unions for unlawful strikes, applied heavier penalties for secondary picketing and provided compensation for those dismissed as a result of closed shops.

Trimble, David (15 October 1944–). Educated at Bangor Grammar School and Queen's University Belfast, where he read law, David Trimble was called to the Bar of Northern Ireland in 1969 before returning to the Law Faculty at Queen's. His political career began in the hardline Vanguard Unionist Party in the early 1970s and he played a leading role in the Ulster Workers' Council successful strike against the Sunningdale Agreement in 1974 but by 1978 he had joined mainstream unionism and entered Westminster as MP for Upper Bann in 1990.

In 1995 he succeeded James Molyneaux as Ulster Unionist leader. To many he seemed to be a hardliner on the right of the party, wishing to take a tougher line on the peace process than Molyneaux. After all, in the previous month he had appeared at the annual Drumcree parade alongside Ian Paisley, saluting the Orangemen after they had won a standoff with the nationalist residents of the Garvaghy

Road. However, Trimble was to surprise everyone by his efforts to further the peace process. In his first speech as UUP leader he made a moderate proposal for an elected Northern Ireland Assembly, with limited powers, as the focus for all-party talks, and he even went to Dublin to talk with the Taoiseach, John Bruton. Finally, in 1998 he risked accusations of betrayal not only by Paisley but by many within his own party by signing the Good Friday Agreement and campaigning with John Hume for a 'Yes' vote in the ensuing referendum (for which actions the two men were jointly awarded the 1998 Nobel Peace Prize).

Despite bitterly condemning the Patten Commission on policing reform and continuing to press Sinn Féin/IRA on decommissioning of weapons by resigning as first minister of the new Northern Ireland Assembly in early 2001, his course of action has encountered rising resistance within his own party and in a haemorrhage of support to the DUP. Matters reached a critical point in the May 2005 general election when the UUP lost all but one of its MPs.

Trimble displayed courage in pushing forward power sharing but was extremely naive in making his and his party's fortunes dependent upon the IRA putting its arms visibly and verifiably beyond use.

Triple Alliance The Triple Alliance was the combination of the Miners' Federation of Great Britain, the National Union of Railwaymen and the National Transport Workers which was formed in 1919 in order to offer one another sympathetic strike action in certain circumstances but it was crippled on 'Black Friday' (15 April 1921) when NUR and NTW support for the miners failed to materialize.

Troubles, The The Troubles is the name given to the sectarian conflict which flared up in Northern Ireland in 1968 when the civil rights movement provoked a backlash which resulted in paramilitary violence and attacks upon the police and British troops (who were sent into the province in 1969). The peace process has seen a reduction but not a complete end to political violence.

Truck Act, 1817. The 1817 Truck Act sought to curb the system whereby wages were sometimes paid in whole or part in vouchers which could only be exchanged for shoddy and overpriced goods at stores run by the employer. It was one of several measures that showed the willingness of the Liverpool government to side with workers against unscrupulous middle-class masters.

U

Ulster Covenant, 1912. The Ulster Covenant, modelled on the Scottish Covenant of 1557, was drawn up in 1912 and signed by almost three-quarters of Ulster's Protestants over the age of fifteen. They pledged themselves to use 'all means which may be found necessary to defeat the present conspiracy to set up a Home Rule Parliament in Ireland', given that the 1911 Parliament Act meant that Home Rule was due to become law in 1914. In practice this meant the creation (in January 1913) of the Ulster Volunteer Force (comprising 100,000 covenanters) and preparations for an 'Ulster provisional government' to assume control of the province in the event of Home Rule passing.

Ulster Defence Association (UDA) The Ulster Defence Association (UDA) was formed in 1971 as an umbrella organization for loyalist paramilitary groups and thereby became the largest loyalist paramilitary group in Northern Ireland. It played a major role in undermining the Sunningdale Agreement. However, the political wing of the UDA – the Ulster Loyalist Democratic Party (ULDP), which later evolved into the Ulster Democratic Party – had only had a negligible impact at the polls.

Ceasefires in support of the Good Friday Agreement have been short lived and by 2000 a feud between the UDA/Ulster Freedom Fighters (UFF) and the Ulster Volunteer Force (UVF) had resulted in several deaths on both sides.

Ulster Democratic Unionist Party (DUP) The Ulster Democratic Unionist Party was founded by the Reverend Ian Paisley in October 1971 out of the Protestant Unionist Party, which in turn had emerged out of Ulster Protestant Action as a hardline Unionist party opposed to any change in the status quo. It played a leading role in the coalition of unionists opposed to the Sunningdale Agreement but ultimately fell out with the Ulster Unionists, and outperformed them in the 1979 European Parliament and 1981 local government elections. For the 1983 and 1987 general elections they negotiated pacts whereby they would not oppose one another in seats where this might let in a republican or a nationalist and they also cooperated in the 'Ulster Says No' campaign against the Anglo-Irish Agreement of November 1985. However, in November 1989 the DUP conference voted to contest all safe Unionist seats for fear that its alliance with the Ulster Unionists was clouding its identity and losing it votes.

The Downing Street Declaration of December 1993 was fiercely condemned by the DUP, although it welcomed the creation of the Northern Ireland Forum, winning 18.8% of the vote then and 18.1% of the vote in the Northern Ireland Assembly elections.

Ian Paisley has provided the DUP with a distinctive, loud and popular voice in Ulster politics and under his stewardship the party eclipsed their UUP rivals in the May 2005 election, gaining four seats, to bring their total to nine, and winning almost double their percentage of the overall poll.

Ulster Unionist Council (UUC) The Ulster Unionist Council was originally launched in Belfast on 3 March 1905 as a means of uniting northern unionism against the threat of internal faction but it drew sustenance from the renewed threat of Irish Home Rule, particularly following the 1911 Parliament Act and the introduction of the Third Home Rule Bill in 1912. The Council was affiliated to Conservative Central Office and its ties with the Conservative Party strengthened once Bonar Law replaced Balfour as its leader.

Ulster Unionist Party (UUP) The Ulster Unionist Party evolved out of the Edwardian Ulster Unionist Council. It dominated Stormont and opposed the Sunningdale Agreement, forming the United Ulster Unionist Council with the Ulster Democratic Unionist party and the Vanguard Unionists to resist power sharing. They left this coalition in 1977 and helped to maintain the minority Labour government in office until it had passed legislation granting extra seats to Northern Ireland, in compensation for the end of Stormont.

Initially attracted by the Conservative promise of two-tier local government for Ireland, the UUP were rapidly disillusioned, boycotting the Constitutional Conference, opposing the creation of the Northern Ireland Assembly (despite winning 29.7% of the vote in the October 1982 Assembly election) and the Anglo-Irish Agreement. Support for the Maastricht Treaty Bill was rewarded by the concession of a Northern Ireland Select Committee, whilst the Downing Street Declaration of December 1993 was framed in such a way as to reassure the party. Under David Trimble the Ulster Unionists won 24.2% in the elections to the Northern Ireland Forum but remained vulnerable to the claims of Ian Paisley and the Ulster Democratic Unionist Party that they were too accommodating to nationalist sentiment. There were also very serious internal divisions regarding Trimble's decision to approve the Good Friday Agreement and participate in the Northern Ireland Assembly, in the elections for which it won more seats but fewer votes than the SDLP. These problems came to a head in the May 2005 general election when the UUP lost five of its six seats. David Trimble resigned and was succeeded as leader by Sir Reg Empey.

Ulster Vanguard Ulster Vanguard under William Craig emerged in opposition to the imposition of direct rule by Ted Heath in 1972 and increasing IRA terrorist activity. Vanguard joined forces with the DUP and the other loyalist organizations opposed to the Sunningdale Agreement to form the United Ulster Unionist Council that in the February 1974 general election won 51.1% of the vote.

Ulster Volunteer Force (UVF) The Ulster Volunteer Force (UVF) was a Protestant loyalist paramilitary body formed on the suggestion of the Ulster Unionist Council in January 1913 to resist Irish Home Rule by force, if necessary (it having become clear that the Asquith government would introduce a Home Rule Bill which the Lords would no longer be able to block, thanks to the 1911 Parliament Act).

The UVF was to be limited, in the first instance, to 100,000 signatories of the Covenant. By the end of 1913 it already numbered 90,000 and had developed into a sophisticated and highly mobile force with motorcar and motorcycle sections, a nursing corps and elaborate mobilization plans. A fund of £250,000 was raised to support UVF members and their dependents in the event of death or injury in the performance of their duties, £10,000 of which was personally donated by Sir Edward Carson.

Later in 1913 the Nationalist community responded to the UVF by creating the larger but less-well-funded, less-well-equipped and less efficient Irish Volunteers. The contrast between the two forces can be seen by comparing their gunrunning operations at Larne and Howth respectively.

Although the UVF and Irish Volunteers presented the spectre of bloody civil war in Ireland, it can be argued that the former helped avoid violence, at least in the short term insofar as it focused loyalist frustrations and aggression against the Westminster government rather than against the Catholic community in Belfast and Londonderry.

Ulster Workers' Council The Ulster Workers' Council was a group of loyalist trades unionists opposed to the power sharing Executive and the Council of Ireland established as a result of the Sunningdale Agreement. In May 1974 it launched the strike that paralysed the province and brought about the collapse of Sunningdale.

Ultras The Ultras were those right-wing Tories who were most bitterly opposed to changes such as Catholic Emancipation and its advocates such as George Canning.

Ironically the passage of Catholic Emancipation converted some Ultras to the cause of parliamentary reform, as a Commons more representative of popular bigotry would have blocked such a measure. Thus in 1830 Ultras such as the Duke of Richmond were prepared to join with Grey and the Whigs and former supporters of Canning such as Palmerston and Melbourne to bring down Wellington's ministry and work for what became the Great Reform Act.

However, the Conservative Party created by Peel continued to have an Ultra wing which once again conceived itself to be betrayed by him over measures such as the 1844 Charitable Bequests Act and 1845 Maynooth Grant.

Unauthorized Programme, 1885. The Unauthorized or Radical Programme was put forward by Joseph Chamberlain and his political associates in the period leading up to the 1885 general election.

Originally published as a series of articles in the *Fortnightly Review*, the pieces were collected in a volume called the 'Radical Programme', for which Chamberlain wrote the preface. The programme's most famous proposal was Jesse Collings' 'Three Acres and a Cow'. However, what was suggested went well beyond what might appeal to the newly enfranchised agricultural labourers, including greater direct taxation, disestablishment and free elementary education.

The programme should, indeed, be seen as part of Chamberlain's strategy for setting the party's agenda and establishing his credentials to succeed

Gladstone in leading the party. The programme was thus a calculated challenge not only to Gladstone but also to Hartington and the Whigs. Historians dispute the extent to which the Unauthorized Programme played well for the Liberals in the ensuing election, where the Irish Nationalists under Parnell ended up holding the balance of power. What cannot be disputed, however, is that Gladstone brilliantly outmanoeuvred Chamberlain and wrested control of the political agenda and party by shortly thereafter embracing the cause of Irish Home Rule.

Union, Act of, 1800/1801. The rebellion of the United Irishmen in 1798 served to emphasize the danger to Britain should the French (at war with Britain since 1793) establish themselves on the island. Pitt thus took the decision to bind Ireland more closely to Britain by uniting the two countries under a single parliament.

Castlereagh persuaded the Dublin parliament to vote for its own extinction by a combination of money involving over £1.5m in compensation for disfranchised boroughs (an average cost of £15,000 per seat), patronage (with thirteen new Irish peerages created and four British peerages bestowed upon Irish peers), and promises, notably of greater economic opportunities for Ireland and of Catholic Emancipation.

The legislation passed through both the Dublin and Westminster parliaments and took effect on 1 January 1801, creating the United Kingdom of Great Britain and Ireland.

Under the terms of the Act Ireland henceforth elected one hundred MPs to the Westminster parliament, whilst four Irish spiritual lords and twenty-eight temporal lords elected for life from amongst the Irish peers were to supplement the House of Lords. In addition free trade was effectively established between the two countries and Ireland was to contribute two-seventeenths of imperial expenditure (although the two exchequers were not united until 1816).

However, Pitt was unable to honour the promise of Catholic Emancipation because George III claimed that such a concession would represent a violation of his coronation oath. The Catholic sense of betrayal fuelled the career of Daniel O'Connell, and the campaign to repeal the Act of Union was barely affected by the eventual concession of Catholic Emancipation in 1829.

Unionist Free Fooders Those Tory dissentients led by Lord Hugh Cecil who were dedicated either to breaking with the Unionists and joining the Liberals or compelling Balfour to disown Joseph Chamberlain over his tariff reform proposals were known as the Unionist Free Fooders. In the event they quarrelled with one another over the best strategy, the Unionist Free Traders, whose most eminent member was Winston Churchill, deciding to join the Liberals.

Unionist Free Traders Those Unionists most violently opposed to the tariff reform crusade launched in 1903 by Joseph Chamberlain became known as Unionist Free Traders. Some of them, like Winston Churchill, felt so strongly on the issue that it led to their crossing the floor of the House of Commons.

United Kingdom Alliance See TEMPERANCE MOVEMENT.

United Kingdom Independence Party (UKIP) The United Kingdom Independence Party was formed in 1991 and has won seats in the European Parliament on a platform of opposing closer European integration in the short term and supporting withdrawal from Europe in the longer term.

University Tests Act, 1871. At the fifth attempt a University Tests Bill became law in 1871 (the 1866 and 1869 bills having been rejected by the Lords, and the 1868 and 1870 bills having had to defer to more pressing parliamentary business). The driving force behind the measure was Coleridge, a Liberal MP, rather than Gladstone himself, although the Liberal leader appreciated that the measure appealed to the non-conformist conscience and, like many Anglicans, felt that the existing state of affairs was no longer defensible.

Thus the Act opened Oxbridge and Durham to non-conformists by stating that persons taking lay academic degrees, or holding lay academic or collegiate offices in these universities, would no longer be required to subscribe to any religious test or formulary (non-conformists still being debarred from the headships of colleges, professorships of divinity, or offices required to be held by persons in holy orders or by churchmen).

Utilitarianism See BENTHAM, JEREMY.

Utilitarians See PHILOSOPHIC RADICALS.

V

de Valera, Eamon (14 October 1882–29 August 1975). Certain mysteries surround the birth of Eamon de Valera in that 'George' was the name recorded on his birth certificate but he was christened 'Edward', only changing his name to the Gaelic 'Eamon' after he had joined the Gaelic League as an adult. He was certainly born in New York City in 1882, the son of an Irish immigrant mother and a Spanish-Cuban father. He thus shared the lot of many nationalists (including Napoleon, Hitler and Stalin) in being born in a sense outside the nation whose politics he was to dominate.

De Valera's impoverished sculptor father died when he was just two years old and he was returned to Ireland by his mother to be raised by an uncle. At the age of sixteen he found true happiness when he left the rural conservative Catholic community that was his home, in order to attend Blackrock College in Dublin, where he excelled in sport and mathematics. After Blackrock he became a teacher in mathematics and increasingly active in militant republican politics.

He joined the Easter Rising and was lucky not only to survive the fighting but to have his death sentence commuted to life imprisonment. The execution of his comrades inflamed public opinion in Ireland, catapulted him into a position of seniority and allowed him to embody the spirit of the 'martyrs'. Released in 1917 he assumed the leadership of Sinn Féin, whose elected representatives boycotted Westminster in favour of their own parliament in Dublin: the Dáil.

De Valera was arrested again in 1918 but managed, with the help of Michael Collins, to escape from Lincoln Jail and returned in triumph to the United States as self–proclaimed President of the Irish Republic. In his absence Collins waged a campaign of urban guerrilla warfare which embarrassed and frustrated the British at the same time as it propelled him into a position to challenge 'the Chief's' leadership within republican circles.

Disagreements over strategy emerged between the two men after de Valera was smuggled back into Ireland at Christmas 1920. De Valera's views prevailed and on 21 May 1921 the IRA reverted to an Easter-Rising style attack upon the Dublin customs house. The rebels were routed, with nearly eighty captured and five killed but the incident helped pressurise Lloyd George into opening negotiations.

De Valera persuaded Collins to attend the conference in London whilst he stayed in Dublin. The simple truth was that he realised that there would have to be compromises and he didn't want to be the one to make them. Thus it was Collins who signed the Anglo-Irish Treaty whereby Ireland would be partitioned and the Irish Free State (comprising the twenty-six counties of the South) would stay in the Commonwealth. The IRA was split over the terms of the Treaty, with the formal point of difference between the factions headed by Collins and de Valera marked by their attitude towards the requirement that an oath of allegiance would have to be sworn to the British crown.

The Four Courts building in Dublin was occupied by IRA hardliners who were shelled by Collins and the official forces of the new state. This marked the emergence of a civil war which was more destructive than the struggle against the British had been and during which de Valera was marginalised by the military commanders and Collins was killed. According to some accounts de Valera tried to prevent the ambush in County Cork which removed his rival but the Neil Jordan film 'Michael Collins' unsurprisingly inclines to the view that 'Dev' played the role of Stalin rather than Lenin to Collins's Trotsky.

With the civil war lost and eleven months of solitary confinement it might have seemed as if de Valera's political career was over but within nine years he was in government at the head of his new party of Fianna Fáil and he was to dominate the politics of the South until 1973 when, at the age of ninety, he finally left the Presidency.

Like de Gaulle, de Valera saw himself, and was seen by many of his compatriots, as embodying his nation. He certainly possessed a thorough understanding of the conservative Catholic rural constituency which formed the backbone of his support, and pandered to its prejudices by having Gaelic made the official language, placing tariffs on British goods and outlawing divorce. He also sought to retain a monopoly on the aspiration of Irish unity by banning the IRA and using every opportunity to hound its members. Not surprisingly de Valera's metamorphosis from gunman to statesman was viewed by succeeding generations of gunmen as a betrayal.

Eire's relations with Britain improved after Neville Chamberlain became prime minister in 1937. The two men saw eye to eye on appeasement and de Valera had hopes that the frontier with Northern Ireland (if there had to be one) might be revised to his advantage just as Chamberlain had accommodated Hitler's desire to incorporate the Sudetenland into the Reich at Munich. 1938 certainly saw a gesture of goodwill on Chamberlain's part with the three treaty ports of the South handed over in return for a vague promise of 'good relations'. Churchill was incensed at the time and his anger was increased when war broke out, France fell and de Valera's Ireland stayed neutral.

Churchill was prepared to pay any price to defeat Hitler and effectively offered Ulster in return for the right to use the ports but de Valera refused. This refusal may have arisen from the belief that Britain was likely to be defeated and that Ireland should not do anything to antagonize Hitler, or it may have reflected the realisation that were Ulster to join Eire it would dilute, if not obliterate, de Valera's personal power base. Whatever, the reason, it hardly reflects well on de Valera.

To his countrymen at the time, however, unaware that the prize of a united island of Ireland had been within his grasp, World War Two was de Valera's finest hour insofar as neutrality averted potential political unrest and – like the Munich Agreement in relation to Prague – saved Dublin from German bombs. However, de Valera's public expression of sympathy to the German Embassy on receipt of the news of Hitler's suicide in April 1945 was a public relations disaster of the first magnitude. His mathematical frame of mind wedded him to forms to such a degree that he could thus display a complete lack of sensitivity.

De Valera nevertheless remained at the centre of power for a further thirty years, only retiring from the Presidency two years before his death in 1975. If Eire was part of his legacy so was Irish partition, whilst continued emigration gave the lie to any claim that independence had brought a land of contentment.

Victoria, Queen (Alexandrina Victoria) (24 May 1819–22 January 1901). Victoria, the only child of Edward, Duke of Kent (the fourth son of George III) and Princess Victoria of Saxe–Coburg, ascended the throne in 1837, following the death of her uncle, William IV. Her gender debarred her from the Hanoverian succession so that the electorate passed to her uncle Ernest Augustus, Duke of Cumberland, and thus brought to an end the union of the two states in the person of the monarch which had begun with the accession to the English throne of George I in 1714.

Victoria's father died when she was eight months old and she was raised by her domineering mother, on whom she largely turned her back on becoming queen. Thanks in large part to the influence of her uncle King Leopold of Belgium, Victoria had a reputation for liberal views that was strengthened by her obvious attachment to Melbourne and received public demonstration in the Bedchamber Incident, at the risk of making the monarch appear partisan. In the same year, Victoria successfully proposed to her cousin, Prince Albert of Saxe–Coburg Gotha, who soon replaced Melbourne as her political mentor (after their marriage in 1840) and who ultimately went on to father their nine children, before his death in 1861. Although the Prince Consort was not very popular with the British people, his influence upon Victoria was largely benign.

However, Albert's demise resulted in Victoria's prolonged withdrawal from public life so that the 'Widow of Windsor' only attended the State Opening of Parliament on six occasions in the remaining forty years of her reign. This fact and the salacious rumours regarding her relationship with John Brown resulted in an upsurge of republican sentiment that was expressed by such rising radical stars as Dilke and Chamberlain. Thus Gladstone commented in 1870 that 'the Queen is invisible and the Prince is not respected'. However, the serious illness and recovery of the Prince of Wales in 1871 prompted an upsurge in royalist sentiment that the Conservative Party successfully exploited first under Disraeli (by means of the Royal Titles Act of 1876), and then under Salisbury, by means of the Golden and Diamond Jubilees (of 1887 and 1897 respectively). The Golden Jubilee saw Victoria return to the public stage for good, although she continued to wear black.

Although during her reign the monarchy increasingly played a ceremonial role, Victoria always played a more active part behind the scenes than most of her subjects realized. In particular, she used her influence at various times in favour of Melbourne and Disraeli and against Palmerston and Gladstone. Nevertheless, Victoria's reign was of crucial importance in marking the transition towards constitutional monarchy, so what Bagehot had described as being the case in *The English Constitution* increasingly came to correspond with reality. That is to say, the monarchy increasingly became one of the 'dignified' rather than 'efficient' parts of the constitution. However, largely by virtue of being Britain's longest reigning monarch, Victoria attained a place in the affections of her subjects by the end of her reign equalled by few, if any, of her predecessors or successors.

Victorian values In an interview with Brian Walden on Sunday 16 January 1983 Margaret Thatcher agreed that her vision was of a Britain more self-reliant, thriftier and less burdened by the state. Moreover, she enthusiastically agreed when Walden characterized these values as essentially Victorian, adding that Victorian values also included the voluntary impulse, whereby the wealthy chose to benefit the community through various benefactions. She also added her wish to create a property-owning democracy or stakeholder society, and cited Winston Churchill in support of her wish to see government provide both 'a ladder ... anyone, no matter what their background, can climb' and 'a fundamental safety net below which no-one can fall'.

This interview sparked a debate, in the media and amongst historians, about just what Victorian values actually were, with critics striving to stereotype Mrs Thatcher as an advocate of *laissez-faire* capitalism, the dismantling of the welfare state, and in favour of gunboat diplomacy (as evidenced by the Falklands War).

War of 1812, June 1812–December 1814. Friction on the American–Canadian border meant that Anglo-American relations were always likely to be strained but they deteriorated to a dangerous degree as a result of the Orders-in-Council of 1807, prohibiting neutral trade with France, in response to the threat posed by Napoleon's continental system.

Although the Orders-in-Council were repealed in June 1812 this came four days too late, the US having already declared war because resentful of the way in which their ships had been stopped, cargoes seized and men impressed by the Royal Navy.

The Americans gained command of the Great Lakes in 1813 but invasions of Canada twice failed. Command of the seas not only enabled the British to blockade the American coast but allowed a British force to land in Chesapeake Bay in June 1814, which proceeded to move north to Washington and set fire to the Capitol and other public buildings.

The war formally lasted until the signing of the Treaty of Ghent on 24 December 1814 but the fighting actually continued into 1815 (including the defeat on 8 January of a British force at New Orleans) because of the time it took for news of the peace to cross the Atlantic.

The war was of greater importance for America than Britain, in stimulating nationalist sentiment and clearing the way for further expansion westward by defeating Britain's Indian allies.

Webbs, the: Martha Beatrice Webb (22 January 1858–30 April 1943) and **Sidney James Webb, Baron Passfield** (13 July 1859–13 October 1947). The future Beatrice Webb was born into the bourgeoisie as Martha Beatrice Potter. Having narrowly missed becoming the third wife of Joseph Chamberlain she entered into social work in London before helping her cousin Charles Booth with his massive study of *The Life and Labour of the People in London.* Her first publication in her own right was *The Co-operative Movement in Great Britain* (1891). In the previous year her researches had led her to tap the brain of Sidney Webb.

The future Baron Passfield of Passfield Corner, like his future wife, was also of middle-class origins but had left school before the age of 16 and only secured admission to the civil service and the bar after attending evening classes. Introduced to the Fabian Society by George Bernard Shaw, Sidney soon made his mark in its service as a lecturer and author and was already a member of its executive and London County Councillor when in 1892 he successfully proposed to Beatrice that their mutual intellectual admiration should lead to wedlock. Theirs was a marriage of minds in a very real sense, as shown by the fact that their honeymoon was spent investigating trade union records in Glasgow and Dublin.

They were intellectual equals in their attempts to provide an ideological underpinning for socialism, although Sidney is generally credited with a remorseless attention to detail whereas Beatrice provided the flashes of inspiration and her private income (of £1,000 per annum) cushioned their decision that Sidney should resign from the civil service and they should attempt to live by their pens.

The pram was not an enemy of promise in the Webb household as there was never need for one. Instead they spawned a small library of books and articles embracing history, economics and current affairs. However, their importance lay as much in institutional innovation as inspirational literature as both of them played a key role (with R. B. Haldane) in founding the London School of Economics and Political Science, in reorganizing the University of London into a federation of research and teaching institutions, and (with Robert Morant) in providing the spadework for what became Balfour's Education Act of 1902, whilst Beatrice's 1909 Minority Report as a member of the Royal Commission on the Poor Laws anticipated several elements of the Beveridge Report, although other features – such as the proposed state regulation of the labour market – were stillborn.

In 1912 the Webbs joined the ILP. In late 1914 they joined the Labour Party and in 1918 Sidney played a key role in drafting what became Clause 4 of the party's constitution. Moreover, his service on the 1919 Sankey Commission facilitated his entry into parliament as Labour MP for Seaham Harbour in Durham in 1922. In Labour's 1924 government Sidney became president of the Board of Trade and in the 1929 government he became colonial secretary with a seat in the Lords as Baron Passfield.

Beatrice continued to offer her husband emotional support and intellectual stimulation. Their last major joint effort was *Soviet Communism: A New Civilization?* (1935). The question mark of the title (removed in later editions) was belied by the contents that comprised an uncritical appreciation of Stalinist Russia. Despite visiting the USSR the Webbs, unlike Malcolm Muggeridge, remained completely impervious to the regime's systematic abuse of human rights. Perhaps this is not so surprising when one remembers that the Webbs were middle-class technocrats who dedicated themselves to serving an abstract conception of mankind and that as time went on they increasingly approached humanity via the medium of statistics rather than through personal contact. They represent a classic example of intellectuals who lacked both common sense and the common touch. They were selfless but soulless, claiming to love their fellow man but emotionally frigid (even in their relations with one another). In these respects and in their influence upon the institutional life of the country they were the spiritual heirs of Jeremy Bentham.

Wellington, Arthur Wellesley, first Duke of (1 May 1769–14 September 1852). Arthur Wesley (from 1798, Wellesley) was the fifth but third surviving son of the 1st Earl of Mornington, an impoverished member of the Anglo-Irish gentry. He left Eton at the age of fifteen in order to attend a military academy at Angers in France. At the age of eighteen he was gazetted ensign in the 73rd Highland Regiment and appointed *aide-de-camp* to the Irish Viceroy, the Duke of Buckingham.

In 1793 he advanced by purchase to a lieutenancy-colonelcy in the 33rd Foot and saw active service in the Low Countries under the Duke of York, 1794–95. In 1796 he was posted to India and was soon joined by his older brother, Richard, Marquess Wellesley, who was appointed governor-general in 1797.

Any insinuations of nepotism were silenced by Arthur's successes on the battlefield, notably at Assaye, on 24 September 1803, when he broke the power of the Marathas by defeating a force six times larger than his own. He returned to Britain in 1805 undefeated and with a knighthood. The following year he married Catherine (Kitty) Pakenham, who had previously refused him. The marriage did not, however, prove to be a success. Nor was Wellesley's military career initially as illustrious as his exploits in the Indian subcontinent might have suggested. His superiors, like Napoleon later, appear to have discounted him as a mere 'Sepoy general'.

Wellesley also fitfully resumed his dual career in politics (having represented the family seat of Trim in the Dublin Parliament, 1790–97). Thus he entered the Westminster parliament (as a Tory) largely in order to defend his brother's Indian record. He also spent two years in Ireland as chief secretary. However, his prospects were transformed in May 1808 when the Spanish revolt against the French broke out and he was ordered to Portugal.

Victory over General Junot at Vimiero (21August 1808) proved to be a false start insofar as superior officers prevented Wellesley pursuing the French because they preferred to sign the Convention of Cintra, which allowed Junot's army to be repatriated. Wellesley briefly returned to Ireland, despite being acquitted by the ensuing court of inquiry, but in April 1809 he was sent back to Portugal by Castlereagh following Moore's death at Corunna

Landing at Lisbon, he surprised Marshal Soult, captured Oporto, and forced the French back onto Spanish soil. However, the victory at Talavera (27–28 July 1809) failed to open the way to Madrid and Viscount Wellington (as he now was) retreated with his greatly outnumbered force to his Portuguese base, defeating Marshal Massena at Bussaco en route (27 September 1810). He had skilfully fortified the famous 'lines of Torres Vedras' across the Lisbon peninsula as his bolthole. In the spring of 1811 the French felt obliged to evacuate Portugal and Wellington felt strong enough to return to the offensive, although it was not until 1812 that he captured the Spanish fortresses of Ciudad-Rodrigo and Badajoz. Following the victory at Salamanca (22 July 1812), Wellington's forces entered Madrid (12 August).

Failure in besieging Burgos resulted in withdrawal once more to Portugal, but Wellington re-entered Spain in May 1813 and routed the French at Vittoria (21 June), thereby opening the way for an attack across the Pyrenees into France itself. On 10 April 1814 Toulouse was taken and Wellington (already a marquis and a field marshal) was created a duke, and was awarded a cash sum and an estate in Hampshire commensurate with his position.

Wellington was appointed ambassador to the restored court of Louis XVIII of France and in February 1815 deputized for Castlereagh at the Congress of Vienna. However, the peacemaking was cut short by Napoleon's descent from Elba and collection of an army. Wellington finally sealed his military reputation by his defeat of the latter at Waterloo (18 June 1815), although he himself admitted that it was 'a damn'd close-run thing' and it was the intervention of Blücher's Prussians that turned a French defeat into a rout.

As commander-in-chief during the occupation of France, Wellington resumed his diplomatic activities, wisely aligning himself with those who argued that the interests of peace would be best served if France were treated relatively leniently. In 1818 he returned home and joined the cabinet of Lord Liverpool as Master General of Ordnance: a post indicative of his unique political position. Wellington enjoyed unparalleled respect as the victor of Waterloo but this was rapidly lost in certain quarters by his being identified with supposedly repressive measures such as the Six Acts and an allegedly illiberal foreign policy pursued at the Congresses of Verona (1822) and St Petersburg (1826).

When Liverpool was forced to resign through ill health and George IV appointed Canning to succeed him in April 1827, Wellington (together with Peel and roughly half of his cabinet colleagues) resigned rather than serve under the politician most closely identified with the cause of Catholic Emancipation. However, following Canning's death after 100 days in office, and the failure of Goderich to form a stable administration, Wellington accepted the King's commission to form a ministry on 9 January 1828. The English, unlike the Americans, have (since at least the time of Cromwell) been very dubious about military men holding executive power. Thus Wellington was obliged to relinquish his role as commander-in-chief upon becoming prime minister.

Superficially Wellington succeeded in recreating the broad coalition of forces that had served under Liverpool. However, the fact that he was not in full control of the political situation was shown by the fact that he had the repeal of the Test and Corporation Acts and a reform of the Corn Laws both forced upon him in 1828. That year also saw the Huskissonite left wing of the government resign over parliamentary reform, whilst the right-wing Ultras were alienated by the decision to allow Catholic Emancipation in 1829. Although Wellington had recognized that Emancipation might be necessary since 1825, his colleagues were taken aback by his apparent betrayal of principle (as symbolized by his duel with the Duke of Winchilsea). His position was further weakened by depression, the accession of William IV in 1830 and the growing demand for parliamentary reform. Although Wellington's ministry survived the general election occasioned by the accession of a new sovereign, it was severely weakened and the final, self-inflicted, blow came on 2 November, when Wellington set his face against any reform of the constitution whatsoever. Thus a combination of Whigs, Huskissonites and Ultras obliged his resignation, and Earl Grey entered office at the head of a reforming coalition.

In May 1832, with apparent stalemate between the Tory-dominated Lords and the Whig-dominated Commons, the King invited Wellington to form a Tory administration to pass a moderate Reform bill. Wellington accepted this responsibility but the attempt foundered not on the slogan 'To stop the Duke, go for gold' but rather on Peel's refusal to lead the Tories in the Commons. As a consequence, Grey returned to office with the King's promise to create sufficient peers to overwhelm the Tories in the Lords but that promise did not have to be redeemed because Wellington persuaded a sufficient number of his followers to allow the Reform Bill to be passed by absenting themselves from the House of Lords. This timely manoeuvre was strategically correct but enhanced the Duke's reputation as a bogey figure with his party's diehard right wing.

In 1834 when William IV dismissed Melbourne and invited the Tories to form a ministry the Duke merely held the fort until Peel could return home from his sojourn in Italy. Wellington served under Peel as foreign secretary (1834–35) and as minister without Portfolio (1841–46). His continued authority helped ensure the safe passage of the repeal of the Corn Laws through the Lords in 1846, after which he retired from active politics, although not from public life, retaining, for example, the post of Commander-in- Chief, which he held from 1842 until his death. He helped contain Chartism without massive bloodshed but equally he bears much of the responsibility for the inadequacies of the army that the Crimean war was soon to reveal. He received a state funeral in 1852 and was buried in St Paul's Cathedral.

The period 1830–50 is commonly referred to as the 'Age of Peel'. This is at least as much due to Norman Gash's dominance over the historiography of the period as to Peel's dominance over the Commons during these years. Indeed, Peel manifestly failed to dominate either his own party or parliament and it was Wellington who played a crucial role, from the House of Lords, in enabling Peel to govern for as long as he did.

Napoleon will always be remembered as Napoleon and there is a danger that Wellington will be remembered primarily as the man who defeated Napoleon. This would be as unjust to Wellington as allowing his political career to be eclipsed by Peel's. The 'Iron Duke' was certainly not without his faults, and sometimes the very qualities that served him well on the battlefield, served him ill on the home front: he expected compliance with his wishes rather than inviting discussion; he was prepared to surrender what he considered to be untenable ground without a fight; and he did his duty whatever the risks to himself or his reputation. Certainly, he was more adept at keeping his forces united in the war zone than at Westminster. Yet not far beneath Wellington's gruff parade ground manner and reactionary image lay the impulses of a pragmatist with a large fund of sympathy for his fellow men.

Welsh Disestablishment, 1920. Irish disestablishment in 1869 gave an enormous boost to the demand for the disestablishment of the Anglican Church in Wales, despite the best efforts of Gladstone to make a case for Irish disestablishment which could not be extended to the mainland. There were bills for Welsh disestablishment, promoted by the Liberation Society, in 1870, 1886, 1889 and 1892.

The policy was official Liberal policy from 1887 but the Tory majority in the Lords appeared to pose an insuperable obstacle until the 1911 Parliament Act, with the result that Welsh disestablishment was finally due to become law in September 1914, only to be further delayed by the outbreak of World War One. On 1 April 1920, the Anglican Church ceased to be the established church in Wales and was also divested of much of its endowments. This represents one of the last triumphs of the non-conformist conscience in British politics.

Westminster, Statute of, 11 December 1931. Although the Balfour Definition of Dominion Status at the 1926 Imperial Conference had done a superb job of soothing dominion sensibilities, continuing calls for definition of the precise nature of the relationship between the mother country and the self-governing colonies resulted in the calling of a special Imperial Conference in 1929.

Its recommendations were approved by a full Imperial Conference in 1930 and embodied in the Statute of Westminster in 1931. This stated that henceforth the imperial parliament at Westminster could not legislate on behalf of a dominion unless that dominion consented and that no law passed by a dominion legislature could be invalidated on the grounds that it ran counter to English law. In other words, equality of status was recognized between the British parliament and the parliaments of the dominions.

Wheatley Housing Act, 1924. The Wheatley Housing Act is the popular name for the 1924 Housing (Financial Provisions) Act which was put on the statute book by minister for health, John Wheatley.

The Act sought to assist local authorities in a fifteen-year programme that built 2.5 million houses. These were to be let at affordable rents for the average working-class family through a national subsidy initially fixed, by agreement with the local authorities, at £9 per house.

The measure was the one significant domestic success of the first minority Labour government, showing its ability to legislate on behalf of the workingman.

Whig party (Whigs, Whiggism) The Whigs originally took their name from the derogatory term 'Whiggamore' which was first applied to cattle-drovers in south-western Scotland and then to seventeenth-century Scottish Covenanters, who were supporters of Presbyterianism.

As a political party they were first identified with opposition to the Roman Catholic Duke of York succeeding his brother Charles II to the throne. They were thus firm supporters of the Glorious Revolution of 1688, which established the supremacy of Parliament over the Crown and assured a Protestant succession. The Whigs gained control of the government in 1714 on the accession of George I and retained it until the accession of George III in 1760. Whilst their leadership was aristocratic and Anglican, they came to represent financial and mercantile interests and to advocate a degree of religious toleration as well as the sovereignty of the people.

In 1830, under Earl Grey, popular support for their policy of parliamentary reform and Tory disunity under Wellington saw them return to office and dominate the following decade. According to Richard Brent the issue of appropriation of the surplus revenues of the Anglican Church in Ireland (as symbolized by Clause 147 of the Irish Church Temporalities Bill of 1833) revealed a three-way split in the party between 'Old Foxites', liberal Anglican Whigs and 'High Churchmen'.

The Old Foxites such as Grey, Lansdowne and Holland were true to the eighteenth-century religious scepticism associated with Charles James Fox, and were chiefly interested in constitutional reform.

The High Churchmen took their Anglicanism seriously and were so doctrinally opposed to the idea of making concessions to Catholics or non-conformists that in 1834 their leading lights – Stanley, Graham, Richmond and Ripon – left the government when Lord John Russell attempted to put the issue of appropriation back on its agenda. Via the Derby Dilly, Stanley (who became the 14th Earl of Derby) and Graham entered the Peel ministry of 1841–46.

The liberal Anglican wing of the party that was prepared to sponsor reforms to attract Catholic and moderate non-conformist support assumed the leadership under Lord John Russell in 1834 and worked closely with the Radicals and Irish following the Lichfield House Compact in 1835. By 1859 these forces had coalesced into the Liberal Party. The Whigs exercised influence within Liberal governments disproportionate to their numbers given the aristocratic connections of Palmerston and Gladstone and the fact that Whigs traditionally received those departments dealing with diplomacy, the colonies and defence.

As Gladstone's retirement appeared to be nearing, the succession was contested by Hartington for the Whigs and Joseph Chamberlain for the Radicals. Lord Salisbury all the while looked for some opportunity to bring the Whigs into the Conservative fold, so that party divisions might more accurately reflect sociological realities. In the event, however, it was Gladstone's Irish Home Rule Bill of 1886 that split the Liberals and resulted in Chamberlain joining most of the Whigs in rejecting Liberalism and ultimately becoming absorbed in what became known as the Conservative and Unionist Party.

Whole hoggers Whole hoggers were those protectionist Unionists who were most radical in their approach to the tariff reform campaign launched in 1903 by Joseph Chamberlain. They were prepared to go 'the whole hog' of imperial preference by adopting food taxes. This was, however, something that the bulk of the party and not just the Unionist Free Traders could not swallow.

William IV (William Henry) (21 August 1765–18 June 1837). Prince William Henry was the third son of George III and Charlotte of Mecklenburg-Strelitz. His father decided that he should follow a naval career and whilst still only thirteen he was posted as a midshipman aboard HMS *Prince George*.

Nelson appears to have genuinely liked and admired the young prince, writing that, 'He has foibles, as well as private men but they are far overbalanced by his virtues. In his professional life he is superior to nearly two thirds, I am sure, of the list; and in attention to orders and respect to his superior officers I hardly know his equal.' However, these words proved very ironic in 1787 when William twice disobeyed orders. Thereafter the Royal Navy only tolerated and promoted him (to Rear-Admiral in 1790) out of deference to his royal connections.

In 1791, the Duke of Clarence and St Andrews, and Earl of Munster, as he now was, began what was to become a twenty-year relationship with the actress Dorothy Jordan. Mrs Jordan was to provide him with ten illegitimate children. But whilst his private life entered a period of contentment, his public life was less happy. He made an embarrassing statement to the House of Lords in 1793 that peace should be made with France, his debts grew to an extent that attracted public attention and his requests for naval employment were repeatedly refused.

When his oldest brother became Prince Regent in February 1811 it appears to have concentrated his mind on his prospects. The Regent's daughter, the Princess Charlotte, and the childless Duke of York, stood between himself and the throne of England, whilst Salic Law debarred the former from the throne of Hanover. William thus awoke to his duty to found a lawful dynasty, threw over Mrs Jordan and joined the Dukes of Kent and Cambridge in scouring the continental courts for a suitable spouse.

William found his bride in Adelaide, the eldest offspring of the Duke of Saxe-Coburg-Meiningen. At twenty-six she was less than half her bridegroom's age. She bore him two children: Charlotte Augusta Louisa and Elizabeth, neither of whom lived long. The death of Princess Charlotte in 1817 made him second in line to the throne and he became heir to the throne with the death of his elder brother, the Duke of York, in 1827. Canning revived the title of Lord High Admiral for William but when he began to take it literally he was prevailed upon to tender his resignation.

In July 1830 George IV died and 'Prince Billy' became King William IV. Despite or because he lacked social graces and intellectual attainments, William – the 'Sailor-King' – was popular with some of his subjects, although such was the contempt in which his predecessor was held that he was bound to benefit from any comparison.

He was sorely tested by the Reform Bill crisis but rose to the challenge well assisted by able advice from his secretary, Taylor, a sense of fair play, and the belief that he should support his prime minister, regardless of party. In April 1831 he acceded to the wish of Grey that he should dissolve parliament in person (notwithstanding personal inconvenience) and despite being depressed by the unrest which attended the consequent election he went even further to facilitate the passage of what became the Great Reform Act by agreeing in principle to the creation of peers to secure the passage of the bill through the Lords and by writing to the opposition peers advising them to avoid making him take that action by ending their resistance to the Bill.

William died on 18 June 1837 and was succeeded by his young niece, Victoria. Set aside her sixty-three years on the throne, his seven-year reign appears little more than a coda to the regency period but by a mixture of good luck and sound judgement in 1830–31 he had acted in a manner which had dispelled all the lingering doubts regarding his fitness to rule and had acted in an impeccably constitutional manner.

Wilson, James Harold, Baron Wilson of Rievaulx (11 March 1916–24 May 1995). Wilson was born into a lower-middle-class Congregationalist household in Huddersfield, Yorkshire and received his education from the Wirral Grammar School and Jesus College, Oxford, where he flirted with Liberalism. He then taught economics at Oxford, first at New (1937) and then at University College (from 1938).

Wilson volunteered for the army but his economic expertise meant that he was drafted into the civil service where he number-crunched for Beveridge and Dalton as Director of Economics and Statistics at the Ministry of Fuel and Power respectively. He entered parliament (as MP for Ormskirk) in 1945 and was soon marked down as a high-flyer serving as parliamentary secretary to the Ministry of Works (1945–47) and as secretary for overseas trade (1947).

As president of the Board of Trade from 1947 to 1951 he exuded competence and even managed to achieve a measure of popularity through his 1949 'bonfire of controls' which somewhat relieved the gloom of 'austerity'. However, it was his departure from office over NHS charges in 1951 that gave him popularity on the party's left. Wilson's 'Bevanite' reputation was not dissipated even when he took Bevan's place in the shadow cabinet, where he emerged as a gifted shadow chancellor and an undistinguished shadow spokesman on foreign affairs.

When Gaitskell fell ill and died unexpectedly in January 1963 Harold Wilson, George Brown and James Callaghan all stood for the leadership of the Labour Party. Callaghan dropped out after the first round and the fact that most of his supporters transferred their allegiance to Wilson secured him victory by 144 votes to 103.

Wilson skilfully exploited Conservative disarray arising out of the Profumo affair and the replacement of Macmillan by Home. In particular he contrasted the image of the old school tie, grousemoor, economically illiterate Toryism of 'the Fourteenth Earl' with the pragmatic, dynamic, modernizing image of the Labour Party under himself. Aristocratic amateurism was opposed by the claims of middle-class meritocracy.

His speech to the 1963 party conference at Scarborough in which he spoke of the need to harness 'the white heat of a second industrial revolution' was part of this process and not only freed the Labour Party from the need to deal with potentially embarrassing specifics (such as the degree of nationalization or level of personal taxation which it stood for) but struck a chord with that section of the public which had been impressed by C. P. Snow's arguments regarding 'The Two Cultures'. Such people believed that Britain was hidebound by tradition and that Labour was best fitted to adapt to the scientific and technological challenges of the future.

Moreover, the British media, anxious to use newsgathering and reportage techniques pioneered for the 1960 Presidential election, were looking for a British JFK. Home could never fit the bill but for a while it looked as if Wilson might, not least because he consciously modelled Labour's 1964 campaign on the Democratic success four years previously.

Once elected in October 1964 with an overall majority of just four votes, Labour underlined its commitment to 'the white heat of a second industrial revolution' by appointing the newly ennobled C. P. Snow as minister of state for the encouragement of science, making Sir Solly Zuckerman the government's Chief Scientific Adviser, and creating a Ministry of Technology under Frank Cousins. However, little in practical terms resulted and Wilson's presidential style increasingly grated as he sought to associate himself with successful celebrities in fields such as sport or pop music (including the Beatles), repeatedly broadcast to the nation (with no less than five 'Panorama' interviews and six ministerial broadcasts in his first eighteen months as premier), or engaged in dramatic headline-grabbing gestures, such as the bombing of the ailing oil tanker *Torrey Canyon*.

In 1966 Wilson successfully increased Labour's majority to 97 seats but suffered a surprising election defeat at Heath's hands in 1970. Perhaps one should not be too surprised. In 1964 Wilson had promised accelerated economic growth through a combination of high socialist purpose and the energetic application of the new techniques of indicative planning. What had followed, however, was an apparent deterioration in Britain's economic standing (at least relative to its major rivals) so that the administration appeared increasingly to be the prisoner than the moulder of events, with devaluation in 1967 providing the classic illustration of this theme. However, the Tories found themselves in a similar situation when they took office, so that in the February 1974 general election Labour emerged as the largest single party albeit with no overall majority. Wilson thus returned to office to head a minority administration.

In addition to lacking a majority, the Labour government was faced with a debilitated economy (not least because of the damage done by the Barber boom) and a deteriorating international economic position (as the shockwaves of OPEC I continued to be felt). The three day week was nevertheless ended and the miners' dispute settled, at the cost of pay rises of 22–32%. Industrial relations were also improved by speedy repeal of the 1971 Industrial Relations Act. Wilson negotiated the 'social contract' with the TUC in September 1974, which helped Labour gain a slim overall majority at the general election in October.

Wilson was meticulous in balancing the left and right wings of the party in his cabinet appointments. Thus the centre-right, like latter day Whigs, tended to monopolize the Treasury, Foreign Office and Defence portfolios, whilst the left enjoyed the high-spending welfare and administrative ministries. In order to prevent a damaging split over Europe, Wilson even broke with constitutional convention in allowing a referendum on continued British membership of the EEC in 1975. Wilson used the 'Yes' vote to demote Benn and steer the party rightwards until he surprised both pundits and the nation by resigning on 16 March 1976.

In 1975 Gerard Noel could write that 'if … MacDonald made Labour government possible, and … Attlee made it respectable, it is … Wilson who has made it successful'. However, Wilson's reputation went into eclipse shortly after his resignation in 1976 for three reasons. Firstly, he largely withdrew from public view (despite attacking Roth's unflattering portrait with twenty-seven counts of libel). Secondly, the cumulative effect of the publication of the Crossman, Castle and Benn diaries and of critical memoirs such as those of Denis Healey did much to confirm the Conservative view of him as a drifting time-server. Thirdly, there seemed little reason to consider a supreme pragmatist like Wilson in the period of 'conviction politics' represented by the triumph of the ideology of the radical right in 1979.

Rehabilitation and revisionism began with the sympathetic treatment of Wilson in the memoirs of Roy Jenkins (somewhat surprisingly perhaps, given that Wilson had intervened in the Warrington by-election to state that he remembered Jenkins as more of a socialite than a socialist as a Labour minister). It continued with Stephen Dorril's and Robin Ramsey's *Smear* which, like Peter Wright's *Spycatcher*, suggested that not all of Wilson's suspicions were unfounded. The reawakened interest in Wilson was demonstrated by the publication of the Morgan, Pimlott and Ziegler biographies within a short space of one another.

This interest drew sustenance because of alleged parallels between the situations in which Kinnock and Blair found themselves and those faced by Wilson. Kinnock, for example, found himself, in 1992, facing an unelected Conservative prime minister after thirteen years of Labour opposition, just as Wilson had confronted Home in 1964, although it was Blair who became the first elected Labour prime minister after Wilson by similarly re-packaging Labour so as to make it avowedly 'modern'.

Women's Social and Political Union (WSPU) In 1903 Emmeline Pankhurst founded the Women's Social and Political Union (WSPU) out of frustration with the more moderate suffragists. WSPU members were suffragettes whose militant tactics certainly drew attention to their cause but also did much to confirm the prejudices of some males that women were not fit to vote.

The tactic of hunger strikes when WSPU members were arrested led to the authorities responding with forcible feeding and then with the 1913 'Cat and Mouse' Act. The suspension of the WSPU campaign for the duration on the outbreak of World War One and the valuable contribution made by many women to the war effort helped the WSPU secure their aim with the concession of votes for women (over the age of 30) in 1918.

World War One, 4 August 1914–11 November 1918. Faced with the prospect of a war on two fronts, Count Alfred von Schlieffen, the German Chief of Staff in 1905, drew up what became known as the Schlieffen Plan. Given the vast distances involved and more primitive state of its transport, he calculated that Russia would be slower to mobilize than its French ally. Schlieffen therefore decided that France should be knocked out first. This was to be accomplished within six weeks not by attacking across the heavily fortified Franco-German border from Alsace-Lorraine but by wheeling the bulk of Germany's western forces through Holland, Belgium and Luxemburg, encircling Paris and then subjecting the French forces on the Franco-German border to a pincer attack, caught between those German troops who had marched in a great arc until they attacked the French in the rear, and those forces which had basically remained static in defending Alsace–Lorraine.

Under Schlieffen's successor the plan was modified in various ways that compromised its effectiveness. For example, von Moltke decided to respect Dutch neutrality, which made passing such a large force through Belgium more difficult. Crucially, however, Belgian neutrality was still violated and this provided the nominal cause of Britain's entry into the war, in line with the 1839 Treaty of London. Despite there being no formal Anglo-French alliance, Asquith was able to unite almost all of his cabinet and the nation thanks to Sir Edward Grey portraying Britain as the stout defender of gallant little Belgium. Haldane had ensured that a small but well-equipped and well-trained expeditionary force could be shipped to the continent, and Churchill, as First Lord of the Admiralty, ensured that the Royal Navy was at battle stations.

The Germans at first considered it unlikely that Britain, wracked by labour disputes, the Ulster crisis and suffragette militancy, would honour the 'scrap of paper' that was the Treaty of London. Even if it did, the calculation was that Britain's 'contemptibly small' 100,000-strong volunteer expeditionary force would be unable materially to affect the outcome. The power of the Royal Navy was acknowledged but the effectiveness of any blockade it was able to mount was dismissed on the grounds that the war would be decided on land 'by Christmas'.

Two of the earliest checks to the Schlieffen Plan were provided by the British Expeditionary Force (BEF) under Sir John French, at Mons, on 23 August, and at Le Cateau, south of Mons, on 26 August, as geography, logistics and French miscalculations conspired to place the British force astride the path of the German juggernaut after it passed through Belgium. Nevertheless, these actions could do little more than delay the German advance, which was not halted until the First Battle of the Marne in September. The so-called 'race to the sea' ended with neither side achieving a breakthrough and with a front line of trenches stretching from the English Channel to the Swiss frontier.

Modern firepower gave the entrenched defender the advantage over any attacker, producing stalemate. Over the next four years efforts would periodically be made to break this deadlock. The British and their French allies more often took the offensive than their foes, given that the success of the Germans in the war's early weeks had given them possession of most of Belgium and Northern France, so that the onus for attack lay with the Allies, whilst the fact that the Germans had generally dug in first meant that they had acquired the best positions.

On 10 March 1915 the British attacked the Germans at Neuve Chapelle but the offensive was called off after just three days. Although the advance of the infantry had been preceded by the heaviest bombardment to date in British military history, the *Times* correspondent, Charles Repington, wrote that British success here and elsewhere was hindered by a 'shell shortage'. This shell scandal helped oblige Asquith to form a coalition government, which included a Ministry of Munitions headed by Lloyd George.

Field Marshal Earl Kitchener, appointed secretary of state for war by Asquith, was one of the few men on either side who had appreciated early on that the war would be a protracted affair and that Britain would therefore need to expand its 250,000-strong army. Whatever his other faults, the secretary of state for war made a great recruiting poster and nearly 2.5 million men answered Lord Kitchener's call for volunteers and his 'new armies' filled the breach caused by the decimation of the pre-war regulars. Many of the new volunteers were members of 'Pals Battalions': friends and workmates who had been recruited from the same areas in towns or cities with the promise that those who joined up together would serve together. All too often, however, this also meant that they would die together.

It was Kitchener who overruled Sir John French and obliged him to mount an attack at Loos in September 1915, although French held back his reserves for as long as possible, for fear that they would be squandered by his field commander, Sir Douglas Haig. These disagreements and the fact that the poison gas employed by the British blew back into their own trenches at the northern end of the battlefield contributed to the failure of the operation and led to French's replacement by his well-connected arch-critic Haig in December.

The stalemate on the Western front and the difficulties of supplying European Russia after Turkey's entry into the war on the side of the Central Powers in November 1914, encouraged the 'Easterners', to attempt to break the deadlock by attempting to force the Straits of the Dardanelles, connecting the Black Sea to the Mediterranean. In early January 1915 the Turkish forts at the entrance to the Straits were bombarded but this merely alerted the enemy to expect a larger-scale attack. This came on 19 February when a pre-Dreadnought battleship fleet was forced to abort its attempt to force the Straits by bad weather. When it returned a week later the Turkish defences had been further strengthened, most notably by the laying of minefields. On 18 March the naval attack was resumed in force but four French and three British capital ships, including the battle cruiser HMS *Inflexible*, were sunk or seriously damaged as a result of enemy shellfire or striking mines.

This setback led to the landings of troops at Cape Helles on 24 April to remove the enemy guns but although the troops got ashore unopposed they failed to make any progress inland. Further forces were landed at Anzac Cove on 25 April but they too found themselves pinned down in conditions reminiscent of the Western Front, with the Turks occupying the higher ground. An additional landing at Suvla Bay in August 1915 did nothing to improve the situation and the decision was eventually taken to evacuate the entire force, which was accomplished without loss of life but with considerable loss of face in December 1915. The political casualties of the expedition included General Sir Ian Hamilton and Winston Churchill. There were other British offensives in other theatres of war, notably General Townshend's disastrous foray into Mesopotamia (Iran), culminating in his defeat at Kut in December 1916, and the more successful campaigns of Allenby in the Holy Land (of which one highlight was his entry into

Jerusalem in time for Christmas 1917). The Arab Revolt, assisted by Lawrence of Arabia, was an exotic offshoot of the latter but it was, it has to be admitted, 'a sideshow of a sideshow', as the war would ultimately be decided, as the 'Westerners' asserted, on the Western Front, and it was there that Haig sought to concentrate Britain's resources.

Haig's name is irrevocably linked with the British offensive on the Somme, 120 miles north-west of Verdun, where the British and French armies met. More particularly, Haig is associated with the first day of the attack – 1 July 1916 – which with 57,000 casualties, of which 19,240 were fatal, can surely be regarded as the single worst day in British military history. When Haig finally called off the offensive, over four months later, Britain had gained less ground, at a cost of 420,000 casualties, than the designated objectives for the first day of the battle.

Haig has been criticized, by Keegan amongst others, for having stubbornly persisted with tactics designed to produce a breakthrough long after it should have been abundantly clear that the battle had degenerated into an attritional slogging match. In Haig's defence, however, historians such as Terraine point out that the German attack on Verdun had resulted in the French substantially reducing their contribution to the offensive and demanding that it be scheduled at least a month earlier than Haig had planned in order to forestall their complete collapse. The tactics may have been crude – a week-long bombardment followed by the infantry walking across no-man's land – but arguably they were the ones best suited to the patriotic and courageous but inadequately trained volunteers provided by Kitchener. Moreover, in the hands of John Charters, military intelligence appears to have been an even greater oxymoron than is usually the case.

In August a film entitled 'The Battle of the Somme', mixing genuine footage with (for the time) plausible reconstructions, began engrossing an audience ultimately estimated at 20 million: half the entire civilian population. It had a sobering effect upon the public mood rather than, as anticipated, boosting morale, but the home front didn't falter and spirits were lifted in September by news of the first appearance in battle of the tank. This innovation was, however, more important psychologically than militarily at this stage as they were too few in number and too prone to mechanical failure to turn the tide of the battle which proceeded grimly until Haig called it off in November.

On 26 February 1917 Lloyd George agreed to place the British army under the command of Robert Nivelle, the new French supreme commander, for the duration of his offensive. This unprecedented decision came about not only because Lloyd George liked both Nivelle and his plan but also because he was increasingly sceptical regarding Haig's fitness for high command. However, the Nivelle offensive failed badly and the gap between expectations and reality fuelled widespread mutiny in the French army. In May Pétain replaced Nivelle and discipline was restored, but the French army would be in no condition to do more than defend for the foreseeable future.

However, Haig had his own offensive planned near the Belgian town of

Ypres, intending to overrun German U-boat bases and achieve a breakthrough on the Front. The campaign started well with the occupation of Messines Ridge, following the detonation on 7 June of nineteen mines under the German positions. However, there was now an ill-advised delay of seven weeks before Passchendaele Ridge was assaulted. The third battle of Ypres, which became better known as Passchendaele, began, after ten days' bombardment, on 31 July 1917. Heavy rain on 1 August marked the beginning of an exceptionally wet summer that turned the battlefield into a bog in which both men and horses sometimes drowned, yet Haig only called off the attack on 10 November. Instead of the intended breakthrough an advance had been made at enormous cost of just five miles: facts which increased Lloyd George's determination to circumscribe Haig's room for manoeuvre, which he proceeded to do by starving his commander-in-chief of reinforcements and forcing the resignation (in February 1918) of Haig's chief ally, Sir William Robertson, as Chief of the Imperial General Staff. Haig successfully resisted Lloyd George's attempts to create a unified Allied Command in 1917, but accepted Foch as his superior in 1918 as the Bolshevik revolution of October 1917 and the conclusion of peace between Russia and the Central Powers at Brest-Litovsk in March 1918 enabled Germany to put the Schlieffen plan into reverse, moving men from the eastern to the western front.

Ludendorff's Spring 1918 offensive in the West was effectively Germany's last throw of the dice as the Royal Navy's blockade was gradually throttling its economy and inflicting serious hardship on its home front. There had been two major efforts to break Britain's stranglehold, namely, the Battle of Jutland in 1916, when the German High Seas Fleet had inflicted greater losses in ships and men upon its adversary but had then returned to harbour, and the campaign of unrestricted submarine warfare from March 1917, intended to starve Britain into submission. However, British countermeasures ensured that it continued to receive the supplies it needed, whilst the German tactics merely provoked the United States into entering the war on the Allied side in April 1917. An important contributory factor was the production of the Zimmermann Telegram by British intelligence, purporting to show Germany inciting Mexico to attack America.

Such was the potential of the United States that it was only a question of time before Germany was defeated, unless she could achieve a breakthrough on the Western Front before American men and supplies were shipped across the Atlantic in decisive numbers. Hence the critical last ditch nature of the Germans' Spring 1918 offensive. Initially successful, getting closer to Paris than at any point since August 1914, the Germans were first halted and then steadily pushed back, although they managed to sign the Armistice in November 1918 whilst still in possession of much Belgian and French soil and with no Allied soldier yet on the right bank of the Rhine.

Niall Ferguson's *The Pity of War* (1998), amongst other orthodoxies, challenges the historiographical consensus that British entry into the war was a necessary evil: to uphold Belgian neutrality, or stop Germany, or both. Indeed, he goes on to hypothesize that had Britain not intervened Germany would have won the war and dominated the continent but allowed Britain to retain her Empire.

By 1914 military technology could produce mass destruction of human life (through barbed wire and machine guns) but it could not (in the absence of radio-telephony, for example) provide a reliable means of communication to give commanders tactical control over the battlefield. Thus World War One was so deadly because it was essentially fought with twentieth-century technology but nineteenth-century tactics.

World War One resulted in a vast expansion of the number and duties of central government departments, including the new Ministries of Health, Labour and Transport. The war had a corresponding impact upon the level of government expenditure and the proportion of national income devoted to public expenditure, which rose from 11.9% of Gross Domestic Product (GDP) in 1913 to 20.5% in 1920 (and which continued to rise thereafter). However, in a desire to return to pre-war 'normalcy' wartime controls were dismantled as soon as possible after peace returned and pressure mounted to reduce the size of the public sector and return to the gold standard at pre-war parity, in line with the prevailing *laissez-faire* ideology and the desire to recover the City's position as an international financial centre. Pressure for the former was unavailing but the latter ultimately, and disastrously, succeeded in 1925. The failure of Britain's return to the gold standard symbolizes the fact that Britain was no longer a superpower after World War One despite the British Empire growing to its greatest ever extent after the peace conference. Indeed it was not until World War Two that Britain's decline as a front-ranking world power became fully apparent.

World War Two, 3 September 1939–2 September 1945. In August 1939 the Nazi–Soviet Pact was concluded. Although the division of Poland between Germany and the Soviet Union was part of its secret clauses, Hitler was convinced that it would dissuade Britain from standing by her Polish guarantee.

Instead, on 3 September 1939 (two days after the German invasion of Poland) Chamberlain broadcast to the nation to explain that Britain was at war with Germany. The French followed suit later in the day. The Poles were also attacked in the east by the Soviet Union on 17 September. Her western allies had already shown themselves to be incapable of offering her practical assistance. A British Expeditionary Force (BEF) was shipped to France but apart from a tentative French foray into the Saar, the two allies were mostly content to await attack: a siege mentality symbolized by the Maginot Line along the Franco-German border. Even after the fall of Warsaw the RAF was ordered to drop leaflets rather than high explosives on the enemy. The period until April 1940 was thus termed the phoney war insofar as the two sides were hardly engaged in conflict, other than on the high seas (notably at the battle of the River Plate). The risk of bombing seemed so remote that by the beginning of 1940 the evacuation of children had gone into reverse and 80% of them had returned home.

In April 1940 the Allies began laying mines in the shipping channel along the Norwegian coast just as Hitler launched a full-scale attack upon Denmark and Norway. The Allies landed troops in an effort to assist Norwegian resistance but to no avail in the face of German air superiority. The failure of the Norwegian campaign sapped confidence in Chamberlain's ability to prosecute the war effectively. He won a no-confidence motion but the drop in his support was so precipitous that he decided to step down as prime minister and Churchill outmanoeuvred Halifax to succeed him.

On 10 May 1940 the Germans launched an offensive against Holland and Belgium and within 10 days had reached the French coast. The bulk of the BEF and some French troops were evacuated from Dunkirk but effectively France was finished: a fact that encouraged Mussolini's Italy to enter the war on Germany's side on 10 June. The French signed an armistice on 22 June that allowed the creation of the collaborationist Vichy government in an unoccupied zone. Fearful that Vichy might allow the powerful French fleet (the fourth largest in the world) to fall into the hands of the Germans, Churchill ordered the destruction of a sizeable portion of it stationed at Mers-el-Kebir in Algeria, once the French rejected the option of scuttling it or surrendering it to British control. In the process 1,300 Frenchmen were killed, bringing Anglo-French relations to a new low, although this action did impress upon the United States Churchill's determination to fight on at all costs and thus helped persuade Roosevelt to sanction the 'destroyers for bases' deal.

As a precondition for launching Operation Sealion – the invasion of Great Britain – the Luftwaffe launched an offensive to gain control of the skies over the Channel. However, the RAF won the Battle of Britain, not least because the Germans made the mistake of launching the Blitz, shifting their attack away from Fighter Command onto the civilian population of London and other major cities.

The year ended with success in the Western Desert, with Major General O'Connor taking some 130,000 Italian prisoners in the course of advancing deep into Tripolitania (Libya). The Italians in Abyssinia, Eritrea and Italian Somaliland were also worsted in the spring of 1941 and the British position in the Middle East was further consolidated by taking control of Syria and the Lebanon from Vichy France, and joining the Russians in invading Iran. However, the Germans bailed out their Italian allies by sending the Afrika Korps to North Africa (in February 1941), where Rommel promptly went on the offensive and besieged Tobruk, and by taking Greece (which the Italians had invaded in October 1940), Yugoslavia and Crete. These reverses led to Churchill's replacing Wavell with General Sir Claude Auchinleck as British Commander-in-Chief in the Middle East.

Hitler's Balkan campaign delayed Operation Barbarossa – the invasion of the Soviet Union – which was eventually launched on 22 June 1941. Churchill, taking the view that my enemy's enemy is my friend, immediately offered to help his former Bolshevik foe. In practical terms this meant stepping up the air offensive against Germany and sending supplies overland via Iran (from August 1941) and by means of perilous Arctic convoys to Archangel and Murmansk. America also entered the war against the Axis powers when Japan bombed Pearl Harbor on 7 December 1941 and Hitler declared war on the United States four days later. The terms of the Tripartite Pact signed by Italy, Germany and Japan in 1940 did not oblige Hitler to do this but he seems to have felt that this merely formalized warlike relations with the United States. Certainly Roosevelt had been straining America's neutral status for some time in order to give succour to Britain, most notably through Lend-Lease, which became law in March 1941.

With both the USSR and the United States fighting alongside Great Britain and the Commonwealth by the end of 1941 it might appear as if the Axis was doomed to suffer defeat but it was not as clear-cut as that. Although the Japanese did not sink any American aircraft carriers at Pearl Harbor they enjoyed a series of runaway successes in late 1941 and early 1942, seizing the Dutch East Indies, Hong Kong, Singapore, Malaya and Burma, together with a string of Pacific islands. They were thus poised to invade India and within bombing range of northern Australia. The British Empire never recovered from this shock, whilst Australia and New Zealand increasingly looked to the United States rather than the mother country for protection. Similarly, in December 1941 Leningrad was besieged and the Germans were just 30 miles (48 kilometres) from Moscow. The Japanese attack on the British, Dutch and American Pacific bases released vital Soviet troops from the Siberian front for a successful winter counter-offensive against the Nazis but Stalin nevertheless constantly urged upon his allies the opening of a Second Front in Europe as soon as possible, in order to relieve pressure upon the Red Army: a demand which was echoed in Britain by the likes of Beaverbrook.

British fortunes in the Middle East in 1942 fluctuated very considerably. The nadir came with the fall of Tobruk on 21 June, which put Churchill under very considerable pressure and persuaded him to recast his commanders, with Auchinleck replaced by Alexander as commander-in-chief, and Montgomery given command of the Eighth Army. 'Monty', greatly assisted by ULTRA intelligence, and possessed of superior forces, boosted British and Allied morale by inflicting the first major defeat of the Germans on land at El Alamein (23 October–4 November 1942).

Although the British were pleased by Roosevelt's determination to make the European theatre of war rather than the Pacific his first priority, they believed that the opening of the Second Front in Europe in 1942 would prove premature: an intuition which appeared to be vindicated by the disastrous large-scale raid upon Dieppe on 19 August 1942. Operation Torch – Anglo-American landings in Vichy – controlled Morocco and Algeria in November 1942, thus representing a compromise: ensuring that American troops would be engaged against German troops at the earliest opportunity and the least risk. However, at the Casablanca conference in January 1943 the British persuaded the Americans that once German–Italian resistance had been smothered in Tunisia (as it was by mid-May 1943), the logical next step consisted of invasion of Sicily (launched in July 1943) and then the Italian mainland (September

1943), although this had the effect of further postponing the cross-Channel attack, whilst offering no soft underbelly for Allied advance, the Italian armistice of September 1943 being counterbalanced by German occupation of northern and central Italy and their determination to contest every foot of ground. However, when the 'Big Three', Churchill, Roosevelt and Stalin, met for the first time at Teheran in November 1943, the tide of war seemed to have turned decisively against the Axis, not least because of the Soviet victory at Kursk, 4–22 July 1943.

1943 also witnessed Allied success in the Battle of the Atlantic as improvements in tactics and technology finally swung the campaign in their favour, after a traumatic period of several months in the previous year and a brief period in March 1943 when Allied shipping losses had mounted catastrophically following the introduction of new cipher arrangements by the Germans which temporarily baffled Bletchley Park. America now lived up to its boast of being the arsenal of democracy, providing the materiel and men (more than a million and a half of them) prior to D-Day on 6 June 1944: the largest amphibious landing in history. It took the Allies over two months to break out of Normandy but thereafter they made fairly swift progress (assisted logistically by Allied landings in the south of France), despite failure at Arnhem in September (when ground forces failed to relieve airborne troops) and the German counteroffensive in the Ardennes in December which became known as the Battle of the Bulge.

By late March 1945 the western allies had crossed the Rhine whilst in the east the Red Army had already penetrated deep into Germany. However, Hitler only committed suicide on 30 April when Russian troops were close to breaking into his bunker beneath the Reich Chancellery in Berlin. VE (Victory in Europe) Day was celebrated on 8 May.

This still left the war in the Far East against Japan. Admiral Yamamoto, the mastermind behind Pearl Harbor, had warned 'we can run wild for six months or a year, but after that I have utterly no confidence' and his prediction had been borne out by events. The Japanese navy had lost the initiative following its aircraft carrier losses at the Coral Sea (7–8 May 1942) and Midway (4–7 June 1942) whilst the army's attempt to invade India was stymied at Kohima and Imphal (March–July 1944). Thereafter the Japanese were pushed back on all fronts, despite fanatical resistance, whilst the cities of the home islands were systematically destroyed from the air. The planned D-Day style invasion of the Japanese homeland was, however, obviated by the two atomic bombs (at Hiroshima and Nagasaki) and, in the period between them, Soviet entry into the Pacific War (in line with the promise made by Stalin at Yalta and confirmed at Potsdam). The wartime alliance was already under severe strain and Hiroshima should be regarded as the West's first shot in the Cold War, being designed to exert diplomatic pressure upon the Soviets as much as military pressure upon the Japanese.

A general election was held in the course of the Potsdam Conference, in which the Conservatives attempted to ride to power on the back of Churchill's reputation as a wartime leader whilst he claimed that Labour's penchant for planning would produce a British form of the Gestapo. However, the Conservatives, who had dominated the National Governments of the 1930s, were identified with the miseries of the Great Depression and the apparent follies of appeasement, whilst Attlee, Churchill's loyal wartime deputy premier, appeared more Grossmith's Pooter than Heinrich Himmler. Moreover, planning and 'fair shares' were widely regarded as having helped win the war whilst equitably sharing the burdens and were thus unlikely to provoke the fears upon which Conservative Central Office counted. Certainly the result was that Labour swept to power with a landslide victory, giving the party its first parliamentary majority.

Britain had rigorously followed the logic of total war to become the most heavily regulated of the combatant nations, with the possible exception of Soviet Russia. It had certainly mobilized a higher proportion of its population than any other nation, making particularly extensive use of women (although they were still denied a frontline role) and it was the experience of war rather than that of mass unemployment during the Great Depression of the thirties, still less the exposure of the theoretical inadequacies of classical economic theory by Keynes in his 'General Theory', which finally discredited the 'Treasury view' regarding the desirability of minimal government. The demands of total war had obliged the substitution of planning for the free play of market forces, the war years accustomed politicians to this idea and provided civil servants with practical experience, and victory set the seal upon the proceedings by apparently providing justification by results.

Moreover, a consensus had emerged during the war, symbolized by the 1944 Employment Policy White Paper, that, in Skidelsky's words, 'The promise to build a Land fit for Heroes could not be betrayed twice with impunity'. In other words, those who had been called upon to risk the ultimate sacrifice in the service of the state should be rewarded for their efforts by, amongst other things, the maintenance of full employment after the war.

Britain thus emerged from the war with a vision of a better-regulated and more just society and enhanced moral authority for its role in resisting fascism. However, more tangible assets had been lost in the fight (including the destruction or damage of one-third of the housing stock, the sale of £1bn of capital assets and the almost complete exhaustion of the gold and dollar reserves). These losses rendered Labour's ability to realize its 'new Jerusalem' highly problematic, as became all too apparent once Lend-Lease was abruptly terminated in August 1945.

Wyndham Land Act, 1903. Irish Chief Secretary George Wyndham's 1903 Land Act was the last, most substantial and most successful in a series of land purchase measures put forward for Ireland by the Conservatives. Under its terms the state provided landlords with a bonus amounting to 12% of sale price and tenants were allowed to borrow purchase money from the Treasury on exceptionally favourable terms (being repaid over 68.5 years by annuities at the rate of 3.25%).

Young England Young England was a four-man ginger group within the Peelite Conservative Party comprising Disraeli, Smythe, Manners and Baillie-Cochrane. They looked back to the Middle Ages as a golden time and were highly critical of the middle classes, particularly those influenced by the ideas of Bentham. Instead they believed in an almost mystic identity of interest between the Crown, aristocracy and the working class and offered a romantic version of paternalism before breaking up over the Maynooth Grant in 1845.

Young Ireland In 1842 Charles Gavan Duffy and Thomas Davis established the *Nation*: a weekly journal which advocated a form of non-denominational nationalism which called for repeal of the Act of Union. The movement which this inspired became known as Young Ireland: a reference to Mazzini's contemporary Young Italy movement.

In 1846, after Davis's death, the movement split, nominally over O'Connell's non-violent tactics, as the Young Irelanders refused to rule out physical force nationalism. Neither the impact of the Great Irish famine nor O'Connell's death in May 1847 healed this division and in early 1848 the more militant John Mitchel broke away to set up the United Irishman. The French revolution of February 1848 healed the latter division because it encouraged the Irish nationalists to think that they might receive French assistance. Although this hope was soon dashed, revolutionary preparations continued apace.

In June 1848 Lord John Russell's government repealed Habeas Corpus and ordered the arrest of O'Brien and his colleagues. O'Brien called the people of County Tipperary to arms to no avail (as they preferred to listen to their priests) and the revolt effectively ended in the battle in the garden of widow McCormack's house near Ballingarry (although sporadic resistance continued until late the following year).

The rebel ringleaders were caught, tried, sentenced to death and then had their sentences commuted to transportation (from which Mitchel and others escaped to America). O'Brien was released in 1854, returned to Ireland in 1856 and lived out the rest of his life quietly there. Other Young Irelanders became involved in Fenianism, with the result that their movement and the 1848 rising has become celebrated as part of the Republican tradition of revolt.

Z

Zinoviev Letter, October 1924. The Zinoviev Letter was a forgery leaked by British intelligence to the *Daily Mail* shortly before the October 1924 general election so as to hinder Ramsay MacDonald from gaining a second term of office.

The letter was supposedly written by the president of the Communist International (Comintern), Grigory Zinoviev, to the British Communist Party, with a view to providing advice on sedition and other practical steps 'to develop the ideas of Leninism in England', including advice on mobilizing 'sympathetic forces' within the Labour Party.

It damaged the Labour Party because MacDonald's government was popularly regarded as 'soft' on communism given the Campbell Case and its attempt to open diplomatic and trading channels with the Soviet Union, including a projected loan.

It is impossible to quantify the damage which this black propaganda did to Labour but it certainly contributed to the Conservative Party's 37% increase in its vote, although a more significant factor in securing a second term for Baldwin was the collapse in the Liberal vote (down from 159 seats in December 1923 to just 40 in October 1924).